Targeting Civilians in War

A VOLUME IN THE SERIES

CORNELL STUDIES IN SECURITY AFFAIRS

edited by Robert J. Art

Robert Jervis

Stephen M. Walt

A list of titles in this series is available at

www.cornellpress.cornell.edu.

Targeting Civilians in War

ALEXANDER B. DOWNES

Cornell University Press

ITHACA AND LONDON

First published 2008 by Cornell University Press

Printed in the United States of America

Library of Congress Cataloging-in-Publication Data

Downes, Alexander B., 1969-
    Targeting civilians in war / Alexander B. Downes.
      p. cm. — (Cornell studies in security affairs)
Includes bibliographical references and index.
    ISBN 978-0-8014-4634-4 (cloth : alk. paper)
  1. Civilian war casualties—History—20th century. 2.
War victims—History—20th century. 3. War and society—
History—20th century. 4. Politics and war—History—20th
century. 5. Military history, Modern—20th century. I.
Title. II. Series.
    U21.2.D587 2008
    172'.42—dc22   2007040729

Cloth printing   10 9 8 7 6 5 4 3 2 1

Contents

[v]

Acknowledgments

Over the course of researching and writing this book, I have benefited from the help and advice of many people. I owe a special debt of gratitude to John Mearsheimer. I arrived at the University of Chicago in the mid-1990s as a former classical musician nervously embarking on what I hoped would be a second career as a political scientist. John took a chance that someone who had until recently spent much of his time practicing the works of Mozart, Beethoven, and Brahms could become an international relations scholar. I am immensely grateful that he did. John read and commented on numerous drafts of this manuscript, giving feedback that was always helpful, and improved the final product immeasurably.

This book literally would not have been possible without the input of Robert Pape, who suggested the question to me in a brainstorming session in January 2001. "What if you could show that democracies were more moral in the way that they fought wars? Now that would be really something," he mused. I came to a different conclusion regarding the impact of democratic war-fighting on civilians, but that in no way diminished Bob's enthusiasm for the project as it progressed. I thank him for his support. Charles Glaser and Stathis Kalyvas helped sharpen my arguments and provided encouragement.

A few other individuals made special inspirational or practical contributions to this book. Benjamin Valentino, for example, was in many ways the trailblazer whose work on mass killing brought the study of civilian victimization into the mainstream of security studies. Ben met with me when I was starting the project and has provided helpful comments on my work as well as encouragement and advice along the way. I have been fortunate to have his path to follow. Ivan Arreguín-Toft generously shared his data on barbarism in asymmetric conflicts and has provided constant encouragement.

Jasen Castillo, Kelly Greenhill, and Sebastian Rosato each offered not only extensive feedback on my ideas but also their friendship, support, and good humor, for which I am tremendously grateful. I thank Roger Haydon at Cornell University Press for his interest in and detailed comments on parts of the manuscript.

I also thank those people who read and commented on various versions of this project over the past several years: Laia Balcells, Barton Bernstein, Kathryn Cochran, Michael Desch, Matthew Fehrs, Martha Finnemore, Christopher Gelpi, Hein Goemans, Peter Gourevitch, Colin Kahl, Robert Keohane, Helen Kinsella, Gregory Koblentz, Matthew Kocher, Eric Mvukiyehe, Richard Price, Dan Reiter, Thomas Spragens, and Elisabeth Wood. I also thank the two anonymous reviewers for Cornell University Press whose comments were especially helpful. I apologize to anyone I may have forgotten.

Several institutions provided generous financial assistance that allowed me to conduct the research and writing for this book. I spent a fruitful year at the Olin Institute for Strategic Studies at Harvard University. I thank Stephen Rosen and Monica Duffy Toft for the opportunity to participate in Olin's program and take advantage of Harvard's many resources. I later received a year of support from the Center for International Security and Cooperation (CISAC) at Stanford University, where I profited from the guidance of Scott Sagan and Lynn Eden. Along the way I also received financial assistance from the Eisenhower Institute in the form of a Dwight D. Eisenhower/Clifford Roberts Graduate Fellowship, and the Harry Frank Guggenheim Foundation, which provided a dissertation fellowship. I also thank the Triangle Institute for Security Studies and the Arts and Sciences Council for Faculty Research at Duke University, both of which gave funds for research in the book's final phases.

Parts of the introduction and chapters 1 through 3 previously appeared in my article "Desperate Times, Desperate Measures: The Causes of Civilian Victimization in War," *International Security* 30, no. 4 (spring 2006): 152–95. Parts of chapter 2 appeared as "Restraint or Propellant? Democracy and Civilian Fatalities in Interstate Wars," *Journal of Conflict Resolution* 51, no. 6 (December 2007): 872–904. Some of the material on the Second Anglo-Boer War in chapter 5 appeared in "Draining the Sea by Filling the Graves: Investigating the Effectiveness of Indiscriminate Violence as a Counterinsurgency Strategy," *Civil Wars* 9, no. 4 (December 2007): 420–44. I thank these journals and their publishers for granting me permission to adapt the material in this book.

For excellent research assistance at Duke University, I thank Soo-Jung Choi, Max Entman, Chad Troop, but especially Katherine Jordan. Katherine was instrumental in helping me prepare the final version of the manuscript and saved me from innumerable errors. I cannot thank her enough. I alone am responsible for any mistakes that remain.

On a personal note, I thank my parents, Bryan and Sheri Downes, for their love and support through thick and thin. They have always been there to help celebrate my successes and to help pick me up when I have stumbled. As a teacher and mentor I only hope I can live up to my father's example, demonstrated by the outpouring of affection and thanks from his former students when he retired in 2001.

Finally, I thank my wife, Tanya Schreiber, who has tirelessly endured many a furrowed brow these last several years. Not only has Tanya served as a sounding board and adviser for my work—I think she can explain my arguments better than I can—but she has coaxed me through the hard times and bad days when I thought I would never finish. Moreover, she has shown me by example how to persevere; her quiet courage in the face of adversity has inspired me more than she knows. I dedicate this book to her.

Targeting Civilians in War

Introduction

War, as it is so often said, is hell. "War is cruelty and you cannot refine it," wrote General William T. Sherman in justifying his decision to evict the inhabitants of Atlanta and burn the city during the American Civil War. One of the principal reasons why war is thought to be hell is the impact it has on innocent civilians, for in addition to consuming the lives of armed combatants, war also devours the lives of those who are not involved in the fighting. Over the past three centuries, for example, civilians (a term I use interchangeably with noncombatants) have comprised half of all war-related deaths. In the twentieth century alone, an estimated 43 million to 54 million noncombatants perished from war-related causes, accounting for between 50 percent and 62 percent of all deaths from warfare.[1]

Even a partial list of the horrors over the past one hundred years is staggering.[2] Tens of thousands of civilians, for example, perished in concentration camps in Cuba, South Africa, and the Philippines at the turn of the last century, and the German war against the Herero people in Southwest Africa resulted in their near extinction. During World War I, the British-led blockade of the Central Powers caused widespread malnutrition and disease and played a large part in the nearly 1 million excess deaths among the civilian population of Germany and Austria-Hungary. Nazi Germany murdered 6 million European Jews and millions of others in Eastern Europe and the Soviet Union during World War II, while Allied strategic bombing killed 300,000 Germans and as many as 900,000 Japanese. United States strategic bombing in the Korean War killed hundreds of thousands of noncombatants, as did indiscriminate American and Soviet counterinsurgency tactics in Vietnam and Afghanistan, respectively. Civil conflicts resulted in massive civilian death tolls in numerous countries, such as

China (1927–49), Spain (1936–39), Guatemala (1966–85), Nigeria (1967–70), Ethiopia (1974–91), and Angola (1975–2002), and the ongoing conflict in the Darfur region of Sudan has killed at least 200,000 and displaced more than ten times that number.[3]

The startling number of civilian casualties in modern wars is puzzling for two reasons. First, there is a widespread belief that killing innocent civilians is morally wrong. According to a recent International Red Cross survey of populations in war-torn societies, for example, "a striking 64 per cent say that combatants, when attacking to weaken the enemy, must attack only combatants and *leave civilians alone.*" By contrast, a mere 3 percent accept the view that belligerents should be permitted to attack combatants and noncombatants alike.[4] The past and present attitudes of Americans are similar: before World War II the American public resolutely opposed urban area bombing as "counter to American humanitarian ideals," whereas hypothetical scenarios regarding an invasion of Iraq in 2003 showed that a majority of Americans consistently opposed going to war if it would result in "thousands" of Iraqi civilian casualties.[5] Why are noncombatants frequently targeted despite the widespread belief that doing so is not only wrong but also illegal according to international law?

Second, killing civilians in war is widely believed to be bad strategy: it rarely helps the perpetrator achieve its goals and can even be counterproductive by strengthening an adversary's will to resist. One recent study, for example, argues that terrorizing civilians in war is self-defeating: "The nation or faction that resorts to warfare against civilians most quickly, most often, and most viciously is the nation or faction most likely to see its interests frustrated and, in many cases, its existence terminated."[6] A leading analyst of interstate coercion agrees, arguing that punishment strategies aimed at an adversary's civilian population—implemented with airpower, seapower, or economic sanctions—rarely extract meaningful concessions.[7]

Given the moral stigma attached to civilian victimization and its supposedly dubious effectiveness, why do governments nevertheless use military strategies that target enemy noncombatants?[8] One school of thought identifies regime type as the key factor but is of two minds regarding its effect. According to some analysts, democracies—which adhere to domestic norms that proscribe killing innocent civilians, whether at home or abroad—are less likely to target civilians than nondemocracies, which are not so constrained.[9] Studies of democratic institutions and war, however, imply just the opposite: democracies could be more likely to target noncombatants because the vulnerability of leaders to public opinion makes them wary of incurring heavy costs on the battlefield for fear of losing support at home.[10] This fear could compel democratic elites to target noncombatants to avoid costs or win the war quickly.

A second explanation emphasizes the "barbaric" identity of the adversary: civilian victimization results from the belief that one is fighting an uncivilized enemy.[11] Sebastian Balfour, for example, in his history of Spain's efforts to conquer northern Morocco, writes that European powers made "a distinction . . . between the treatment of fellow Europeans and that of colonials who resisted European advance. The standards of warfare that could be applied to the colonial enemy were different because these opponents were not 'fully civilized.' "[12] The choice of strategy, in other words, depends on one's view of the adversary: the laws of war apply only in wars against "civilized" opponents, not "barbarians."

A third set of arguments focuses on military organizations. One variant contends that organizational culture—defined as the "the pattern of assumptions, ideas, and beliefs that prescribes how a group should adapt to its external environment and manage its internal affairs" is what steers militaries toward or diverts them away from civilian victimization.[13] Specifically, when a military's organizational culture dictates a strategy that relies on the targeting of civilian populations, states will typically escalate to the intentional killing of noncombatants and sometimes even genocide during the course of a war.[14] A different organization-centered argument maintains that militaries target civilians when a particular service branch believes doing so will serve its parochial interests. This is likely to be the case when multiple services are competing to make the largest contribution to victory so as to capture the lion's share of postwar military spending, or when an organization is struggling to achieve independence as a separate service.[15]

Although these arguments are intuitively plausible, the evidence does not support them: as this book will show, democracies are somewhat more likely than nondemocracies to target civilians, but democracy alone is not the principal driving factor. Preexisting cultural differences between states (such as race or religion) that might engender perceptions of barbaric identity, moreover, fail to predict civilian victimization. Nor do organizational cultures or parochial interests reliably explain decisions to target noncombatants.

Based on an investigation of interstate and colonial wars over the last two centuries, this book identifies two other factors that are primarily responsible for civilian victimization. First, desperation to win and to save lives on one's own side in costly, protracted wars of attrition causes belligerents to target enemy civilians. According to the desperation logic, states that are embroiled in costly and prolonged struggles become increasingly desperate to snatch victory from the jaws of defeat and reduce their own losses. States that find themselves in this situation target noncombatants because doing so allows them to keep fighting, reduce casualties, and possibly win the war by coercing the adversary to quit. In short, states—including democracies—tend to prize victory and preserving the lives of their own people above humanity in warfare: desperation overrides moral inhibitions against killing noncombatants.

Civilian victimization motivated by desperation in wars of attrition rarely intends to destroy the victim group.[16] Rather, the targeting of non-combatants in these wars is primarily a coercive strategy: it is a means to persuade an enemy government (in a conventional war) or rebel group (in a guerrilla war) to accede to the coercer's political or military demands. As a form of coercion, civilian victimization can follow the logic of punishment or the logic of denial.[17] In the former, violence is directed at noncombatants in the hope that they will rise up and demand that their government end the war. In other words, civilian victimization as punishment targets the enemy civilian population's will to resist. The punishment logic commonly underpins violence against noncombatants during sieges, naval blockades, and strategic bombing of urban areas.

In the denial logic, on the other hand, civilian victimization is meant to undermine an adversary's military capability to resist. In counterguerrilla wars, for example, killing civilian supporters of the other side—or evacuating them from targeted areas—intimidates other civilians (or simply prevents them) from providing assistance to the rebels and hence undermines the insurgents' logistical ability to continue fighting. Even some bombing campaigns have aimed to reduce enemy output of military goods by killing the civilian workforce. Civilian victimization as a coercive mechanism is typically a tactic of later resort, because coercion—whether of the punishment or denial variety—does not work quickly.[18] States, therefore, frequently turn to coercion later, only after their initial strategy to win the war quickly has failed.

The second mechanism that leads to civilian victimization is belligerents' appetite for territorial conquest: when states seek to conquer and annex territory that is inhabited by enemy noncombatants. This scenario typically occurs in wars of territorial expansion or when hostilities break out between intermingled ethnic groups that claim the same territory as their homeland. In this circumstance, attacking enemy civilians often makes good strategic sense because it eliminates "fifth columns" that could rebel in an army's rear area and also heads off potential revolts that might occur later on. Furthermore, purging an enemy's civilian population reduces the likelihood that the adversary will attempt to reconquer the disputed territory in the future by removing a major reason for war: rescuing their national brethren trapped behind enemy borders. One's claim to territory, moreover, is strengthened by facts on the ground, foremost among them the national character of the population. The Kosovo Albanians' claim to self-rule in Kosovo, for example, is enormously strengthened and legitimized by the fact that more than 90 percent of the population in Kosovo is Albanian. Each of these factors makes it likely that when states try to seize territory from each other, they will seek to change the demographic situation in the conquered area by targeting civilians.

Civilian victimization produced by the appetite to annex territory from a neighbor—contrary to civilian victimization in protracted wars of attrition—tends to be a tactic of early rather than later resort. The reason is that enemy civilians are readily accessible to the invader and expelling or killing them pays real dividends by removing the threat of rebellions in the rear, eliminating the possibility that the opponent might try to rescue its people in the future, and solidifying the attacker's claim to the land. Moreover, because it is not usually produced by desperation, civilian victimization for territorial reasons can occur when a belligerent is winning or doing well.

Democratic regime type by itself increases the likelihood that a state will victimize enemy noncombatants in warfare. At first glance, democracies appear to target civilians at a slightly higher rate than nondemocracies do. This difference, however, is accounted for by democracies' being more likely than autocracies to use force against civilians in protracted wars of attrition. Outside of such wars, there is no difference in the propensity of the two regime types to target noncombatants. The evidence therefore indicates that once democratic leaders find themselves in costly or losing wars, something about democracy, such as the additional pressure generated by electoral institutions of accountability, may force leaders to take measures to reduce losses or deliver victory—including civilian victimization—even if it means violating the strictures of liberal norms. This demonstrates a potential "dark side of democracy": how institutions designed to ensure domestic peace and tranquility may lead democracies to perpetrate injustices abroad.[19] It also shows how the norms and institutions characteristic of democracies can contradict rather than reinforce each other in wartime.

Leaders need not be certain that a strategy of targeting civilians will succeed for civilian victimization to be a rational choice; they merely need to believe that it might contribute to victory (or stave off defeat) or lower their costs of fighting. Leaders might also perceive themselves as having no other option than to attack noncombatants to achieve their war aims. If civilian victimization offers even a small chance of reversing a grim situation, or delivering a state's goals at a cost it can afford to pay, leaders may rationally take that chance. Once states become committed to victory, therefore, if the costs of fighting increase or the war begins to appear unwinnable, they tend to victimize civilians first before abandoning their goals. The fact that civilian victimization is often chosen in the most difficult circumstances also helps to explain why it has a relatively low success rate, at least in conventional interstate wars.

Understanding the causes of civilian victimization in warfare should be of interest to analysts in a variety of disciplines as well as policymakers. Scholarly interest in the question why—and under what circumstances—civilians become victims in war has increased in recent years, yet it remains understudied relative to other topics in security studies.[20] This is a sad state of affairs given the millions of innocent people who died in armed conflicts in the twentieth century alone. This question until recent years was investigated largely by genocide scholars, who found a striking correlation between war and genocide, but have not adequately explored how the dynamics of armed conflict sometimes lead to mass killing of noncombatants. Admirable exceptions to this trend exist in the study of guerrilla wars,[21] but by their own admission these studies cannot explain the many instances of large-scale killing that occur in conventional wars.[22] This book, therefore, aims to increase our understanding of this important phenomenon and contributes several causal mechanisms—protection of friendly forces, the need to win, and the threat posed by enemy civilians to securely holding contested territory—that transcend the guerrilla-conventional divide and explain civilian victimization in both types of conflicts.

This book has relevance for several debates that are of central concern to security studies.[23] First, as already mentioned, understanding the roots of civilian victimization may help explain the historical prevalence of punishment strategies despite their seeming inefficacy. The extant coercion literature equates inflicting pain on civilians with punishment and destroying military targets with denial. A closer examination of civilian victimization, however, shows that violence against noncombatants can be employed to sap the enemy's will to resist *or* his capability to resist. Differentiating civilian victimization as punishment from civilian victimization as denial also helps explain the puzzle why some coercive strategies commonly described as punishment are more successful than others, an issue I explore further in the book's conclusion.

Second, the treatment of noncombatants by democracies in war provides a new venue for testing arguments regarding the effect of liberal norms and democratic institutions originally devised to explain peace between democracies. I follow the lead of some democratic peace theorists and their critics by deducing further implications from these arguments and testing them against new evidence.[24] To the extent that the debate between proponents and detractors of democratic peace has bogged down owing to the limited time period in which data are available (1816 to the present), the small number of democracies, and the scarcity of interstate wars, this procedure may help move the debate forward by providing new evidence for or against different normative and institutional causal mechanisms.

[6]

Third, this book also supplements the literature on norms and force in international relations. To date, this literature has focused on explaining the rise of (and adherence to) normative restrictions on the use of force against noncombatants. In particular, scholars have studied the development of taboos against the use of certain weapons, such as nuclear weapons, chemical and biological munitions, and antipersonnel land mines.[25] By contrast, I look at the problem from the opposite perspective: which factors lead states to violate norms? Under what circumstances do norms protecting innocent people break down? When do seemingly "civilized" people revert to "uncivilized" methods of fighting?[26] More generally, the resort to civilian victimization may provide insights into the poorly understood question of escalation in war.[27]

Finally, my findings regarding democracy and civilian victimization question the view that democracies' responsiveness to the electorate and their relative restraint toward civilians in war renders them more vulnerable to coercion by punishment, such as suicide terrorism. Some argue, for example, that terrorists are emboldened to strike democratic states because "their publics have low thresholds of cost tolerance and high ability to affect state policy." Moreover, democracies are perceived to be relatively restrained in the level of force they will employ in response to terrorist attacks.[28] By contrast, I find little support for the view that democracies treat civilians better in interstate wars, or that democracies are more likely to be targeted for civilian victimization by autocracies.

From a practical perspective, greater knowledge of the causes of civilian victimization in warfare can also help answer policy questions. For one, such understanding could help policymakers assess the risk that particular conflicts will descend into brutalization of civilians and thus guide decisions about whether and how to intervene abroad in order to prevent the abuse of noncombatants. It should not come as a surprise to policymakers, for example, when theaters of battle characterized by extensive ethnic intermingling—such as Bosnia—result in major depredations against civilians. Moreover, curtailing civilian victimization will typically require more than airpower because bombing is rarely effective at stopping ethnic cleansing or preventing widely scattered counterinsurgent forces from operating.

Understanding the causes of civilian victimization, furthermore, can also help us determine whether the spread of democracy in the international system will lead to fewer noncombatant casualties in warfare. Democratization is often touted as a win-win situation: democracies respect human rights at home and refrain from fighting each other abroad. Consequently, spreading democracy has become the cornerstone of American foreign policy in the post–Cold War world. If democracies also fight their wars in accordance with the principle of noncombatant immunity, civilian victimization may become just a bad memory.

The study of civilian victimization is particularly relevant for the United States, which—owing to its preponderance of power, tremendous military technological advantages, and most recently the impetus provided by the open-ended war on terror begun by the George W. Bush administration—is the most militarily active state in the world. American power and technology lower the bar against using force by making it appear relatively easy and low cost, while fighting terrorism gives the United States a compelling reason to intervene abroad: to oust regimes that sponsor or harbor terrorists and to prevent the development of weapons of mass destruction by regimes that might pass them to terrorists.

Skeptics might argue that a liberal democracy like the United States in the twenty-first century would not resort to violence against civilians to achieve its objectives. When a quick show of force fails to cow or defeat an enemy expeditiously, however, American policymakers—as in past conflicts—will face pressures to escalate militarily, which may involve inflicting harm on civilians. The key factors, I argue, are the cost and protractedness of the war, not the regime type of the states involved. Some authoritarian states may be quicker to put civilians in the cross-hairs nowadays, but democracies historically have shown a striking tendency to target noncombatants or use indiscriminate tactics that lead to large-scale civilian deaths when faced with costly fighting or uncertain victory. Moreover, the cost-sensitivity of modern democracies like the United States places additional stress on policymakers to fight cost-free wars. Even if leaders are reluctant to kill civilians intentionally and openly, this pressure can still lead to noncombatant suffering in indirect ways, such as through the targeting of infrastructure and reliance on economic sanctions that adversely affect civilian health. I explore this possibility in chapter 7.

The U.S. military is geared to fight high-intensity conventional warfare and is not nearly as effective at fighting guerrilla insurgencies. America's opponents may be able to exploit this weakness to deflect U.S. power, lengthen wars, and frustrate U.S. forces, which could lead the United States to target noncombatants. The guerrilla insurgency in South Vietnam, for example, proved deeply frustrating to American political and military leaders and did not fit into the high intensity conventional strategy the U.S. Army had developed to defeat a Soviet invasion of Western Europe. The attrition strategy implemented by U.S. commanders in Vietnam—which depended on racking up a high body count—demanded indiscriminate firepower, which killed large numbers of Vietnamese noncombatants.[29] More recently, American officials recognize that the open-ended war on terror and Islamic radicalism begun by the Bush administration and described by the president as "the defining struggle of our time" could take a generation or more to prosecute.[30] This conflict has already caused Bush and his advisers to sanction open-ended detention without trial of suspected militants, a redefinition of torture to maximize the legal techniques available to American interrogators to extract information from suspects, and the practice of "extraordinary rendition," whereby terrorist suspects are turned over to third countries that are known to practice torture.[31] Finally, large-scale conventional conflicts—such as a potential war with China over Taiwan—could also prove costly and difficult to win, perhaps leading to serious bombing campaigns that would kill many civilians.

THIS book joins and builds on a small but growing literature dedicated to explaining why states and rebel groups target noncombatants. Two of the most prominent contributions are Benjamin Valentino's *Final Solutions: Mass Killing and Genocide in the 20th Century* and Stathis Kalyvas's *The Logic of Violence in Civil Wars*. Readers familiar with this literature might wonder how my work relates to theirs.

The degree of overlap between this volume and Kalyvas's is relatively small. Kalyvas offers a theory of violence in civil (or, more accurately, guerrilla) wars in which each belligerent aims to secure control over—and hence collaboration and support from—the population. These conflicts are characterized by divided sovereignties, zones controlled to various degrees by incumbents and insurgents. The purpose of violence is to obtain the collaboration of the population in the various zones. In areas where each actor exerts monopoly control, little violence occurs since it is unnecessary. Violence is also generally absent in zones where control is up for grabs, because neither side possesses sufficient information to target civilians selectively. Indiscriminate violence under these circumstances is counterproductive because it alienates people and may cause them to support the adversary. Violence is most likely in zones where one side is locally dominant (although not hegemonic) but its control is slipping as the opponent makes inroads into the area. The declining belligerent targets actual and potential defectors to deter them from switching allegiances and thus maintain its grip on the population.[32]

This book, by contrast, deals mostly with interstate wars, almost none of which are insurgencies. In conventional conflicts, belligerents employ indiscriminate violence against an enemy's civilian population—to the extent they are able and the circumstances warrant—to gain coercive leverage over the adversary's government. Belligerents also use indiscriminate violence in conventional conflicts to eliminate unwanted populations from conquered territory. In neither case is exerting control over—or seeking the collaboration of—enemy populations a relevant mechanism. The main point of overlap with Kalyvas is my chapter on counterinsurgency, but even here I identify a set of cases that defy Kalyvas's logic of selective violence.

Rather than becoming increasingly discriminate in their employment of violence over time, the British in South Africa moved in the opposite direction, interning entire populations as they became increasingly desperate to suppress the Boer insurgency. Indeed, selective violence in this conflict was ineffective at extracting meaningful collaboration from the civilian population. Similar trends are evident in other colonial wars, such as the Spanish-Cuban (1895–98), U.S.–Filipino (1899–1902), and Second Italo-Sanusi (1923–32, in Libya) wars.

The common ground between this book and Valentino's is more extensive. Valentino seeks to explain incidences of large-scale (fifty thousand or more killed) government violence against noncombatants in the twentieth century, whether inflicted in the course of a war or not. He argues that the key to understanding these violent episodes lies not in regime type, moments of national crisis, or a society's cleavage structure—factors stressed by previous studies of genocide—but rather in the goals of state leaders. Three types of objectives in particular can trigger mass killing. First, leaders "seeking to achieve the radical communization of their societies," such as Joseph Stalin, Mao Zedong, and Pol Pot, have used mass killing to eliminate elements of the population that opposed this transformation or which did not fit into the communist view of society. Second, mass killing occurs when leaders want to expunge an ethnic group in order to "implement racist or nationalist ideologies calling for the ethnic, national, or religious purification" of the state or to "resolve political or military conflicts between ethnic groups over the control of territory." Finally, leaders seeking to defeat guerrilla insurgencies use mass killing to eliminate the civilian support that fuels guerrilla movements.[33]

There are important areas of synergy between this book and Valentino's, but also several areas where we diverge. The most important similarity is that we both argue that state violence against noncombatants is largely the result of rational strategic calculations rather than emotion, dehumanization, or irrational hatred. For example, my research shows that states hope to win quick and decisive victories by force of arms and turn to targeting civilians only when their countermilitary strategies are frustrated. States are also sensitive to the possibility that civilian victimization may trigger enemy retaliation against their own population or prompt influential third parties to enter the war. Each of these factors sometimes deters states—at least temporarily—from opting for civilian victimization. In a similar vein, Valentino documents how leaders explore a variety of steps to achieve their aims without violence and turn to bloodshed only when other avenues are blocked. Another point of convergence is that we both generally downplay the role of cultural factors in producing violence. I contend, for example, that perceptions of an adversary's identity are unrelated to the occurrence of civilian victimization, while Valentino argues against social cleavages and dehumanization.

There are a few differences, however. One concerns the dependent variable. This book focuses specifically on war, and the reasons that states target noncombatants in armed conflicts, whereas Valentino uses a numerical threshold of civilian fatalities to identify his case universe. One of Valentino's three causal mechanisms, therefore—the collectivization of agriculture under communist regimes—plays no role in my work since it typically does not occur during wartime. A second difference is substantive: although many of the cases I examine fall into Valentino's category of "terrorist mass killing," he devotes little attention to these cases in his book.[34] My book can thus be seen as complementary to his in that it opens up and explores the dynamics of this category of cases. My other causal mechanism for civilian victimization—appetite for conquest—to some extent combines Valentino's ethnic and territorial categories of mass killing because I look at cases where one state attempts to seize land from another, and particular ethnic groups may be viewed as obstacles to control over that territory. Although Valentino breaks decisively with previous genocide literature in many respects, he retains its emphasis—at least in the case studies that form the bulk of his book—on mass killing as a phenomenon of domestic politics.

A third difference is theoretical. My research places much less emphasis than Valentino's on the role of individuals and their ideologies and beliefs. Valentino, in advocating a "strategic perspective" on mass killing, argues for the importance of individual leaders and their goals, depicting mass killing as a "brutal strategy designed to accomplish leaders' most important ideological or political objectives and counter what they see as their most dangerous threats."[35] The centrality of leaders fits well with the communist and ethnic cleansing scenarios, but less well with the third scenario, counterinsurgency. Here Valentino sheds his emphasis on leaders' goals for the simple logic that targeting civilians makes good strategic sense for combating insurgencies. No particular ideology or goal is needed to explain mass killing in this situation; all one needs to posit is a preference for victory. Most of the cases in this book are of exactly this type: conflicts in which one or both belligerents simply seek to win and use increasingly violent instruments to coerce the adversary to concede. In other cases, states fight not only to win but to obtain territory, and civilian victimization arises out of the perception that some groups pose a threat to the assimilation of that territory.

The next chapter defines civilian victimization in greater detail, lays out the various types of civilian victimization, and then presents a series of theories to explain it, including my own desperation and territorial annexation arguments. The remainder of the book is devoted to empirical tests of the competing theories, starting with a statistical analysis of civilian victimization in interstate wars in chapter 2 and proceeding in chapters 3–7 through a series of case studies of blockade, strategic bombing, counterinsurgency, ethnic cleansing, and cases where civilian victimization did not happen. I conclude with a discussion of the theoretical and policy implications of my findings.

[1]

Defining and Explaining Civilian Victimization

What is civilian victimization, and why do governments victimize civilians in warfare? I begin by defining the concept of civilian victimization, the phenomenon I seek to explain in this book. Civilian victimization is a military strategy chosen by political or military elites that targets and kills noncombatants intentionally or which fails to discriminate between combatants and noncombatants and thus kills large numbers of the latter. I then outline the common forms of civilian victimization and provide illustrative examples.

In the second part, I summarize three competing perspectives on civilian victimization: regime type, civilized-barbaric identity, and organization theory. The regime-type view maintains that domestic norms and institutions are the most important causes of civilian victimization. The civilized-barbaric identity argument, by contrast, contends that states kill an adversary's noncombatants when they view the enemy as outside the community of civilized nations. Organization theory, finally, suggests that the cultures or parochial interests of military organizations are the prime causes of civilian victimization.

The third section presents my theory of civilian victimization, which identifies two crucial factors: the growing sense of desperation to win and to conserve on casualties that states experience in protracted wars of attrition, and the need to deal with potentially troublesome populations dwelling on land that an expansionist state seeks to annex. I discuss the logic underpinning these two factors and the differing implications they have for the timing of civilian victimization. I also explain why targeting civilians—even though it does not always work—is not an irrational gamble, but rather a calculated risk. I conclude with a short discussion of methods and cases.

Defining Civilian Victimization

Civilian victimization as I define it consists of two components: (1) it is a government-sanctioned military strategy that (2) intentionally targets and kills noncombatants or involves operations that will predictably kill large numbers of noncombatants. Civilian victimization violates the principles of noncombatant immunity and discrimination as enshrined in the Geneva Conventions and just-war theory, which require that belligerents must distinguish between combatants and noncombatants and refrain from taking aim at the latter.[1] Common forms of civilian victimization include aerial, naval, or artillery bombardment of civilians or civilian areas; sieges, naval blockades, or economic sanctions that deprive noncombatants of food; massacres; and forced movements or concentrations of populations that lead to widespread deaths. As with Benjamin Valentino's definition of mass killing, civilian victimization "is not limited to 'direct' methods of killing, such as execution, gassing, and bombing. It includes deaths caused by starvation, exposure, or disease resulting from the intentional confiscation, destruction, or blockade of the necessities of life. It also includes deaths caused by starvation, exhaustion, exposure, or disease during forced relocation or forced labor."[2]

Several aspects of civilian victimization bear elaboration. First, in accordance with the Geneva Conventions, I define combatants as "all organized armed forces, groups and units which are under a command responsible to that Party for the conduct of its subordinates," as well as individuals involved in the construction of weapons.[3] Noncombatants, by contrast, do not participate in armed conflict by fighting, carrying weapons, serving in the uniformed military or security services, or building weapons. Two general principles can be used to demarcate the line between combatants and noncombatants. One view, articulated by Michael Walzer, maintains that people have the right to be free from violence unless they forfeit that right by participating in military activity, such as taking up arms or working in a munitions factory. As Walzer puts it, "No one can be threatened with war or warred against, unless through some act of his own he has surrendered or lost his rights."[4] A second perspective focuses on the degree of threat an individual poses to the adversary to draw the combatant/noncombatant line. Only those individuals who actively participate in hostilities—by serving in the armed forces, for example—constitute an immediate threat of harm to the enemy and thus qualify as combatants.[5] I argue that individuals who build bombs and other munitions also pose a significant threat of harm and should thus be included in the combatant category. If they are not, attacks on munitions factories (or targeted killings of terrorist bomb-makers, for that matter) would have to be classified as intentional targeting of civilians. This violates the common-sense understanding that such individuals are not owed the same degree of protection as those employed in other sectors of the economy, and that killing them is not morally wrong.[6] Thus, whichever of these general principles one subscribes to, both point to an understanding of noncombatants as outside the realm of military activity either as fighters or makers of weapons.

Skeptics contend that nationalism and industrialization have eliminated the noncombatant category altogether because all citizens in modern states contribute to the war effort if only by going to work, paying taxes, or consenting to the use of force.[7] This view clashes with the obvious fact that even in modern societies, there are many people who contribute little if anything to the war effort, and further that this relative disengagement (and absence of threat) makes a difference as to whether they may be killed.[8] Many individuals work in sectors of the economy unrelated to the war effort; some, particularly children and the elderly, do not work at all. One study estimates that 75 percent of the population of an industrial country does not labor in war-related industries, and that even in industrial cities, 66 percent of the inhabitants are civilians.[9]

Second, civilian victimization is a government-sanctioned policy or strategy, as opposed to random or uncoordinated attacks by a few military units. Intentional attacks on civilians, as Christopher Browning has pointed out, can take the form of arbitrary explosions of violence or revenge inspired by "battlefield frenzy," on the one hand, or can represent "official government policy" or "standing operating procedure," on the other hand.[10] Only the latter comprises civilian victimization as defined in this book: it consists of a government policy of sustained violence against a noncombatant population, rather than haphazard outbursts of brutality by frustrated troops. This does not mean, however, that civilian victimization must be initiated by civilian leaders; in fact, it is sometimes initiated by the military on the ground, but once political leaders become aware of the strategy and approve it—or decline to stop it—it becomes de facto government policy.[11]

Third, civilian victimization consists of strategies that intentionally target civilian populations but also strategies that—although not purposefully aiming at noncombatants—nevertheless fail to distinguish between combatants and noncombatants. A strategy of civilian victimization, in other words, either targets civilians on purpose, or employs force so indiscriminately that it inflicts large amounts of damage and death on noncombatants. In certain cases, for example, belligerents openly declare or make statements of policy that designate noncombatants as the target of a strategy. British bombing policy in the Second World War, which charged Bomber Command with destroying urban areas in Germany to undermine "the morale of the enemy civil population and in particular, of the industrial workers," falls into this category.[12] British policy clearly meant to kill German civilians in order to bring about the collapse of Germany's will to fight. The 300,000 fatalities caused by this strategy were not a side-effect of strikes on military targets, or a product of a refusal to discriminate between soldiers and civilians, but rather the intended object of the strategy.

In other cases, however, belligerents mount a pattern of repeated attacks over an extended period that fail to distinguish between combatants and noncombatants and thus kill tens of thousands of civilians. Although killing noncombatants is not the avowed purpose of such a strategy, this outcome is nevertheless foreseeable, predictable, and often desired, and thus constitutes civilian victimization. The U.S. Army Air Forces during World War II, for example, launched seventy self-described attacks on a "city area" in Germany, raids that qualify as intentional civilian victimization. United States bombers also devoted about half of their total effort to radar bombing, which—although not purposefully directed at civilians—American military officers knew was the functional equivalent of British area bombing. According to Thomas Searle, "USAAF commanders essentially acknowledged this fact by using a large percentage of incendiary bombs (the preferred weapon against cities) on these raids even though such bombs were ineffective against rail yards, the official targets."[13] The adoption and exploitation of this indiscriminate form of attack thus constitute civilian victimization.

Contrast each of these strategies with the U.S. strategic bombing campaign during the 1991 Persian Gulf War. In that conflict, for example, F-117 aircraft bombed the Al-Firdos bunker in Baghdad, an installation that U.S. air planners believed was a command-and-control center. Unknown to these planners, however, the Iraqi regime was using Al-Firdos as a bomb shelter for civilian dependents of Iraqi officials. The air strike killed approximately two hundred to three hundred civilians. These deaths, although tragic, did not result from a government policy of targeting noncombatants. Nor did the casualties stem from a refusal to discriminate between soldiers and civilians, as the U.S. military did not even know there were noncombatants present at the target. Moreover, immediately after the Al-Firdos disaster, U.S. officials declared Baghdad off-limits to further air strikes, and few targets were struck in the Iraqi capital for the remainder of the war.[14] Table 1.1 highlights the differences among these types of violence and provides examples of each.[15]

Clearly there are cases in which establishing the intentionality or deliberateness of civilian victimization is harder than in the British case. Policymakers do not always speak openly or truthfully when it comes to killing innocent people: there is no mention in the memoirs of British leaders, for example, that the policy of blockade in World War I was meant to starve the German people. President Truman, moreover, spoke of Hiroshima and Nagasaki as purely military targets.[16] These cases highlight the importance of examining internal government documents and private communications whenever possible to supplement leaders' official pronouncements. They

Table 1.1. A typology of civilian casualties

	Intentional	Indiscriminate	Collateral
Government-sanctioned strategy	British blockade of Germany, 1915–19	Prussian shelling of Paris, 1871	Civilian deaths inflicted by U.S. bombing of Iraq, 1991, or Serbia, 1999
	British bombing of Germany, 1942–45	U.S. radar bombing of Germany, 1943–45	
	U.S. firebombing of Japan, 1945	German "Blitz" on Britain, 1940–41	
	Bulgarian, Greek, Serbian, and Turkish massacres in the Balkan Wars, 1912–13	U.S. bombing of North Vietnam (Rolling Thunder), 1965–68	
	German Einsatzgruppen massacres in U.S.S.R., 1941–42	Boer and African civilian deaths in concentration camps, 1900–1902	
Not government-sanctioned or a strategy	Massacre at Deir Yassin by Jewish militias, 1948	Shelling of Vicksburg, U.S. Civil War, 1863	Civilians shot or bombed in crossfire between opposing forces
	My Lai massacre, Vietnam War, March 1968		
	Haditha massacre, Iraq, 2005		

also underline the importance of observing behavioral indicators that may indicate a shift toward civilian victimization—increasing indiscriminateness, decreasing concern for civilian life, or variation in the types of weapons used (incendiary versus high explosive bombs, for example).

Other analysts have chosen to include only intentional civilian deaths in their studies. Kalyvas, for example, looks only at the deliberate killing of noncombatants—homicide—excluding deaths inflicted unintentionally (collateral damage) and nonviolently (famine and disease). Valentino also focuses on intentionality, differentiating intentional from unintentional deaths based on the civilian or military nature of the target: when the target is military, civilian deaths are always unintended; when the target is civilian, deaths are always intended.[17] This definition undesirably stretches the concept of intentionality. Valentino, for example, argues that if noncombatants are the direct object of the policy, their deaths should be considered intentional if they are a foreseeable result of the policy. But this statement equates the mere knowledge that civilians will die with intending or desiring their deaths. Valentino thus contends that the fatalities of Boer women and children in British concentration camps during the Second Anglo-Boer War (1899–1902) were intentional because the civilians themselves were the object of the policy. This judgment is belied by the evidence, however, which shows that British officials did not purposefully try to kill these people, or hope to bring about the deaths. According to historian Thomas Pakenham, "Kitchener no more desired the death of women and children in the camps than of the wounded Dervishes after Omdurman, or of his own soldiers in the typhoid-stricken hospitals of Bloemfontein. He was simply not interested."[18] Civilians were the direct object of the reconcentration policy, but this does not necessarily make their deaths intentional.

Valentino also excludes from his definition all civilian fatalities that result from strikes on military targets, deeming these casualties to be unintended collateral damage. This, too, involves conceptual stretching, this time of collateral damage. When a strategy ostensibly directed at military targets generates tens of thousands of noncombatant fatalities, can these deaths still be considered collateral? Excluding these cases also ignores substantial evidence that some attackers simply did not make any attempt to distinguish between combatants and noncombatants, did not care that large numbers of civilians were being killed, or sought to capitalize on the fear these deaths created among the enemy population.

I argue, therefore, that civilian victimization should include all cases where it can be determined that belligerents intended to kill an adversary's noncombatants, but it should not be limited to such cases. The concept should also include strategies that cause large numbers—tens of thousands—of civilian deaths owing to belligerents' inability or refusal to discriminate between combatants and noncombatants or their failure to exercise due care in their treatment of civilians.

Finally, the scope of this book is limited to the killing of enemy noncombatants during international wars. Victimization that occurs within the perpetrator's recognized borders is included only insofar as it occurs during an interstate war and the targeted population shares the nationality of the enemy state (e.g., Greeks in Turkey during the Greco-Turkish war, 1919–22).[19] Cases of killing perpetrated by nonstate actors—such as insurgent groups or terrorists—are excluded, as are instances of anticivilian violence that occur during civil wars, after an international war is over, or outside of war altogether.[20]

[18]

Policies of Civilian Victimization

I consider civilian victimization to have occurred when belligerents make widespread, repeated, and systematic use of any of the following tools: massacre, starvation, indiscriminate bombardment, or forced relocation or concentration of civilians in circumstances that belligerents foresee will result in many deaths. Massacres consist of "large-scale, face-to-face violence against civilians targeted as groups" and occur in a number of contexts.[21] Some massacres, as noted above, are generated by passions aroused in the heat of battle, but others are perpetrated as part of a strategy to decimate or intimidate the population. The customs of siege warfare, for example, decreed that defenders and civilians in towns that refused to surrender could be massacred indiscriminately or sold into slavery after an assault captured the city.[22] The Wehrmacht made systematic use of massacres in combating the Greek insurgency during the German occupation of Greece from 1941 to 1944. In the Soviet Union, the Germans employed special killing units—known as *Einsatzgruppen*—to murder as many as 1.5 million Jews in 1941 and 1942.[23] Serbian irregulars also repeatedly massacred Bosnian Muslim civilians as these militias advanced across eastern Bosnia in the spring of 1992.[24]

Intentional bombardment of civilians or indiscriminate bombing of non-combatant areas constitute the second mode of civilian victimization. Indiscriminate bombardment with explosive projectiles intended to terrorize towns often accompanied siege warfare, and naval bombardment of port cities has also been used to frighten people on shore.[25] The successful launch of the winged, propeller-driven aircraft in 1903, however, ushered in the strategic bombing era, which became the dominant form of bombardment in the twentieth century beginning in World War I. Strategic bombing victimizes civilians when it has the avowed goal of causing civilian casualties either to undermine civilian morale or an adversary's ability to fight.[26]

Civilian victimization may also be a consequence of attempts to deprive an enemy of food. Besiegers, for example, often used hunger and starvation as a weapon to induce their victims to surrender, as the Romans did at Jerusalem in AD 72.[27] During the deadly winter of 1941–42 in German-besieged Leningrad, "The city was filled with corpses. They lay by the thousands on the streets, in the ice, in the snowdrifts, in the courtyards and cellars of the great apartment houses." As one woman wrote in her diary that cold winter, "Today it is so simple to die. . . . You just begin to lose interest, then you lie on the bed and you never again get up."[28] Naval blockades can also be employed in a similar fashion. A member of the British Admiralty before the First World War, for example, "held that (in a protracted war) the mills of our sea-power (though they would grind the German industrial population slowly perhaps) would grind them 'exceedingly small'—grass would sooner or later grow in the streets of Hamburg and wide-spread dearth and ruin would be inflicted."[29] In a lesser-known conflict that occurred during World War I, Italy prevailed on its Triple Entente allies to help it institute a blockade of northern Libya aimed at the rebellious Sanusi sect. According to Rachel Simon, "This economic pressure—the starving of the population—was used to win specific political goals: the surrender of the rebels and the imposition of a new leadership."[30] Similarly, during the Nigerian Civil War (1967–70), one government commander told journalists that "I want to prevent even one Ibo having even one piece to eat before their capitulation."[31]

Hunger and starvation of civilians may also result from systematic devastation of the environment. According to Vegetius, devastation of an adversary's land dominated the conduct of war in medieval Europe: "The main and principal point in war," he wrote, "is to secure plenty of provisions and to destroy the enemy by famine." "To attack your enemy's economic base, isolate his castles, starve his population," writes historian John France, "these were surer methods and more applicable to the usually limited objectives for which men fought" in medieval times.[32] The infamous French devastation of the Palatinate in the late seventeenth century, for example—designed "to create an artificial desert that would preclude the enemy from undertaking offensive operations"—inflicted widespread civilian suffering not only in the Palatinate, but in Baden and Württemberg as well.[33] Destruction of crops and food supplies—with the attendant civilian suffering—also occurred in wars of colonial conquest. French general Saint-Arnaud, for example, described France's scorched-earth policy (known as *razzia*) in Algeria in the 1840s as follows: "We have burned everything, destroyed everything. How many women and children have died of cold and fatigue!"[34] "Grass no longer grows where the French army has set foot," agreed another Frenchman. In a clear reference to Voltaire, he continued: "We have ravaged the countryside, killed, burned, carved up, and chopped down, all for the best in this best of all possible worlds."[35]

Finally, civilian victimization occurs when belligerents coerce groups of people to move in circumstances that are sure to kill many or most of them. In the process of fighting the Filipino insurgency from 1899 to 1902, for example, the U.S. Army forced much of the rural population—including the entire population of certain islands—into camps where many died owing to sickness and disease.[36] According to one American congressman who visited the Philippines, "You never hear of any disturbances in Northern Luzon . . . because there isn't anybody there to rebel. . . . The good Lord in heaven only knows the number of Filipinos that were put under ground."[37] High mortality rates similarly followed Britain's incarceration of Boer and African women and children in South Africa (1899–1902) and Spain's concentration of Cuba's rural population (1895–98).

Evicting people entirely from their homes and forcing them to travel long distances also commonly generate significant fatalities, a process made worse by the violence that is often needed to compel people to abandon their dwellings. As many as eight thousand Cherokee Indians died along the Trail of Tears in the late 1830s after being forced by the U.S. government to leave their homes in Georgia.[38] According to a veteran of this expulsion, "I fought through the civil war and have seen men shot to pieces and slaughtered by thousands, but the Cherokee removal was the cruelest work I ever knew."[39] Turkey's removal of its Armenian population from Eastern Anatolia during World War I caused substantial mortality even without the attendant massacres and brutality.[40] In the Second Balkan War in 1913, the Greek Army burned at least 161 villages and massacred thousands in a "war of devastation" to ensure that "no Bulgarian subjects" remained in Greek-controlled territory.[41]

In short, civilian victimization is a government-sanctioned policy in wartime that targets enemy civilians intentionally or fails to discriminate between combatants and noncombatants. Belligerents need not put a gun to their victims' heads for a wartime strategy to constitute civilian victimization. Widespread noncombatant suffering and mortality can be generated by systematic devastation of the environment, cutting off supplies of food, or forced relocation. Next, I elaborate the various theories that have been offered to explain civilian victimization, before turning to my own desperation and annexation arguments and a discussion of the methods and cases I use to test these competing theories.

REGIME TYPE AND CIVILIAN VICTIMIZATION

Two alternative explanations for civilian victimization focus on regime type. One argues that autocracies account for the lion's share of noncombatant targeting because democracies are uniquely restrained by their domestic norms, whereas the other contends that democracies are more likely to target civilians because institutions of accountability make democracies more cost-sensitive and needful of victory.

Democracy: Restraint or Propellant?

Scholars who invoke democracy to explain civilian victimization disagree over the effect that it has, and this dispute reflects the norms versus institutions divide in the broader democratic peace literature. Most of the empirical studies to date find that democracies are less likely than nondemocracies to inflict civilian victimization and base their explanations in norms. R. J. Rummel, for example, notes that democracies are less likely to commit mass murder in foreign wars. In an examination of all wars since 1945, Benjamin Valentino, Paul Huth, and Dylan Balch-Lindsay find that democracies are less likely than authoritarian states to engage in mass killing. After examining twenty-five cases of counterinsurgent warfare by democracies and autocracies between 1945 and 1990, Michael Engelhardt concludes that the "literature confirms the assumption that non-democratic regimes are free to use much harsher tactics in dealing with insurgency than are democratic regimes." Finally, Gil Merom argues that "democracies fail in small wars because they cannot find a winning balance between the costs of war in terms of human lives [to their own military forces] and the political cost incurred by controlling the latter with force, between acceptable levels of casualties and acceptable levels of brutality."[42]

The most common argument advanced to explain the powerful aversion to civilian victimization by democracies is that the norms inherent in democratic societies proscribe killing the innocent.[43] Valentino, Huth, and Balch-Lindsay, for example, argue that democratic norms are the key restraint against killing civilians: "If democratic values promote tolerance, nonviolence, and respect for legal constraints, then democracies should wage their wars more humanely than other forms of government."[44] Other scholars, however, argue that norms of nonviolence and respect for innocent life have their origins in liberal rather than democratic theory. Liberal norms forbid violating the rights of others or treating people as means to an end. These norms apply even to the citizens of enemy states in wartime.[45] Michael Doyle, for example, contends that restraints on violence against civilians have their origin within liberal thought and endorses Kant's view that liberal democracies must "maintain . . . a scrupulous respect for the laws of war."[46]

A contrasting perspective on democracy rooted in institutions, however, implies that democracies should be more likely to inflict civilian victimization on their foes. The logic is simple: as wars become protracted and the costs of fighting increase, public support tends to decline.[47] Knowing this, democratic elites labor to keep casualties down and maintain public backing for the war effort, which may produce civilian victimization as a means to manage costs. Moreover, because losing a war—or even fighting to a protracted draw—threatens leaders' tenure in office, democratic executives have incentives to fight hard and make sure they win. "Fighting hard" could be interpreted to include civilian victimization.[48] The threat of removal for losing a war also gives democrats incentives to pick easier fights in the first place. This implies that democratic war initiators should be less likely to victimize noncombatants because these conflicts are unlikely to become wars of attrition.[49] Autocracies, by contrast, are less vulnerable to either of these forces because leaders in such regimes are not subject to public recall.

Problems with Regime-Type Arguments

Several problems confront either version of the regime-type argument. First, it is unclear if democracies actually externalize their domestic norms. Liberal democracies, for example, are supposed to go to war for "liberal" reasons only—that is, in self-defense or to prevent human rights abuses. Yet liberal states routinely attacked and subjugated African and Asian tribes in the nineteenth century for reasons not remotely connected to security and have rarely intervened abroad to stop genocide.[50] Liberal democracies often sponsor war crimes tribunals, but hardly ever allow their own soldiers or statesmen to be tried for such violations.[51] Democracies have also undermined or overthrown other democracies and supported brutal dictators when it suited their interests, such as fighting communism during the cold war or terrorism today.[52]

Second, publics in liberal democracies—just as they do not always oppose war—do not uniformly disapprove of civilian victimization. A principled minority can always be counted on to denounce attacking noncombatants, but the majority of people—although firm believers in civilian immunity in theory—are prepared to countenance civilian deaths when their country goes to war.[53] This is why some authors argue that democratic institutions facilitate civilian victimization, either by forcing elites to attend to vindictive public opinion or by putting pressure on leaders to win wars quickly and at low cost.[54]

Third, several analysts question the view that democracies are the only regime type whose domestic institutions systematically affect leaders' behavior. Democratic peace theorists argue that the risk of removal from office gives democrats incentives to avoid antagonizing voters. However, while the *risks* of losing power in a democracy from policy failure are no doubt higher than in less open political systems, the *costs* of being removed are much lower: democratic rulers are never punished by exile or death, whereas leaders of authoritarian regimes sometimes do suffer this fate. It is unclear whether the incentives created by the risks of losing power dominate those created by the potential costs. Indeed, recent scholarship on war termination has found that—contrary to the democracy argument—the costs of removal are the most important factor. Leaders in oligarchic regimes, because they are likely to be removed and punished for even a moderate loss in war, tend to gamble for resurrection, risking catastrophic defeat (and sure punishment) for a slim chance at victory (and continuing in office).[55] Democratic leaders, by contrast, are willing to settle on moderately losing terms because although they will lose office, they will not lose their lives. Dictators, too, will settle for small losses because they can repress any domestic unrest that results. Focusing solely on the risk of removal and ignoring the potential costs of removal, therefore, is misleading.[56]

Finally, the democracy argument erroneously assumes that public opinion acts as a brake on leaders' ability to conduct foreign policy but that leaders lack the ability to shape citizens' views. In fact, leaders in democracies are not cravenly dependent on public opinion, but possess substantial leeway to act independently, particularly when it comes to state security.[57] Furthermore, the initiation of force abroad by a democracy is frequently met with a "rally-round-the-flag" effect whereby much of the public closes ranks behind the executive.[58] Two-thirds of the American public, for instance, initially favored U.S. intervention in Korea and Vietnam, wars that are now widely viewed as the nation's least popular conflicts.[59] Moreover, opposition parties hardly ever dissent from governments' choices to threaten or use force. This fact renders the support of the opposition—thought by some to be a signal of credibility to potential targets—rather uninformative.[60] The restraining power of public opinion on democratic leaders' choices to go to war, therefore—or to victimize noncombatants once in a war—appears frail.

PERCEPTIONS OF CIVILIZED VERSUS BARBARIC IDENTITY

Other scholars argue that mistreatment of civilians is more likely to occur in conflicts in which belligerents view each other as "barbaric" or subhuman. John Dower, for example, has documented how racial hatred between Japan and the United States in World War II contributed to battlefield atrocities and eased the way toward incendiary bombing of Japanese cities.[61] Other historians have advanced this thesis to explain brutality in wars between Christian Europe and the Islamic Middle East, the mass extermination of native civilizations in the New World, and violence in wars of empire, arguing that the "rules, objectives and conduct of war were altogether different once civilization had been left behind." Against barbarians, notes another analyst, "Methods of warfare that in Europe were morally and legally barred were considered legitimate in the face of an enemy who did not seem to subscribe to the same cultural code." As a Greek officer put it after the Balkan wars of 1912–13, "When you have to deal with barbarians, you must behave like a barbarian yourself. It is the only thing they understand."[62]

Problems with the Argument

Three flaws undermine the identity argument. First, it is not clear that objective differences in identity correlate with civilian victimization. For every historian who argues that wars between Christian Europe and the Islamic world were particularly brutal, for example, others contend that wars between Europeans were often just as savage.[63] Similarly, Imperial Japan treated British and American prisoners-of-war with great brutality during World War II, but behaved just as atrociously toward fellow Asians in Korea, China, and elsewhere.[64]

Furthermore, if the identity argument were correct, civilian victimization should have been more frequent in colonial and imperial wars than in interstate wars, since colonial conflicts were fought almost exclusively between white, Christian Europeans and nonwhite non-Christian peoples of Africa and Asia. My coding of the Correlates of War project's list of "extrasystemic" wars undercuts this hypothesis.[65] Using a wide variety of sources, I was able to judge in 84 of the 112 cases in the dataset whether the state actor employed a strategy of civilian victimization. Of those 84 cases, states targeted noncombatants in 29 percent of them. The frequency of civilian victimization in interstate wars—as shown in chapter 2—is about 30 percent for states that had a realistic ability or opportunity to kill enemy noncombatants.

Similarly, data collected by Ivan Arreguín-Toft on the incidence of "barbarism" (a strategy involving the systematic violation of the laws of war) in asymmetric conflicts since 1809—wars in which the strong side had at least a ten-to-one advantage in material power—contradict this hypothesis. Arreguín-Toft found that states used barbarism only about 20 percent of the time.[66] Although the majority of the cases in Arreguín-Toft's dataset comprise wars of imperial expansion, maintenance of empire, or decolonization, there are also a substantial number of interstate wars and civil wars. To eliminate overlap with my dataset but still retain my focus on international conflict, I dropped these two types of conflicts and reanalyzed the data. Eliminating interstate and civil wars resulted in a slight increase in the frequency of barbarism, from 20 to 23.6 percent (N = 106), but this figure is still somewhat smaller than the frequency of civilian victimization in interstate wars. Arreguín-Toft also included many conflicts that do not appear in any conflict dataset (including eleven between the United States and Native American tribes in the nineteenth century) as well as clashes that are ambiguous as to whether they are civil or colonial wars, such as rebellions by groups against land empires like the Ottoman or Russian Empires. Dropping these conflicts yields precisely the same result: barbarism occurred in 23.6 percent of the cases (N = 72). Thus, it does not appear that civilian victimization is more frequent in imperial and colonial conflicts than it is in interstate conflicts.

A second reason to doubt the identity argument for civilian victimization is that demonization of the enemy is ubiquitous in war, yet civilian victimization is relatively rare. States in conflict almost always vilify each other, and political elites have considerable incentives to use such rhetoric, both to convince their populations that war is justified and to mobilize them to fight the conflict.[67] The occurrence of civilian victimization in war, however, varies. Demonization, moreover, when it does occur, is likely to be motivated by clashes of interest rather than actual beliefs about the barbaric nature of the enemy. Germany's transformation in American rhetoric from advanced constitutional state to autocracy before World War I, and the transformation of Saddam Hussein from a bulwark against Islamism in the 1980s to another Hitler after his invasion of Kuwait in 1990, both reflected changes in American relations with Germany and Iraq rather than objective modifications in those countries' institutions or identities.[68] Similarly, when Greece and Bulgaria fought together against Turkey in the First Balkan War, they had friendly relations and viewed each other positively. When the interests of the former allies clashed in 1913, however, and "policy dictated a breach," the Greek press (on cue from the government) spewed forth anti-Bulgarian invective and the previously friendly attitudes between the two nations completely reversed.[69] In short, demonization occurs all the time, but civilian victimization does not, and demonization tends to be instrumental, having little or nothing to do with leaders' views regarding the enemy's actual identity.

Third, although a sophisticated proponent of the identity thesis might argue that perceptions of identity are endogenous to war—that is, the process of fighting brutalizes the participants and convinces them over time that the enemy is barbaric—this, too, is unlikely to account for many cases of civilian victimization. For one thing, it is natural for men who are trying to kill each other to develop feelings of hatred for the enemy. Brutalization in this sense is ubiquitous, but civilian victimization again varies. Moreover, brutalization is most likely to occur in protracted wars of attrition and is thus at least partly a response to rising costs of fighting and desperation. Finally, brutalization affects soldiers on the battlefield more than those responsible for the strategic direction of the war and is thus probably a better explanation for battlefield atrocities than for policies of civilian victimization.[70]

MILITARY ORGANIZATIONS AND CIVILIAN VICTIMIZATION

Like the regime-type perspective, organization theory contains two different arguments on the origins of civilian victimization: organizational culture and parochial organizational interests.

Organizational Culture

Proponents of organizational culture argue that the prevailing culture inside a military organization determines whether it will advocate a strategy that targets civilians. The culture of an organization refers to the beliefs, ways of doing business, and standard operating procedures that develop over time inside an organization based on its members' perception of the organization's mission and goals. In a military organization, "each service develops a culture to guide war fighting. These 'paradigms' either advocate or ignore specific means of warfare. Those means compatible with the dominant war-fighting culture will be adopted and advocated by the military, those means not compatible will suffer benign neglect."[71] Importantly, militaries tend to prefer escalation in those areas that fit with their cultures: "An organizational-culture perspective posits that state preferences on restraint originate in the fit between a particular means of warfare and the collective beliefs of the military services that deploy the means in question. . . . *States will prefer mutual restraint in a particular mode of force if it is antithetical to the war-fighting culture of their military bureaucracy. States will favor escalation when the organizational cultures of their military bureaucracies are compatible with use.*"[72]

This hypothesis, although formulated as a general proposition regarding militaries' willingness to escalate, can be recast more narrowly in terms of noncombatant immunity: states will target enemy civilians if the cultures of their militaries embrace strategies predicated on defeating an adversary by punishing its civilian population. States will observe noncombatant immunity and kill relatively few civilians when they have military cultures that favor counterforce targeting. Legro, for example, argues that the culture of land power in the German armed forces explains why the Luftwaffe generally refrained from bombing civilians early in World War II. Britain, on the other hand, ultimately adopted punishment bombing of German noncombatants owing to the culture of area bombing that developed in the RAF during the interwar period.[73] Others argue that the culture of the German Army in the Wilhelmine period—in particular its obsession with battles of annihilation and total victory—could generate fearful violence against noncombatants in order to achieve the absolute triumph of force the army's culture demanded. When a quick and total victory eluded the kaiser's soldiers—as it did in Southwest Africa in 1904—the relentless pursuit of the enemy in an attempt to achieve total conquest resulted in the near extermination of the Herero people.[74]

Parochial Organizational Interests

Arguments based in parochial organizational interests, by contrast, argue that all organizations tend to want the same kinds of things—autonomy from outside oversight, control over their own affairs, greater levels of prestige and resources—and thus similar organizations across different countries or different issue areas should behave similarly. Organization theorists of military doctrine, for example, contend that all militaries exhibit a bias toward the offensive since attacking tends to require greater resources and expertise than defending.[75] This perspective on civilian victimization implies that should a military organization—or key individuals within the organization—perceive that targeting civilians might advance the organization's parochial interests—or enhance their own job security— the organization will be more likely to lobby for—and the state more likely to adopt—a strategy of civilian victimization.

The strategy of firebombing Japan in World War II is frequently cited as an example of the power of organizational imperatives. Proponents of strategic airpower in the U.S. Army Air Forces, such as General Henry "Hap"

Arnold, knew that if strategic bombing could defeat Japan on its own and alleviate the need for a costly invasion of the Japanese home islands, this would be a powerful argument for making the air force independent of the army. Arnold pressured his subordinates to achieve results in the Pacific with the new B-29 bomber, going so far as to sack General Haywood Hansell and replace him with General Curtis LeMay as commander of B-29s in January 1945. LeMay, too, was told he was expendable if he did not prove the worth of airpower. LeMay's shift to firebombing in March 1945, according to this account, was motivated primarily by his desire to keep his job, which was in jeopardy owing to Arnold's wish to prove that airpower could win wars on its own and should therefore constitute an independent service coequal with the army and the navy.

Problems with Organizational Arguments

One problem shared by both versions of these organization theory arguments is that they apply to the era of professionalized military bureaucracies, which began to emerge in Europe only in the mid-to-late nineteenth century. Civilian victimization, however, has existed since the beginning of recorded history. The contribution of organizational arguments, therefore, is limited to the relatively recent past. Similarly, arguments that focus on military organizations as the key actors fail to explain how militaries get their preferences implemented as state policy when there is civilian control of the military. Civilian policymakers ultimately make the decisions, and they are not affected by the dynamics of military cultures or interservice rivalries.

Accounts featuring organizational culture amply demonstrate that the preconceived assumptions and ideas regarding the appropriate way to fight that permeate military organizations affect the doctrine these organizations develop to wage wars and even how militaries choose to fight in the early stages of armed conflicts. Still, cultural arguments are plagued by two significant weaknesses. First, as an empirical fact, few states plan to implement policies of civilian victimization before wars break out, and even fewer military organizations formulate such strategies in peacetime. Exceptions, of course, exist. The development of an area bombing doctrine in the interwar period by Britain's Royal Air Force is one example. Similarly, the Eisenhower administration's New Look strategy in the 1950s emphasized massive retaliation in the event of Soviet aggression, entailing the obliteration of more than one hundred Soviet cities and millions of civilians in the process.[76] But these examples are few and far between. Moreover, even when militaries do have strategies that call for civilian victimization, these are not automatically and immediately carried out on the outbreak of war. It took two years for Britain to shift to area bombing in World War II as British leaders generally steered clear of targeting German civilians in the war's early phases to avoid giving Hitler an excuse to bomb British cities.[77]

Second, the vast majority of systematic targeting of noncombatants that occurs during wars happens when militaries' initial counterforce strategies fail to deliver a quick and decisive victory. The enemy's ability to retaliate against the state's own civilians also sometimes dictates a strategy that avoids noncombatants in a conflict's early phases (as in the example above). Escalation to civilian victimization, however, eventually occurs whether or not it is compatible with military culture because it is a logical response to the rising costs of battle and/or the need to achieve victory or stave off defeat. A "culture of punishment" is thus neither necessary nor sufficient for a state to target civilians.

The parochial organizational interest argument also faces difficulties. For one, it seemingly overpredicts civilian victimization, since military branches are always competing for resources and influence yet civilians are rarely targeted. Moreover, if the argument is restricted to services trying to secure organizational independence, such as the U.S. Air Force in World War II, the question is why did services that were already independent—such as the RAF in Britain and the Luftwaffe in Germany—also bomb civilians? Finally, if securing organizational independence is such an important motivation for civilian victimization, why did the U.S. Air Force behave similarly in Korea—after achieving organizational autonomy—to the way it did in World War II, firebombing cities in North Korea?

DESPERATION, CONQUEST, AND CIVILIAN VICTIMIZATION

I argue that states are prone to target civilians for one of two reasons: first, desperation to achieve victory and lower costs in protracted wars of attrition—in which case civilian victimization is a coercive strategy meant to sap the morale of an adversary's population or undermine the enemy's ability to fight—and second, an appetite for territorial conquest that causes states to use force to subdue or eliminate an adversary's population to gain control over the conquered area. States that are less tolerant of costs and in greater need of victory—such as democracies—are likely to be more susceptible to desperation.

Desperation and Civilian Victimization

Imagine two belligerents go to war over issue X. Each country wants to win a quick and decisive victory, achieving its aims at relatively low cost to itself. Imagine further that events do not unfold as planned, and the belligerents' strategies for prevailing quickly and cheaply are foiled. The war bogs down into siegelike operations, trench warfare, and costly battles of attrition. Alternatively, suppose a country is attacked by a rival, and owing to the geographic or military circumstances realizes that the war is going to be a difficult and costly slog. Battlefield stalemates like these—or the knowledge early on that there is no easy way to prevail—give rise to two mechanisms that can trigger civilian victimization. First, such deadlocks induce desperation to win: belligerents will use any means that has the potential to pull victory from the jaws of defeat. Second, the costs of fighting generated by wars of attrition cause desperation to save lives and lead to targeting of noncombatants as a cost-reduction strategy that allows a state to continue prosecuting the war at an acceptable price in casualties.[78]

In protracted wars of attrition, civilian victimization is a form of coercion, that is, the attempt to influence an adversary's behavior by manipulating costs and benefits. Specifically, civilian victimization inflicts costs on noncombatants to coerce a government or rebel organization to cease fighting. Traditionally, scholars have equated inflicting pain on noncombatants with punishment. Punishment is a coercive strategy that erodes the adversary's will to fight, either by convincing the government that the civilian costs outweigh the benefits of resistance, or by turning the civilians themselves against the war and hoping that they will pressure the government to end the war. The logic of punishment is clearly reflected in Lord Cherwell's "dehousing" memo, which became the basis for British urban area bombing during World War II. Cherwell—Prime Minister Winston Churchill's scientific adviser—argued that relentless bombing of cities would destroy German morale by rendering the population homeless.[79] Of course, the British proposed to do much more than simply destroy German homes: the real targets were the occupants of those homes. But the objective of the strategy is nonetheless clear: kill noncombatants to break the will of survivors, thereby inducing the enemy to give up.

Victimizing civilians can also follow the logic of denial, intended more to undermine the adversary's ability to prosecute its military strategy than to break its will to resist. According to internal military documents from 1943 and 1944, for example, American planning to use incendiary bombs against Japanese cities was not a punishment strategy. Rather, the objective was to destroy Japan's dispersed system of industrial production and to generate a labor shortage by killing workers.[80] Similarly, in response to Chinese intervention in the Korean War in early November 1950, the commander of UN forces—General Douglas MacArthur—unleashed U.S. bombers to create a cordon sanitaire between the Chinese border and UN lines. According to one historian, "MacArthur told the American ambassador to South Korea that he intended to turn the narrow stretch of territory between UN lines and the border into 'a desert' incapable of supporting Communist troops."[81]

The denial logic of civilian victimization is even more apparent in counterguerrilla warfare. Insurgent forces rely on the assistance they receive from the civilian population. Counterinsurgency strategies use civilian victimization to sever the link between the guerrillas and the populace by one of two means: deter people from helping the insurgents, or physically prevent such support by removing the population from areas where guerrillas operate. The deterrence tactic employs murders and massacres of known or suspected insurgent supporters to frighten those left alive. The interdiction method, by contrast, concentrates people under government control or simply kills them, rendering them unable to support the guerrillas.

Desperation to Win. When wars become protracted with little chance of victory on the immediate horizon, belligerents are more likely to employ civilian victimization out of desperation to win the war. In an anarchic world, states are concerned with survival. While the consequences of defeat in war are not always catastrophic, at the very least defeat can endanger the state's power position or reputation, leaving it vulnerable to future predation or challenges by its neighbors. In wars of attrition, moreover, the consequences of losing may be severe, including the loss of significant amounts of territory, national independence, or even enslavement or genocide. The perils of defeat, therefore, make decision-makers desperate to win and may cause leaders to target civilians.

A classic case of desperation to win occurred in the latter days of World War I. Despite increasing pressures from the admirals of the High Seas Fleet, both Chancellor Theobald von Bethmann-Hollweg and Kaiser Wilhelm II had steadfastly rejected launching a campaign of unlimited submarine warfare against British commerce with German U-boats. Such a strategy, they believed, ran too great a risk of provoking the United States to enter the conflict, a risk they did not feel was warranted given Germany's relatively favorable military position. In the summer of 1916, however, blow after blow struck the Central Powers—failure at Verdun, the British offensive on the Somme, the Brusilov offensive against Austria-Hungary, and the entry of Romania into the war on the side of the Entente powers—radically changing the German leadership's perception of the likelihood of victory. A sense of desperation that something had to be done to stem the tide of defeats finally caused Bethmann-Hollweg to acquiesce in the military's desire for U-boat warfare against ships importing food to Britain. As naval historian V. E. Tarrant concludes, "The demands of the military and naval leaders, the Kaiser's acquiescence and the Chancellor's abdication of authority had a common denominator—realistically there was no alternative but to make the ultimate decision with regard to the strategic use of the U-boats, because Germany's situation was desperate."[82]

Desperation to win is also behind many instances of civilian victimization in wars against guerrilla insurgencies. Rebel movements that choose to employ a guerrilla strategy do not hope to defeat their more powerful foes by inflicting massive casualties. Rather, guerrillas hope to prolong the war indefinitely, inflicting small but steady casualties on their adversary in the hope that the more powerful side will tire of the conflict and give in to the insurgents' demands instead of continuing to prosecute a seemingly un-winnable war. The stronger forces, therefore, have an incentive to strike at the guerrillas' Achilles heel—the civilian population from which they draw recruits, supplies, shelter, and information—in order to shorten the war.[83] Rebels, too, tend to target noncombatants as they become increasingly desperate, which tends to occur when government forces begin to infiltrate areas the insurgents have previously controlled, causing the rebels to lash out against defectors to deter other potential turncoats.[84]

Desperation to Save Lives. As the costs of fighting mount, states need to conserve their military forces while still putting pressure on the enemy. Given that the manpower resources of most countries are not inexhaustible, suffering large numbers of casualties threatens to deplete the state's most important military asset, which could eventually result in an inability to continue the war. Taking huge casualties is also bad for the military's morale, as demonstrated by the French army mutinies after the disastrous Nivelle offensive of 1917. Terrific combat losses, moreover, sap morale on the home front, causing civilians to lose faith in victory and pressure the government to stop the war. And, in the words of George Kennan, "Government is an agent, not a principal. Its primary obligation is to the *interests* of the national society it represents." The interests of mankind as a whole rate—if anything—a distant second.[85] This obligation, or "statesman's duty," disposes leaders to value and protect the lives of their people over those of foreigners.[86] Targeting enemy civilians (or using force less discriminately)—because it can provide a way to continue attacking the enemy yet decrease one's own losses at the same time—is a rational solution.[87] Over time, therefore, even if leaders did not previously believe in the efficacy of civilian victimization or think that they would use such a morally objectionable strategy, the costs of the fighting convince them that something must be done to win the war but also to limit losses. Civilian victimization is a promising option on both counts.

The costs of fighting come in two forms: costs of actual military operations, and costs expected to result from future operations. In the former, increasing losses from combat threaten to destroy a belligerent's forces. This can occur in the context of a particular military campaign or in the war as a whole. When U.S. daylight precision bombing of Germany in World War II became unsustainably costly in the fall of 1943, for example, American airmen—rather than abandon bombing altogether—adopted radar techniques that radically reduced accuracy and increased noncombatant casualties, but drastically reduced U.S. bomber losses.[88] In World War I, as the expectations of each of the belligerents regarding the costs of fighting and the duration of the war as a whole changed as 1914 turned to 1915, leaders in many of these countries decided to add civilian victimization—in the form of primitive strategic bombing and naval blockade—to their repertoire of strategies to coerce their enemies to end the war and limit their own combat losses.

Civilian victimization may also result when belligerents expect that the costs of future fighting will inflict serious military costs. The anticipation of high costs of fighting can occur before the war actually starts or during the war itself. The prospect or expectation that a war will be costly induces states to develop strategies that will achieve the state's aims but avoid paying a high price.[89] The mere prospect of future costs before a war begins is thus generally not powerful enough to cause states to target civilians because states desire quick and decisive victories, and civilian victimization—to the extent that it works—works slowly.

When the costs of an impending military operation promise to be very high during an ongoing war, however, the state is already committed, fewer alternatives are available, and hence civilian victimization is more likely to be chosen. In one scenario, a state is attacked and knows immediately that the war cannot be won quickly. This was the case in the Pacific after Japan struck the United States in the Philippines and at Pearl Harbor. Driven out of the Far East and with much of the Pacific fleet destroyed, the United States simply did not have the means at its disposal to defeat Japan quickly. Moreover, American leaders understood that penetrating Japan's defense perimeter would require difficult fighting well before U.S. forces got anywhere near the Japanese homeland. In short, U.S. leaders knew that they were in for a long war of attrition and began to plan accordingly for how they might employ airpower against Japanese cities to lower the costs of victory and shorten the war.

The classic example of impending costs during an ongoing war is siege warfare: assaulting walled cities was difficult because of the advantages held by the defender, and thus besieging forces would try to reduce the town with indiscriminate bombardment and starvation. A more recent example on a grander scale was the endgame of the Pacific War. Military planners forecast that the projected invasions of the Japanese home islands would exact a heavy toll in U.S. casualties. Confronted with this prediction, U.S. leaders tightened the naval blockade, firebombed Japanese cities, and ultimately used atomic weapons to avoid a costly invasion.

A Tactic of Later Resort. Because states prefer to win quick and decisive victories, they typically seek to defeat an adversary's military forces at the outset of wars. Unless states specifically intend to seize and annex territory populated by the enemy, therefore, civilian victimization tends to be a "tactic of later resort."[90] When states face the prospect of a protracted war of attrition, they more often than not are deterred from initiating a conflict, or they postpone an attack until they devise a plan that promises to deliver a victory on the cheap. The problem with initiating a war with a strategy of civilian victimization is that such strategies—when they work—take time to have an effect. States tend not to elect civilian victimization as a war-initiating strategy, therefore, because it possesses little utility for winning quick and decisive victories.[91]

Robert Pape has elaborated a number of reasons why coercive strategies do not succeed quickly. It is important to remember that these reasons apply especially to civilian victimization, which Pape argues is unlikely to succeed in major wars because states are able to adapt and minimize their vulnerability, punishment cannot inflict sufficient pain on nationalistic societies to compel them to sacrifice important interests, and hurting civilians more often turns them against the attacker than against their own leaders. Beyond these factors, coercion produces success late in wars for Pape because leaders face significant costs for admitting defeat. Democratic leaders confront the prospect of being voted out of office for losing the war, whereas autocratic leaders may be overthrown, exiled, jailed, or killed. Leaders thus tend to hold out, hoping for a miracle to reverse the tide of battle and save their political futures. Even when political leaders are ready to throw in the towel, sometimes the military opposes surrender.[92]

Other factors reinforce the tendency for civilian victimization as a tactic of later resort. The most important of these is deterrence, the ability of both adversaries to strike each other's noncombatants. When both belligerents have the ability to kill their adversary's civilians, each may be deterred from striking by the prospect of retaliation, much like mutual assured destruction discouraged the United States and the Soviet Union from using nuclear weapons during the cold war. Mutual deterrence of this kind, for example, restrained the onset of urban aerial bombing by Britain and Germany in the early years of World War II.[93] When only one side possesses the capability to target civilians—or when a conflict has progressed to the stage that one side is safe from retaliation by the enemy—the deterrence view would not predict restraint to hold up.

Belligerents may also be deterred from victimizing noncombatants by the fear of alienating a powerful third party or even provoking it to enter hostilities. In the early months of World War I, British leaders worried that implementing a total blockade of Germany might provoke the neutral states of northern Europe to enter the conflict on Germany's side and cost them much needed American support. Similarly, the Germans feared that unrestricted submarine warfare would trigger American intervention on the side of the Entente, and thus German political leaders refused to unleash the U-boats until after the tide of the war turned decisively against them in 1916.

Furthermore, the desire to avoid international criticism of their conduct or damage to the state's reputation could deter leaders from early resort to civilian victimization. Although the norm against killing civilians has never been internalized so as to make attacking noncombatants unthinkable, violating it imposes a cost by sullying a state's reputation.[94] Belligerents often attempt to curry favor with influential neutral states or the international community more generally by proclaiming their intention to wage war in conformity with international humanitarian norms, or by denouncing supposed violations of those norms by their opponent.[95]

Finally, and most simply, states must have the ability to reach an adversary's homeland to employ civilian victimization, and this is sometimes not the case early in a conflict. After Japan's surprise attack on American bases in Hawaii and the Philippines in December 1941, for example, the United States had few means with which to inflict damage on the Japanese home islands. Only after a protracted island-hopping campaign did the United States acquire bases close enough to Japan to contemplate a serious campaign of civilian victimization.[96]

Appetite for Conquest and Civilian Victimization

The desperation model assumes nothing about the nature of the belligerents' war aims, only that states go to war over an unspecified issue. In some conflicts, however, the objective of one or both combatants is to conquer and annex a piece of the adversary's territory. Land, of course, is rarely uninhabited, and the people living there can be more or less hostile to the change in ownership. When the chancellor of Prussia, Otto von Bismarck, sought to annex the historically German provinces of Alsace and Lorraine (acquired by France under Louis XIV) in the Franco-Prussian War, much of the population did not oppose the transfer of sovereignty. The Prussians, moreover, viewed the inhabitants as "German" and capable of being assimilated without much trouble.[97] Mass violence against civilians was therefore absent in this case. Other cases, however, turn out differently. What distinguishes these from the outcome in 1870?

I argue that the presence of civilian populations sharing the nationality of the enemy in areas a belligerent wishes to annex generates civilian victimization to cow such people into submission or, more commonly, to evict them from the territory altogether.[98] On the one hand, these civilians sometimes pose a real threat of subversion or rebellion, a potential fifth column that can create serious immediate or future problems for the occupier. Demographically intermingled ethnonational groups, for example—such as Arabs and Jews in Palestine (1947–49) or Serbs and Muslims in Bosnia (1992–95)—occasionally go to war. At least one side in such conflicts—and often both—seeks to establish a national state on all or part of the territory inhabited by another group. A national state with a substantial minority of "nonnationals," however, is unlikely to be secure or stable over time because this group poses a permanent threat of rebellion. As one Zionist leader commented in 1938, "We cannot start the Jewish state with ... half the population being Arab. ... Such a state cannot survive even half an hour."[99] Moreover, leaving concentrations of enemy nationals intact behind the front lines risks leaving a fifth column that could take up arms and create a two-front war. After the Haganah (the main Jewish defense force) captured the town of Beisan in May 1948, for instance, Jewish officers—who viewed this concentration of Arab civilians so close to the front lines as a security threat—sought and received approval to expel them.[100] Believing that there is little or no possibility of gaining the support of members of the opposing group, belligerents in these situations attack the other group's civilians to avoid the risk—if not always the actuality—of being attacked themselves.

Expelling or killing civilians of the enemy group not only reduces the costs of the present fighting—by depriving their fighters of manpower and materiel—but it also reduces the threat of future costs from an uprising or a rescue operation by the group's coethnics from outside the state. The presence of these civilians creates a standing invitation for their conationals in neighboring states to intervene to rescue them, as well as giving the territory's former owner a claim to the land. In the first Balkan war (1912–13), for example, Serbia, Montenegro, Bulgaria, and Greece invaded Ottoman territory with the explicit intention of seizing land and annexing it to their national states. To ensure the viability—and permanence—of these conquests, and to reduce the possibility that the Turks would seek to reconquer lost territories, the Balkan states quickly set about persecuting and expelling Turkish civilians. When the former allies turned on each other in the second Balkan war (1913), they likewise killed and banished civilians who shared the nationality of their new enemy, the losing Bulgarians suffering the most.[101]

In interstate wars, the group most likely to be viewed as hostile or threatening is the noncombatant population that shares the enemy's nationality. Occasionally, however, a regime identifies one particular group in the enemy society as the most serious threat, such as Nazi Germany's classification of Jews as a racial and ideological menace. Groups like this may then be singled out for especially harsh treatment, deportation, or even total annihilation. This may also occur when a state at war perceives a particular domestic population as sympathetic to the enemy and thus constituting a potential fifth column. Examples include Turkey's treatment of its Armenian population in World War I, and Stalin's deportation of ethnic Germans from European Russia and several other groups from the Caucasus during World War II.[102] Nor is ethnonational identity the sole line of difference: some states are governed by particular political ideologies and may persecute their ideological foes on invading another country.[103] These special motivations for identifying the "hostile" population granted, however, the basic logic of territorial annexation still holds, and no special murderous ideology is needed to generate civilian victimization in these conflicts.

A Tactic of Early Resort. Civilian victimization in wars in which the annexation of enemy-inhabited territory is the goal tends to be a tactic of early resort because civilians are readily accessible, and attacking them pays immediate military and political dividends by removing threats of rebellion and subversion in the army's rear area. Furthermore, deterrence is unlikely to act as a restraint because one side may have exclusive access to the adversary's civilians as a consequence of invading enemy territory. Eliminating fifth columns in one's midst may also seem necessary for survival and hence override fears that the enemy might launch reprisals elsewhere. Moreover, states involved in aggressive wars to seize and colonize territory, or locked in struggles for survival to eliminate fifth columns, are probably less susceptible to norms against harming noncombatants.

The Rationality of Civilian Victimization

As noted in the introduction, civilian victimization is commonly thought to be irrational because attacking noncombatants is generally ineffective and sometimes even steels the enemy's resolve to resist.[104] This raises a puzzling question: If governments know that victimizing civilians will not help achieve their objectives, then why would they do it?

Those who uncritically condemn policies of civilian victimization wrongly assume that such policies are always ineffective.[105] There is significant variation in the success rate of civilian victimization over time and across different types of warfare. In the past, sieges regularly succeeded at capturing enemy towns by starving the besieged civilian population. The hunger, deprivation, sickness, and death inflicted on noncombatants during the Siege of Paris by Prussia in 1870–71, for example, significantly hastened French officials' decision to surrender the city. By late January 1871, according to one history of the conflict, "Cases were reported of people dropping dead in queues outside food-shops, and undernourishment, cold and disease took their toll of thousands more. . . . Faced with the imminent prospect of famine on a horrifying scale, the Government decided that it could not delay negotiating an armistice any longer."[106]

Besieging entire countries and attempting to coerce them into ending a war via civilian victimization is more difficult, owing to the resiliency of the modern nation-state, but does not always fail. The Anglo-American naval blockade of Germany in World War I, for example, is credited by some—including Philipp Scheidemann, the leader of Germany's Social Democratic Party at the end of the war—with contributing to Germany's eventual collapse in the fall of 1918.[107] Similarly, the U.S. blockade of Japan during World War II debilitated Japanese war production by 1945. Had the war continued, Japan would have faced widespread famine owing to its inability to import food.[108] By contrast, all three attempts by continental powers to interdict Great Britain's food supply—Napoleon's Continental System, and the U-boat campaigns of Wilhelmine and Nazi Germany—produced disappointing results for the coercer, owing to Britain's ability to adjust to projected shortages, substitute other goods for those in short supply, and place more land under cultivation.[109]

Judicious use of terror against civilians can pay high military dividends in guerrilla wars: insurgents employ it to coerce civilians into supporting their movement, while incumbents rely on it as a means of counterpersuasion. The Vietcong, for example, made widespread use of assassination to terrorize rural villagers in South Vietnam. According to Stathis Kalyvas, "In a hamlet they would pick out a couple of people who they said cooperated with the United States, and shoot them, to set an example. Apparently, this worked." Similarly, the Phoenix Program instituted by U.S. and South Vietnamese forces "appears to have been quite effective in getting South Vietnamese peasants to minimize their collaboration with the Vietcong after 1971."[110] But even indiscriminate violence—such as forced concentration or mass killing intended to reduce guerrillas' ability to fight by cutting them off from the civilian population—has succeeded in several wars. Indiscriminate violence can succeed against smaller populations and land areas—such as the Second Anglo-Boer War, the U.S.–Filipino War, the Second Italo-Sanusi War—because the government is able to target the entire population, preventing it from providing any material support to the rebels.[111] Such strategies tend to backfire when states are unable to exert physical control over the territory or population in question, as the Germans could not do in the Soviet Union or the Balkans during World War II.[112]

Many states have successfully expanded their territory (or that of an ally) by targeting enemy civilians in wars of conquest. Just looking at interstate wars, for example, Russia assisted in the creation of a Bulgarian state by killing and expelling Muslim Turks in the Russo-Turkish war (1877–78); Serbia, Bulgaria, Greece, and Montenegro each expanded at the expense of Ottoman Turkey in 1912–13, driving out much of the remaining Muslim population in Europe in the process; Israel consolidated and expanded its territory in the 1948 war, as most of the Palestinian Arabs fled the fighting or were expelled by force; and Turkey established a Turkish Cypriot enclave in northern Cyprus in 1974 by forcibly removing Greek Cypriots. Clearly, some ethnic cleansing campaigns also backfire: Germany's quest to conquer much of the Soviet Union in World War II is the most spectacular example. Greece's expulsion of Turks from western Anatolia also miscarried when Mustafa Kemal rallied the Turkish Army and ejected the invaders, ending the Greek presence in Anatolia.

Further evidence regarding the effectiveness of civilian victimization can be derived from large-N data (see table 1.2). Returning to Arreguín-Toft's data on asymmetric conflicts, for example, strong actors that used barbarism as a strategy won 78 percent of the time, compared to 69 percent for strong actors that employed conventional strategies. Furthermore, barbarism is much more effective than conventional approaches against insurgencies, winning in 77 percent of cases versus 50 percent in which this approach was not used.[113] An examination of the Correlates of War project's "extrasystemic" war data yields similar results. Civilian victimization in these conflicts is no more or less effective than fighting conventionally—79 versus 83 percent—but it still works in four out of every five cases. Against guerrillas, however, civilian victimization wins somewhat more often than conventional approaches, 71 to 60 percent.[114] Finally, in interstate wars, states that target civilians win 62 percent of their wars as opposed to 42 percent of states that use exclusively countermilitary strategies. This relationship holds—although not as strongly—in wars of attrition, where the figures are 61 versus 44 percent.[115] These correlations, of course, do not prove that civilian victimization was a cause of victory. However, if civilian victimization were as ineffective as some critics maintain, there should be some evidence that states that target civilians lose in the majority of cases. Instead, the evidence indicates precisely the opposite: targeting civilians seems to be at least as effective—and sometimes more effective—than conventional strategies.[116]

A key point to remember, finally, is that civilian victimization is often driven by perceived strategic necessity: leaders may see themselves as having little choice but to target noncombatants if they wish to prevail at a price they can afford, avoid defeat, or annex desired territory. Leaders, therefore, need not be certain that civilian victimization will succeed; they merely need to believe that it might lower their costs of fighting, contribute to victory (or stave off defeat), or consolidate their hold over territory. If civilian victimization offers a chance of reversing a grim situation, or delivering a state's goals at a cost it can afford to pay, leaders may take that chance rather than abandon their goals. Civilian victimization is thus a calculated risk, not an irrational gamble.

Table 1.2. Civilian victimization and victory

	Percentage of victories		Percentage of victories in guerrilla wars/ wars of attrition	
	Barbarism/civilian victimization	Conventional strategy	Barbarism/civilian victimization	Conventional strategy
Asymmetric wars	78	69	77**	50**
Extrasystemic wars	79	83	71	60
Interstate wars	62***	42***	61	44

Sources: Data on the effectiveness of barbarism in asymmetric wars are from Ivan Arreguín-Toft, "How the Weak Win Wars: A Theory of Asymmetric Conflict," *International Security* 26, no. 1 (summer 2001): 93–128. Data on outcomes in interstate and extrasystemic wars is from Correlates of War Interstate and Extra-State War Data, version 3. http://cow2.la.psu.edu. Coding for civilian victimization in these conflicts was performed by the author.

Note: Asterisks indicate that the difference between the two strategies is statistically significant; ** = < 0.05; *** = < 0.01.

METHODS AND CASES

The theories sketched in this chapter predict different patterns of outcomes. The remainder of this book is devoted to testing these competing arguments and determining which provides the superior explanation for civilian victimization in warfare. I employ both large-N statistical techniques as well as process tracing of historical cases to investigate the causes of civilian victimization. This combination of methodologies allows me to compile evidence on the incidence of civilian victimization in a large sample of cases and investigate its causes in particular instances.

The comparative advantage of statistical methods lies in establishing correlations between independent and dependent variables in a wide variety of cases. The analysis in chapter 2, for example, includes all countries that participated in an interstate war in the past two centuries, a total of 323 countries in 100 conflicts. These states are coded along a variety of dimensions, including whether or not they used a strategy of civilian victimization and how many civilians they killed. Using this data, I am able not only to establish correlations between individual independent variables and civilian victimization, but I can also determine the relative importance of each variable controlling for the effects of the others, as well as estimate how much each of the independent variables increases or decreases the likelihood that a state will victimize noncombatants. This large-N methodology permits greater confidence in the results than were I to examine only a few cases in depth. In particular, the statistical aspect of this book demonstrates the generalizability (or external validity) of my arguments regarding desperation, appetite for conquest, and civilian victimization, suggesting that these arguments are not the product of case selection or unique to a few particular cases but hold across many wars.

Large-N methodologies are less adroit, however, at showing causality—that changes in an independent variable actually cause (rather than correlate with) changes in the dependent variable. Every theory, in addition to having a hypothesis that predicts a relationship between two variables, contains a causal logic that explains why this relationship obtains. If a theory is correct, we should observe leaders in individual cases reasoning and behaving in ways that the causal logic of the theory predicts. Investigating these causal logics is the strength of qualitative methods, particularly process tracing: demonstrating that as leaders' perceptions of the costs of fighting rise or their estimates of the likelihood of victory fall, they choose to adopt less discriminate means of combat or deliberately target civilians. The two methods, therefore, complement each other, and strengthen the inferences that may be drawn from the evidence presented.

Within the qualitative section of this book, the criteria I used to select cases for closer examination allow me to make relatively strong claims about causality. First, I chose cases that contained variation on the primary independent variables: regime type, identity, organizational culture and interests, desperation, and annexationist war aims. Because it is not possible to obtain variation on all of these variables in a single case, I selected several in order to be able to make comparisons across cases. Some cases, for example, pit a democracy against a nondemocracy. Others pit two belligerents that share a similar cultural code whereas in a third group of cases, two belligerents who view each other as barbarians square off. There are also cases in which desperation and the desire to annex territory vary. My arguments are strengthened to the extent that similar behaviors emerge across regime types and different views of the adversary's identity, and variation in behavior accords with variation in desperation and annexationist war aims.[117]

Second, although I placed a high priority on covering the four main forms of civilian victimization—bombing, blockade/siege, counterinsurgency, and cleansing—selecting only cases in which victimization occurred would bias my results because of the problems associated with selecting on the dependent variable. I thus examine not only cases where civilian victimization was present, but also several cases—such as the 1991 Persian Gulf War—in which the states concerned did not victimize noncombatants in order to observe if the variables I assert cause civilian victimization are absent or take low values in these cases.

Third, many of the cases of desperation I examine are characterized by within-case variation in both costs and expectations of victory, on the one hand, and civilian victimization on the other. This permits what George and Bennett label a "before-after design" in which the researcher can observe whether change in the independent variables resulted in corresponding change in the dependent variable.[118]

Finally, I chose cases that—by spanning the twentieth century—allow for a longitudinal analysis to test for period effects, such as improvements in weapons technology that allow for greater precision, or stronger international ethical norms against harming innocent civilians.

[2]

Statistical Tests

Civilian Victimization, Mass Killing, and
Civilian Casualties in Interstate Wars

The purpose of this chapter is to evaluate empirically the competing explanations for civilian victimization outlined in chapter 1 against evidence from a large number of cases. The analysis uses evidence from a new dataset that includes data on 323 belligerents in interstate wars between 1816 and 2003 as well as 53 cases of civilian victimization. The statistical results provide solid support for the view that desperation to win and to save lives on one's own side, as well as an appetite for territorial conquest and annexation, are the primary drivers of civilian victimization. Indicators of desperation, such as battle deaths, war duration, total war aims (like regime change or unconditional surrender), and attrition warfare correlate strongly with civilian victimization, mass killing, and the number of civilian fatalities a state inflicts. Similarly, when a belligerent intends to annex territory from another state, civilians are also likely to be targeted and killed.

By contrast, I find scant support for the argument that belligerents are more likely to target civilians in wars fought across cultural boundaries than against opponents with similar identities. This variable is never statistically significant in the predicted positive direction with any dependent variable. In fact, controlling for other determinants of civilian victimization, cultural differences tend to have a negative effect, reducing the likelihood of civilian targeting and the number of noncombatant fatalities.

The findings for regime type are interestingly nuanced. The effect of democracy on civilian victimization, mass killing, and civilian casualties is uniformly positive and sometimes significant, especially with the first two dependent variables. This finding is subject to two qualifications. First, the positive result for democracy is driven mainly by the conduct of these regimes during wars of attrition, when they are more likely than autocracies to victimize noncombatants. Second, a reversal occurs around 1970, after which time democracies become less likely than other regimes to target civilians.

It is not possible to test organizational arguments in a large-N setting: hardly any militaries have "punishment" cultures, for example. Moreover, military services are always jockeying with each other for increased funding, but very few are trying to achieve organizational independence during wars. These mechanisms are better examined in case studies.

This chapter is divided into two parts. The first part describes the analysis and my main findings in terms that should be easily comprehensible by the general reader. The second part consists of a pair of appendixes, which go into far greater detail for those readers interested in the statistical analysis. In the first appendix, I describe the dataset, operationalize the variables, discuss the methodology, and present the results of several different types of regression models of the determinants of civilian victimization, mass killing, and numbers of civilian casualties. The second appendix addresses the issue of sequencing, looking specifically at civilian victimization in wars of attrition to be sure that desperation precedes civilian victimization.

DATASET

To test the hypotheses about civilian victimization generated in this volume, I compiled a dataset consisting of all states that participated in an interstate war between 1816 and 2003. This list of wars and belligerents draws primarily on the Correlates of War (COW) Interstate War Participants dataset, which I modified in two ways.[1] First, I added seven wars to the list that were either omitted by COW, were ongoing at the time of the dataset's last release, or occurred later: Chad-Libya (1987, Azou Strip), Armenia-Azerbaijan (1992–94, Nagorno-Karabakh), Ethiopia-Eritrea (1998–2000, border), United States–Yugoslavia (1999, Kosovo), India-Pakistan (1999, Kargil), United States–Afghanistan (2001, Taliban support for al-Qaeda), and United States–Iraq (2003, remove Saddam Hussein). In these wars, Armenia, Azerbaijan, and Yugoslavia victimized civilians, but the Yugoslav case is omitted because it was committed inside the country's borders against a domestic population. Second, I disaggregated long, multiparticipant, and multiphase wars into their components. Following recent quantitative work on war initiation and victory, for example, I divided World War II into nine separate wars, and the First World War into four individual conflicts.[2] I also divided the Vietnam and Persian Gulf wars into two conflicts each (1965–73 and 1973–75 for the former, Iraq versus Kuwait and Coalition versus Iraq for the latter). These changes resulted in a list of 100 wars, 323 belligerents, and 53 cases of civilian victimization.

Outcomes

The analysis in this chapter employs three different measures of civilian targeting and civilian casualties: civilian victimization, mass killing, and number of civilian fatalities. The reason is to test the robustness of my findings: do the same variables that explain decisions to target noncombatants also explain the numbers of civilians who are killed? To the extent that the results remain consistent across these different dependent variables, we gain greater confidence that the findings are not a fluke.

Civilian Victimization

Civilian victimization is defined as a military strategy in which civilians are either targeted intentionally or force is used indiscriminately such that tens of thousands of civilians are killed. As outlined in chapter 1, civilian victimization typically takes one of several forms: bombardment of urban areas; starvation blockades, sieges, or sanctions; population concentration or relocation, massacres, and destruction of the environment in the context of counterinsurgency strategies; and depredations against civilians in the service of ethnic or ideological cleansing. The dependent variable was coded 1 if a state employed such a strategy and zero otherwise. Fifty-three belligerents—16 percent of all interstate war participants, and 30 percent of those deemed capable of targeting civilians—victimized noncombatants according to my criteria. Civilian victimization occurred in one-third of interstate wars. These instances—and the casualties they generated—are displayed in table 2.1.[3]

Mass Killing

One criticism of civilian victimization is that it does not convey any information about the severity of the violence. This could be a potential source of bias: what if democracies, for example, are just as likely to target civilians, but when they do, democracies do not kill as many noncombatants as autocracies? The next two dependent variables are designed to alleviate this problem by measuring in various ways the number of civilians killed by belligerents in wars. One such variable already exists in the literature: mass killing, defined by Benjamin Valentino as an instance where a belligerent intentionally kills fifty thousand or more noncombatants over a maximum period of five years.[4] Because I am interested in civilian victimization that states inflict on noncombatants outside their borders during armed conflicts, mass killing for the purposes of this analysis consists of cases of intentional or indiscriminate killing of civilians in enemy countries that result in at least fifty thousand civilian fatalities during an interstate war. Between 1816 and 2003, there were eighteen cases of mass killing according to this definition.

Table 2.1. Cases of civilian victimization and mass killing in interstate wars, 1816–2003, with estimates of civilian fatalities

War	State	Years	Mass killing*	Civilians Killed		
				Low	Medium	High
Franco-Prussian	Prussia	1870–71	1	6,987	50,000	50,000
Russo-Turkish	Russia	1877–78	1	262,000	262,000	262,000
Boxer Rebellion	China	1900	0	32,284	32,284	32,284
Boxer Rebellion	Russia	1900	0	*5,000*	*5,000*	*5,000*
Boxer Rebellion†	United Kingdom	1900	0	*1,000*	*1,000*	*1,000*
Boxer Rebellion†	United States	1900	0	*1,000*	*1,000*	*1,000*
Boxer Rebellion†	France	1900	0	*1,000*	*1,000*	*1,000*
First Balkan	Serbia	1912–13	0	453	*11,000*	*11,000*
First Balkan	Bulgaria	1912–13	0	1,345	*15,000*	*15,000*
First Balkan	Greece	1912–13	0	210	*1,000*	*1,000*
Second Balkan	Serbia	1913	0	9,453	*15,000*	*15,000*
Second Balkan	Greece	1913	0	1,180	*10,000*	*10,000*
Second Balkan	Bulgaria	1913	0	671	*1,000*	*1,000*
Second Balkan	Turkey	1913	0	2,648	*7,500*	*7,500*
World War I West	Germany	1914–18	0	11,369	11,446	11,446
World War I West	France	1914–18	1	374	297,374	410,374
World War I West	United Kingdom	1914–18	1	891,374	297,374	410,374
World War I West	United States	1917–18	1	0	297,000	410,000
World War I East	Turkey	1914–18	1	50,000	75,000	75,000
Hungarian†	Romania	1919	0	126	*1,000*	*1,000*
Greco-Turkish	Greece	1919–22	0	10,000	15,000	15,000
Greco-Turkish	Turkey	1919–22	0	25,000	25,000	100,000
Franco-Turkish†	France	1919–21	0	*1,000*	*1,000*	*1,000*

(Continued)

(Table 2.1.—Cont.)

War	State	Years	Mass killing*	Civilians Killed		
				Low	Medium	High
Franco-Turkish†	Turkey	1919–21	0	20,000	27,600	30,000
Sino-Soviet†	USSR	1929	0	2,000	2,000	2,000
Sino-Japanese	Japan	1931–33	0	6,080	10,000	16,120
Italo-Ethiopian	Italy	1935–36	1	250,000	250,000	250,000
Sino-Japanese	Japan	1937–45	1	1,578,000	3,949,000	6,325,000
Poland	Germany	1939	0	26,000	41,000	56,000
Russo-Finnish†	USSR	1939–40	0	640	650	700
World War II West	Germany	1940–45	1	53,000	53,000	53,000
World War II West	United Kingdom	1940–45	1	305,000	305,000	305,000
World War II West	United States	1941–45	1	100,000	100,000	100,000
German-Yugoslav	Germany	1941	0	3,000	17,000	17,000
World War II East	Germany	1941–45	1	6,074,000	10,000,000	14,000,000
World War II East	USSR	1941–45	1	500,000	500,000	500,000
World War II East	Romania	1941–44	1	400,000	400,000	400,000
Pacific War	United States	1941–45	1	268,157	330,000	900,000
Palestine	Israel	1948–49	0	850	1,130	2,000
Korea	N. Korea	1950–53	1	29,000	129,000	129,000
Korea	United States	1950–53	1	100,000	406,000	1,000,000
First Vietnamese	United States	1965–73	1	91,936	313,936	313,936
First Vietnamese	N. Vietnam	1965–73	0	41,294	42,194	44,140
Cyprus	Turkey	1974	0	3,250	3,250	3,250
Cyprus	Cyprus	1974	0	500	500	500
Cambodia-Vietnam	Cambodia	1975–79	0	2,000	2,000	30,000
Uganda-Tanzania	Uganda	1978–79	0	2,000	2,000	2,000

War	State	Years	Mass killing*	Civilians Killed		
				Low	*Medium*	*High*
Iran-Iraq	Iran	1980–88	0	1,000	1,000	1,000
Iran-Iraq	Iraq	1980–88	0	11,000	12,420	15,050
Lebanon	Israel	1982	0	5,000	10,000	15,485
Persian Gulf†	Iraq	1991	0	14	14	14
Armenia-Azerbaijan	Armenia	1992–94	0	*7,500*	*7,500*	*7,500*
Armenia-Azerbaijan	Azerbaijan	1992–94	0	*7,500*	*7,500*	*7,500*

* Coding based on mid-range estimate of civilian fatalities; italics indicate author's estimates.
† Borderline cases.

Number of Civilian Fatalities

The final dependent variable consists of the number of civilian deaths inflicted on an adversary's population by belligerents in interstate wars. Owing to limits on the availability and reliability of data in the nineteenth century, analysis using this particular measure is limited to cases occurring from 1900 to 2003. I obtained data for 82 percent of the cases occurring on or after 1900 (196 out of 239). For each war, I gathered estimates of civilian casualties on both sides from multiple secondary sources. It is not uncommon to find several different estimates, although they tend to cluster around a few figures. Whereas some analysts have chosen to use the average of the various estimates, I recorded low, medium, and high figures, and ran the analysis on each as a separate dependent variable.[5] The results reported below were obtained using the mid-range figures. Results using the low and high estimates do not differ substantively from what is reported.

POTENTIAL CAUSES

Next, I coded a variety of features about each country and the war itself. For more detail on each, see the discussion in appendix 2.1. To test regime-type arguments, I coded each state's level of democracy at the beginning of the war. To test the identity argument, I coded whether states belonged to different civilizational blocs, such as Western European, Eastern Orthodox, Islamic, Hindu, Sinic, Japanese, African, or Latin American. To test the desperation argument, I coded indicators of costly and protracted wars, such as battle deaths, war duration, rising or total war objectives, and whether a conflict was a war of attrition. Finally, to test the annexationist argument,

I coded whether a belligerent intended to conquer and incorporate territory from another country into its own state.

I also coded a variety of other factors that might have an influence on states' choices to target civilians: the relative material capabilities of the parties to the conflict; deterrence, defined as both sides in a war having the ability to target noncombatants; whether a state's civilian population was targeted by the adversary; and whether the conflict took place after World War II or the Vietnam War to see if civilian victimization has become rarer in recent times. For the analyses of mass killing and number of civilian fatalities, I also included a measure of the size of the enemy's population.

The unit of analysis in the dataset is the state in a war. Unfortunately, data on some important variables—battle deaths and civilian fatalities, for example—are not available on a monthly or even an annual basis for most conflicts, precluding a more fine-grained, time-series statistical analysis. The desperation model, however, predicts that rising costs of fighting and doubts about the likelihood of victory should precede civilian victimization. As a check on the statistical results, therefore, in appendix 2.2 I examine each case of civilian victimization in a war of attrition to determine whether it occurred before or after desperation kicked in. I find that in the vast majority of cases, attrition preceded civilian victimization.

Civilian Victimization, Civilian Fatalities, and the Historical Record

What does the historical record reveal about the causes of civilian victimization in interstate wars?

Targeting Civilians in War

Tables 2.2 to 2.5 present a series of cross-tabulations displaying the relationships between democracy, cultural differences, attrition, annexation, and civilian victimization. The first half of each table includes all states in the dataset, whereas the second half includes only those thought to be capable of striking their adversary's civilian population.

These tables nicely foreshadow the results of the regression analysis. Table 2.2, for example, shows that roughly one quarter of all democracies in interstate wars targeted civilians, compared to about 15 percent of nondemocracies. Democracies were thus about 83 percent more likely than nondemocracies to target civilians in the dataset that includes all belligerents, a difference that is statistically significant.[6] Cultural differences also have a positive effect, as shown in table 2.3, but the size of the effect is smaller: the presence of cultural differences between belligerents increases the chance

Table 2.2. Cross-tabulation of democracy and civilian victimization in interstate wars, 1816–2003

		Democracy All belligerents			Democracy Capable belligerents		
		Yes	No	Total	Yes	No	Total
Civilian victimization	Yes	18 26.9%	35 14.7%	53 17.4%	18 41.9%	35 27.1%	53 30.8%
	No	49 73.1%	203 85.3%	252 82.6%	25 58.1%	94 72.9%	119 69.2%
	Total	67 100.0%	238 100.0%	305 100.0%	43 100.0%	129 100.0%	172 100.0%

Pearson Chi²(1) = 5.3843 Pr = 0.02   Pearson Chi²(1) = 3.2816 Pr = 0.07

Table 2.3. Cross-tabulation of cultural differences and civilian victimization in interstate wars, 1816–2003

		Cultural differences All belligerents			Cultural differences Capable belligerents		
		Yes	No	Total	Yes	No	Total
Civilian victimization	Yes	35 20.0%	18 13.3%	53 17.1%	35 32.4%	18 27.7%	53 30.6%
	No	140 80.0%	117 86.7%	257 82.9%	73 67.6%	47 72.3%	120 69.4%
	Total	175 100.0%	135 100.0%	310 100.0%	108 100.0%	65 100.0%	173 100.0%

Pearson Chi²(1) = 2.3897 Pr − 0.12   PearsonChi²(1) = 0.4245 Pr = 0.52

of civilian victimization by about 50 percent in the dataset that includes all belligerents. This disparity is not statistically significant.

Tables 2.4 and 2.5, on the other hand, reveal powerful correlations between indicators of desperation, appetite for territory, and civilian victimization. States involved in wars of attrition, for example, targeted enemy civilians 50 to 60 percent of the time, a figure that is between four and seven times the rate for states that fought quick and decisive wars. Moreover, belligerents that intended to annex enemy territory struck at enemy noncombatants fully 82 percent of the time, a rate that is four to nine times the rate for states that do not have this as a war aim.

Desperation in wars of attrition and an appetite for territorial conquest continue to exert the largest and most significant effects on the likelihood of civilian victimization in a multivariate regression. Both of these variables are statistically significant at the highest level controlling for other factors

Table 2.4. Cross-tabulation of wars of attrition and civilian victimization in interstate wars, 1816–2003

		War of attrition All belligerents			War of attrition Capable belligerents		
		Yes	No	Total	Yes	No	Total
Civilian victimization	Yes	36 50.0%	17 7.2%	53 17.2%	36 61.0%	17 15.0%	53 30.8%
	No	36 50.0%	219 92.8%	255 82.8%	23 39.0%	96 85.0%	119 69.2%
	Total	72 100.0%	236 100.0%	308 100.0%	59 100.0%	113 100.0%	172 100.0%

Pearson Chi²(1) = 70.9248 Pr = 0.00   PearsonChi²(1) = 38.4270 Pr = 0.00

Table 2.5. Cross-tabulation of wars of annexation and civilian victimization in interstate wars, 1816–2003

		War of annexation All belligerents			War of annexation Capable belligerents		
		Yes	No	Total	Yes	No	Total
Civilian victimization	Yes	27 81.8%	26 9.4%	53 17.1%	27 81.8%	26 18.6%	53 30.6%
	No	6 18.2%	251 90.6%	257 82.9%	6 18.2%	114 81.4%	120 69.4%
	Total	33 100.0%	277 100.0%	310 100.0%	33 100.0%	140 100.0%	173 100.0%

Pearson Chi²(1) = 109.1456 Pr = 0.00   Pearson Chi²(1) = 50.2698 Pr = 0.00

that might influence civilian victimization, and each also exerts strong substantive effects. Table 2.6 shows the significance level for all variables as well as the change in the expected probability of civilian victimization obtained by shifting each variable from a low to a high value while holding the others constant at their averages. The column labeled "initial probability" gives the likelihood of observing civilian victimization when the variable in question takes a low value, either zero for dichotomous variables or the twentieth percentile value for continuous variables. The next column shows the increase or decrease in the probability of civilian victimization that results from changing each variable from low to high, whereas the fourth column simply sums the two previous columns to show the new total probability. This is the likelihood of civilian victimization occurring when the variable in question takes a high value and all other variables are at their means. The final column calculates the percent change: the new total probability divided by the initial probability (minus one), which is the same as dividing the change in probability by the initial probability.

States involved in wars of attrition, for example, were nearly eleven times more likely to target enemy noncombatants than states that did not fight wars of attrition. States that intended to annex territory from their enemy were more than twenty-three times as likely to victimize civilians as states that did not fight for this reason. Democracy also increased the likelihood of civilian victimization in war—by nearly 300 percent—but the joint effect of democracy and wars of attrition shows that the higher likelihood of civilian targeting by democracies is driven by their behavior in costly, protracted wars. When a state is both a democracy and fighting a war of attrition, the probability of civilian victimization jumps more than twelve times. This is a larger effect than for autocracies waging attrition wars. Cultural differences between states, by contrast, controlling for these other factors, had a slight negative effect on the probability of civilian victimization, reducing it by 29 percent. As opposed to its uncontrolled effect, therefore, when other causes of civilian targeting are accounted for, the presence of cultural differences exerts a small downward effect on the probability that a belligerent targeted enemy noncombatants.

Table 2.6 also shows the impact that some of the control variables had on the likelihood of civilian victimization. Unsurprisingly, greater levels of material power more than tripled the likelihood that a state would target civilians, as did having one's own civilian population targeted by the enemy. Interestingly, deterrence did not exert a restraining effect: when a state and its adversary in a conflict both had the capability to strike their adversary's population, the state was five times as likely to target noncombatants. Finally, states that fought in wars after 1945 were 58 percent less likely to use civilian victimization.

In short, the statistical analysis of civilian victimization lends strong support to my suppositions regarding desperation to win and to save lives on one's own side in wars of attrition, and the intention to seize and annex territory from an adversary. Democracy, too, increases the likelihood of civilian victimization. This is mainly due to the very high rate at which democracies target civilians in wars of attrition (thirteen out of fourteen cases, or 93 percent) rather than an overall propensity to victimize noncombatants.[7] This finding lends support to a qualified version of the institutional argument: democratic accountability makes it imperative for democracies to prevail and keep the costs of fighting low—which in turn increases the likelihood that civilians will be targeted—but this occurs only when the war takes a turn for the worse. Conditional on desperation, therefore, democracies are differentially more likely than autocracies to target civilians. Finally, the identity argument receives no support from this analysis, often taking the wrong sign and failing to achieve statistical significance.

Table 2.6. Change in the expected probability of civilian victimization associated with each independent variable (participants in interstate wars, 1816–2003)

Variable	Initial probability	Absolute change in probability	Probability after change in variable	Percent change
Democracy (Polity)**	.0353219	.0963727	.1316946	273
Democracy (Doyle)	.0396394	.0347853	.0744247	88
Cultural difference	.057475	−.0164136	.0410614	−29
War of attrition***	.0259146	.250324	.2762386	966
Battle deaths*	.0410597	.0652245	.1062842	159
War duration**	.041675	.0821061	.1237811	197
Expansive war aims**	.0559286	.1167311	.1726597	209
Democracy in war of attrition***	.0435926	.495236	.5388286	1136
Annexationist aims***	.0298331	.6697002	.6995333	2245
Relative capabilities**	.0266487	.0602836	.0869323	226
Deterrence***	.0267747	.1111811	.1379558	415
Target of civilian victimization**	.0394613	.1013937	.140855	257
Post-1945*	.0653265	−.0380322	.0272943	−58

Note: * = < 0.10; ** = < 0.05; *** = < 0.01. Estimates for all variables except democracy (Doyle coding), battle deaths, war duration, expansive war aims, and democracies in wars of attrition are generated from model 1 in table 2.9. Estimates for the other five variables come from models 2 and 5–7 in table 2.9, and model 8 in table 2.10. All variables except the variable of interest are held constant at their mean values. The independent variables are shifted from 0 to 1 in the case of dummy variables, or from 20th to 80th percentile in the case of continuous variables. All calculations were performed using CLARIFY: Software for Interpreting and Presenting Statistical Results, version 2.1, by Gary King, Michael Tomz, and Jason Wittenberg. http://gking.harvard.edu/stats.shtml.

Mass Killing

As discussed earlier, one downside of civilian targeting as a dependent variable is that it does not tell us anything about the severity of violence against noncombatants. For this reason, I collected data on two alternative measures: whether or not civilian deaths exceeded the threshold of fifty thousand, and the total number of civilians killed per belligerent. If the statistical results remain consistent across these different indicators of civilian victimization, we gain confidence that the findings are not an accident but instead reflect real trends.

Are the same factors correlated with mass killing and civilian casualties as were correlated with civilian targeting? The answer is yes. As table 2.7 shows, democracy, wars of attrition, and annexationist aims significantly increase the

Table 2.7. Change in the expected probability of mass killing associated with each independent variable (participants in interstate wars, 1816–2003)

Variable	Initial probability	Absolute change in probability	Probability after change in variable	Percent change
Democracy (Polity)***	.0017243	.0127621	.0144864	740
Democracy (Doyle)***	.0018928	.0082327	.0101255	435
Cultural difference	.0050915	−.0028613	.0022302	−56
War of attrition***	.001339	.0399991	.0413381	2987
Battle deaths***	.0001617	.0030132	.0031749	1863
War duration***	.0001696	.0070492	.0072188	4156
Expansive war aims***	.0024116	.0297793	.0321909	1235
Annexationist aims***	.0019093	.068022	.0699313	3563
Relative capabilities	.002563	.0044278	.0069908	173
Enemy population***	.001037	.0094451	.0104821	911
Deterrence	.0026233	.0011354	.0037587	43
Target of civilian victimization	.0026182	.0015141	.0041323	58
Post-1945	.0032631	.000566	.0038291	17

Note: *** = < 0.01. Estimates for all variables except for democracy (Doyle coding), battle deaths, war duration, and expansive war aims are generated from model 1 in table 2.11. Estimates for the other four variables come from replications of model 1 in which each variable is substituted for Polity democracy and war of attrition, respectively. All other procedures are the same as for table 2.6.

probability of mass killing. The substantive effects are larger than for civilian victimization: democracy results in an eightfold increase in the likelihood of mass killing, attrition boosts the probability of mass killing nearly thirty-one times, whereas annexation makes mass killing about thirty-seven times more likely. The size of the enemy population also matters: increasing this variable from a low to a high value increases the chance of mass killing by a factor of ten. Cultural differences, by contrast, halve the likelihood of mass killing rather than increasing it as the identity argument hypothesizes.

These findings in some ways mesh with those in the existing literature and in other ways clash with them. The positive effect of costly wars of attrition, for example, accords with the finding by Benjamin Valentino, Paul Huth, and Dylan Balch-Lindsay that guerrilla warfare—particularly waged by strong rebel groups with large numbers of civilian supporters—increases the likelihood of mass killing. My positive result for democracy, however, contradicts their finding that democracies are less likely to kill more than fifty thousand noncombatants in wars after 1945.[8]

In one sense, these contradictory findings may be reconcilable. Valentino, Huth, and Balch-Lindsay's study, for example, includes civil wars as well as interstate conflicts and wars of decolonization. Many analysts maintain that democracies are less brutal than nondemocracies in waging internal conflicts.[9] Moreover, my analysis of democracy and civilian victimization reveals that the effect of democracy has changed over time. Other studies examine only the period after World War II and thus are unable to trace the effect of variables over longer time periods. My data show that after World War II, democracies started to become less likely than autocracies to target civilians, but the difference between the two regime types was not significant in statistical terms. Starting from the latter stages of the Vietnam War (about 1970), however, accounting for other factors, democracies became significantly less likely than nondemocracies to employ civilian victimization. This period effect extends, in weaker form, to mass killing and the number of civilians a state kills in war. It may be the case, therefore, that democracies were more likely than autocracies to target and kill massive numbers of civilians before 1945, but have become less likely to do so in recent times.

Looking exclusively at international wars fought by democracies since World War II, however, points to a familiar trend. Although democratic states have fought few costly international wars since 1945, democracies not only victimized civilians in most of them—the Dutch in Indonesia (1945–49), France-Madagascar (1947–48), France-Indochina (1945–54), the United States in Korea (1950–53), France-Algeria (1954–62), United States in Vietnam (1965–73), and Israel-Lebanon (1982)—they often committed mass killing (in all but the Dutch and Israeli cases) as well.[10] At least in international wars, therefore, it appears that costly wars of attrition have still tended to induce a resort to civilian victimization by democracies after 1945.[11]

Civilian Fatalities

Finally, desperation in wars of attrition and fighting to seize and annex territory from one's rivals also results in states inflicting significantly larger numbers of noncombatant fatalities. Because the dependent variable for this analysis is the count of civilian deaths inflicted per belligerent, table 2.8 shows numbers of civilian casualties rather than probabilities of civilian victimization or mass killing. Otherwise, however, the tables are similar: the initial count column shows the count of civilian deaths with all variables at their average values. The next column shows how many more or less casualties occur when the variable in question is increased by one unit. The two counts are then summed and the percent change calculated in the same manner as in the previous tables.

Table 2.8. Marginal effects of independent variables on number of civilian fatalities inflicted by participants in interstate wars, 1900–2003

Variable	Initial count	Absolute change in count	Count after change in variable	Percent change
Democracy (Polity)	4734	1766	6500	37
Democracy (Doyle)	4520	2661	7181	59
Cultural difference*	4734	−5322	−588	−112
War of attrition***	4734	30505	35239	644
Battle deaths***	4495	5464	9959	122
War duration***	7721	11512	19233	149
Expansive war aims**	7663	13737	21400	179
Democracy in war of attrition***	4087	42488	46575	1040
Annexationist aims***	4734	54340	59074	1148
Relative capabilities**	4734	9617	14351	203
Enemy population***	4734	8179	13307	176
Deterrence	4734	−342	4392	−7
State's own civilians killed	4734	−3383	1351	−71
Post-1945	4734	−2237	2497	−47

Note: * = < 0.10; ** = < 0.05; *** = < 0.01. Estimates for all variables except for democracy (Doyle coding) battle deaths, war duration, expansive war aims, and democracies in wars of attrition are generated from model 1a in table 2.12. The estimate for democracies in wars of attrition is from model 2a. Estimates for the other four variables come from replications of model 1 in which each variable is substituted for Polity democracy and war of attrition, respectively. Values in the table were generated using Stata's "mfx compute" command, and represent the effect of a one-unit change in each independent variable on the number of civilian casualties, holding all other variables at their mean values. Note that this procedure understates the effects of the continuous variables. Clarify (used in the previous two tables) does not support the zero-inflated negative binomial model. Thus, I was not able to manipulate the continuous variables from low to high values.

As shown in table 2.8, states in wars of attrition kill approximately seven and a half times as many civilians as states not involved in such wars. Similarly, annexing territory from a rival increases the number of civilian deaths more than twelve times. Cultural differences, net of other factors, reduce the number of noncombatants a state kills by about 112 percent.[12] Democracies kill between 37 to 59 percent more civilians than nondemocracies, but most of their killing is done in wars of attrition: the combination of these two variables increases the number of civilian deaths inflicted more than eleven times.

Again, as with the analysis of mass killing, some of these findings are consistent with the current literature whereas others diverge from it. Benjamin

Valentino, Paul Huth, and Sarah Croco, for example, found strong positive effects for attrition strategies, total war aims, and war duration in twentieth-century interstate wars. They also found little independent effect for identity. Our results for regime type, however, are somewhat at odds: I find that democracy has a mostly positive effect on the number of civilians killed, and a large and significant positive effect in wars of attrition. Valentino, Huth, and Croco, on the other hand, find no consistent positive impact for democracy, and although their interaction term for democracies in wars of attrition is positive, it falls just short of statistical significance.[13] This difference probably stems from a number of factors that I discuss in appendix 2.2.

THE statistical analyses performed in this chapter lend strong support to my hypotheses regarding the causes of civilian victimization in warfare. Desperation in protracted wars of attrition and the intention to conquer and annex enemy territory significantly increase the chances of civilian victimization and mass killing in interstate wars between 1816 and 2003, and correlate with higher totals of civilian fatalities in interstate wars after 1900.

By contrast, the statistical evidence failed to lend much support to the argument that civilian victimization is more likely when wars are fought between states that are from different races, religions, or cultures. Cultural differences even appear to lower the number of noncombatant fatalities, exactly the opposite of the predicted relationship. One possible interpretation of these results is that while dehumanization probably plays a role in the harming of enemy civilians, even culturally similar people can be demonized as "barbaric" when the need arises. As this is most likely to occur in wars of attrition or wars to annex territory, when these factors are controlled for, the effect of cultural differences disappears or even becomes negative.

My findings regarding the effect of democracy run counter to some of those in the existing literature. Contrary to Valentino, Huth, and Balch-Lindsay, I find that democracies do not typically externalize their domestic beliefs about humane treatment of individuals to enemy civilians during wartime. In fact, and in contradiction to Valentino, Huth, and Croco, democracies appear to be particularly vindictive in costly wars, where they victimize noncombatants at a higher clip than nondemocracies and kill larger numbers of civilians. These findings lend partial support to the institutional argument, which contends that because leaders in democracies are vulnerable to public recall, they fight tenaciously to secure victory and their political future. Other predictions of the institutional theory, however—such as the argument that democracies select easy wars that can be won quickly and decisively without civilian victimization—are not strongly upheld (for more, see below). The effect of democratic institutions, therefore, is a question to which we must pay close attention in the case studies.

[56]

Appendix 2.1

A Multivariate Analysis of Civilian Victimization,
Mass Killing, and Civilian Fatalities

A NOTE ON THE DATASET

As mentioned above, the dataset used in my analysis contains 323 states in interstate wars between 1816 and 2003. It is not clear, however, that each of these 323 states should remain in the analysis. Including them all assumes that each belligerent was equally capable of attacking enemy noncombatants, and that each also had the option of making this choice. The Franco-Spanish War (1823), for example, was fought entirely on Spanish soil. Spain simply had no ability to target French civilians even if it had wanted to. Equating Spain's inability to victimize civilians with France's decision not to conflates two different types of nonevents. Subordinate alliance partners, furthermore, typically have little freedom to implement policies independently in a war in which they fight alongside a great power ally. A long list of countries technically participated on the United Nations' side in the Korean War, for instance, but the United States was in charge and was the only belligerent to deploy large air, ground, and sea forces. When "UN" forces bombed North Korean cities to rubble in the late fall and winter of 1950–51, it was not an Ethiopian, Belgian, or Filipino decision, it was a U.S. decision.

Some argue that observations like these—where the outcome of interest is absent but was impossible—are irrelevant for testing causal hypotheses. Relevant cases are those in which the outcome of interest is present and those where the outcome is not present but could have occurred.[14] Excluding such cases, however, might conceivably introduce a selection bias: states that would consider using civilian victimization as a war strategy are more likely to acquire the capabilities to do so than states that refuse to contemplate killing noncombatants on a widespread scale. States that refused to harm noncombatants for normative, institutional, or identity reasons would thus disappear from the sample and bias the analysis against finding any effect for those factors.[15]

To address this issue, I performed the analysis using two versions of the dataset: one that included all states regardless of their capability to harm enemy civilians, and the second containing only those belligerents that had the capability or opportunity to kill enemy noncombatants. A participant in an interstate war was coded as having the opportunity/capability to target enemy civilians if it was not a subordinate alliance partner, meaning that it had independent decision-making ability on military strategy, and it met either of the following two criteria: (1) the state's ground forces invaded the territory of the enemy country; or (2) the belligerent had air, missile, or naval forces to bombard or blockade the enemy homeland. Dropping belligerents that lacked opportunity/capability leaves 175 belligerents from the original 323. Substantial numbers of auxiliary belligerents, for example, were dropped from the Austro-Prussian (1866) and Franco-Prussian (1870–71) wars, World Wars I and II, and the Korean, Vietnam, and Persian Gulf wars. Similarly, I eliminated states that lacked the capability to strike their adversary's homeland, such as Spain in the Franco-Spanish war (1823), Morocco in the two Spanish-Moroccan wars (1859–60, 1909–10), China in the Sino-Japanese war (1894–95), and Ethiopia in the Italo-Ethiopian war (1935–36).

Although this is a useful check on the results, ultimately I choose to report the results including all states on the assumption that a state's capability to target civilians is largely a function of its relative power. States that control a very small percentage of relative power in any conflict are unlikely to be able to do much harm to enemy civilians. More powerful states, by contrast, are typically more able to direct force against an adversary's noncombatant population. This assumption is generally borne out in the analyses below. Moreover, there does not appear to be any selection effect operating, since the results using the two sets of cases rarely differ.[16]

INDEPENDENT VARIABLES

Because my data are limited to interstate wars, very few of which involved guerrilla warfare or counterinsurgency, it is not possible to test hypotheses regarding the effect of insurgency on civilian targeting or casualties. I fold counterinsurgency into the war of attrition variable defined below since it shares many qualities with these conflicts.[17] Furthermore, organizational culture is difficult to test in a large-N format because few militaries develop cultures in peacetime predicated on killing civilians in wartime. The cultural hypothesis is best studied by performing detailed case studies comparing the few instances of "punishment" cultures that exist with the conduct of militaries that lacked such cultures.[18]

Regime Type

To code countries' regime types, I use the Polity 4 dataset, which focuses strictly on governmental institutions rather than civil or economic rights and freedoms. Polity uses an index to measure a country's democratic and autocratic features based on the competitiveness of political participation, openness and competitiveness of executive recruitment, and constraints on the power of the executive. The indices for democracy and autocracy range from zero (least democratic or autocratic) to 10 (most). As is now common in the large-N literature, I subtract the latter from the former to create a 21-point scale ranging from −10 to 10 measuring a state's overall level of democracy. I follow convention and code as democracies states that score 7 or above on this scale (21 percent of the countries in the dataset).[19]

Institutions, however, are a very inexact proxy for norms, which many scholars hypothesize are the cause of peace among democracies and restraints on targeting civilians. I use Michael Doyle's list of liberal democracies to represent the norms argument. Doyle employs four criteria to judge whether or not states are liberal: (1) respect for civil and political rights and freedoms, (2) elected representative government, (3) respect for private property, and (4) a free-market economy. Twenty-five percent of the states in the dataset are coded as liberal.[20]

Barbaric Images of the Enemy

As a proxy for perceptions of the adversary as barbaric, I code whether belligerents belonged to different civilizations as defined by Samuel Huntington. This may strike some readers as anachronistic because Huntington's categorization is meant to describe the fault lines along which conflict will occur in the future rather than in the past. Of the various indicators available, however, such as religion and race, this is the one that best approximates the real and perceived lines of difference that have existed over the past two hundred years. Civilizational difference, for example, divides Eastern Europe and Russia from Western Europe, European from Islamic countries, Muslim from Jew, Muslim from Hindu, Hindu from Chinese, and Chinese from Japanese. In fact, this coding rule is almost identical to coding for difference in religion and including Eastern Orthodox as separate from Protestant/Catholic.[21]

This measure leaves much to be desired as a representation of the actual causal mechanism in the identity argument but is the best that can be done in a quantitative study. A better way to test the argument is to use in-depth process tracing of how elites and masses in a country perceived the enemy and whether this had any effect on how that state subsequently treated civilians in the war. This task I leave to the case-study chapters. In the meantime, I test whether ex ante differences in identity—captured here as civilizational differences—are associated with an increased propensity to target and kill enemy civilians.

Desperation

I use four indicators to capture the desperation logic.

- *War of attrition.* Wars of attrition are conflicts in which the defense has the advantage and thus tend to be enormously costly and protracted.

Attrition warfare is essentially siege warfare: wars generally lacking in maneuver or movement, which are instead dominated by static, linear, or trench operations. Actual sieges—such as the siege of Leningrad in World War II or the siege of Paris in the Franco-Prussian War—clearly qualify as attrition, but so, too, do wars that resemble sieges on a larger scale. The dominance of firepower over movement in World War I on the western front, for example, quickly transformed that conflict into trench warfare in which thousands of lives were required to conquer a few hundred yards of territory. In another example, the United States was forced to fight its way across the Pacific from 1942 to 1945, assaulting prepared Japanese defenses on island after island. Other conflicts have taken a similar form, such as the Crimean, Russo-Japanese, Chaco, Korean, Iran-Iraq, and Ethiopian-Eritrean wars.[22] Finally, I code counterinsurgent warfare as a type of attrition war, as it typically "involves using small mobile units to seek out and destroy guerrillas directly."[23]

Importantly, a war is coded as an attrition war not based solely on countries' initial strategies, but rather on the predominant mode of combat during the war. Germany, for example, quickly sliced through Poland's defenses in September 1939 and reached Warsaw but then bogged down in the face of Polish defenses inside the city and faced a protracted siege. Later, the Germans employed a blitzkrieg to invade the Soviet Union, but after the initial offensive was thwarted, the fighting was dominated by desperate attrition warfare as well as actual sieges (Leningrad) and urban warfare (Stalingrad).[24]

- *Battle deaths.* The most direct indicator of the human costs of war is the number of fatalities a state's forces suffer in battle, available in the Correlates of War (COW) dataset, supplemented by a variety of secondary sources. I have updated these figures through the Iraq War of 2003. Because the spread of these figures is so broad, I use the log of battle deaths in the analysis.
- *War duration.* The longer a war goes on, the more costly it is likely to be, and the more desperate belligerents are likely to become. I measure war duration in days (again taken from COW) and use the log of that number in the analysis.
- *Expansive or expanding war aims.* Wars in which one or more belligerents demand unconditional surrender from the adversary, or raise their political objectives during the course of the war, are likely to induce greater resistance from the enemy. This in turn causes the first state to employ greater levels of force, and an escalatory spiral ensues leading to civilian victimization. Moreover, it is simply more militarily difficult to conquer whole states and overthrow regimes than it is to achieve more limited war aims, and thus the costs of the war are likely to be higher.[25] I coded this variable by examining belligerents'

war aims and how they changed in each war. Examples of total war aims include World War II and the 2003 Iraq War. Cases in which war aims expanded after the war began include the Franco-Prussian War, World War I, and Korea.

Annexation of Territory

To gauge the effect that territorial expansion exerts on civilian victimization, I code a dummy variable that takes the value of 1 when a state aims to conquer and permanently annex land from a neighboring state. This variable is coded by examining how leaders describe their goals before the war starts and whether those aims included taking and digesting enemy territory. Examples include the Balkan Wars (1912–13), Greco-Turkish War (1919–22), World War II Eastern Front (1941–45), and the Palestine War (1947–49).

Control Variables

A number of control variables are also included in the analysis.

1. *Relative capabilities.* States that have higher levels of material capabilities should have a greater capacity to target enemy civilians. I code relatives capabilities as the percentage of total capabilities of all states in the war controlled by each belligerent. Each state's capability is taken from COW's National Material Capabilities dataset and consists of population, urban population, iron and steel production, energy consumption, military expenditure, and military personnel.
2. *Deterrence.* If both sides in a conflict have the ability to attack each other's civilian populations, the possibility of retaliation may deter them from carrying out such attacks, or curb the parties from utilizing the full destructive power at their disposal. In such cases—like Britain and Germany with airpower in 1939 and 1940—each country is scored 1 on a dummy variable for deterrence.
3. *Retaliation.* If one belligerent engages in countercivilian strikes, however, the target state may reply with attacks of its own. The victim may simply wish to exact revenge for the deaths of civilians on its side, or it may desire to target the population as a reprisal: to teach the enemy a lesson that killing noncombatants does not pay because it invites retaliation. When a state becomes a target of civilian victimization, therefore, it receives a 1 on this dummy variable.[26]
4. *Post-1945.* World War II was such a catastrophe for civilian populations that it sparked a renewed effort to codify, legalize, and enforce norms prohibiting the use of force against noncombatants. Ward Thomas, for

example, argues that the norm against bombing civilians has recovered and grown gradually stronger since 1945, and the death toll from bombing campaigns has progressively shrunk over time.[27] This norm has been reinforced by improvements in weapons technology that allow one or two bombs to destroy a target that required hundreds of bombs in World War II. The spread of global media, in this view, has also helped limit civilian casualties by increasing public awareness of the plight of civilians in wars. In short, there should be less targeting of civilians and fewer civilian casualties in the post-1945 period. Some might argue for a later turning point, however, contending that the heightened media focus on the Vietnam War, and the invention of precision-guided munitions late in that conflict, gave rise to global norms against targeting civilians as well as improved means to avoid inflicting civilian casualties. I thus also code a dummy variable taking the value of 1 for conflicts that occurred after 1970.

5. *Enemy Population.* Finally, when numbers of civilian fatalities are the dependent variable, it is necessary to control for the size of the enemy's population, since greater numbers of casualties could simply be a function of a larger population. I use the log of the target state's population.

METHODOLOGY

Because civilian victimization and mass killing are dichotomous variables, traditional ordinary least squares (OLS) regression—which assumes a continuous and unlimited dependent variable rather than a binary and limited one—yields biased estimates. What is needed is a statistical technique that estimates whether the independent variables increase or decrease the probability that civilian victimization or mass killing occur. The logit estimator is the one that I employ.

Civilian casualties as a dependent variable present a number of difficulties. Casualties are technically a count. Count variables—such as the number of times per week an individual dines out, or the number of traffic tickets one accumulates per year—typically have more zero observations and a greater dispersion than the normal distribution assumed by linear regression, causing OLS to produce biased estimates.[28] In the civilian fatality data I have collected, in fact, the variance of the data greatly exceeds the mean because the minimum observation is zero and the maximum is in the millions. Moreover, in addition to having a large variance, roughly half the observations are zeros, meaning the distribution is skewed to the left, bearing little resemblance to the bell-shaped normal distribution. Finally, civilian casualty counts are always either zero or positive whereas the normal distribution that underlies OLS assumes that observations may take values less than zero.[29]

Other scholars, however, have pointed out that civilian fatalities also violate certain assumptions of count models. As Valentino, Huth, and Croco note, for example, "Count models assume a data-generating process based on a sequence of identical Bernoulli trials in which the outcomes of the trials are binary (for example, success or failure, heads or tails)." They argue that because civilians are often killed in large numbers by single attacks, "Civilian deaths during war are not generated by an identical binary process (1 killed or 0 killed)," and thus count models are inappropriate.[30] Count models also assume that each observation is of the same length, but wars vary greatly in duration from a few days to several years.

Because the data does not fully conform to the assumptions of count models or OLS, rather than simply choose one or the other, I employ both and supplement them with a third (ordinal logit, explained below). To the extent that the results are consistent across these different models and ways of measuring the dependent variable, our confidence in the robustness of the findings increases. First, I use a zero-inflated negative binomial model to analyze counts of civilian casualties.[31] The ZINB model assumes that there are two groups of states: belligerents for which killing enemy civilians is an actual possibility, and belligerents that cannot kill enemy noncombatants because they simply do not have the opportunity or ability to do so. Zero counts can occur because a belligerent that could have killed civilians for a variety of reasons did not, or because a belligerent was unable to kill civilians. The ZINB model thus calculates two separate equations: a logit model which estimates the effects of the independent variables on the probability that a state falls in the zero category, and a negative binomial model that calculates the effect of the variables on the number of civilians killed.

Second, I use ordinal logit to analyze a transformation of the raw civilian fatality data. One criticism of count models is that they estimate the mean of the distribution, which in this case—owing to a handful of very high casualty cases and the low overall number of cases—is quite large. For civilian deaths in interstate wars after 1900, for example, the mean exceeds 92,000 even though half of the observations are zeros and many others are less than 1,000 or 5,000. Another way to compensate for this high degree of dispersion—besides using OLS on logged values of noncombatant deaths—is to transform the data into categories (0, 1, 2, etc.) corresponding to ranges of fatalities and use ordinal logit. The major assumption of this approach is that the exact numbers are not necessarily of intrinsic importance, but rather what is important are the differences between none versus some, little versus big, and big versus huge. This is a reasonable assumption that is especially well-suited to a dependent variable like civilian casualties that is characterized by uncertainty as to the exact number of deaths. Often we know the order of magnitude of civilian fatalities—hardly any, hundreds, thousands, tens of thousands, hundreds of thousands, or millions—better than the actual numbers themselves. I discuss the particular categorizations employed below.

Finally, I follow Valentino, Huth, and Croco and analyze civilian casualties using linear regression, correcting for the wide dispersion of the data by taking the log.

Civilian Victimization: A Multivariate Analysis

The statistical analysis of civilian victimization strongly supports the desperation and annexation hypotheses. The first four models in table 2.9, for example, show that my main indicator of desperation—the war of attrition dummy variable—is positive and significant at better than the 1 percent level whether all belligerents or only capable belligerents are included in the analysis. Models 5–7 demonstrate that other proxies for desperation, such as war duration, battle deaths, and expansive war aims also significantly increase the likelihood of civilian victimization. In all seven models in table 2.9 the variable signifying the intention to annex territory also strongly predicts civilian victimization. These results robustly support the argument that desperation and appetite for territorial conquest cause states to target civilians.

Turning to the competing hypotheses, it is clear that the identity argument fares poorly. Cultural differences between belligerents at the outset of a war, for example, are either weakly negative or weakly positive depending on which proxy for desperation is included in the model. Results for the regime-type hypothesis, by contrast, show that democracy consistently correlates positively with civilian victimization. Liberal democracy as coded by Doyle—included in models 2 and 4—is positive but does not approach statistical significance, suggesting that regime type does not exert a strong effect on the probability of civilian victimization. The coefficient for democracy as coded by Polity, however, is substantively larger and attains significance in each of the five models in which it appears in table 2.9. This result suggests that democratic regimes may actually be more likely to target civilians than nondemocracies.[32]

Why this divergence in results for regime type? A closer look at the data points to four crucial coding differences between Polity and Doyle that result in more positive cases and fewer negative cases in the Polity version. First, Doyle labels Greece as liberal from 1864 through 1911 only, whereas Polity codes Greece as a democracy until 1915. This difference is important because Greece fought—and victimized civilians—in both Balkan Wars (1912–13).[33] Second, Polity codes Israel in 1948 (War of Independence) and Armenia in 1992 (Armenian-Azerbaijani War) as democracies, whereas for Doyle Israel does not become liberal until 1949 and Armenia does not appear on his list at all. Each of these countries is coded as employing civilian

Table 2.9. Determinants of civilian victimization by participants in interstate wars, 1816–2003 (logit estimates)

	1 All states	2 All states	3 Capable states	4 Capable states	5 All	6 All	7 All
Democracy (Polity dummy)	1.52** (0.64)	–	1.43** (0.62)	–	1.54** (0.58)	1.27** (0.55)	1.30** (0.53)
Democracy (Doyle dummy)	–	0.72 (0.56)	–	0.53 (0.56)	–	–	–
Cultural difference	−0.38 (0.45)	−0.31 (0.46)	−0.31 (0.46)	−0.19 (0.46)	0.18 (0.45)	0.01 (0.46)	0.10 (0.46)
War of attrition	2.84*** (0.63)	2.72*** (0.61)	2.81*** (0.69)	2.69*** (0.66)	–	–	–
Battle deaths	–	–	–	–	0.52* (0.27)	–	–
War duration	–	–	–	–	–	0.89** (0.35)	–
Expansive war aims	–	–	–	–	–	–	1.30** (0.54)
Territorial annexation	4.49*** (0.76)	4.44*** (0.75)	3.87*** (0.82)	3.82*** (0.81)	3.75*** (0.63)	4.00*** (0.68)	3.75*** (0.59)
Relative capabilities	2.38** (0.94)	2.42** (0.95)	1.86* (1.11)	1.93* (1.08)	1.80** (0.76)	1.74** (0.74)	1.33* (0.73)
Deterrence	1.84*** (0.49)	2.20*** (0.54)	1.04* (0.62)	1.42** (0.70)	1.96*** (0.54)	2.16*** (0.51)	1.87*** (0.47)
State is target of CV	1.44** (0.59)	1.35* (0.58)	1.69*** (0.66)	1.59*** (0.63)	1.75* (0.72)	1.62** (0.68)	1.93*** (0.69)
Post-1945	−1.16 (0.62)	−1.23* (0.63)	−1.02 (0.65)	−1.09 (0.63)	−0.88 (0.68)	−1.18** (0.58)	−1.22** (0.56)
Constant	−5.58*** (0.94)	−5.54*** (0.95)	−4.59*** (1.13)	−4.58*** (1.13)	−6.56*** (1.35)	−6.42*** (1.07)	−4.54*** (0.61)
N	298	300	169	170	291	300	300
Log likelihood	−56.05	−58.64	−51.23	−53.87	−67.72	−68.05	−68.30
Wald Chi²	54.21***	57.25***	39.87***	44.72***	77.66***	75.96***	81.74***
Pseudo-R²	0.60	0.58	0.51	0.49	0.50	0.51	0.51

Note: Huber-White robust standard errors (clustered on each war) in parentheses.
* = <0.10; ** = <0.05; *** = <0.01

victimization in their respective wars. Third, Polity considers Britain to be nondemocratic until 1880, whereas Doyle codes Britain as liberal from the 1832 reforms broadening the franchise. The final difference concerns Sardinia-Piedmont/Italy, coded by Doyle as liberal from its independence in 1849 until Mussolini seized power in 1922, but judged by Polity to be nondemocratic from its founding until after World War II. These last two differences matter because Britain and Italy fought several interstate wars in the periods when the respective codings clash, but did not harm noncombatants in any of them, meaning that there are several more negative cases using Doyle's coding.[34]

Among the control variables in table 2.9, relative power matters: the more powerful a state grows, the more likely it is to employ civilian victimization as a war strategy, probably because powerful states simply have greater capabilities. Attacks on noncombatants, furthermore, appear to cluster in particular wars, as states whose civilian populations are targeted tend to strike the civilians of their opponents. Surprisingly, deterrence is also positive and significant. I interpret this to mean that the ability to retaliate against an opponent's civilians may delay resort to civilian victimization in particular cases but is unable to prevent it. Indeed, when both belligerents have the capability to target civilians, if the war fails to end quickly, not even the threat of retaliation can dissuade the combatants from exploiting that capability. The deterrence variable in that case simply captures a state's capability to strike enemy noncombatants.[35] Finally, the consistently negative and frequently significant coefficient for the variable "post-1945" shows that interstate wars after World War II are less likely to be characterized by civilian targeting.

Table 2.10 shows three models with interaction terms that provide further tests of the impact of democracy on civilian victimization. Model 8, for example, tests the hypothesis that democracies are more prone than autocracies to target civilians in costly wars of attrition owing to democracies' heightened cost-sensitivity and aversion to defeat. I created an interaction term by multiplying together the dummy variables for democracy and war of attrition. The coefficient for this interaction term in model 8 is positive, significant, and substantively larger than for attrition alone (i.e., nondemocracies in wars of attrition), indicating that even though all states tend to target noncombatants in wars of attrition, democracies are differentially more likely to do so than nondemocracies. Indeed, democracies targeted civilians 93 percent of the time they were involved in wars of attrition, compared with 40 percent for autocratic states.[36] This finding supports the argument that the heightened cost-sensitivity and defeat-phobia of democracies increase the likelihood that these states will target civilians should they become involved in protracted wars of attrition.

Models 9 and 10 test the hypothesis that democracies are less likely to victimize noncombatants in recent wars. One could argue that equating

Table 2.10. Determinants of civilian victimization by participants in interstate wars, 1816–2003: democracy interaction terms (logit estimates)

	8 *All states*	9 *All*	10 *All*
Democracy (Polity)	0.01 (0.85)	1.87** (0.77)	2.22*** (0.69)
Cultural difference	−0.32 (0.46)	−0.26 (0.48)	−0.09 (0.51)
War of attrition	2.01*** (0.61)	2.87*** (0.64)	3.07*** (0.66)
Democracy * attrition	3.49*** (1.34)	–	–
Democracy * post 1945	–	−1.01 (1.00)	–
Democracy * post-1970	–	–	−2.95** (1.39)
Territorial annexation	4.36*** (0.61)	4.50*** (0.80)	4.78*** (0.77)
Military balance	2.32** (0.98)	2.53*** (0.95)	1.98** (0.91)
Deterrence	1.74*** (0.47)	1.82*** (0.50)	1.05** (0.47)
State is target of CV	1.50** (0.61)	1.43** (0.59)	1.53** (0.62)
Post-1945	−1.11* (0.63)	−0.85 (0.72)	–
Post-1970	–	–	1.64 (1.10)
Constant	−5.09*** (0.81)	−5.81*** (0.97)	−6.07*** (0.80)
N	298	298	298
Log likelihood	−52.34	−55.72	−55.59
Wald Chi²	71.09***	52.68***	62.03***
Pseudo-R²	0.62	0.60	0.60

Note: Huber-White robust standard errors (clustered on each war) in parentheses.
* = <0.10; ** = <0.05; *** = <0.01

"democracy" in the nineteenth and early twentieth centuries with "democracy" in recent decades unfairly biases the analysis against finding a restraining effect for domestic norms or institutions. According to this argument, only recently have democracies actually become "liberal" or "democratic" in the sense that we understand these terms today. The United States, for example, scored +10 on the Polity index at the time of the Mexican-American War, when slavery was a legal and accepted practice. To claim that the United States in 1846 and the United States in 1965, 1991, or 2003 are equivalent observations is simply wrong. A better test of liberal/democratic restraint would be to limit the analysis to the post–World War II era, or the post-Vietnam period when democratic institutions and norms were more fully developed.

To test these propositions, I inserted a variable in model 9 that is the product of the democracy and post-1945 dummy variables. This interaction term compares the effect of regime type after World War II with its effect before that conflict. As shown, democratic regimes after 1945 are associated with smaller probabilities of civilian victimization, whereas the reverse is true before 1945. The former effect is not significant, but the latter is. Model 10, by contrast, moves the cutoff date forward to 1970, with the result that the difference between democracy before and after this date becomes significant. The results in model 10 support the conclusion that until the Vietnam War, democracies were more likely than nondemocracies to target civilians. Only after Vietnam have democracies reversed course and become less likely than other regimes to victimize noncombatants.

The statistical data, therefore, provides strong evidence that until very recently democracies were not restrained from targeting civilians in interstate wars. Large cultural differences between belligerents appear to be unrelated to the danger of civilian victimization. The increased sensitivity to costs engendered by democratic institutions, on the other hand, does seem to have increased the propensity of democracies to use civilian victimization as a means to win wars and conserve on their own losses, but only in long, costly conflicts.[37] Wars of attrition, and wars to conquer and annex enemy territory, however, are the key drivers of civilian victimization for all types of states.

Specification Checks

I performed a number of specification checks to gauge the sensitivity of the results to small changes in the coding of the independent and dependent variables. Several of the cases in table 2.1, for example, are coded as borderline cases of civilian victimization (indicated by daggers) because they resulted in low numbers of casualties, or it is unclear if there was an actual policy of targeting civilians.[38] In the first specification check, therefore, I recoded these borderline cases from 1 to 0 and reestimated model 1 from table 2.9. Nothing much changes: democracy remains positive but loses its significance; cultural difference is negative and insignificant; and attrition and annexationist aims are positive and significant ($p < 0.01$).

Second, I performed a battery of tests to check the stability of the democracy finding. For starters, I recoded only those borderline cases of civilian victimization involving democracies, but left those committed by autocracies unchanged. Reestimating model 1, these alterations reduced the coefficent on democracy to 0.65 (p = 0.36). Another possible objection concerns coding France and the United States as having engaged in civilian victimization in World War I as part of the British-led blockade of the Central Powers. The argument would be that this was a British policy; France and the United States played only a subsidiary role. Recoding these two cases lowers the democracy coefficient to 1.08 (p < 0.08). Some critics might also object to characterizing Israel as a democracy in the 1948 War of Independence. Changing Israel's regime type to nondemocratic in this conflict lowers the coefficient of democracy to 1.51 (p < 0.05). Adopting Doyle's coding of Greece as a nondemocracy during the Balkan Wars results in a coefficient of 1.42 (p < 0.05). Even if one makes the unlikely assumption that all of these coding decisions concerning democracy and civilian victimization were made in error, incorporating all of the suggestions in this paragraph for recoding still fails to generate even a negative effect for democracy on the likelihood of civilian targeting (0.31, Pr = 0.67). These tests make it clear that although the statistical significance of the correlation between democracy and an increased likelihood of civilian victimization is not robust, the variable is consistently positive, and it is nearly certain that there is no negative relationship between the two variables.

Third, proponents of institutional accountability arguments for democratic peace and military effectiveness might argue that democracies—because they are better at choosing wars they are likely to win quickly and decisively—should be less likely to victimize civilians in wars they initiate, but more likely to attack noncombatants in wars in which they are the targets. Wars that democracies choose, according to this logic, should not become protracted wars of attrition, and thus democracies would not be put in a position of having to target civilians. I tested this argument by coding a variable for war initiation, generating an interaction term for democratic war initiators, and inserting these variables into model 1.[39]

The results show that although the effect of democratic war initiator on the probability of civilian victimization is in the expected negative direction, it misses statistical significance (B = −1.61, p = 0.17). Democratic targets, on the other hand, are more likely to use civilian victimization as a war strategy than democratic initiators (B = 2.34, p < 0.01). Thus, there is only tepid support for the hypothesis that democracies choose easier wars that are less likely to become wars of attrition and necessitate the targeting of noncombatants.

Fourth, some would argue that differentiating among regime types based exclusively on the risk of removal from office is misleading; the pivotal factor instead is the potential cost of removal to the leader. This perspective identifies "semi-repressive, moderately exclusionary regimes" (also known as mixed regimes or oligarchies) as the type of government most likely to engage in civilian victimization because leaders in these states are most vulnerable to being arrested, exiled, or killed if they lose a war moderately *or* disastrously. This danger gives oligarchs an incentive to gamble for resurrection and employ high variance strategies—such as civilian victimization—to avoid defeat.[40]

I tested this argument by creating a dummy variable for mixed regimes if they scored between −6 and +6 on the Polity index. Plugging this variable into model 1 yields a surprising result: oligarchies are significantly less likely than democracies or dictatorships to target civilians ($B = -2.04$, $p < 0.01$). This negative relationship obtains even in protracted wars of attrition, when oligarchs would presumably have the greatest incentive to gamble for resurrection ($B = -1.23$, $p = 0.21$ for the interaction term). This is a perplexing result for scholars who argue that the institutional structures of mixed regimes—which result in oligarchs being removed and punished for even minor war losses—should cause leaders to avoid defeat at all costs.

This interesting result for oligarchies highlights another finding of note: on closer inspection, the relationship between regime type and civilian victimization is nonlinear. In fact, it is U-shaped: the regime types at the two ends of the spectrum—democracies (states scoring 7 or above on the Polity index) and dictatorships (states scoring −7 or less)—are each more likely to target civilians than are mixed regimes, those states that fall between 6 and −6. Forcing this curvilinear relationship to be linear generates an insignificant result for the 21-point Polity variable.[41]

Finally, one might argue that certain countries or regimes, such as Nazi Germany, are inherently more likely to target civilians than others. To test for these country-specific effects, I coded a dummy variable that takes the value of 1 for Germany in wars between 1933 and 1945. When included in the regression, this variable is positive but not significant ($B = 2.18$, $p = 0.15$) and has no effect on the other variables.[42] Nor are dummy variables significant for Germany or the United States from 1816–2003. Country-specific effects do not appear to influence the results.

MASS KILLING

Table 2.11 shows the results of four logit regressions using mass killing—whether or not a belligerent in an interstate war killed at least fifty thousand enemy noncombatants—as the dependent variable. The first thing to notice is that the decision to include all belligerents (model 1) rather than only those deemed capable of targeting civilians (model 2) has no impact on the results, as there is very little difference in the coefficients for almost all of the variables. The second thing to notice is that restricting the analysis to the period 1900–2003 (model 3) does not much affect the results, either.

Table 2.11. Determinants of mass killing in interstate wars, 1816–2003 (logit estimates)

	1 All states	2 Capable states	3 All states 1900–2003	4 All states
Democracy (Polity)	2.40*** (0.89)	2.31*** (0.84)	2.37*** (0.87)	2.73** (1.08)
Democracy * post-1945	–	–	–	−1.29 (2.08)
Cultural difference	−1.83 (1.22)	−1.77 (1.25)	−1.66 (1.27)	−1.68 (1.30)
War of attrition	4.33*** (1.42)	4.19*** (1.41)	3.95*** (1.38)	4.54*** (1.50)
Territorial annexation	4.06*** (1.43)	3.77*** (1.43)	3.68** (1.63)	4.13*** (1.16)
Relative capabilities	4.27 (3.38)	3.97 (3.51)	3.78 (3.84)	4.64 (3.40)
Enemy population	2.37*** (0.87)	2.23*** (0.85)	2.17** (0.83)	2.44*** (0.90)
Deterrence	0.48 (1.00)	0.17 (1.02)	0.52 (1.05)	0.52 (0.94)
State's own civilians targeted	−0.34 (1.01)	−0.27 (1.04)	−0.29 (1.03)	−0.51 (0.96)
Post-1945	−0.90 (1.63)	−0.87 (1.59)	−0.89 (1.71)	−0.36 (1.75)
constant	−19.23*** (5.32)	−17.97*** (5.34)	−17.78*** (5.08)	−20.10*** (5.71)
N	298	170	224	298
Log likelihood	−24.97	−24.46	−24.23	−24.79
LR Chi²	20.75**	17.13**	18.09**	21.54**
Pseudo-R²	0.63	0.57	0.58	0.64

Note: Huber-White robust standard errors (clustered on each war) in parentheses.
* = <0.10; ** = <0.05; *** = <0.01

Turning to the substantive results, the models displayed in table 2.11 indicate that desperation and appetite for territory correlate positively and significantly with decisions to engage in mass killing at the 1 percent level in all four models. Other proxies for desperation to win and to save lives— such as war duration, battle deaths, and expansive war aims—also significantly increase the likelihood of mass killing in interstate warfare (p < 0.01 for each). Overall, therefore, table 2.11 offers strong support for desperation and appetite for conquest as determinants of massive killing of civilians.

The results for democracy and mass killing are even stronger than those reported above for civilian victimization, and the opposite of those found in earlier studies of mass killing in wars after 1945: democracy strongly and significantly increases the probability of mass killing in models 1–4.[43] The relationship between democracy and mass killing, however, ceases to be significant after 1945: an interaction term signifying democracies in wars after World War II in model 4 is weakly negative (but not significant) whereas democracy (in this case meaning democracy before 1945) remains positive and significant.

The surprising positive result for democracy and mass killing highlights an important but heretofore unknown fact about regime type and civilian casualties: campaigns of civilian targeting by democracies in interstate wars are 52 percent more likely to escalate to mass killing than those by autocracies.[44] This finding would appear to support the old adage that democracies are slow to anger, but once aroused, their wrath is terrible. Less surprisingly, the data show that democracies are more likely than autocracies to inflict mass killing in wars of attrition, thus corroborating the similar finding for civilian victimization above. Unfortunately, introducing an interaction term into the regression for democracies in wars of attrition is not possible because there is no instance of a democracy committing mass killing outside of an attrition war. Thus democracy and the interaction term are perfectly collinear. Cross-tabulations, however, show that democracies engage in mass killing 57 percent of the time in wars of attrition, compared to only 15 percent for nondemocracies (p < 0.01).[45]

Moving on to other explanations, cultural differences fail to exert a discernible effect on the likelihood of mass killing in warfare, but the effect (while insignificant) is consistently in the opposite of the predicted direction. Differences in civilizational membership actually correlate with a lower probability of mass killing. Cultural clashes are thus marginally less likely—controlling for other factors—to result in massive civilian bloodshed than are wars between culturally similar states. One possible reason for this unexpected finding is that wars between countries from different civilizations are also wars of attrition or wars of annexation. Cultural differences are not highly correlated with either of these variables, though (0.13 and 0.11, respectively), and excluding attrition and annexation from the model still leaves cultural differences with a negative coefficient, if smaller in absolute terms.[46]

The only control variable to reach statistical significance is enemy population: the greater the population of the adversary state, the more likely mass killing becomes. This is not surprising, since there are simply more civilians to kill when a population is large. The findings for relative capability, while not significant, are suggestive. The variable for material power is consistently positive, indicating that the more powerful states in particular conflicts are more able to inflict mass killing. None of the other controls—including being the victim of civilian targeting, or the war occurring after 1945—is statistically significant.[47]

Civilian Fatalities

Finally, I turn to actual numbers of civilian war deaths. I present this analysis in three steps. First, I use a zero-inflated negative binomial estimator to gauge the effect of the independent variables on the number of civilians killed in interstate wars from 1900 to 2003. Second, I transform the raw civilian casualty counts into categories based on their severity and reestimate the model with ordered logit. Finally, I examine logged value of civilian deaths using OLS.

As with the previous analyses of civilian targeting and mass killing, desperation and appetite to annex territory stand out as the most important determinants of civilian casualties in interstate wars. Democracies in wars of attrition kill larger numbers of civilians than democracies not fighting such wars, and about the same number of noncombatants as autocracies in wars of attrition. Cultural differences, finally, consistently reduce the number of noncombatant fatalities, contrary to the expectations of the identity perspective.

A Count Model of Civilian Fatalities

Models 1 and 2 in table 2.12 display the results of zero-inflated negative binomial (ZINB) regressions using the midrange estimate of civilian fatalities in all wars starting in or after 1900 as the dependent variable. Each ZINB model contains two sets of coefficients: a negative binomial estimate of the influence of each variable on the number of casualties observed and a separate logit estimate that reports the influence of each variable on the probability of an observation taking the value of zero. A positive sign for the negative binomial half of the equation means that the variable in question increases the number of civilians killed. A positive sign for the logit model, by contrast, means that the variable increases the likelihood that the number of civilians killed will be zero. In table 2.12, the negative binomial coefficient is listed in the first column of each model (1a and 2a) while the logit estimate follows in the second column (1b and 2b).

Looking at model 1, protracted wars of attrition and the intention to annex enemy territory are the two most powerful predictors of civilian fatalities. Other indicators of attrition—war duration, battle deaths, and high or expanding war aims—also significantly increase civilian war deaths when substituted into the model ($p < 0.01$ for the first two, $p < 0.05$ for the third). The clash of cultures argument is again turned on its head, as cultural differences between the belligerents reduce the number of civilian fatalities in interstate wars.[48] The effect of democracy, by contrast, is interestingly nuanced. In model 1, the effect of democracy on the number of civilians killed is weakly positive, and at the same time democracies are less likely to be in the group that kills no civilians (as shown by the negative and significant

Table 2.12. Determinants of civilian fatalities in interstate wars, 1900–2003

	Zero-inflated negative binomial estimates Dependent variable: counts of civilian fatalities				Ordered logit estimates Dependent variable: categorical measure of civilian fatalities		OLS estimates Dependent variable: logged counts of civilian fatalities	
	1a NB	1b Logit	2a NB	2b Logit	3	4	5	6
Democracy (Polity)	0.28 (0.38)	−1.03* (0.56)	−1.00** (0.46)	−0.74 (0.64)	0.94** (0.44)	0.43 (0.49)	0.50** (0.23)	0.18 (0.23)
Cultural difference	−0.99* (0.57)	−0.55 (0.50)	−0.86* (0.45)	−0.63 (0.48)	−0.31 (0.45)	−0.30 (0.42)	−0.10 (0.20)	−0.08 (0.18)
War of attrition	2.58*** (0.53)	−2.83*** (0.51)	1.61*** (0.56)	−2.51*** (0.54)	2.75*** (0.45)	2.31*** (0.45)	1.90*** (0.31)	1.53*** (0.26)
Democracy * attrition	—	—	2.58*** (0.73)	−20.83*** (0.85)	—	1.87 (1.20)	—	1.39** (0.67)
Territorial annexation	2.74*** (0.47)	−23.86*** (0.83)	3.14*** (0.33)	−23.63*** (0.79)	3.39*** (0.64)	3.71*** (0.67)	2.48*** (0.31)	2.62*** (0.33)
Relative capabilities	1.79** (0.76)	−3.04*** (0.91)	1.94*** (0.57)	−3.03*** (0.84)	2.32*** (0.53)	2.30*** (0.54)	1.38*** (0.31)	1.38*** (0.31)

Enemy population	1.68***	−0.57	1.50***	−0.51	0.83**	0.73**	0.47***	0.41**
	(0.38)	(0.46)	(0.36)	(0.45)	(0.32)	(0.32)	(0.17)	(0.16)
Deterrence	−0.18	−1.36**	−0.08	−1.23**	0.98**	0.84*	0.63**	0.53**
	(0.72)	(0.60)	(0.51)	(0.61)	(0.47)	(0.48)	(0.24)	(0.23)
State's own civilians killed	−0.81	−0.43	−0.39	−0.47	−0.33	−0.29	−0.19	−0.16
	(0.55)	(0.65)	(0.53)	(0.66)	(0.42)	(0.42)	(0.23)	(0.22)
Post-1945	−0.58	−1.23*	−0.21	−1.32**	0.10	0.19	0.17	0.22
	(0.64)	(0.66)	(0.49)	(0.62)	(0.48)	(0.46)	(0.24)	(0.23)
Constant	0.73	6.97***	1.23	6.66***	−	−	−2.12**	−1.79**
	(1.67)	(2.53)	(1.60)	(2.40)			(0.81)	(0.77)
N	190		190		190	190	190	190
Log likelihood/F	−937.06	−	−931.03	−	−174.55	−171.89	31.47***	28.76***
LR Chi²/R²	326.02***	−	453.84***	−	112.76***	121.70***	0.63	0.65
Vuong Statistic	7.52***	−	7.64***	−	−	−	−	−

Note: Huber-White robust standard errors (clustered on each war) in parentheses; * = <.10; ** = <.05; *** = <.01 The F and R^2 statistics apply only to the OLS estimates in models 5 and 6. The Vuong Statistic (models 1 and 2) determines whether ZINB significantly improves the fit of the model over a normal negative binomial regression. The significance level indicates that it does.

coefficient in model 1b). Model 2, however, shows that the effect of democracy is conditional on whether the conflict is a war of attrition. Democracies kill larger numbers of civilians than nondemocracies in wars of attrition, but kill fewer civilians than autocracies do when the war is not a war of attrition. Democracies in attrition wars are also highly unlikely to kill zero civilians. Looking at the other interactive hypotheses, democratic war initiators do not kill fewer civilians (B = 0.35, p = 0.78). Finally, democracies do not appear to kill significantly fewer noncombatants than autocracies in interstate wars after 1945 or after 1970.[49]

Among the control variables, a few points are worth mentioning. As expected, increases in relative capabilities and the size of the enemy population result in larger numbers of civilian fatalities. Greater gaps in relative capabilities also strongly decrease the likelihood of observing zero fatalities. On the other hand, having one's own civilians killed brings about an apparent reduction in the number of civilian casualties a state inflicts. This latter variable remains negative even in the reduced sample of states having the capability to harm enemy civilians, meaning it is not simply an artifact of some states being unable to strike back. The way this variable is measured—as a dummy signifying that a state suffered some non-zero number of civilians killed rather than how many died—may be contributing to this odd result. Finally, wars after 1945 are less likely to have zero civilians killed. This finding may be the result of a reporting bias, as the quality and availability of data are better for more recent conflicts.[50]

An Ordinal Logit Model of Civilian Fatalities

I also analyzed civilian casualties using an ordinal logit model. The dependent variable for this analysis is based on the following categories of noncombatant deaths: 0; 1–500; 501–5,000; 5,001–50,000; 50,001–500,000; 500,000–5 million; and over 5 million.[51] The results of this analysis again strongly support desperation and annexation as causes of civilian fatalities. Measures of wars of attrition (including war duration, battle deaths, and expanding or total war aims), are positive and significant at the highest level, as is the variable for territorial annexation. Cultural differences, on the other hand, have a small and insignificant negative effect on civilian casualties. Democracy is positive and significant in model 3, a change from the ZINB analysis, but that significance disappears when an interaction term for democracies in wars of attrition is included in model 4. The interaction term just misses significance (p < 0.12), and this time is smaller than war of attrition by itself (meaning autocracies in wars of attrition), although the two are close in value. Democratic war initiators do not kill significantly fewer civilians in the ordinal logit analysis, nor do democracies kill significantly fewer civilians in wars after 1945 or 1970.[52] Finally, as before, increases in relative capabilities and the size of the adversary's population lead to larger numbers of civilian dead.[53]

OLS and Civilian Casualties

Finally, models 5 and 6 show results obtained by using OLS on logged values of civilian fatalities. These results are nearly identical—in terms of coefficient signs and significance levels—to the ordinal logit estimates just discussed. Democracy, attrition (in all its forms), annexation, relative power, size of the enemy population, and deterrence are all positive and significant; democracy in wars of attrition (model 6) this time is significant and about the same size as attrition alone. Democratic war initiators do not kill fewer civilians, nor do democracies kill fewer noncombatants after 1945 or 1970.[54]

IN SUM, three different analyses of the data on civilian fatalities strongly support the desperation and annexation theses. The results also accord well with Valentino, Huth, and Croco's findings on the importance of attrition, total war aims, and war duration for civilian casualties. We also agree that cultural or identity differences between belligerents do not seem to increase civilian deaths. A few differences emerge between us, however, on the role of democracy. Valentino, Huth, and Croco, for example, find no significant effect for regime type on numbers of civilian casualties in interstate wars, whereas I find some evidence of a positive relationship driven primarily by democratic victimization of civilians in wars of attrition. This latter finding is stronger—but not much different—from their positive and nearly significant interaction term for regime type and attrition strategy.

What explains this difference? One possible explanation is that I include all civilian deaths inflicted by belligerents whereas Valentino, Huth, and Croco include only intentional fatalities. In additional tests, however, my results remain stable (and in fact become slightly stronger) if I restrict the analysis to intentional deaths. A second potential explanation is missing data: there are forty-three belligerents in my dataset (in eighteen wars) for which I was unable to obtain a figure for the number of civilian fatalities inflicted, and a handful of other cases are missing data on an independent variable. Third, our datasets include different wars: Valentino, Huth, and Croco include twelve wars of occupation in their dataset, whereas my dataset is comprised exclusively of interstate wars. Fourth, there are some differences in the way we measure certain variables. I measure regime type once for each belligerent at the beginning of each war, for example, whereas they use the average of each state's democracy score for all the years the war was ongoing. Moreover, while most of the wars in Valentino, Huth, and Croco's dataset consist of one state on each side, cases with multiple states fighting on the same side are combined into coalitions. In these cases, "the values of the independent variables are averaged across

the members of the coalition and weighted based on the troop contributions of each coalition member."[55] In my dataset states are not combined
into coalitions: each state's regime type is measured separately. Finally,
I measure attrition as a dummy variable whereas they measure it as the
percentage of the war during which each belligerent fought an attrition
strategy.[56]

Appendix 2.2

Determining Cause and Effect:
Does Desperation Precede Civilian Victimization?

One limitation of my dataset is that it is not a time series: it codes whether
a conflict was a war of attrition or territorial annexation and whether a belligerent targeted civilians, but it does not specify the order in which these
two events occurred. The desperation model, however, implies that attrition precedes civilian victimization (in the appetite for conquest model,
civilian victimization may occur at any point in the conflict, but it often
occurs early). To ensure that the relationship between wars of attrition and
civilian victimization is not the reverse of what I hypothesize—that is, that
civilian victimization occurs early in wars and leads to wars of attrition
because it is not very effective—it is necessary to ascertain whether cause
came before effect.

I compiled a list of all cases of civilian victimization in wars of attrition
and compared the approximate date that the conflict became a war of attrition with the date that civilian victimization was first used by a belligerent
(see table 2.13). I found that in thirty-one out of thirty-seven instances—84
percent—the war became static or a siege occurred before or around the
same time belligerents targeted civilians. Regarding the six apparent out-
liers—Russia (Russo-Turkish War, 1877–78), Greece (Greco-Turkish War,
1919–22), Germany (Poland, 1939), Germany and Romania (versus the Soviet
Union, 1941–45), and North Korea (1950–53)—three points are noteworthy.
First, each of these cases was also a war of territorial annexation. The reason
that civilian victimization preceded the transformation of the conflict into a
war of attrition, therefore, was that it was triggered by a different cause: the
perceived need to repress or eliminate unwanted or threatening groups in
conquered territory. Russia, for example, killed and expelled Turks from Bulgaria to ensure "the existence of an overwhelmingly Slavic Bulgaria after the
war."[57] Greece, too, targeted ethnic Turks on landing in western Anatolia in
1919; Germany killed Poles and Polish Jews in 1939; Germany and Romania

Table 2.13. Timing of civilian victimization in wars of attrition

War	State	Years	Onset of attrition	Onset of CV	Comments
Franco-Prussian*	Prussia	1870–71	September 1870	September 19, 1870	Siege and bombardment of Paris
Russo-Turkish*	Russia	1877–78	July 20, 1877	July 1877	Cleansing of Bulgarian Turks begins in July
				October 24, 1877	Siege of Plevna begins in October
Boxer Rebellion	China	1900	June 20	June 20	Sieges of Tianjin and Western embassies in Beijing
Boxer Rebellion	Russia	1900	June 20	July 13(Tianjin); August 14 (Beijing)	Reprisal massacres by Western armies after lifting sieges of Tianjin and Beijing
Boxer Rebellion	United Kingdom				
Boxer Rebellion	United States				
Boxer Rebellion	France				
First Balkan*	Bulgaria	1912–13	October 29, 1912	November 1912	Ethnic cleansing of Turks in Balkans begins in early November
First Balkan*	Serbia	1912–13		November 14, 1912	Siege of Adrianople by Serbs and Bulgarians begins in mid-November
World War I West	Germany	1914–18	Fall 1914	December 21, 1914 February 1917	Zeppelin bombings of Britain Unrestricted submarine warfare
World War I West	France	1914–18	Fall 1914	March 1915	Blockade of Central Powers expanded to deny food imports
World War I West	United Kingdom	1914–18	Fall 1914	March 1915	
World War I West	United States	1917–18	April 1917	April 1917	
World War I East*	Turkey	1914–18	Fall 1914	1918	Invasion of Transcaucasia and massacre of Armenians

(Continued)

(Table 2.13.—Cont.)

War	State	Years	Onset of attrition	Onset of CV	Comments
Greco-Turkish*	Greece	1919–22	September 1921	May 15, 1919 August 1922	Greeks massacre Turks upon landing in Smyrna Greeks burn Turkish villages after defeat on Sakkaria River
Greco-Turkish*	Turkey	1919–22	September 1921	September 1922	Destruction of Smyrna
Sino-Japanese	Japan	1931–33	January 28, 1932	January 29, 1932	Bombardment of Shanghai after Japanese attack bogs down in the city
Sino-Japanese*	Japan	1937–45	August 13, 1937	December 13, 1937	Battle of Shanghai; Rape of Nanking
Poland*	Germany	1939	September 8	First week of September September 25	Massacres of Poles and Polish Jews Siege and bombardment of Warsaw
Russo-Finnish*	USSR	1939–40	December 1939	December 1939	Bombing of Finnish cities
World War II West	Germany	1940–45	August 1940	September 1940 April 1942 June 1944	The Blitz Baedeker raids V-1 (flying bomb) and V-2 (rocket) attacks on Britain
World War II West	United Kingdom	1940–45	August 1940	February 1942	Area bombing of German cities
World War II West	United States	1940–45	August 1943	November 1943	Radar bombing of Germany (plus 70 urban area raids)
World War II East*	Germany	1941–45	December 1941 September 1941	June 1941 October 7, 1941 August 23, 1942	Massacre of Soviet Jews by German Einsatzgruppen Siege of Leningrad Bombing of Stalingrad
World War II East*	USSR	1941–45	1941	1945	Massacre of Germans by Red Army troops
World War II East*	Romania	1941–44	December 1941	June 1941	Massacre of Soviet Jews

Pacific War	United States	1941–45	1942	November 1944	Strategic bombing of Japanese cities
Palestine*	Israel	1948–49	March 1948	April 1948	Massacre and expulsion of Palestinian Arabs
*Korea**	*N. Korea*	*1950–53*	*September 1950*	*June 1950*	*Massacre of anti-communists in Seoul*
Korea	United States	1950–53	October 1950	November 5, 1950	Strategic bombing of North Korean cities
First Vietnamese	United States	1965–73	1965	1965 1968	Indiscriminate use of firepower Phoenix campaign
First Vietnamese*	N. Vietnam	1965–73	1965	1965	Assassination of government officials (continued from civil war phase of conflict)
Iran-Iraq	Iraq	1980–88	End 1980	1982	War of the cities
Iran-Iraq	Iran	1980–88	End 1980	1982	War of the cities
Lebanon	Israel	1982	Mid-June 1982	July 4, 1982	Siege and bombardment of Beirut
Armenia-Azerbaijan*	Azerbaijan	1992–94	January 31, 1992	February 1992	Siege and bombardment of Stepanakert
Armenia-Azerbaijan*	Armenia	1992–94	January 31, 1992	February 1992	Massacre of Azeris at Khojaly

* Conflict is also a war of territorial annexation. Italics = civilian victimization occurred before conflict became war of attrition.

attacked Jews in the Soviet Union in the summer of 1941; and the North Koreans killed anticommunist Koreans on taking Seoul in late June 1950.

Second, in four of the six cases, belligerents implemented additional strategies of civilian victimization after the conflict bogged down into a war of attrition: Russia at the siege of Plevna in autumn 1877; Greece after its defeat on the Sakkaria River in September 1922; Germany at the siege of Warsaw in September 1939; and Germany again at the sieges of Leningrad and Stalingrad.

Finally, recoding these six cases as nonwars of attrition does not affect the results reported in table 2.9: the coefficient for war of attrition remains positive and significant at better than the 1 percent level.

A closer look, therefore, reveals that in most wars of attrition, desperation was the sole cause of civilian victimization, and in most of the others, attrition was one cause of civilian victimization. In only two of the thirty-seven cases (Romania in 1941 and North Korea in 1950) did attrition not influence a choice to target noncombatants. The relationship between wars of attrition and civilian victimization, therefore, does not suffer from endogeneity.

[3]

The Starvation Blockades of World War I

Britain and Germany

The First World War is remembered mainly for the years of carnage and futility of trench warfare on the Western front that followed the defeat of Germany's Schlieffen Plan. The naval aspect of the war—of which so much was expected after the prolonged Dreadnought race between Germany and Great Britain—was anticlimactic. Both sides anticipated a titanic clash of battleships in the North Sea, but a decisive battle failed to materialize because each had settled on a largely defensive strategy. The British, for example, implemented a policy of distant blockade, hoping that the ships of the German High Seas Fleet would sortie away from the German coast and give battle in the open where British superiority in numbers could destroy them. But the Germans had no such plan: wary of being outnumbered and defeated in detail, Germany's admirals planned to wage a limited guerrilla war (*Kleinkrieg*), making only restricted forays into the North Sea with surface ships and submarines in the hope of attriting British forces and evening the odds. This policy failed, and thus a stalemate prevailed at sea. Germany's surface raiders were swept from the world's oceans by the end of 1914, and aside from one near miss at Jutland, the massive fleets—which had contributed so much to Anglo-German tensions—swayed at anchor for four years.

Instead, the focus of naval warfare shifted to an unexpected venue: economic warfare. The main belligerents in World War I attempted to throttle their opponents' seaborne trade by way of naval blockades in order to defeat the enemy by hunger. This chapter focuses on the two largest and most famous of these operations: the Allied (mainly British) surface naval blockade of the Central Powers, and Germany's U-boat blockade of the British Isles. In the first half of the chapter, I trace the British decision to impose a starvation blockade on the Central Powers. This embargo aimed to break the morale of the enemy civilian population through their stomachs: the Allied blockade cut off imports of food to the Central Powers starting in March 1915. British leaders decided to target enemy civilians, I argue, as they came to perceive that the costs and duration of the war would be far greater than they had originally believed, and because they thought that denying food to noncombatants might help win the war. With so much at stake, British decision-makers felt that they had no choice but to "use every weapon in our hands to bring to an end this horrible War."[1]

The choice to wage unrestricted submarine warfare also evolved gradually in Germany, receiving fresh impetus every time Germany's prospects for victory took a turn for the worse. As Germany's western offensive ground to a halt in autumn 1914, German naval officers began to push for unlimited use of U-boats against British and neutral commerce. But Kaiser Wilhelm II and his chancellor, Theobald von Bethmann-Hollweg, repeatedly rebuffed the admirals on the grounds that such a move would provoke neutral countries—particularly the United States—to join the ranks of Germany's foes. However, 1916 was the year of crisis for the Central Powers. Reeling under the combined impact of Verdun, the Somme, the Brusilov Offensive, and Romania's entry into the war, German officials grew more desperate as the year passed. Finally, in December, the Admiralstab (the German Admiralty Staff) convinced Bethmann-Hollweg and the kaiser to gamble that a campaign of unrestricted warfare with submarines would finish off Great Britain before the United States could come to the rescue. As defeat appeared certain if Germany remained on the defensive, German leaders believed they had nothing to lose by unleashing the U-boats.

Each of these cases qualifies as a case of civilian victimization. In each instance the strategy was aimed squarely at the civilian population: the British interdicted all of Germany's seaborne trade starting in March 1915, and Germany attempted to cut off British grain imports. The British blockade, in fact, contributed to conditions that took the lives of about half a million Germans, and a similar number of Austrians as well. Although the German blockade had little impact on the British food supply, it was clearly a case of civilian victimization because a conscious choice was made to target the civilian food supply.

CIVILIAN VICTIMIZATION IN CONVENTIONAL WARS OF ATTRITION

When conventional wars between regular armies bog down into stalemates, belligerents have incentives to use military force against civilians to coerce the enemy government or leadership to quit the war. As discussed in chapter 1, civilian victimization as a coercive tool can follow both punishment and denial logics. As punishment, civilian victimization attempts to inflict enough pain on enemy noncombatants that the civilian population rises up and demands that the government stop the fighting, or even replaces the government with more dovish leaders. Alternatively, civilian victimization convinces the enemy government to concede the issue at stake rather than allow its population to continue suffering. One Iraqi officer, for example, explained his country's decision to initiate bombing of Iranian cities in 1985 by arguing: "We want to bring the Iranian people into the front lines of the war. . . . We hope this will encourage the Iranian people to rebel against their government and bring the war to an end."[2]

Civilian victimization, however, can also serve a denial function by undermining an enemy's military strategy for achieving victory. The most common way that this occurs in conventional interstate wars is when belligerents attack their adversary's civilian population in order to decrease the adversary's production of war matériel. The American firebombing of Japan, for example, was not primarily intended to induce the Japanese people to demand an end to the war, but rather to eliminate Japan's war production, which was highly decentralized and scattered throughout residential neighborhoods.[3]

Starvation blockades and sieges typically fall into the punishment category, seeking to coerce an adversary by depriving its civilian population of food. In siege warfare, according to Michael Walzer, "The death of the ordinary inhabitants of the city is expected to force the hand of the civilian or military leadership. The goal is surrender; the means is not the defeat of the enemy army, but the fearful spectacle of the civilian dead."[4] One way to hasten the day when hunger so weakens the defenders that cities can be taken with a minimum of resistance is for the besieger to prevent the besieged's civilian population from leaving the town, thereby increasing the number of mouths that must be fed from scarce provisions. During the Russian siege of Plevna in 1877, for example, "When Osman Pasha's food supplies began to fail, he turned out the old men and women who were in the town and demanded free passage for them to Sofia or Rakhovo. General Gourko [the Russian commander] refused and sent them back." Similarly, General Ritter von Leeb forbade Soviet noncombatants from escaping through German lines during the siege of Leningrad, in which about 1 million civilians died.[5]

Belligerents also sometimes use naval blockades to starve entire countries into submission. In the Nigerian Civil War, for example, the government blockaded the secessionist Ibo region, viewing "starvation [as] a legitimate weapon of war . . . [and] regarding it as a valid means of reducing the enemy's capacity to resist, a method as old as war itself."[6] According to a classified report by an American epidemiologist in 1969, "Slow, creeping starvation of almost the entire population is the key impression today in Biafra." The survey also found that "the Biafran people were suffering from the highest rate of famine ever recorded in history," including the siege of

Leningrad.[7] Sapping the will of an adversary by starving its civilian population is difficult to accomplish against an entire nation-state; thus some starvation blockades—such as Napoleon's Continental System and Germany's U-boat campaign—kill few if any civilians.[8] Other times, however, blockade (and its modern equivalent, economic sanctions) proves quite deadly: the Nigerian embargo and the sanctions on Iraq in the 1990s each helped kill hundreds of thousands.[9]

THE BRITISH BLOCKADE OF GERMANY

On March 1, 1915, the governments of Britain and France announced that they intended to expand the objectives of the naval blockade of the Central Powers to include the interdiction of food. The Entente powers worked assiduously thereafter to throttle Germany's ability to import foodstuffs. Britain and France, for example, concluded a series of rationing agreements with northern European neutral countries such as the Netherlands, Denmark, Norway, and Sweden, whereby those countries agreed voluntarily to restrict their exports to Germany. The addition of the United States to the Entente fold in 1917 made the food blockade even more effective. The United States ended all remaining trade with Germany and slashed its exports to the northern European neutrals, further reducing those countries' ability to export goods to the Second Reich.[10]

The blockade was largely responsible for shortages of key products in Germany. Without access to imported fertilizers, the yields of German harvests declined over the course of the conflict, rendering Germany unable to replace lost grain imports with increased domestic production. The Second Reich grew 4.4 million tons of wheat in 1913, for example, but only 2.5 million tons in 1918.[11] Bread was the first foodstuff to be rationed in Germany (in 1915), the daily ration being set at 225 grams per day, but both the quality and quantity of bread declined over time.[12] Similarly, German consumption of meat products plummeted from 1,050 grams per week in 1913 to 135 in 1918.[13] The meat shortage in turn yielded a shortage in fats: weekly consumption plunged to less than one-third of prewar levels by the last year of the war.

Predictably, reductions in the quantity and quality of food adversely affected the health of the civilian population. Living on the official government ration in Bonn, for example, German nutritionist R. O. Neumann lost 25 percent of his body weight in seven months. Another nutritionist estimated the average weight loss of Germany's urban citizenry at 20 percent. Fatalities from tuberculosis increased 68 percent between 1914 and 1917, which translated into 41,678 extra deaths. Malnutrition took a terrible toll on Germany's children: one wartime survey showed that of 2,154 children surveyed, 39 percent had rickets owing to a deficiency of Vitamin D.[14]

[86]

Children and workmen alike displayed the bloated abdomens of hunger edema, caused by the retention in the body of unwanted fluids.

As a result of this deprivation and disease, Germany suffered somewhere between half a million and a million excess civilian deaths—deaths over and above the prewar death rate—during World War I. Official German statistics, for example, put the excess civilian death toll at 763,000, not counting 150,000 fatalities due to influenza in 1918. Another estimate performed ten years after the war arrived at a figure of 424,000 excess civilian deaths, and put fatalities from influenza at an additional 209,000.[15] Austria-Hungary suffered grievously as well, losing an estimated 467,000 civilians to the effects of the blockade.[16] Women were hit particularly hard: by 1918 the female death rate in Germany had increased 50 percent over the rate in 1913, and was also 50 percent higher than the corresponding rate in England.[17]

The exhaustion of the civilian population owing to the blockade was so severe it may have contributed to Germany's quick collapse in 1918. Illustrative is the comment by Philipp Scheidemann, leader of the Social Democrats in the Reichstag, on October 17, 1918, when asked if Germany could continue the war: "That is a question of potatoes. We have no more meat. Potatoes cannot be delivered because we are short four thousand [railroad] cars every day. We have absolutely no fats left. The distress is so great that one stands before a perfect puzzle when one asks: How does North Berlin live and how does East Berlin live? As long as this puzzle cannot be solved, it is impossible to improve morale."[18] As Avner Offer has put it, "The Allied offensive was the hammer, the home front provided the anvil."[19]

Why did the Entente governments—and particularly the British—implement a strategy that sought to coerce the German regime through the empty stomachs of the civilian population?

British War Aims and Expectations

In the ten years prior to the outbreak of the First World War, British planning for a war with Germany changed from a strategy of "splendid isolation" to one of "continental commitment," which in turn entailed a shift in primacy from the navy to the army. Rather than remaining aloof from a Franco-German war, or employing only maritime means to fight, British leaders decided that maintaining the balance of power in Europe and preventing the channel coasts from falling under German control required that a British Expeditionary Force (BEF) fight alongside France. Naval power alone was insufficient because it could not affect the course of fighting on land, and by the time the effects of a blockade began to be felt, France might already be defeated. The Admiralty bitterly opposed a continental strategy but failed to articulate a compelling alternative. The navy eventually settled on a policy of distant blockade, but its purpose was not starvation: the admirals hoped that interdicting Germany's overseas commerce would compel the High Seas Fleet to give battle.[20] As John Coogan observes, "No one in the Admiralty believed that any economic pressure the navy could bring to bear in a few months would force the enemy to accept peace on terms acceptable to the Allies."[21]

Britain went to war in August 1914 for limited objectives and expected a brief, low-cost conflict. Despite Foreign Secretary Edward Grey's tireless attempts to convince the cabinet that Britain's security rested on preventing a single power from dominating the continent, the ministers initially endorsed "a much narrower definition of what constituted British interests, namely the independence of Belgium and the exclusion of the Germans from the Channel ports."[22] But British objectives quickly escalated: by September, Grey and Chancellor of the Exchequer David Lloyd George were publicly calling for the destruction of "Prussian militarism," in other words, regime change in Germany.[23] British leaders, however, did not envision committing the military means to match their ambitious political goals. Britain, they thought, "would fight a relatively inexpensive naval and economic war while France and Russia would crush Germany on land." The expansion of British war aims to include the overthrow of the German government and its rebirth as a democracy, incongruously, had little effect on this view. "In 1914–15 they [the Cabinet] sought to carry out these aims by employing strictly limited means, by relying on economic pressure and their allies to defeat the enemy whilst Britain itself stood largely aloof from the land war."[24]

The British policy of limited liability was combined with a belief that the war would be short. First Lord of the Admiralty Winston Churchill, for example, "thought the weight of evidence pointed to a short though terrible war," a sentiment shared by fellow cabinet member David Lloyd George. General Sir Archibald Murray, the chief of staff of the BEF, told Lord Esher, a member of the Committee of Imperial Defense (CID), that "the war will last three months if everything goes well, and perhaps eight months if things do not go so satisfactorily." In fact, the only prominent Briton who dissented from this view was Lord Kitchener, but even he predicted a quick German defeat of the French. Most of Kitchener's colleagues found his belief that the war would last three years to be "unlikely, if not incredible . . . [and] believed the war would be over before a million new men could be trained and equipped."[25]

Early Constraints on Using Hunger as a Weapon

Aside from the fact that British policymakers believed the war breaking out on the continent would be over quickly, three other factors constrained immediate resort to a starvation blockade. First, by the time the effects of such a blockade began to be felt in Germany, France might already be defeated. The realization that sole reliance on a naval strategy "could not make their homeland secure" contributed to the decision to send an expeditionary force to fight alongside the French Army in the event of a war with Germany: "A limited expeditionary force was designed to sustain the allies in the field while the blockade did its slow work."[26]

Second, British leaders feared that restricting German trade too aggressively might push the north European neutrals into the war on Germany's side or—more importantly—cause a breach with the United States. Indeed, repeated controversies flared in autumn 1914 between the United States and Britain over restrictions on American trade with Germany.[27] United States leaders were not concerned about the moral rectitude of starving German civilians; rather, they worried that U.S. businesses would suffer from an all-encompassing British embargo. Appeasing American concerns was crucial to Britain's war prospects because the War Department intended to purchase large amounts of arms and munitions from Bethlehem Steel, a vital source of supply that the U.S. government could easily cut off.[28] Aware of this possibility, British officials repeatedly assured the United States that the aims of the blockade were limited and did not include an embargo of food. As Foreign Minister Grey put it in a telegram to Britain's ambassador in Washington in late September 1914: "We have only two objects in our proclamations: to restrict supplies for the German Army and to restrict the supply to Germany of materials essential for making munitions of war."[29] "The surest way to lose the war would be to antagonize America," Grey wrote in his memoirs. British policy should be "to secure the maximum blockade possible that could be enforced without a rupture with the United States."[30] In short, as Coogan notes, "Most British leaders believed by the end of September 1914 that economic pressure might help win the war. Few questioned that a conflict with the United States could lose it."[31]

Finally, the reigning norms and laws of naval warfare—codified in the Declaration of London, negotiated by the leading naval powers in 1908–9—undercut Britain's ability to starve its adversary. "The Declaration of London," argues Avner Offer, "preserved the essence of the Declaration of Paris [in 1856]. It extended neutral rights and immunities by defining contraband, and defining it narrowly, and especially by the introduction of a 'free list.'" Under these rules, as Paul Vincent points out, "foodstuffs consigned to the German government but unloaded at Rotterdam would have been immune from capture by British cruisers during World War I."[32]

The London Declaration established three categories of goods. The first category, absolute contraband, consisted of items useful solely for military operations, such as arms and ammunition. Conditional contraband, the second category, included articles that could be used either for civilian or military purposes, including foodstuffs, forage, fuel, and lubricants. Finally, the declaration established a free list of items that could never be declared contraband, such as cotton, rubber, fertilizers, wool, raw hides, and several metallic ores.[33] Whether a cargo was subject to seizure by a blockading force depended on the military or nonmilitary nature of the goods in question as well as their destination. Absolute contraband, for example, could be seized if it was destined for the enemy country, territory occupied by the enemy, or the adversary's armed forces. Similarly, conditional contraband was subject to capture if these items were consigned to the enemy's armed forces or government. The difference between the two categories was that while absolute contraband could be seized no matter what its immediate destination so long as its ultimate destination was the enemy, conditional contraband was not liable to capture if delivered to a neutral port, even if its final destination lay in the enemy homeland. Put simply, the doctrine of "continuous voyage" applied to absolute contraband but not conditional contraband.

Changes in Costs and Likelihood of Victory

British dreams of a short, low-cost war collided head-on with reality in the fall of 1914. By the time the Battle of the Marne began on September 5, the BEF had already lost more than 15,000 troops killed, wounded, or taken prisoner. "Despite continued optimism at BEF headquarters," Coogan writes, "London was coming [in September] to accept Kitchener's prediction of a long and bloody war."[34] Another 24,000 British soldiers were killed in October and November in the fighting at Ypres, bringing total British casualties by the end of the year to almost 100,000, nearly two-thirds of the BEF's original strength. At the conclusion of the First Battle of Ypres, which ended the race to the sea, both sides dug in along a front of three hundred miles from the Flemish coast in Belgium to the border of Switzerland.[35]

The results of the five months of combat in 1914 shattered the British cabinet's strategy of obtaining "maximum victory at minimum cost," and "most decision-makers realized that the magnitude of the issues at stake now pointed to a prolonged conflict." Already in October, Lord Esher wrote in his journal: "Anticipations of an early defeat by the Allies of Germany have been falsified by events, and all indications to-day point to a long continuance of the struggle." Esher's early recognition gradually dawned on the cabinet by the end of 1914. In late December Herbert Asquith, the prime minister, noted that he was "profoundly dissatisfied with the immediate prospect—an enormous waste of life and money day after day with no appreciable progress."[36]

Both Lloyd George and Churchill cited the expectation of costly fighting for little gain on the western front as the rationale for opening new fronts in separate letters to Asquith at the end of the year.[37] Lloyd George commented after a visit to the front in late 1914 that "any attempt to force the carefully-prepared German lines in the west would end in failure and in appalling loss of life." The prime minister did not need much convincing, noting in a private letter on December 30, 1914, that "the losses involved in the trench-jumping operations now going on on both sides are enormous & out of all proportion to the ground gained." Similarly, Esher attributed the deadlock to "the physical and material conditions of modern war, that appear to tend rather in the direction of siege than of free manoeuvre."[38]

Britain's losses, although small in absolute terms, were staggering as a percentage of its total strength and represented the bulk of the country's professional army. The losses of Britain's allies, however, made the "business as usual" strategy impossible: French casualties numbered almost 1 million men, while those of the Russians approached 2 million.[39] The Entente had successfully halted the German juggernaut, but the cost of doing so had severely weakened Britain's continental allies, on whose shoulders the British had hoped to put most of the burden of fighting the Germans. "By December 1914," David French argues, "it was clear that this was unrealistic. Although the French and Russians thwarted the Germans' plan to achieve a quick victory in a two-front war their armies suffered horribly in doing so and by the end of 1914 the enemy was in occupation of large tracts of Allied territory."[40] Germany began to extend peace feelers in the hope of detaching one of these powers from the Entente. Fearful of defection, the British strategy of "fight to the last Russian" was no longer tenable. By the beginning of 1915, "British strategy therefore shifted towards being seen to be doing whatever they could to give their allies material and moral assistance."[41] Sending a large British Army to the continent was no longer avoidable, which meant that the costs of the war would vastly exceed what Britain had initially anticipated.

Institution of the Starvation Blockade, Phase I

It is interesting to note that although the British blockade would eventually target the food supply of German civilians, that was not its initial intent. In fact, the impetus for establishing a blockade was a perceived German military vulnerability. When the cabinet voted to deploy the BEF to the continent on August 6, the Royal Navy appeared to have been relegated to a supporting role in the unfolding war. Two events quickly changed this. First, although the Central Powers lost their ability to reprovision themselves with their own ships (most were seized or interned in neutral ports), Germany—as allowed under the Declaration of London—began transferring its seaborne trade to neutral ships docking in neutral ports. Second, the British media erroneously reported that the German armies traversing Belgium were desperately short of food. At the same time, the British government discovered that large shipments of grain were underway from New York to Rotterdam and assumed that the Germans intended to obtain supplies for the military through the Netherlands. Churchill pointed out that intercepting these food shipments could have a decisive effect on the outcome of the fighting in France.

In response to this apparent military vulnerability, the British moved to interdict German imports by promulgating the Order in Council of August

20, 1914. The key provision of the order was its application of the doctrine of continuous voyage to conditional contraband, such as food. The order stated that "conditional contraband destined to enemy armed forces, or to contractors known to be dealing with the enemy state, was liable to capture regardless of the port to which the vessel was bound."[42] Under the Declaration of London, by contrast, conditional contraband shipped through neutral ports was not liable to seizure. The British justified this violation of the declaration's terms by arguing that food was now absolute contraband because the German government had taken over the food system (this assertion, too, was based on bogus reporting). The order, however, apparently did little to interdict German trade: because Entente agents "had not yet collected any of that sufficient evidence upon which particular cargoes could be condemned . . . the order in council of 20th August was still no more than the assertion of a legal principle."[43] The British government seemed to be grasping at straws, notes Coogan: "Grey proposed application of the doctrine of continuous voyage to conditional contraband because he had the vague hope that intercepting food imports might somehow defeat Germany." Britain, having "plunged into a Continental war fought on a scale Europe had not seen since the days of Napoleon," aiming for decisive victory, but without a strategy to achieve it, "grasped any plan that seemed to promise quick and easy victory."[44]

In the face of mounting evidence that the quantity of goods reaching Germany through neutral countries was increasing rather than decreasing, London issued a second Order in Council on October 29. This proclamation stated that the British would presume that conditional contraband aboard any vessel headed to a neutral port was bound for the enemy and thus liable to capture if such cargoes (1) lacked a specific recipient, (2) were consigned "to order" of the shipper, meaning that they could possibly be shipped on to Germany, or (3) were consigned to an individual in enemy territory. Moreover, article 2 of the order proclaimed the right to designate a neutral country an enemy base of supply if it could be shown that Germany was drawing supplies for its army through that country. In other words, Britain threatened to treat a neutral country supplying Germany's armed forces as if it were a part of German territory. This measure would allow Britain to seize shipments of conditional contraband headed for these ports and compel the shippers to present evidence that the cargo was not on its way to the enemy.[45]

The changing beliefs of British leaders about the type of war they were fighting caused them to take aim at German food imports. What began as an opportunistic tactic to intercept supplies to Germany's armies in August evolved toward a strategy to starve German civilians as Britain's military fortunes declined in autumn 1914. "The War Office," notes Coogan, "continued to emphasize the need to break the German armies on the Western Front. But London, shocked by the casualty lists, turned increasingly to economic warfare as a relatively bloodless path to victory."[46]

Despite the repudiation of some of the Declaration of London's key provisions, however, the British at this time were still not waging an all-out war on German commerce. The August and October Orders in Council asserted the Entente's rights to condemn cargoes bound for the enemy, but these rights were still largely hypothetical and only occasionally included efforts to interdict food supplies bound for civilians. "Consequently," observes Paul Vincent, "the fleet rarely interfered with neutral trade during the first three months of the war," arresting only three neutral vessels, although it detained many more without officially bringing charges.[47] Official historian of the blockade, A. C. Bell, in a statement that must be considered sympathetic to Britain, summarizes blockade policy at the end of 1914:

> The British government were not, at this date, committed to what may be called unlimited economic warfare; for, in the autumn of 1914, the economic campaign against the central empires was being waged for the limited purpose described in the war orders to the fleet. The government had not enlarged or augmented these objects since the war began, nor had military or naval advisers urged them to do so. The authorities did not, therefore, contemplate measures for controlling and stopping all the enemy's supplies; indeed, at the time, they did not even contemplate stopping foodstuffs, if they were to be consumed by the civil population of the central empires.[48]

Comments made by British officials seemingly affirmed the limited nature of the blockade. Churchill, for example, the top civilian at the Admiralty, remarked in the House of Commons as late as February 15, 1915, that although "there are good reasons for believing that the economic pressure which the Navy exerts is beginning to be felt in Germany. . . . So far . . . we have not attempted to stop imports of food."[49]

This official rhetoric, however, is contradicted by evidence that the Royal Navy stopped many ships carrying food to German and neutral ports in the war's first few months. As noted earlier, the British stopped grain shipments in August that were supposedly destined for the German Army. Beginning in November, moreover, the navy began seizing neutral vessels in what Coogan judges to be "part of a deliberate attempt to deny food to the German civilian population."[50]

Institution of the Starvation Blockade, Phase II

As British leaders realized that the war would be far more costly and protracted than they had originally believed, they sought ways to continue to prosecute the war without paying the awful blood price of trench warfare on the western front. Several members of the cabinet advocated a peripheral strategy of attacking Germany's weaker allies, what Lloyd George described as "bringing Germany down by the process of knocking the props under her."[51] Several such operations were mounted, including opening fronts at Gallipoli, Salonica, in the Middle East, and seizing German colonies in Africa, but none was decisive.

Another weapon Britain employed was to tighten the naval blockade and use it to "stop all German trade, imports and exports alike, without reference to its contraband or noncontraband character," including food.[52] This strategy was formalized in the Order in Council of March 1, 1915, which declared: "The British and French governments will hold themselves free to detain and take into port ships carrying goods of presumed enemy destination, ownership or origin."[53] The German declaration of submarine warfare on February 4, a result of a series of tit-for-tat escalations since the beginning of the war and Germany's perception that Britain was already trying to starve German civilians, provided Britain with an excellent pretext to interdict German food imports in a way that avoided offending neutral opinion. Indeed, as the costs of the war rose and the prospect of it ending any time soon plummeted, the deterrent effect of alienating the powerful United States eroded: as Foreign Secretary Grey's "confidence in the war's quick termination lessened, his determination to preserve American friendship [through restraints on the blockade] similarly weakened."[54]

Admiralty officials, however, did not believe that German U-boats posed a serious threat to British trade: "Losses no doubt will be incurred," Churchill warned, "but we believe that no vital injury can be done." "The submarine business is annoying but that is all," opined another government minister.[55] Thus it was not the threat to British trade represented by the U-boats that sparked the order to cut off all German imports and exports. Rather, British authorities seized on the perceived intention of Germany to sink indiscriminately all merchant vessels in the North Sea to institute terms that were not previously acceptable to neutral states, calculating that the heinousness of the German violation of international law would pave the way. In this estimation the British were correct: U.S. protests were muted, and the Scandinavian countries confined themselves to a pro forma note of protest. As David Stevenson summarizes, "In reality submarine warfare was simply used as a pretext for a policy the British were determined on anyway, in response to the pressure of their own public opinion and the growing evidence that defeating Germany would be long and costly."[56]

The underlying cause of this escalation against Germany's civilian population was the British realization at the end of 1914 and beginning of 1915 that Britain was engaged in a protracted war of attrition in which the country would need to use every weapon at its disposal to prevail. As leader of the Conservative opposition in Parliament Andrew Bonar Law put it after hearing Asquith read the reprisal order on March 1, "in taking that course the Government will have, not the support of the House of Commons only, but it will have the support to the end, of the whole of the people of this country when they determine that no power which is in their hands will be

left unused to bring at the earliest moment this terrible conflict to an end."
Maurice Hankey, secretary of the Committee of Imperial Defense, agreed,
writing at the end of 1914: "If our main military effort against German territory is unattainable for the present, the principal weapon remaining is
economic pressure, and this, in the writer's opinion, is the greatest asset we
have in the war." Asquith himself acknowledged that denying food to Germany might cause "hardship" to the civilian population, but averred "that
under existing conditions there is no form of economic pressure to which
we do not consider ourselves entitled to resort."[57]

Despite a concerted effort to conceal their true intentions after the war,
there is little doubt that British leaders intended to starve the German people and hoped that the suffering inflicted would destroy their morale.[58] In
response to a memorandum by Lord Crewe in June 1915 querying "whether
we should lose anything material by ceasing to prohibit the import of all
foodstuffs into Germany through neutral ports and by falling back, as far as
foodstuffs are concerned, upon the ordinary rules that apply to conditional
contraband,"[59] the British government frankly admitted its intention to
starve German civilians in an internal memo. "Although we cannot hope to
starve Germany out this year," Hankey wrote, "the possibility that we may
be able to do so next year cannot be dismissed. . . . In view of this possibility
it would appear to be most inexpedient at the present time to decide even
in principle on a relaxation of our blockade." Hankey argued that although
neither battlefield reverses nor "economic and food pressure" would prove
decisive on their own, the combination of the two could lead to the collapse
of enemy resistance. Moreover, Hankey argued, "in view of the moderate
degree of success which has attended our military pressure, we cannot afford to forgo any one of these means."[60] United States leaders expressed
similar sentiments when they entered the war two years later: comment-
ing on the U.S. policy of total embargo, a *Times* correspondent remarked,
"While it is realized here that this complete starving out of Germany will
bring keen suffering to non-combatants, the United States takes the position
that every measure tending to hasten the end of the war will save thousands of American lives and millions of American dollars, and that it would
be folly to permit supplies to reach Germany directly or indirectly, as the
only effect would be to prolong the sufferings of the world."[61] The blockade,
Bell concludes, "originally directed solely against the armed forces of the
enemy . . . had been diverted from them, by pressure of circumstances, and
redirected against the enemy population."[62]

The abortive British plan to burn German and Austro-Hungarian grain
crops using incendiary devices dropped from aircraft provides further evidence of British intentions. In a detailed report dated April 1, 1915, Hankey
and two others concluded that one-third of German wheat and rye was
vulnerable to air attack from Britain, France, and Russia, whereas about half
of Austro-Hungarian wheat and 35 percent of the empire's rye lay within

the range of Allied aircraft.[63] The report's authors contemplated using small incendiary bombs to burn the enemy's ripe corn.[64] The scheme appears to have been vetoed by the French, who feared German retaliation against their own crops.[65]

British government officials were by no means unanimous that the starvation blockade would succeed, yet they proceeded with it anyway. Some officials—notably Hankey—were optimistic about the effects of blockade. Others disagreed: "The process of economic exhaustion alone," opined Lloyd George, "will not bring us a triumphant peace as long as Germany is in possession of these rich allied territories. No country has ever given in under such pressure, apart from defeat in the field."[66] Indeed, the British could only hope that the cumulative effect of future military victories and economic deprivation would prove decisive, as there was little evidence in 1915 that the blockade would lead quickly to a German collapse.[67] Despite these uncertain views, British leaders believed they could not afford to abstain from the use of every means at their disposal that might contribute to subduing Germany.

Alternative Explanations

This section considers alternative explanations for Britain's institution of the starvation blockade. I argue that the identity and organization theory arguments do not provide much leverage on this case. British public opinion, however, strongly favored blockade; the press and opposition politicians pressured the government to impose more stringent measures on Germany and neutral trade with Germany. Although the Asquith and Lloyd George governments did not always respond to this pressure, Britain's democratic system reinforced strategic arguments for civilian victimization.

Regime Type. There is little evidence that liberal norms or democratic accountability acted as a restraint on British blockade policy. On the contrary, the parliamentary opposition and the press routinely pilloried the Asquith and Lloyd George governments for being too soft on Germany and on the neutral countries supplying the Germans with foodstuffs.[68] Public pressure to interdict enemy food supplies appeared in the first weeks of the war, according to John Coogan. "Although the campaign of economic warfare initiated under the Order in Council of August 20 far exceeded the limits of international law, it did not satisfy the British public. The press demanded that a Germany supposedly on the verge of starvation not be permitted to 'feed herself through Holland,' whatever the law said."[69] Some critics actually charged that the Foreign Office was preventing the British Navy from doing all that it could.[70] In December 1916, for example, the City of London passed a resolution condemning the feeble enforcement of the blockade and calling on the government to permit the British Navy to tighten the ring around Germany.[71] One member of Parliament went so far as to say that "the policy of agreements with neutral countries was exceedingly unpopular. The attitude of the ordinary Englishman was that he did not like to have any truck with any kind of arrangement which would directly or indirectly benefit his enemies."[72] Late in the war, British attitudes became downright vindictive. F. W. Wile, for example, wrote an article for the *Weekly Dispatch* in September 1918 in which he commented, "I know that not only are ten thousands of unborn Germans destined to a life of physical inferiority . . . but also that thousands of Germans, not even yet conceived, will have to face the same fate."[73]

Even after the war ended, many Britons argued that the blockade should be maintained to punish the Germans for starting the war. A few days after the armistice, several British newspapers denounced German pleas for food as "Hun food snivel" and later denounced candidates for Parliament who displayed "any tenderness for the Hun."[74] "In December 1918," writes Vincent, "few Englishmen were prepared to be receptive to German accounts of starvation. According to the generally accepted consensus, appeals for food were likely to be another instance of 'Hun' trickery."[75] Indeed, article 26 of the armistice continued the blockade, which the Allies used to wring compliance with its terms from Germany since they "were not prepared to occupy Germany and dismantle its sovereignty."[76] The first shipment of food relief did not arrive in Germany until late March 1919; the blockade itself continued until July.

Although the policy of starving Germany won widespread public approval, and members of Parliament and the public applied substantial pressure to the British government, the evidence on democracy as a cause of civilian victimization is mixed. British officials, for instance, did not respond to repeated calls early in the war to declare cotton absolute contraband for fear of unduly alienating the United States. Later on, despite intense parliamentary criticism of the rationing agreements with neutral countries, the government refused to enact total embargoes that would have pleased its domestic constituency but also probably would have driven those states into the enemy camp or triggered their invasion by Germany.

In short, public preferences in Britain were punitive toward "the Hun" and viewed the blockade as a means to penalize Germany for starting the war, revenge for the sinking of passenger liners and merchant ships, and a useful tool for winning the war. And this sentiment undoubtedly influenced the government: "As the people became more determined to win a total victory during September," writes John Coogan, "the British government became more willing to employ whatever weapons might be necessary to smash Germany to its knees." Still, it is unclear just how much urging from their domestic audience British leaders needed, since cold military logic pointed in the same direction: "The casualty lists from the western front were coming to dominate any discussion of maritime rights."[77] Government leaders viewed the blockade primarily as a tool to help win the war at an acceptable cost for Britain, and ratcheted up the pressure slowly so as to avoid driving neutral countries into the arms of Germany.

Identity. The identity argument predicts no civilian victimization in this case because England and Germany actually shared something of a common identity through their "similar Nordic or Teutonic stock" and the German origins of the British royal family.[78] The two countries also shared similar forms of worship. Yet despite these cultural similarities, Britons soon adopted a view of Germans as bloodthirsty brutes with no respect for law or civilization. The development of these opinions, however, followed the outbreak of the war and the commission of real atrocities. Popular views of German identity also had little effect on the formation of policy.

Almost from the beginning of the war, German atrocities in Belgium served as evidence of German barbarism. In late August 1914, a British magazine printed a drawing entitled "The Triumph of 'Culture'" depicting a German soldier standing over the dead bodies of a woman and child in the midst of a burning Belgian village. "'Vandals,' 'Huns,' and the image of the barbarian hordes descending on 'civilization' saturated the representation of the atrocity issue," write John Horne and Alan Kramer, complete with "the Kaiser as the 'modern Attila.'"[79] The drawings of Dutch cartoonist Louis Raemaekers, who composed many representations of German atrocities in Belgium, were immensely popular in Britain. Wellington House—the British War Propaganda Bureau—churned out a diverse array of atrocity propaganda, an effort for which it enlisted several prominent English academics, such as James Bryce and Arnold Toynbee.[80] Some went so far as to argue that because "the Germans appeared to show all the atavistic characteristics of the original Huns," that "there might even 'be force in the contention of those who believe that the Prussian is not a member of the Teutonic family at all, but a "throw-back" to some Tartar stock.'"[81] "The cumulative effect" of this propaganda campaign, concluded two British authors, "was the creation of a national stereotype of the German as a 'Beastly Hun' capable of the worst crimes imaginable to civilised man and whose rules of war were barbaric and inhumane."[82]

Even if all of this public anger and vilification of the Germans were predicted by the identity theory, there is little evidence that barbaric images of Germans preceded the conflict or that these perceptions had much influence on strategy. British decision-makers did not frequently cite Germany's barbaric qualities as a reason for imposing the blockade, nor—as noted above—did policymakers succumb to public hatred for Germany when doing so would have compromised the war effort. Moreover, British perceptions of Germany as beyond the pale of civilization crystallized almost immediately, whereas the decision to impose a starvation blockade on Germany did not occur until nine months later. British decision-making tracks better with leaders' perceptions of the cost of the war and likelihood of victory. Demonizing the enemy surely eased the way toward civilian victimization, but was not the primary cause.

Organization Theory. An organizational culture argument for civilian victimization in this case would contend that the Royal Navy had a "blockade culture," which aimed from before the war to defeat Germany by means of economic pressure. The navy had perfected the art of blockade in the Napoleonic Wars, and the economic strategy had a strong advocate in Admiral Sir John "Jacky" Fisher, First Sea Lord from 1904 to 1910. There were at least two other views on naval strategy within the Admiralty, however. One, espoused by Captain Slade of the Naval War College and firmly situated in the Mahanian tradition, hoped for "the prospect of a single great battle that would decide the command of the sea . . . [and] only allowed commercial blockade a secondary role in a possible war."[83] Indeed, one could easily make the case that the British had a "battleship culture" before World War I rather than a "blockade culture." After all, it was the great Dreadnought race with Germany that did so much to increase Anglo-German tensions, and many naval officers expected to fight a climactic battleship engagement in the war's early days. A second school of thought, represented by Fisher's successor as First Sea Lord Admiral Arthur K. Wilson, recommended combined operations with "a floating army, making raids on different parts of the German coasts and so diverting troops from the main theatre of war."[84]

The influence of these various strategies ebbed and flowed in the decade before World War I, and the plan that was actually implemented in 1914 did not envision a total blockade of Germany. The economic strategy dominated under Fisher, and the Committee on Imperial Defense endorsed this strategy in 1909: "We are of the opinion that a serious situation would be created in Germany owing to the blockade of her ports, and that the longer the duration of the war the more serious the situation would become."[85] But the fortunes of the economic strategy declined when Admiral Wilson took over as First Sea Lord in 1910. Wilson favored a close blockade of Germany's North Sea Coast supported by amphibious landings by the army. The advent of the submarine, aircraft, mines, and coastal artillery, however, had rendered this strategy untenable, and it was scrapped after Wilson's departure.

By the time the war orders of 1914 were published, the navy's strategy had attained its final form: a "distant blockade" was to be imposed by placing the Grand Fleet in the North Sea between Norway and Scotland and the Channel Fleet in the Straits of Dover, thus bottling up the High Seas Fleet and allowing the British to regulate all merchant shipping. Some scholars have argued that this disposition of forces meant "the economic operations that had been tentatively ordered in the 1908 plans had finally assumed greater importance than the traditional military operations."[86]

[99]

Others maintain to the contrary that the "wartime blockade in fact had no prewar roots," but rather was "improvised" on the fly in response to rumors of food shortages among German troops and "to satisfy a vague desire to strike some sort of blow."[87] Those who assign primacy to economic warfare neglect the Admiralty's hope that it could provoke the High Seas Fleet to fight. Rather than tangle with the German ships on their own turf, however, the British wished to entice the Germans away from the German coast where the English flotillas could bring their superior numbers to bear. The economic argument also forgets that the fleet had no orders to intercept contraband when the war began. The evidence thus tends to support the view that the economic strategy was not predominant before the war started; rather, the blockade was initially viewed as an instrument to bring about the destruction of the German Fleet, and economic objectives only ascended in importance as the war progressed.

As for the parochial organizational interests argument—that naval officers advocated blockade to promote the interests of the navy—there is some truth to this in the decade before the war, but not once the war began. The economist faction within the Admiralty clearly viewed blockade as an alternative to the army's plan to send an expeditionary force to the continent, a plan Fisher once dubbed "an act of suicidal idiocy."[88] If blockade was the primary British strategy, it would obviously necessitate devoting the lion's share of budgetary resources to the navy rather than the army. The Admiralty managed to obtain governmental support for a limited blockade in the decade before the war, but could not prevent the continental commitment. The fact remains, however, that the navy received huge resources to build Dreadnoughts to sink German battleships, not destroyers or cruisers to enforce a blockade: increases in the naval estimates were driven by investments in big-gun ships to maintain a sufficient edge over Germany's capital ships.[89] Finally, membership in the navy did not determine support or opposition to blockade once hostilities commenced: although one of the principal advocates of starvation blockade was Maurice Hankey, a marine officer, many of Britain's leading civilian politicians similarly supported blockade. Most importantly, however, the professional naval officers at the Admiralty unanimously opposed the initial suggestion to embargo conditional contraband in August 1914 because it violated the Declaration of London and such cargoes would never be condemned by British Prize Courts.[90]

THE British blockade of Germany aimed to break the morale of the German civilian population through their stomachs: the Allied blockade cut off imports of food to the Central Powers starting in March 1915. British leaders decided to target enemy civilians, I argue, as they came to perceive that the costs and duration of the war would be far greater than they had originally believed, and because they thought that denying food to non-combatants might help win the war. Democratic politics in Britain provided a further impetus for civilian victimization as the public, the press, and the opposition each called for harsher policies, forcing the government to walk a precarious tightrope between pressuring the enemy and alienating potential allies.

Germany's Gamble with Unrestricted Submarine Warfare

Germany's leaders in World War I viewed Great Britain as their most dangerous foe, yet also the most vulnerable one. The Germans never quite accepted that Britain was truly committed to the war, and thus hoped that the British could be coerced to withdraw by blows to their civilian morale. When the Second Reich suffered battlefield reverses in autumn 1914 and again in 1916, therefore, it was against Britain that Germany struck with attempts to victimize civilians from the air and by sea. Unfortunately for the Germans, they lacked the capabilities to subdue England by aerial bombardment or starve it with U-boats: German aerial attacks killed a total of 1,336 Britons during the entire war, whereas the U-boat blockade failed to kill any civilians in Britain itself, although sinkings of merchant ships and passenger liners drowned twelve thousand British sailors and fewer than two thousand civilians.[91] As I will show below, however, German bombing intended to terrorize the civilian population and break its morale, and the blockade hoped to cut off Britain's food supply, "lead to the premature starvation . . . and therefore to the overthrow of the enemy coalition."[92]

The Failure of the Schlieffen Plan

In autumn 1914, as the leaves fell from the trees, rather than returning to victory parades in Berlin, the German Army retreated from the outskirts of Paris, failed to outflank the French and British forces, and was finally forced to dig in for a protracted war of attrition it had not expected.[93] This turn of events "filled [Chief of the General Staff Erich von] Falkenhayn with a deep pessimism" and convinced both he and Chancellor Bethmann-Hollweg that Germany could not hope to prevail if the enemy coalition remained unified.[94] The 1915 U-boat campaign—as well as the use of zeppelins to bomb Britain—was spurred in large part by the failure of the Schlieffen Plan to deliver a quick and decisive victory.[95]

As a result of Germany's failures in the field, German military officers soon began to advocate escalation against civilians in two forms: unrestricted submarine warfare against British shipping, and zeppelin air raids against British cities. German naval memoranda in December 1914, for example, argued strongly that "we dare not leave untried any means of forcing England to her knees, and successful air attacks on London, considering the well-known nervousness of the public, will be a valuable measure."[96] The military men, however, had trouble obtaining the kaiser's consent: "The Kaiser, so often represented as the blood-thirsty advocate of *Schrecklichkeit,* was in fact the chief obstacle to the air war on England." Wilhelm at first refused to sanction aerial attacks on London, the home of his royal cousins, and zeppelin raids in the first few months of 1915 were confined to the eastern coastal areas of Britain. Only in May did the kaiser approve attacks on London east of the Tower, and all remaining restrictions were finally lifted in July. In general, the zeppelins aimed to hit targets of military value and did not purposefully target residential areas. The primitive nature of the bombing, however, and the fact that it took place at night, severely curtailed accuracy in practice, resulting in harm to civilians. In September, Falkenhayn "cautioned the Imperial Navy . . . to try to avoid excessive civilian damage in London, perhaps by limiting bombing to the area of the docks, for fear that the French and British raids might be turned into more severe reprisals."[97] The personal qualms of the kaiser, therefore, and fear of Allied reprisal attacks, both worked to limit the harshness of German aerial attacks.

Similar limits were placed on the U-boat campaign that commenced in February 1915. In the first three months of the 1915 campaign, for example, 94 of the 116 merchant vessels destroyed were sunk according to prize regulations, that is, the submarine surfaced and allowed the merchant crew to abandon the ship before sinking it.[98] In the face of mounting American anger in the wake of the torpedoing of the liners *Lusitania* and *Arabic,* however, the German government first announced that neutral merchant vessels and large enemy or neutral passenger ships would be exempt from submarine attack, and then eventually cancelled the entire offensive.[99] The reason was that Germany's key decision-makers, wary of alienating the United States, felt that—as Falkenhayn put it—the "submarine campaign, with its relatively small actual results, was not worth this price."[100]

By 1916, however Falkenhayn had changed his mind about submarine warfare and viewed it as essential to his one-two punch against France and Britain.[101] Falkenhayn's increasingly pessimistic view of Germany's chances drove his embrace of the U-boats. As Falkenhayn put it in his December 1915 memo to the kaiser, "Our enemies, thanks to their superiority in men and material, are increasing their resources much more than we are. If that process continues a moment must come when the balance of numbers itself will deprive Germany of all remaining hope."[102] "Falkenhayn," according to H. E. Goemans, "was convinced Germany would have its last chance at victory in 1916," and must use all of the weapons at its disposal.[103] Top naval officers lined up in support of Falkenhayn, but Bethmann and the kaiser remained skeptical. The chancellor, for example, argued that Germany's "military situation was not so bad that we had to make such a desperate move."[104] Kaiser Wilhelm agreed: "The present military situation is not such as to force us to stake everything on one throw of the dice"; thus "the time had not yet come to risk the armed intervention of America."[105] The kaiser ordered the resumption of a limited submarine offensive that permitted German U-boats to sink without warning only enemy ships in the war zone. Again, as in 1915, when friction developed with the United States over the sinking of a civilian ship (the French steamer *Sussex*), Germany retreated and returned to cruiser warfare, which precipitated an end to the campaign. "The unrestricted submarine campaign," remarks Holger Herwig, "had been blunted primarily by United States reaction to the indiscriminate sinking of passenger liners rather than to British antidotes," which were still largely ineffective at sinking German U-boats.[106]

The Four Hammer Blows Induce German Pessimism

With the Verdun offensive in tatters by spring 1916, calls for Falkenhayn's head were not long in coming. By early July, when the British unleashed their attack on the Somme, Verdun had cost the Germans 250,000 casualties.[107] A month earlier, the Russians had opened their great summer offensive by ripping through Austro-Hungarian forces and penetrating deep into Hungary. To contain this advance the German High Command committed much of its strategic reserve, which was badly needed in the West. To cap it all off, Romania entered the war on the side of the Entente. Bethmann—who had tolerated Falkenhayn while the general opposed unrestricted submarine warfare but began intriguing against him when Falkenhayn changed sides in late 1915—was convinced by this string of catastrophes that the chief of staff had to go.[108] Germany's fading fortunes also persuaded the chancellor that the country should seek a negotiated settlement to the war at the earliest possible opportunity.

The Romanian declaration of war was the last straw. The kaiser—who was close to Falkenhayn and distrusted his likely successors Generals Paul von Hindenburg and Erich Ludendorff—had no choice but to make a change, dismissing Falkenhayn on August 28. Hindenburg became chief of the General Staff with Ludendorff as his First Quartermaster General.

Immediately thereafter the top military and political leaders assembled for a conference on strategy at Imperial headquarters in the town of Pless. Predictably, Admiral Holtzendorff, head of the Admiralstab, pleaded for unrestricted submarine warfare: "Motivated by the dilemma in which Germany found herself by the August of 1916," Holtzendorff argued that a "country in danger must make every exertion possible, and that unrestricted U-boat warfare was on that account inevitable and had better commence at once. *Finis Germaniae* . . . consists not in the use, but in the withholding of a weapon which cripples England's ability to support her allies and continue the war."[109]

Holtzendorff's argument failed to persuade Hindenburg and Ludendorff who—although favorably inclined toward unrestricted submarine warfare in general—did not believe that the time had come to use the last weapon in Germany's arsenal. With Romania still to deal with, Germany's manpower reserves were nearly exhausted. The duo, therefore, took seriously the argument that unlimited U-boat warfare would prompt the Netherlands and Denmark to declare war on Germany:

> Only with extreme regret could we refuse to pronounce in favour of unrestricted submarine warfare on the ground that, in the opinion of the Imperial Chancellor, it might possibly lead to war with Denmark and Holland. We had not a man to spare to protect ourselves against these States, and even if their armies were unaccustomed to war, they were in a position to invade Germany, and give us our death-blow. We should have been defeated before the effects, promised by the Navy, of an unrestricted U-boat campaign could have made themselves felt.[110]

The conferees, therefore, decided to postpone a final decision on U-boats until the defeat of Romania, but "the question is no longer whether the [U-boat] campaign should, or should not, be pursued without restraint, but only what will be the best moment for removing every restriction."[111] Crucially, while stressing the danger of alienating America and the other neutrals, Bethmann conceded a critical part of his authority by agreeing that the unrestricted underwater campaign—a highly political decision—should commence when the High Command felt the military conditions were right.

Shortly after the conclusion of this conference, Hindenburg and Ludendorff visited the Western front to gain a firsthand appreciation for the problems that had bedeviled their predecessor. At Cambrai on September 7, "the Army Group and Army commanders had painted a frightening picture of warfare in the west; of the crushing Allied material superiority in what the Germans came to call '*die Materialschlacht*' (the battle of matériel), and the 'fearful wastage' of the German forces on the Somme and at Verdun."[112] Deeply impressed by these conditions, the duo decided to assume a defensive posture in the West. The new commanders ordered construction to begin on a new line of fortifications, what would soon be known in Germany as the Siegfried Line and to the Allies as the Hindenburg Line. This formidable barrier of concrete and steel bunkers, when completed, stretched for seventy miles in three parallel lines. In February 1917, the German Army left its positions and withdrew to the Hindenburg Line.

Although Germany waged cruiser warfare with submarines in the fall of 1916, it was clear to all that this was an interim measure. Indeed, as early as September 10, Ludendorff assured Captain von Bulow of the Naval Staff that he favored the institution of unrestricted submarine warfare as soon as the military situation cleared up.[113] Two months later, Admiral Scheer visited Hindenburg and Ludendorff at Pless, and found them in agreement that a campaign of unlimited submarine warfare should begin by February 1, 1917, at the latest.[114] Then, in early December, Bucharest fell to General von Mackensen's forces, thereby removing the final impediment to U-boat warfare. Later in the month, the French counterattacked at Verdun, capturing eleven thousand German prisoners and retaking nearly all of the ground surrendered earlier in the battle. This event made an impression on Ludendorff, who wrote to the chancellor that "what had occurred on the western front had persuaded him that unrestricted submarine warfare must begin in January . . . the whole matter was reduced to the simple proposition: that the empire was hard pressed, and must make every exertion in the coming year."[115]

In sum, Germany's top political and military leaders perceived their country's predicament at the end of 1916 to be grim. The fighting that year had gone against them on all fronts, and though they had managed to staunch the bleeding at Verdun, the Somme, in eastern Galicia, and in Romania, there was little prospect for improvement in the immediate future. The Allies heavily outnumbered German troops in the West, 3.9 million to 2.5 million.[116] As Roger Chickering puts it,

> The two sides seemed condemned to an extended ordeal of attrition—a prolonged, massive investment of men and *matériel* with negligible strategic returns. While this prognosis pleased the generals nowhere, it was particularly disquieting to the Germans, for it meant that they were eventually going to lose the war. The Germans faced a coalition that could, as the Battle of the Somme had already demonstrated, outproduce them in every area that was relevant to combat in this mode—whether munitions, machinery, food, or men.[117]

It had taken two long years, but by late 1916 "most German leaders, including Hindenburg and Ludendorff, had reluctantly concluded that Germany was fighting a war of attrition, as Falkenhayn had been insisting for two years."[118]

The Decision for Unrestricted U-Boat Warfare

Pressure on the Chancellor. As the war progressed, German lawmakers in the Reichstag increasingly criticized Bethmann-Hollweg for opposing unrestricted submarine warfare. In the spring of 1916, for example, both the Conservatives and National Liberals sponsored resolutions in the Reichstag backing unfettered use of submarines, but the chancellor was able to divert them to the secret proceedings of the Budget Committee. By the fall, however, a majority of the Reichstag clearly approved of setting the U-boats free. On October 7, deputies passed a resolution suggested by the Center

Party which, while "stressing the chancellor's responsibility" for the final decision to wage unrestricted U-boat warfare, argued that the views of the High Command "'have to be nearly decisive. . . . If Hindenburg resolves upon ruthless submarine warfare . . . no chancellor can take a different position.'"[119] Described by Gordon Craig as "an act of collective irresponsibility in a matter affecting the very heart of the constitution, the principle of civilian dominance over the military," the measure passed and effectively tied the chancellor's hands.[120]

Bethmann's only escape from the increasing pressures to escalate the war by declaring unrestricted submarine warfare was to secure an armistice. As Konrad Jarausch puts it, "This naval challenge signaled the beginning of a race between peace and the expansion of war."[121] To this end, Bethmann announced in the Reichstag on December 12 Germany's willingness to open negotiations with Entente representatives in a neutral country.[122] American president Woodrow Wilson—having secured reelection—then sent a peace note in which he invited the warring parties to state their war aims as a preliminary step toward negotiations. The whole effort came to naught, however, as the Allies resoundingly rejected Bethmann's olive branch and "condemned Germany as an immoral aggressor seeking to justify her crimes and impose her own form of peace on the civilized world."[123] With that, the door slammed shut on any hopes of a negotiated peace in 1917.

Holtzendorff's Memorandum. Against this depressing military and diplomatic background, chief of the Admiralstab Holtzendorff circulated another memorandum on unrestricted submarine warfare dated December 22. In this famous memo, Holtzendorff argued that Britain could be brought to the brink of ruin in six months. The genesis of this memo lay in a series of studies performed by members of Department B1 of the Admiralty Staff beginning in early 1915. From the beginning, Hermann Levy—in peacetime a professor of economics at Heidelberg and the leading figure in this inquiry—focused on the effects of cutting off Britain's ability to import wheat.[124] He found that Britain maintained a low level of grain on hand relative to the amount imported. Unlike most countries, which stockpiled grain that lasted most of the year, Britain "relied on an 'uninterrupted stream' of grain, and did not hold much of it in storage. At their highest, stocks rose to seventeen weeks' supply; at their lowest, they would last only six and a half weeks."[125] "Here was a target," notes Avner Offer, "small enough for the submarines to destroy, and yet critical for Britain's survival," which would allow Germany's U-boats "to deliver a decisive blow with limited means."[126] Levy argued that if imports could be shut off when domestic stocks were already depleted, wheat prices would rise to such astronomical levels that a panic would ensue and London would be unable to continue the war effort.[127]

Department B1's study of economic warfare against Britain culminated in Holtzendorff's memorandum.[128] Holtzendorff argued that the poor world-wide grain harvest in 1916 presented Germany with a unique opportunity. Britain normally imported most of its wheat from the United States and Canada, but it appeared that neither country would have any excess wheat for export after domestic consumption.[129] The meager harvest meant that the British would have to look to more distant suppliers, such as Argentina, India, and Australia. The increased distances, in turn, meant that the same tonnage of shipping could carry only half the amount of grain as it could carry from North America, thus utilizing a greater proportion of the merchant fleet and making it more vulnerable to interdiction.

Holtzendorff calculated that Britain had roughly 10.75 million tons of shipping available to carry its trade—6.75 million tons owned by the British, 900,000 tons of captured Central Powers shipping, and 3 million tons flying neutral flags.[130] Submarines operating according to the prize rules in the last three months of 1916 had been able to sink about 300,000 tons per month.[131] Holtzendorff and his staff estimated that the U-boats could double this monthly average if allowed to sink ships without warning. Moreover, the fear of being sent to the bottom would scare off, according to Holtzendorff, about 40 percent of neutral ships trading with Britain. Over the course of five months, the losses incurred by this campaign—4.2 million tons—would amount to 39 percent of Britain's combined merchant tonnage. Holtzendorff and his economic team believed that this loss would prove decisive: "England would not be able to put up with such a loss, whether considered with regard to its effects upon the situation which would develop after the war or with regard to the possibility of continuing further with the war at the present time."[132] "The rise in prices, and then the actual shortages of bread," argues Offer, "would create such panic and outcry that Britain would not be able to continue the war."[133]

Although the blockade ended up having little effect on civilian food supplies in England, there is no doubt that German policy intended to starve the British population. In 1915, German naval officers were disappointed that with the means at their disposal they were "not in a position to cut off England's imports to a degree that the country will suffer hunger." In 1916, Holtzendorff's memorandum "stressed that the unrestricted submarine campaign was to be directed, not merely, or even primarily, at ships carrying munitions, but against all imports necessary to life in the British Isles."[134] The blockade Germany meant to impose was total: just as the British stopped all trade with Germany, so the Germans sought to sink all ships doing business with Britain.

The flaws in the Admiralstab's reasoning were large and numerous. For starters, the memo assumed that the British would not adapt to the submarine campaign by building more ships, allocating more tonnage to carrying trade, or adopting a convoy system. Furthermore, wheat occupied only a small fraction of total British merchant tonnage, so the weight of ships sunk was not the proper measure by which to evaluate the success of the campaign.[135] The correct metric was the amount of wheat destroyed or the supply of grain on hand in England. These measures demonstrate the true failure of the campaign: wheat losses per month averaged about 6 percent, and the country's stockpile actually *increased* over the crucial first several months of the campaign—when shipping losses, by contrast, were at the highest—from five and a half weeks' supply to fourteen weeks.[136] Finally, the assertion that Britain would collapse in six months had no actual basis in fact or logical argument.

The Pless Conference. Unrestricted submarine warfare as the last hope for victory now possessed unstoppable momentum, however, and the defeat of Romania in December and the rejection of Germany's peace feelers removed the final obstacles. On January 8, 1917, Hindenburg, Ludendorff, and Holtzendorff, in an audience with the kaiser, demanded the initiation of a U-boat campaign or the termination of the chancellor, and this time Wilhelm gave way. Not even Bethmann—the staunchest opponent of the submarine clique—resisted when presented with this *fait accompli* when he arrived at the conference the next day, stating meekly that "if the military authorities consider the U-boat war essential, I am not in a position to contradict them."[137] The campaign was set to begin on February 1.

The Reasons Why. The testimony of German decision-makers is unanimous in arguing that Germany's grim prospects in the war plus the belief that unrestricted submarine warfare offered a chance to avoid defeat were the main factors in determining whether to target Britain's food supply.[138] Ludendorff, for example, argued that because of the Entente's superiority in every category, "If the war lasted our defeat seemed inevitable." Unrestricted submarine warfare, therefore, "was now the only means left to secure a victorious end to the war within a reasonable time. If submarine warfare in this form could have a decisive effect—and the Navy held that it could—then in the existing situation it was our plain military duty to the German nation to embark on it."[139] Admiral Scheer expressed similar sentiments in his memoirs: "But if we did not succeed in overcoming England's will to destroy us then the war of exhaustion must end in Germany's certain defeat. There was no prospect of avoiding such a conclusion by the war on land. . . . *In such a situation it was not permissible to sit with folded hands and leave the fate of the German Empire to be decided by chance circumstances.*"[140] Germany's note to the American government, delivered the day before the campaign began, put the matter succinctly: "Every day by which the war is shortened preserves on both sides the lives of thousands of brave fighters, and is a blessing to tortured mankind. The Imperial Government would not be able to answer before its own conscience, before the German people, and before history, if it left any means whatever untried to hasten the end of the war."[141] In short, as naval historian V. E. Tarrant concludes, "The demands of the military and naval leaders, the Kaiser's acquiescence and the Chancellor's abdication of authority had a common denominator—realistically there was no alternative but to make the ultimate decision with regard to the strategic use of the U-boats, because Germany's situation was desperate."[142]

Alternative Explanations

Regime Type. The coding of Germany's regime type has been the center of some controversy in the context of the democratic peace (DP) debate. Supporters of DP argue that the kaiser's autonomy from the Bundestag in foreign policy, and the lack of civilian control over the military, rendered Germany a nondemocracy.[143] The Polity dataset, which focuses on the openness of domestic political institutions, also codes Imperial Germany as an autocracy. Critics, by contrast, contend that when compared to countries thought to be democratic at the time, such as France and Britain, the similarities far outweigh the differences, and Germany certainly was—and was perceived to be—a much more advanced constitutional state than other countries sometimes mentioned as liberal at the time, like Chile or Colombia.[144]

Wherever the truth lies in this debate (I have followed the practice of most large-N studies and coded Germany as a nondemocracy), public opinion—contrary to what one would expect in an autocratic state—exerted a serious influence over German policymakers. The German public from the early days of the war clamored for retribution against Britain. This vengeful sentiment is well-captured by public reaction to an interview given by Admiral Alfred von Tirpitz to an American reporter in February 1915. Asked whether Germany was considering imposing a blockade on Great Britain, Tirpitz replied, "Why not if we are driven to extremities? England is endeavouring to starve us; we can do the same, cut off England and sink every vessel that attempts to break the blockade."[145] The Tirpitz interview caused a public sensation in Germany, coming at a time when the chance for a quick victory had disappeared and the public was receptive to any weapon that promised to shorten the war and end it in Germany's favor. According to Gordon Craig,

> Tirpitz divined that the thought of a wonder weapon would excite public opinion to the point where it would demand enough submarines to defeat Britain, and, by and large, he was right. From the very beginning of the war, the great mass of the public accepted the idea of unrestricted submarine warfare (that is, the sinking of ships without warning) with an uncritical enthusiasm and had no sympathy with the argument that resort to this kind of war would be an affront to humanity and would alienate neutral opinion.[146]

Germany's civilian leadership, however, like their British counterparts, did not simply bow before public sentiments and immediately implement a policy that would (in their opinion) harm Germany's cause. The kaiser's personal predilections in the case of aerial bombardment of London, and the threat of American intervention on the side of the Entente in the case of unrestricted submarine warfare, caused delays in each of these campaigns. In the U-boat case, the government held out for two years against mounting public agitation and political intrigue, demonstrated by the words of Count Hertling, the minister-president of Bavaria, in a letter from August 1916:

> The government has no idea of the wild passions with which the opponents of the Chancellor are working. They have just one central idea: England is the enemy, England must be destroyed and this can be achieved in a few months, if only the navy is given a free hand to launch unrestricted submarine warfare. But the government refuses to budge, the Kaiser continues his love affair with England . . . and the Chancellor is too weak to oppose him.[147]

The German nondemocratic decision-making process, in fact, looks remarkably similar to the British democratic one. Critics might respond that as the war progressed Germany increasingly came to resemble a military dictatorship, and the important decisions were made by generals, not statesmen. The generals undeniably exerted greater influence over German policy as time passed. One cannot argue, however, that Hindenburg and Ludendorff seized the reins of power from Germany's civilian leaders and forced them to order unrestricted submarine warfare. Such a view ignores the nearly unanimous support that the submarine strategy enjoyed in German society. In fact, it was the Reichstag that tied Bethmann's hands in October 1916 by resolving that U-boat warfare should begin when the High Command deemed the time to be right. Unrestricted submarine warfare, argues one author, "may well rank as the most popular military campaign of the entire war."[148] Bethmann began to have second thoughts, "and he could not help feeling that a policy that was backed by all of the military leaders, the Emperor, the Reichstag majority, and most politically active Germans might, after all, be sounder than he had believed."[149] "Resolutely opposed only by the Socialists," concludes Jarausch, "the unleashing of the U-boats was therefore Bethmann's most democratic decision."[150]

Identity. Contrary to the expectations of the identity hypothesis, in the weeks and months following the outbreak of war, Britain became public enemy number one in Germany. "Like all the belligerents," comments a historian of German propaganda in World War I, "Germany in the months following the outbreak of war was gripped by a jingoistic wave of hysteria that sought release through an intense hatred of the enemy." Like the Entente, German propaganda emphasized supposed enemy atrocities to foster the view that the adversary was barbaric, most commonly the story of Belgian women gouging out the eyes of wounded German soldiers. According to one Englishwoman in Germany at the start of the war, "The Allies loomed in most people's eyes as horrible, blood-soaked, sadistic savages. In fact very much the same sort of savages that were being created in English and French minds, and labelled [sic] Boches and Huns."[151]

Britain's decision to enter the war against Germany, however, provoked widespread outrage and caused the English to emerge as the most hated of Germany's foes, a striking reversal from prewar attitudes, which were harsher toward France and especially Russia. In a November 1914 interview, for example, Hindenburg spoke highly of the fighting qualities of the Russians and the French, but viewed "the English as the most hated enemy." Similarly, a traditionally francophobic German newspaper noted in January 1915: "The English have become the most hated of all our enemies. . . . Germany will ultimately come to terms with France [and] with Russia, again, but never with England."[152] That the German public felt the same way is demonstrated by the speed with which the phrase "Gott strafe England"—God punish England—became ubiquitous, being printed on all manner of articles and used as a greeting among children and in telephone conversations. Moreover, the villain of Ernst Lissauer's "Hymn of Hatred," a popular war song, was not France or Russia, but England.

Given the sense of betrayal Britain's declaration of war provoked—as well as the excuse it provided to deflect blame for the causes of the war away from Germany—the venom directed at England is understandable, but it does not provide support for the identity argument. Although Germans expressed hatred and loathing for the British, and viewed them as foul betrayers, they did not generally depict their cross-channel neighbors as barbarous brutes exempt from the protection of the rules of civilization. Moreover, as noted above, the two countries shared similar ethnic origins as well as royal ties. Indeed, some German commentators predicted before the war that Britain would intervene in favor of their "'Germanic' cousins."[153] By contrast, the "case against an inferior and barbarous Russia was even easier to make" than one against England, particularly given the low regard with which Russia was held before the war and the proximity and magnitude of the Russian threat.[154] Yet Germans reserved their most withering hatred for Britain. In short, the Germans directed their hatred at the wrong enemy as far as the barbaric identity hypothesis is concerned.

Organization Theory. Organizational arguments do a poor job of explaining the German case. Despite the central importance that submarines played in warfare at sea in the First World War, their role was almost entirely a product of wartime circumstances rather than prewar planning. In fact, German naval plans for war against Great Britain envisioned no independent role for U-boats and had hardly even considered the possibility of a submarine offensive on English commerce. Typical of Admiralstab thinking on the subject is a December 1912 paper, which established three targets for German U-boats: the main body of the British fleet, British bases, and the ships carrying the BEF to the continent.[155] The only study on the interdiction of British seaborne trade with submarines is a May 1914 report by Ulrich-Eberhard Blum, an officer in the Submarine Inspectorate. Blum estimated that Germany would need 222 U-boats to establish a blockade of the British Isles.[156] By contrast, in August 1914 the German Navy disposed of a total of 30 submarines capable of operating against Great Britain.[157]

Parochial organizational interests, by contrast, explain the navy's sudden conversion to the submarine in fall 1914 but cannot account for state policy. Almost to a man, German naval officers believed that the English Grand Fleet would storm into German coastal waters seeking battle. Instead, Britain's battleships remained in port at Scapa Flow while its cruisers imposed a distant blockade at the exits to the North Sea. Chief of the High Seas Fleet Admiral von Ingenohl, deprived of a chance to tangle with the Royal Navy in friendly waters, ordered his forces to implement the naval equivalent of guerrilla warfare, but in reality the Germans could not force the British to fight. The High Seas Fleet was bottled up and the admirals knew it.

Suggestions to use Germany's U-boats against British shipping began to percolate within the Admiralstab beginning in October, but the first official recommendation came from chief of the Navy Staff, Admiral Hugo von Pohl, in a memo sent to the kaiser the day after the British declared the North Sea to be a war zone. Considering that before the war broke out the navy possessed no plans at all to use U-boats for commerce warfare, as well as the presence of fewer than thirty submarines in the entire fleet, this was a surprising recommendation. Simple frustration at not being able to have any impact on the course of the war goes a long way toward explaining this sudden change of heart. The navy as an organization would look impotent if, after having built dozens of warships, they sat rusting in port while the army fought and bled on land. The navy's desire as an organization, therefore, to contribute to the war effort helps to explain the new fondness for submarines.

The navy's newfound faith in commerce warfare notwithstanding, civilian control of the military in Germany turned out to be quite robust. Kaiser Wilhelm and his chancellor repeatedly rebuffed the navy's arguments for unrestricted submarine warfare on the grounds that the risks such a strategy entailed were not worth the rewards. Only when Germany's military position soured considerably in 1916 did Germany's civilian leaders become desperate enough to gamble on the unlimited use of U-boats against British commerce.

Ultimately, unrestricted submarine warfare failed to knock out the British, brought the Americans into the war, and helped seal Germany's doom. But this undesirable outcome does not mean that the decision was irrational at the time. True, Holtzendorff's estimates and calculations were flawed, and German leaders failed to appreciate likely British countermeasures and the impact of America's contribution to the Allied war effort. Even so, the U-boats actually sank nearly 2 million tons of merchant shipping in the first three months of operations—an average of 648,000 tons per month—a figure that exceeded the level envisioned by Holtzendorff.[158] Moreover, although the actual danger to British wheat supplies on reflection was slight, the massive shipping losses frightened British officials at the time.[159]

The fact was that by the end of August 1916, Germany's situation looked untenable. Besieged on all fronts, outnumbered by a wide margin, inferior in materiel, and plagued by a hungry population and an ally tottering on the brink of collapse, Germany's defeat was certain without some sort of miracle. Ironically, had the submarine decision been postponed but a few months, Russia's collapse might have made a German victory—or at least a favorable negotiated settlement—possible in the West. Unfortunately, the Russian Revolution was not foreseeable in 1916; in fact, the Russians had just finished giving Austria and Germany a vicious beating on the Eastern front. It was at least as likely that the Austro-Hungarian Empire would be rent asunder by national revolutions as Russia would fall victim to a class-based revolution. These historical counterfactuals notwithstanding, German leaders simply felt they could not stand idly by while their country went down to defeat.

CONCLUSION

This chapter has demonstrated that as British and German policymakers' perceptions of the costs and length of the Great War rose, and their belief in victory diminished, they adopted coercive strategies that targeted civilians. The means employed were primarily naval—surface ships on the British side and submarines for the Germans—and the goal was to deprive the enemy population of food. Germany also employed its advantage in airpower to bomb British cities when the battlefield situation turned against them, first with zeppelins in 1914–15, and with zeppelins and Gotha bomber aircraft in 1916–17. Britain took longer to develop a bombing capability, but had the conflict continued beyond 1918 the newly formed Independent Force would likely have taken the war to German cities.[160] The British blockade turned out to be far more effective than the German one in terms of its impact on the civilian population. The British were able to drastically lower the availability of grains, meats, and fats, which adversely affected the health of millions of Germans. The U-boat blockade, by contrast, never seriously threatened Britain's food supply even though millions of tons of shipping were sunk. Nevertheless, the intent was the same: to reduce the import of foodstuffs, thereby inducing hunger in the civilian population, which would demand that its government quit the war.

These case studies reveal two other interesting points. First, Britain and Germany each feared triggering the intervention of a powerful third party—the United States—if they implemented a strategy of civilian victimization more than they worried about retaliation by their opponent. The key restraint on British blockade policy was the possible reaction of the United States if Britain too severely curtailed American trade with Germany. Note that the U.S. objection was not a moral one about the ethics of starving civilians; rather it was concerned with protecting the access of American businesses to foreign markets. The critical civilian leaders in Germany—Kaiser Wilhelm and Chancellor Bethmann-Hollweg—also continually cited the possibility of U.S. entry into the war as a reason against unrestricted submarine warfare. These fears regarding the reactions of a third party show a different, less direct way that deterrence can affect choices to target civilians.

Second, public opinion in democratic Britain and autocratic Germany was rabidly problockade, and decision-makers in both countries felt tremendous pressure from the media, the legislature, and the public generally to impose a starvation blockade on the enemy. In neither country, however, did this pressure automatically translate into policy, as leaders sought to balance the positive effects of increased coercive leverage on the enemy against the negative effects of possible third-party intervention. Moreover, the decision-making process for unlimited submarine warfare in Germany cuts against the image of the Second Reich as a military dictatorship, as civilian leaders repeatedly overruled military preferences. By late 1916, support for U-boat warfare was virtually unanimous, and—in truly democratic fashion—the policy was implemented. In fact, once one examines the nuances of the decision-making process, Germany appears to have been more restrained than Britain in terms of choosing civilian victimization as a strategy.

[4]

Strategic Bombing in World War II

The Firebombing of Japan and the Blitz

This chapter discusses in detail two cases of civilian victimization via aerial bombardment in World War II: the United States versus Japan (1944–45) and Germany versus Great Britain (1940–41). In each case, a state—a democracy in the former and a dictatorship in the latter—faced a costly seaborne invasion of its enemy's homeland and reacted in similar ways: by shifting the potential costs to enemy civilians. Against Japan, American officials understood from the start that the war would be a protracted affair. The bloody nature of the fighting in the Pacific then convinced top American political and military officials that an invasion of the Japanese home islands would probably be necessary to subdue Japan, and that this invasion was likely to entail high American casualties. Moreover, the extraordinary weather conditions over Japan largely frustrated American attempts to bomb industrial targets with high explosives. The belief that destroying Japan's major cities by fire would shorten the war and save American lives was ubiquitous among those responsible for the decision.

By contrast, Germany expected a quick and decisive victory when it invaded France and the Low Countries in May 1940. Indeed, the German blitzkrieg crushed the combined forces of Britain, France, Belgium, and the Netherlands in six weeks, resulting in the conquest and occupation of the latter three countries and the ejection of British troops from the continent. Britain, however, did not capitulate, forcing Hitler to consider an invasion. Such an attack could not proceed until the Luftwaffe destroyed the British fighter force. When this proved impossible, Hitler and his air commanders—in a last-gasp effort to persuade Winston Churchill's government to come to terms—sent their bombers against British urban industrial areas an indiscriminate night bombing offensive known as "The Blitz" that killed tens of thousands of Britons.

THE FIREBOMBING OF JAPAN

On the night of March 9, 1945, General Curtis LeMay, commander of Twenty-first Bomber Command based in the Marianas Islands, launched Operation Meetinghouse against Tokyo, a mission that marked the official beginning of the destruction of Japan's cities by fire.[1] That night, 279 B-29s dropped 1,665 tons of incendiary bombs—almost 500,000 individual munitions, mostly of the M-69 type—on a ten square mile section of the Japanese capital from altitudes between forty-nine hundred and ninety-two hundred feet. The targeted sectors of the city were among the most densely populated in the world, counting an average of 103,000 residents per square mile. Ninety-eight percent of the buildings were constructed of paper and wood, and the proportion of the targeted area covered by roofs (and thus highly inflammable) was also high, reaching 40 to 50 percent in Asakusa ward. The Tokyo Fire Department, moreover, was utterly inadequate for dealing with large or multiple fires, and the capacity of the city's eighteen concrete bomb shelters was a paltry five thousand people.[2]

In the event, Tokyo's firefighters were quickly overwhelmed. High winds brought the many small conflagrations together and generated a firestorm. "Unlike the firestorm that sucks everything to its center," such as the one that destroyed much of Hamburg in July 1943, Michael Sherry writes that "the conflagration that swept Tokyo was rapaciously expansive, a pillar of fire that was pushed over by the surface winds to touch the ground and gain new fury from the oxygen and combustibles it seized. LeMay had chanced upon just the right use of incendiaries, and the wind served as a giant bellows to superheat the air to eighteen hundred degrees Fahrenheit." Many people seeking refuge from the fires headed to the city's rivers and canals, only to be burned or boiled to death. According to an eyewitness, "In the black Sumida River . . . countless bodies were floating, clothed bodies, naked bodies, all as black as charcoal. It was unreal. These were dead people, but you couldn't tell whether they were men or women. You couldn't even tell if the objects floating by were arms and legs or pieces of burnt wood." Five of the city's thirty-five wards were listed as mostly destroyed, seven were about half destroyed, and another fourteen were partly wiped out. Eighty-two percent of the ten square mile target area was leveled, and almost sixteen square miles of eastern Tokyo was razed to the ground. Nearly eighty-eight thousand died and more than 1 million were left homeless and fled the city. During the raid, "B-29 crews fought superheated updrafts that destroyed at least ten aircraft and wore oxygen masks to avoid vomiting from the stench of burning flesh." The glow from the fires was visible a hundred miles out to sea.[3]

But this was only the beginning. Following the success of Operation Meetinghouse, Twenty-first Bomber Command went on a ten-day fire blitz against Nagoya (twice), Osaka, and Kobe, stopping only when the raiders expended their entire stock of incendiaries. The details of these attacks may be found in table 4.1. Overall, including the Tokyo raid, these five missions burned out 31.9 square miles of Japan's four largest cities. This was more damage than the combined bomber offensive inflicted on the six most-bombed German cities and amounted to 41 percent of the destruction visited on Germany in the entire war, all accomplished with fewer than 1 percent of the bomb tonnage! Moreover, Twenty-first Bomber Command's sortie rate skyrocketed: LeMay's force launched about the same number of sorties in the blitz as were sent against Japan in the previous four months. Yet the number of B-29s lost in this flurry of activity was only about one-quarter the number lost in that four month period, twenty-two as compared to seventy-eight.[4]

The fire raids were interrupted for several weeks so Twenty-first Bomber Command could support the invasion of Okinawa, but they picked up again in mid May. Large forces of B-29s again pounded Japan's largest cities before turning their attention to medium-size urban areas in mid June, and then to small cities and towns in July as the larger cities were progressively destroyed. Chief of Staff of the Army Air Forces (AAF) General Henry "Hap" Arnold's prediction that "Japan . . . will become a nation without cities" was rapidly being realized.[5] Table 4.2 summarizes these raids. Over the course of the campaign against Japan, incendiary munitions composed 61 percent of Twentieth Air Force's total tonnage, and roughly 70 percent of the total bomb weight was dropped on urban areas (as opposed to particular targets in cities).[6] Almost every town with more than thirty-eight thousand people was bombed. The record of destruction is impressive:

> In all, sixty-six cities (including Hiroshima and Nagasaki)—home to 20.8 million people—were attacked. The airmen destroyed 178 square miles (about three times the area of the District of Columbia) and 43 percent of the built-up areas of these cities. Thirty-five of the cities lost 1 or more square miles of their central sections. . . . According to Japanese reports, the bombing killed 241,000, seriously injured 313,000, and destroyed 2.3 million homes. The United States Strategic Bombing Survey (USSBS) put the death toll at 330,000, number of injured at 476,000, and buildings destroyed at 2.5 million. The bombing forced 8.5 million people to flee their homes.[7]

Why did the United States unleash this reign of fire on Japanese civilians? I argue that three factors explain the outcome. First, U.S. leaders from President Roosevelt on down understood that a war against Japan could not be won quickly and was likely to involve significant human costs. The vast distances involved and the oceanic nature of the theater meant that it would be impossible to land large armies and advance across land as in most wars. Instead, troops would have to be moved across vast expanses of ocean and landed on tiny islands to assault prepared defenses. Put simply, the terrain of the Pacific War favored the defense and would require much time and many

Table 4.1. The fire blitz on Japan, March 1945

City	Date	Square miles burned	Deaths	Homeless	Homes destroyed	Bombers over target	Bomb tonnage	Bombers lost
Tokyo	March 9	15.8	84,000–100,000	1–1.15 million	267,171	279	1,665	14
Nagoya	March 11	2.1	2,700	NA	25,000	285	1,790	1
Osaka	March 13	8.1	3,000–4,000	500,000	130,000–200,000	274	1,733	2
Kobe	March 16	2.9	2,600–8,000	242,000–650,000	65,951	307	2,355	3
Nagoya	March 18	3	828	NA	40,000	290	1,858	2
Total		31.9	93,128–115,528	1,742,000–2,300,000	528,122–598,122	1,435	9,401	22

Sources: Figures compiled from Kenneth P. Werrell, *Blankets of Fire: U.S. Bombers over Japan during World War II* (Washington: Smithsonian Institution Press, 1996), 159–68; E. Bartlett Kerr, *Flames over Tokyo: The U.S. Army Air Forces' Incendiary Campaign against Japan 1944–1945* (New York: Donald I. Fine, 1991), 207, 215–19; Edwin P. Hoyt, *Inferno: The Firebombing of Japan, March 9–August 15, 1945* (Lanham, MD: Madison Books, 2000), 45–92; and Wesley Frank Craven and James Lea Cate, eds., *The Army Air Forces in World War II*, vol. 5, *The Pacific: Matterhorn to Nagasaki, June 1944 to August 1945* (Washington: Office of Air Force History, 1983), 614–23.

Table 4.2. Incendiary Missions of XXI Bomber Command, March–August 1945

Month	Raids	Cities struck	Square miles burned	Bombers lost	Loss rate	Percentage incendiaries
March	5	Tokyo, Nagoya (2), Osaka, Kobe	31.9	22	1.3	72
April	2	Tokyo, Kawasaki, Yokohama	21–22.5	19–21	1.6	24
May	5	Nagoya (2), Tokyo (2), Yokohama	35.9–37	55–61	1.9	64
June	7	Osaka (3), Kobe, 11 medium-size cities	27.6	30	0.8	65
July	9	35 small cities	32.1–35.4	13	0.3	74
August	5	12 small or medium cities	10.5–13.1	3	0.3	57

Sources: Data compiled from Kenneth P. Werrell, *Blankets of Fire: U.S. Bombers over Japan during World War II* (Washington: Smithsonian Institution Press, 1996), 159–68, 177–82, 187–89, 192–94, 201–3, 206–8, 220–23; E. Bartlett Kerr, *Flames over Tokyo: The U.S. Army Air Forces' Incendiary Campaign against Japan 1944–1945* (New York: Donald I. Fine, 1991), 207, 215–19, 226–77, 324–36; and Wesley Frank Craven and James Lea Cate, eds., *The Army Air Forces in World War II*, vol. 5, *The Pacific: Matterhorn to Nagasaki, June 1944 to August 1945* (Washington: Office of Air Force History, 1983), 635–44, 653–58, 674–75.

Note: The figures for August omit damage inflicted by the two atomic bombs (4.7 square miles of Hiroshima and 1.5 square miles of Nagasaki destroyed). The "bombers lost" category includes only those lost on fire missions. The loss rate, however, is for all bombing operations, not just incendiary missions. In general, at least as many aircraft were lost to operational or noncombat causes as were destroyed by enemy action.

men to overcome. For this reason, U.S. political and military men expressed keen interest from the beginning in strategies that might provide a shortcut to victory, such as unrestricted submarine warfare and incendiary bombing. Although the United States was able to initiate submarine attacks against Japanese merchant shipping soon after Pearl Harbor, it could not bomb Japan until it acquired bases close to the country. The distance to be covered explains the two-and-a-half-year delay between the Japanese attack and the first sustained U.S. bombing of the home islands (in June 1944, launched from bases in China), but planning for a bombing campaign had long been underway and quickly focused on the potential of firebombing to defeat Japan.

Second, although the eventual outcome of the war was not in doubt, the tenor of Japanese resistance in Pacific battles caused top U.S. officials to believe that an invasion of the home islands would be necessary to subdue Japan. Despite the U.S. Strategic Bombing Survey's optimistic conclusion after the war that Japan would have surrendered by November 1945 without an invasion or the atomic bomb from the effects of continued bombing and the naval blockade, few U.S. leaders believed this in early 1945.[8] In battle after battle, Japanese troops repeatedly fought to the last man rather than surrender; the desire to avoid the costs of invading Japan motivated the shift to incendiary bombing, and later the use of atomic weapons.

Finally, U.S. precision bombing efforts in the Pacific had proven largely futile owing to the extreme distance involved from the principal U.S. bases in the Marianas Islands, environmental factors like the jet stream, and Japanese air defenses. Operational failure and relatively high bomber loss rates created a crisis for bombing; shifting to incendiary attack was one way to increase effectiveness, lower losses, and do enormous damage to Japanese urban areas and hence Japan's industrial productivity—damage that might render an invasion unnecessary and save the lives of countless American servicemen. LeMay alone made the actual decision to shift to incendiary tactics, but the preferences of top AAF officers and the substantial planning for fire attack made it clear that an incendiary campaign would eventually occur no matter who was in command.

The Pacific War: A War of Attrition

The sinking of much of the Pacific Fleet at Pearl Harbor left the United States on the defensive in early 1942. The loss of the Philippines also deprived the United States of the ability to strike directly at the Japanese homeland in any meaningful way.[9] The dramatic U.S. victory at the Battle of Midway in June, however, during which four Japanese aircraft carriers were sunk, marked the high tide of Japanese eastward expansion and paved the way for the American counteroffensive. But U.S. forces still faced a tough fight against a fanatical foe to make their way across the Pacific.

Indeed, the tenor of Japanese resistance in the Pacific from the very beginning indicated that an attack on the Japanese home islands might be a difficult and costly proposition. On island after island, Japanese troops simply refused to surrender. On Guadalcanal in August 1942, for example, Japanese troops fought nearly to the last man: of one unit's eight hundred men, only fifteen were captured, twelve of whom were wounded. At Tarawa in the Gilbert Islands in November 1943, American troops on one island took eight Japanese prisoners out of a defending force of 2,571, a death rate of 99.7 percent. In the Marshall Islands in early 1944, the death rate on Kwajalein Island was 98.4 percent, while on Roi-Namur it was 98.5 percent.[10] As one marine commander described the combat on Guadalcanal, "I have never heard or read of this kind of fighting. These people refuse to surrender. The wounded wait until men come up to examine them . . . and blow themselves and the other fellow to pieces with a hand grenade."[11]

The bloodletting continued in the Marianas in the summer of 1944 (see table 4.3). On Saipan, for example, 97 percent of the thirty thousand Japanese personnel died. Hundreds of Japanese civilians also chose death to American capture: convinced that "the Americans would rape, torture, and

Table 4.3. Japanese, American, and civilian casualties in major Pacific battles, 1944–1945

		Japan				United States
Battle	Date	Manpower	POWs	Percent KIA	Civilian dead	Total casualties (killed)
Saipan	June 1944	30,000	921	97	1,000	14,111 (3,426)
Iwo Jima	February 1945	21,000	1,083	95	0	24,733 (6,913)
Okinawa	April 1945	120,000	7,400	94	42,000– 122,000	51,450 (12,850)

Sources: Figures for Saipan and Iwo Jima are from Richard B. Frank, *Downfall: The End of the Imperial Japanese Empire* (New York: Random House, 1999), 29–30, 60–61. Figures for Okinawa are from Gordon L. Rottman, *World War II Pacific Island Guide: A Geo Military Study* (Westport, CT: Greenwood Press, 2002), 443–44.

Note: Figures for Iwo Jima and Okinawa include casualties suffered by the U.S. Navy, primarily from Japanese kamikaze attacks: 2,634 (982 killed) at Iwo Jima and 9,700 (4,900 killed) at Okinawa. United States forces also suffered 26,200 nonbattle casualties on Okinawa.

murder them. . . . Whole families died in full view of the invading Allied forces by killing themselves with hand grenades provided by the Japanese military or leaping from high cliffs into the sea or onto the rocks below."[12]

In addition to resulting in the wholesale annihilation of Japanese forces, the reluctance of the enemy to surrender in these Pacific battles exacted a deadly toll on American soldiers as well. Total U.S. combat fatalities in both theaters, which had totaled only 62,092 from the war's outset in December 1941 through the end of 1943, quickly doubled in the seven months from January to July 1944 to 125,274 as U.S. troops were fully engaged in Europe and the Pacific.[13] In the invasion and battle for Saipan (June 15–July 9, 1944), U.S. forces suffered 14,111 casualties, 20 percent of the invading force. The carnage was even worse on Iwo Jima, where nearly 30 percent of the 75,000 marines who landed in February 1945 were killed or wounded in five weeks of fighting. The marines captured only 1,083 Japanese troops out of the 21,000 on the island before the invasion.[14] The battle for Okinawa, which began in April, truly demonstrated what an invasion of Japan might look like: American forces suffered more than 51,000 casualties in subduing 120,000 Japanese defenders. Tens of thousands of civilians also died in the midst of the furious fighting. This staggering death toll led President Truman to comment that invading Japan might be like "an Okinawa from one end of Japan to the other."[15]

In sum, two years of combat in the Pacific convinced U.S. civilian and military leaders of two things: Japan would not surrender without an invasion of its homeland, and assaulting the home islands was likely to be a costly bloodletting. There was simply no precedent for expecting Japan to give up: in none of the Pacific battles had Japanese troops capitulated in large numbers. Indeed, it was the total annihilation of Japanese forces on Saipan in July 1944—and the willingness of many civilians to kill themselves rather than be captured by Americans—that helped prompt the shift in policy. General Marshall explained to the Combined Chiefs on July 14: "As a result of recent operations in the Pacific it was now clear to the United States Chiefs of Staff that, in order to finish the war with the Japanese quickly, it will be necessary to invade the industrial heart of Japan."[16] The Joint Chiefs of Staff (JCS) reached this conclusion before the firebombing began and well before the debate over the atomic bomb.

The Saipan operation also had a major impact on estimates of how costly an invasion might be. The Joint Strategic Survey Committee of the JCS, working on a document entitled "Operations Against Japan Subsequent to Formosa," used the results of the Saipan fighting to generate estimates of the potential price in U.S. lives of attacking the Japanese home islands. Assuming that the Japanese would have roughly 3.5 million troops available, the planners applied what came to be known as the "Saipan ratio"— "one American killed and several wounded to exterminate seven Japanese soldiers"—and concluded that "it might cost us a half million American lives and many times that number in wounded to exterminate the Japanese ground forces that conceivably could be employed against us in the home islands."[17] Other army studies came to much lower estimates, and many analysts have argued for fatality figures in the twenty-five thousand to forty-six thousand range.[18] The Japanese buildup in southern Kyushu (the site of Operation Olympic, the first invasion) during the summer of 1945 casts doubt on these lower figures, but even if one accepts casualty figures in the range of 100,000 to 200,000 implied by the lower fatality estimates, this was still plenty high enough to trigger a search for alternatives to an invasion, including firebombing and the atomic bomb.[19]

The Potential of Fire as a Weapon against Japan

American civilian and military officials knew well that Japan was a much better target for incendiary attack than Germany. This awareness manifested itself in extensive prewar interest in the potential of fire as a weapon against Japanese cities by civilians both inside and outside of government, as well as a few air officers, although most cleaved to their doctrine of precision bombing. Concerted planning inside the air force began in 1943 for an incendiary campaign.

Prewar Interest in Incendiary Attack. In contrast to the bombing of Germany, American officials expressed great interest in using fire as a weapon against Japan. The main reason for this interest was the greater vulnerability of Japanese urban construction to fire. Eighty percent of Japanese cities were built out of wood and paper, whereas 95 percent of German cities were constructed of stone and brick. The 1923 earthquake, which started devastating fires in Tokyo, brought this fact to the attention of American leaders, and the potential of firebombing figured prominently in their minds in the years leading up to the outbreak of the Pacific War. Former General Billy Mitchell, for example, pointed out in the 1920s and 1930s that the wood and paper construction of Japan's towns "form the greatest aerial targets the world has ever seen. . . . Incendiary projectiles would burn the cities to the ground in short order."[20] Claire Chennault, who came out of retirement to command Chiang Kai-shek's air force in China, wrote to Hap Arnold in 1940 to inform him of the potential for incendiary attack on Japan's cities. "Whereas Arnold and the airmen rejected the idea" as contrary to the AAF doctrine of precision bombardment, writes Kenneth Werrell, "[President] Roosevelt was delighted by the proposal and ordered his top cabinet officials to work on the project. Certainly, this was a radical shift from the president's appeal to the warring parties in September 1939 to refrain from bombing civilians."[21] A mere three weeks before Pearl Harbor, army chief of staff General George C. Marshall held a secret news briefing for seven correspondents, the contents of which were leaked to the Japanese. In an attempt to deter a Japanese movement against Southeast Asia, Marshall warned: "If war with the Japanese does come, we'll fight mercilessly. Flying fortresses will be dispatched immediately to set the paper cities of Japan on fire. There won't be any hesitation about bombing civilians—it will be all out."[22] Marshall's remarks—although indicative of U.S. officials' interest in fire as a weapon against Japan—were likely part of the larger U.S. strategy in 1941 of deterring a Japanese attack by threatening retaliation against Japan with B-17s and B-24s being deployed to the Philippines.

Nor did the potential for fire attacks on Japan escape analysts outside of government. An article that appeared in *Harper's* magazine in 1942 compared the flammability of several major Japanese cities, concluding that Osaka, Kobe, and Kyoto offered the most promising targets for American incendiaries. According to the authors, "In a really congested neighborhood, crowded with buildings from the bank of one canal to the next, with only shoulder-width runway between, the chance of the [incendiary] bomb starting an immediate fire is just about as good as if it fell into a full waste-paper basket." Although the authors drastically underestimated the number of incendiaries needed to start uncontrollable fires, suggesting that only five bombers could burn Osaka, three Kyoto, and two Kobe, they maintained that "the fact remains that this [firebombing] is the cheapest possible way to cripple Japan. It will shorten the war by months or even years and reduce American and Allied losses by tens of thousands."[23]

On the whole, however, discussions inside the AAF before the war regarding the possibility of bombing Japan followed the theory of precision bombing developed and taught in the interwar period at the Air Corps Tactical School. This theory—variously called the industrial web or critical node theory—argued that wartime economies were deeply interdependent. Destroying one or a few critical components or nodes in the economy could bring production to a grinding halt. "Resting on assumptions about the complex and fragile nature of modern industrial economies," comments Tami Davis Biddle, "the 'industrial fabric' approach postulated that by carefully choosing the right card at the base of an intricate structure, an air force could bring the whole house of cards crashing down."[24]

American air doctrine, unlike that developed contemporaneously in Great Britain, largely eschewed targeting civilians directly in favor of bombing an enemy state's economic infrastructure, but like British doctrine it still hoped to achieve decisive morale effects.[25] Morality did not drive the Americans' stand against targeting civilians directly, however: American airmen largely viewed bombing the population as inefficient rather than immoral.[26] United States air leaders, however, wanted to avoid giving the American public the impression that bombing strategy was based on targeting civilians because they believed most Americans disapproved of the practice. But AAF planners did foresee circumstances in which noncombatants might be attacked. In fact, AWPD/1—the air corps blueprint for a potential war with Germany written in 1941—advocated outright attacks on civilians as potentially decisive when the enemy was on the ropes.[27] This eventuality aside, however, "American air strategy aimed not at killing large numbers of civilians directly but at causing general social collapse through the precision bombing of key industrial nodes." "Human beings," wrote Generals Hap Arnold and Ira Eaker in their 1941 book *Winged Warfare,* "are not priority targets except in special situations."[28] Against Japan, AAF officers before the war intended to carry out their precision doctrine, resisting suggestions made by Chennault, Marshall, and Roosevelt that they attack Japanese urban areas with incendiaries. As Arnold put it in a discussion with Marshall in 1941, any strategic bombing of Japan would be intended to destroy "Japanese factories in order to cripple production of munitions and essential articles for maintenance of economic structure in Japan."[29]

In sum, U.S. government officials, civilian commentators, as well as some air officers manifested considerable interest in the possibility of urban incendiary attack on Japan before Pearl Harbor. The key underlying factor that explains this interest was the well-known vulnerability of Japanese cities to fire. Some of the statements and policies made before the war began, however, are attributable to the hopes of members of the Roosevelt administration that Japan could be deterred from launching a war by the threat of aerial retaliation against its cities. The official position and plans of the air force itself remained committed to precision attack.

The Evolution of Wartime Plans Toward Firebombing. Planning inside the AAF for a bombing campaign against Japan did not begin until 1943.[30] The first compendium of targets, compiled by the Intelligence Section of the

Air Staff in March 1943, omitted any mention of area attacks. But the chief of plans requested "a study of the vulnerability of Japanese target areas to incendiary attack" in May, which led to a revised report issued in October. This document, entitled "Japan, Incendiary Attack Data, October 1943," contained a detailed analysis of the vulnerability of twenty cities to fire-bombing. According to Thomas Searle, "The first page of the report listed four reasons why Japanese cities were better targets than German cities for incendiary attack: the greater inflammability of Japanese residential construction, the greater building congestion in Japanese cities, the proximity of factories and military objectives to residential construction in Japan, and the concentration of Japan's war industry in a few cities. Thus, by October of 1943, the Air Staff had determined that incendiary area attacks on Japanese cities would be dramatically more effective than they had been against German cities."[31] This conclusion was reinforced by tests of the new M-69 incendiary bomb on models of Japanese villages at Dugway Proving Grounds in Utah from May to September 1943, which proved its ability to start numerous fires.[32]

A second study of the potential of bombing in Japan performed by the Committee of Operations Analysts (COA)—a separate group of (mainly civilian) planners assembled by Arnold—in November 1943 largely echoed the conclusions of the Air Staff. The COA report, entitled "Economic Objectives in the Far East," listed six important target systems in Japan, one of which was urban industrial areas. According to Ronald Schaffer, "The committee believed that a series of massive firebomb attacks on urban areas would produce a major disaster for Japan." Not only would incendiary raids devastate Japanese war production by burning out workshops based in homes, they would also "dislocate war workers" "through death, injury, and destruction of homes."[33]

General Arnold endorsed the principle of area attacks in his plan for an air campaign against Japan that he presented to the president in February 1944. The plan emphasized the ease of starting "uncontrollable conflagrations" in Japanese cities, as did the JCS when it approved the COA's report two months later.[34] That attacks on urban areas were explicitly designed to kill civilians is confirmed by a JCS document from April 1944 that listed "the absorption of man hours in repair and relief [and] the dislocation of labor by casualty" as among the intended effects of incendiary raids. As Searle notes, "the JCS in 1944, like the Air Staff in 1943, wanted to use civilian casualties as a means of cutting Japanese industrial production."[35] The following September, a report by a subcommittee of the COA (the Joint Incendiary Committee) explicitly estimated that "full-scale [incendiary] attacks on six large urban areas" would kill or wound approximately 560,000 Japanese and succeed in "dehousing" nearly 8 million workers.[36] The next month, the COA "recommended an incendiary assault on Japan's cities to come after a precision campaign," ideally in March 1945 when weather conditions would be best suited to inflicting maximum fire damage.[37] By September 1944, concludes Michael Sherry, although no clear-cut directives were issued, "the air staff apparently had committed itself to a major incendiary campaign the following spring."[38] The rationale for such a campaign was clearly articulated in an October memo written by chemist Raymond Ewell of the National Defense Research Committee. Ewell thought the AAF should dispense with precision bombing altogether and immediately shift to firebombing, which he believed could be "the key to accelerating the defeat of Japan, and if as successful as seems probable, . . . might shorten the war by some months and save many thousands of American lives."[39]

Evidence indicates that Arnold and the air planners did not want to initiate an incendiary campaign until the AAF had amassed sufficient numbers of B-29s in the Marianas to inflict massive destruction. Members of the COA, for example, were concerned that attacking too early with fewer aircraft "would merely create firebreaks against a later heavy attack." Moreover, striking several Japanese cities in a short, violent burst increased the likelihood that the Japanese would be overwhelmed and unable to adapt to the change in American tactics.[40] Similarly, when Arnold's deputy, General Lauris Norstad recommended in late November that the AAF memorialize the fourth anniversary of Pearl Harbor by bombing the Imperial Palace in Tokyo, Arnold responded, "Not at this time. Our position—bombing factories, docks, etc.—is sound—Later destroy the whole city."[41] This comment indicates Arnold's preference for husbanding the B-29s until large sections of Japanese cities could be incinerated.

In short, in 1943 and 1944, U.S. air planners began to think about how to employ incendiary weapons to kill Japanese workers and disable Japanese industry and to plan for an eventual incendiary campaign against Japanese cities. As Searle puts it, "The orders for the 9 March 1945 raid [on Tokyo] reflected the longstanding interest of the Air Staff and the JCS in using urban incendiary raids to cut Japanese industrial production by (among other things) killing Japanese civilians."[42]

The Bombing of Japan up to March 1945

Thus far I have established that the Pacific War quickly became a war of attrition, with Japanese resistance convincing U.S. leaders that a costly invasion of the home islands would be needed to obtain Japan's surrender. With this realization came a renewed interest in reducing the costs of such an invasion by using airpower. Moreover, I have examined prewar interest in incendiary attack on Japan and wartime planning for such operations, showing that although many civilian leaders expressed interest in firebombing Japan before the war, AAF doctrine called for precision bombing and U.S. airmen seriously began to contemplate a fire campaign only in 1943. Once the various planning agencies recommended firebombing, however, they argued it should not commence until sufficient resources were available to burn large areas and make the biggest impact.

This section traces the actual course of bombing up until the shift to sustained incendiary attack in March 1945. I argue that the operational difficulties faced by Twenty-first Bomber Command operating from the Marianas—along with pressure from air force commanders in Washington—were the immediate cause of LeMay's decision to inaugurate the fire campaign. LeMay gave the order for systematic fire attacks to begin, but the long-standing interest in—and planning for—incendiary raids ensured that such attacks would have occurred at about the same time whoever was in command. LeMay determined only the manner in which the raids would be flown and their timing.

Operations from China. Early in the war, the United States lacked both the resources and bases in proximity to Japan to launch a major strategic air offensive. As the first new B-29 aircraft became available in early 1944 Arnold decided to deploy them to India and stage missions out of China in a campaign called Matterhorn.[43] Operations began in early June and followed the AAF's precision doctrine, dropping primarily high-explosive ordnance (HE) from high altitudes on specific industrial targets. The results of the first raid—against railroad shops in Bangkok—were typical of Twentieth Bomber Command's operations from India and China: 16–18 bombs (4–4.5 tons of 353 tons dropped) landed in the target area with little damage inflicted.[44]

Two factors handicapped Twentieth Bomber Command's operations in the Far East. First, the logistic effort required to sustain bomber operations was extreme, as ferrying the materiel necessary to launch one attack sortie from China required seven trips over the Himalayas from India.[45] These logistical limitations made it nearly impossible to mount substantial attacks. Second, only a small part of southern Japan was within striking distance of B-29s operating from China, drastically limiting the available targets. In fact, during Twentieth Bomber Command's ten-month stint in China, the B-29s flew only nine missions against Japan (out of forty-nine total), delivering a scant 961 tons of bombs (of 11,244 total) on targets in Kyushu, the southernmost of the Japanese main islands.[46]

Operations from the Marianas. American conquest of the Marianas Islands (Saipan, Guam, and Tinian) in the summer of 1944 provided the AAF with bases from which B-29s could bomb almost all of Japan. This was by no means an easy trip, however: the round-trip flight to Japan from Saipan was thirty-one hundred miles, nearly the operational limit of the B-29. General Haywood "Possum" Hansell was appointed commander of the newly constituted Twenty-first Bomber Command. Hansell had taught at the Air

Corps Tactical School (ACTS) in the 1930s and was one of the principal architects and foremost advocates of the industrial web theory and precision bombing. Hansell was also one of the authors of AWPD/1, the blueprint for U.S. bombing in Germany. Unsurprisingly, Hansell began a campaign against Japan intended to destroy the following targets (listed in descending order of importance) with HE: aircraft industry, industry in cities, shipping, and coke, steel, and oil.

In general, Hansell achieved poor results. In the first mission, flown on November 24, 1944, against the Nakajima Musashino aircraft engine factory in Tokyo, only 24 of the 111 B-29s that left Saipan bombed the primary target; another 64 attacked urban areas.[47] Roughly 1 percent of the buildings and 2 percent of the machine tools were damaged. Eighty-one Superfortresses headed back to the same plant on November 27 but were foiled by clouds and forced to bomb by radar. The bombers returned to Musashino again on December 3 and 27, inflicting little damage: twenty-six bombs fell in the target area on each occasion.[48] Meanwhile, Hansell mounted three raids in December against the Mitsubishi aircraft engine plant in Nagoya with varying degrees of success. Arnold, however, was not satisfied with the achievements of the B-29s; desiring a "full-scale test of the potential for firing Japanese cities," Arnold (through his deputy Norstad) urged Hansell on December 19 to fly an incendiary raid on Nagoya.[49] Hansell resisted, arguing that success with HE bombing was just around the corner, but these results failed to materialize quickly enough to save Hansell's job, as Arnold sacked him in favor of LeMay on January 7, 1945.

By all accounts, Hansell "left a legacy of miniscule accomplishment in terms of target destruction coupled with serious losses."[50] During Hansell's tenure, Twenty-first Bomber Command undertook fourteen missions, ten of which were daylight HE efforts against particular industrial targets. As Kenneth Werrell observes, "On the ten raids against the aircraft targets, only three achieved results considered good: two against Nagoya, and the one attack [Hansell's last, coming on January 19] on the Kawasaki plant" in Akashi.[51] Only 14 percent of bombs fell within a thousand feet of the target on these three raids, as opposed to 2 percent on the other seven missions. Thirty-four B-29s were lost, fifteen to enemy fire and nineteen to operational causes.[52]

Contrary to conventional wisdom, the nature of operations did not change drastically when LeMay took charge in January 1945. In fact, LeMay's first eight missions bear a striking resemblance to those launched under his predecessor: six were daylight attacks against industrial targets (mostly aircraft plants) and two were experimental area raids with incendiaries.[53] Half of the precision missions, however, were complete failures, with no bombers dropping their cargoes on the primary target. It could no longer be denied that HE bombing in the Pacific theater was a failure, a conclusion the AAF Evaluation Board had already reached in mid January 1945.[54]

As indicated by the accuracy statistics cited in the previous paragraphs, it is a misnomer to describe U.S. bombing from November 1944 to March 1945 as "precision bombing." Precision was what these strikes aspired to rather than what they achieved. In fact, many raids were conducted by radar—which at this time was inherently imprecise—and the secondary targets for the bombers were often "urban areas."[55] Even raids conducted in clear weather that struck the primary target managed to place less than 15 percent of their bombs within a thousand feet of the aim point. Finally, more than one quarter of Twenty-first Bomber Command's missions were self-described urban area raids mounted largely with incendiary munitions.

Because of the overall indiscriminate nature of these attacks, U.S. forces were already engaging in low-level civilian victimization in the Pacific. From November 1944 to March 1945 U.S. bombers (for the most part) sought to destroy Japanese industry directly with HE rather than purposely kill Japanese civilians, although many died nevertheless. From March to August 1945, by contrast, civilian casualties were a specific objective, even if the ultimate goal was the same: destruction of Japanese war production. In general, the early months of the campaign may be viewed as something of a warm-up for what came later: neither Hansell nor LeMay had sufficient numbers of B-29s to launch the all-out devastating incendiary raids air force planners envisioned. The number of aircraft available to bomb in the theater, for example, did not much exceed 100 until early February 1945. Twenty-First Bomber Command had 140 B-29s on hand in late January; this number doubled on February 5 to 285, and increased again to 356 on February 25.[56] Moreover, as Schaffer points out, "In its final report, delivered October 11, 1944, the COA recommended that until the AAF was ready to obliterate the Honshu cities it should send its B-29s against vital precision targets like aircraft plants." As soon as Twenty-first Bomber Command accumulated the necessary forces, gained needed data from experimental fire raids, and the weather became conducive to starting large blazes, firebombing commenced, according to plan. The difficult conditions for precision bombing in the Far East also played a contributory role in prodding LeMay to change tactics, however, and it is to these conditions I turn next.

A Crisis for Bombing in the Pacific. By early March 1945, therefore, B-29 operations had failed to make a significant contribution to the defeat of Japan. Strategic airpower in the Pacific so far was a flop. Why? Several factors complicated bomber operations in the Pacific theater and reduced bomber effectiveness. First, the weather over Japan presented difficulties similar to those over Germany but with an added twist. Cloud cover, which had so limited early operations over the Reich, also proved a problem over Japan, breaking up formations on the way to the target and frequently rendering visual bombing impossible.[57] According to Hansell, "Weather over Japan was our most implacable and inscrutable enemy"; LeMay estimated that prevailing weather conditions over Japan allowed for a maximum of seven days of visual bombing per month, and three to four days on average.[58] Even worse, Twenty-first Bomber Command discovered the jet stream, which produced headwinds of up to two hundred knots. These heavy winds played havoc with bombing accuracy.[59]

Second, Japanese industry was heavily concentrated in a few cities, but was broadly dispersed *within* those cities. Japan's twenty largest cities, for example, contained 22 percent of the total population, 53 percent of all precision targets, and 74 percent of the highest priority targets.[60] But destroying factory complexes was not sufficient to stop Japanese war production, as cottage industries contained in nearby homes fed each plant. As LeMay recalled in his memoirs, "I'll never forget Yokohama. That was what impressed me: drill presses. There they were, like a forest of scorched trees and stumps, growing up throughout that residential area. Flimsy construction all gone . . . everything burned down, or up, and drill presses standing like skeletons."[61] Precision attacks on plants, therefore, could slow output, but were unable to bring production to a halt.

Third, the long distances the B-29s had to fly to strike Japan reduced the weight of bombs they could carry, which in turn limited their destructive power. Fourth, the AAF's daylight precision tactics required bombers to fly in formation at high altitude, but this approach played into the strengths of Japanese defenses. Japan's day-fighter force was far superior to its night-fighters, and the antiaircraft artillery protecting Japanese targets was mostly long range, able to inflict more damage to high-flying planes than those at lower altitudes. B-29s attacking from high altitude in daylight thus met relatively heavy fighter opposition. For example, the first two missions conducted after LeMay took command—daylight raids against the Mitsubishi (January 23) and Nakajima (January 27) aircraft facilities—experienced 691 and 984 fighter attacks, respectively. While only two B-29s were lost on the former attack, nine fell victim to enemy defenses on the latter.[62]

In short, the weather and physical conditions in the Pacific theater favored the defense and rendered achieving decisive results with HE bombing almost impossible.

The Shift to Firebombing

Given the failure of bombing with HE, Washington continued to push for further incendiary raids in February 1945 to gauge the effectiveness of fire attacks on Japanese cities. LeMay launched two—against Kobe and Tokyo—the latter of which burned out one square mile of the Japanese capital. Both of these missions were flown at high altitude, however, which limited their effectiveness: the aircraft could not carry many bombs, and the extreme winds at high altitude scattered the relatively lightweight incendiaries across a wide area, preventing large fires from starting. In view of these difficulties, LeMay improvised and ordered his B-29s to attack at night with incendiaries from lower altitudes. Although his antiaircraft artillery experts uniformly predicted disaster, LeMay believed (correctly) from examining intelligence photos that the Japanese possessed few low-level flak guns. Night flying would further protect his bombers from flak as well as fighter opposition, since the Japanese had only two night-fighter units deployed in the homeland. Moreover, low-level attacks would consume much less fuel because the planes would not have to fight the jet stream. To further decrease aircraft weight, LeMay stripped his Superfortresses of their defensive guns and the gunners needed to man them. This savings in fuel could be translated into an increased bomb load. The resulting modifications more than doubled the B-29s' average bomb load from three to six-and-a-half tons.[63]

LeMay had found the magic formula. Over the next five months, he and his bomber crews gutted Japan's cities and towns. Moreover, U.S. bomber losses on incendiary missions were but a fraction of those on precision raids. LeMay's new tactics, designed "to inflict the maximum damage on the enemy with the minimum casualties on the American side," proved devastatingly effective.[64] No order ever came from Arnold, Norstad, or anyone else in Washington instructing LeMay to shift to an incendiary campaign: LeMay alone made the decision to firebomb Tokyo. Precision bombing was already a failure; Arnold did not want to take responsibility for a new strategy that he was unsure would succeed. What LeMay did receive from his commanders was a strong unwritten message in the form of suggestions and hints, "polite nudges and the occasional injunction," as Sherry puts it, combined with frequent reminders to maximize the number of bombs dropped.[65] The preferences of the AAF's top leadership, as well as the planning for an incendiary campaign underway inside the AAF since 1943, lead most historians to argue that fire would have come to Japan's cities sooner or later no matter who was in command of Twenty-first Bomber Command. Indeed, LeMay's decision was embraced after the fact by his superiors in the AAF and civilians in Washington, who congratulated LeMay on his smashing success.[66]

Explaining the Change to Incendiary Bombing

To adequately explain the adoption of incendiary area bombing in the Pacific theater, it is necessary to account for the preferences of three sets of actors: (1) the top civilian leadership, namely the president; (2) the top military leadership, in this case—because of the enormous autonomy of the different armed services—General Arnold, chief of staff of the AAF; and (3) the local military commander, Curtis LeMay.

Roosevelt. President Roosevelt did not micromanage the conduct of the war or closely monitor the actions of his military commanders. American civil-military relations in World War II were thus far different from those in the Vietnam War, where President Johnson exercised strict control over military operations, particularly the Rolling Thunder bombing campaign against North Vietnam. FDR rarely intervened in the air war, and certainly did not prescribe or proscribe particular targets. As Sherry puts it, "The machinery was in place; Roosevelt was largely content to let it turn." Arnold kept him apprised of developments in the bombing campaigns, however, and FDR voiced no objections when informed of incendiary attacks on Japan.[67]

The slow and bitter progress of U.S. forces in the Pacific was a key factor in convincing President Roosevelt to support a campaign of incendiary bombing in the "hope . . . that air power would help defeat Japan without an invasion." Although his desire to deter a Japanese attack spurred Roosevelt's interest in firebombing before the war, and the political need to assist China explains the president's keenness to deploy B-29s to the Far East, it was the possibility that an intense aerial assault on Japan might bring about an early surrender and save American lives that best explains Roosevelt's support for bombing. FDR wanted to avoid a Pacific campaign that moved "forward inch by inch, island by island" and "would take about fifty years before we got to Japan." In August 1943, for example, the president cited the precedent of the recent RAF attack on Hamburg to his military advisers, suggesting that "we can use Siberian air fields . . . to attack the heart of Japan in a manner that she will find it hard to endure."[68] Given the context, presumably that manner was to start uncontrollable conflagrations in Japanese cities. Overall, FDR's few comments on the subject indicate an impatient commander-in-chief willing to support incendiary bombing because it might circumvent a slow, bloody slog across the Pacific.

Arnold. Even though the air force was technically part of the army, in practice it was highly autonomous, and Arnold basically had a free hand when it came to targeting. The president, the Joint Chiefs, and the army chief of staff, George Marshall, exercised little oversight of bombing policy. The command arrangements in the Pacific increased this independence even further because unlike the Atlantic, there was no overall theater commander, and Arnold himself ran the Twentieth Air Force from Washington. Historians disagree regarding the extent of Arnold's control over bomber operations in the Pacific. Some argue that he and his deputies kept a tight rein on the subordinate commands whereas others maintain that control from Washington was tenuous, especially after Arnold suffered another heart attack in January 1945. Whichever one of these views one accepts, Arnold's command style in the case of incendiary weapons was indirect. Given the failure of precision bombing, he was loath to stick his neck out and order a change to firebombing in case it, too, failed. He and Norstad thus poked and prodded LeMay to firebomb but did not order it directly.

Although officially Arnold adhered to the jointly agreed policy that an invasion of Japan's industrial heartland would be necessary to end the war, privately he never abandoned the hope and belief that airpower could convince the Japanese to surrender and obviate a costly invasion. In April 1945, for example, Arnold wrote to Barney Giles, his chief of air staff, "In my opinion we can bring Japan to her knees by B-29 bombing before the ground troops or the Navy ever land on the shores of the main island of Japan." The next month Arnold told LeMay that "combined with mining the maximum [incendiary] efforts of the near future will perhaps do more to shorten the Pacific war than any other comparable military engagement."[69]

Clearly Arnold believed that airpower could defeat Japan by burning down cities, which would avert the costly invasion of the Japanese heartland. Securing the early surrender of Japan, however, would also serve Arnold's other major objective: independence for the air force. Michael Sherry, for example, downplays operational factors and the desire to preclude invasion as motivations for firebombing, arguing that the shift to fire was made because "incendiary bombing was easy and because doing it rescued the AAF's flagging fortunes."[70] The failure of precision bombing endangered the AAF's quest to become an independent service after the war, and even raised the possibility that Twenty-first Bomber Command would be diverted to other missions subordinate to the army or navy in the Pacific. In short, "achieving victory and enhancing the air force's reputation were inseparable objectives for the AAF"; incendiary bombing appeared to be the most promising way to inflict the maximum damage on Japan with airpower. Thus Arnold became a fervent supporter of firebombing.[71]

Other voices in the AAF also expressed the view that incendiary bombing could shorten the war and save American lives. Norstad, for example, told LeMay in April 1945, "We can only guess what the effect [of continued firebombing] will be on the Japanese. Certainly their warmaking ability will have been curtailed. Possibly they may lose their taste for more war." An officer in the Fifth Air Force described U.S. air strategy in a July newsletter as follows: "We are making War and making it in the all-out fashion which saves American lives, shortens the agony which War is and seeks to bring about an enduring Peace." Historian Ronald Schaffer summarizes these views: "The idea of shortening the war appears repeatedly in statements by air force officers. . . . The implication was that if the war could be won more quickly, fewer people would suffer."[72]

LeMay. Two factors pushed LeMay to adopt incendiary tactics in March 1945. First, HE bombing was a failure. Four months of daylight HE bombing from the Marianas (and several months before that from China) had hardly destroyed a single target in Japan. LeMay knew that he, like Hansell before him, was expendable if he did not achieve some success for bombing against Japan. Norstad, LeMay's immediate superior, reinforced this message in person, telling LeMay in no uncertain terms exactly whose job was on the line when LeMay took command of Twenty-first Bomber Command: "You go ahead and get results with the B-29. If you don't get results, you'll be fired."[73] LeMay also surely knew that a successful bombing campaign in the Pacific might help secure organizational independence and strategic priority for the air force after the war. As his second month in command drew to a close, LeMay "woke up . . . to the fact that I hadn't gotten anything much done any better than Possum Hansell had."[74]

Not only was LeMay under pressure to achieve results or be relieved, it was clear which strategy his superiors thought would be most effective: firebombing. LeMay knew of the many studies performed inside the AAF on the efficacy of incendiary attack against Japan, and had received multiple suggestions and requests from Washington to experiment with starting fires. Although no direct orders from Arnold or Norstad were forthcoming, it was clear which way the wind was blowing. LeMay's contribution was that he put together all the pieces that made it possible to burn large urban areas, not that he came up with the idea in the first place.

The second factor that motivated LeMay to become a fire starter was his belief that by torching Japanese cities, air power could induce Japan to surrender before an invasion, thus shortening the war and saving countless lives. Norstad briefed LeMay on the "Saipan ratio" when LeMay replaced Hansell as commander of Twenty-first Bomber Command in January 1945, warning his subordinate: "If you don't get results it will mean eventually a mass amphibious invasion of Japan, to cost probably half a million more American lives." As LeMay later put it, "Our whole goal was to try to end the war before the invasion. We were not going to be able to do it continuing on like we were, given the weather and the problem of high-altitude visual bombing. We just didn't have enough airplanes and enough time. So we had to do something radical. We had always been thinking about incendiary attacks against the vulnerable Japanese cities."[75]

The stated rationale for the firebombing (at least initially) was not the classic punishment logic of crushing civilian morale, but rather to inflict maximum damage on Japanese war production. Indeed, the orders for the first Tokyo fire raid bear out this rationale: "Employment at scores of war plants throughout Tokyo and environs would be directly affected by casualties, movement of workers out of the area, use of manpower in reconstruction, and probably lowered worker morale."[76] As Thomas Searle observes, "Casualties were again explicitly mentioned, and regarded as desirable because they would directly affect employment at war plants. . . . Lowering morale was a means of lowering industrial production—not a means of inciting either rebellion or popular demands for surrender."[77] As LeMay put it colorfully in his memoirs,

We were going after military targets. No point in slaughtering civilians for the mere sake of slaughter. Of course there is a pretty thin veneer in Japan, but the veneer was there. It was their system of dispersal of industry. All you had to do was visit one of those targets after we'd roasted it, and see the ruins of a multitude of tiny houses, with a drill press sticking up through the wreckage of every home. . . . We knew we were going to kill a lot of women and kids when we burned down that town. Had to be done.[78]

The architect of the fire raids certainly believed that he had found a way to bring hostilities to a rapid close, thereby saving American lives. LeMay told Lieutenant Colonel St. Clair McKelway, the public relations officer for Twenty-first Bomber Command, while the bombers were winging their way to Tokyo on the night of March 9: "If this raid works the way I think it will, we can shorten this war. . . . He hasn't moved his industries to Manchuria yet, although he's starting to move them, and if we can destroy them before he can move them, we've got him. I never think anything is going to work until I've seen the pictures after the raid, but if this one works, we will shorten this damned war out here."[79] LeMay reiterated these views in his press release on March 11: "I believe that all those under my command on these island bases have by their participation in this single operation shortened this war. . . . They are fighting for a quicker end to this war and will continue to fight for a quicker end to it with all the brains and strength they have."[80] In his memoirs, LeMay explicitly made the argument that he believed his fire raids had saved American lives:

No matter how you slice it, you're going to kill an awful lot of civilians. Thousands and thousands. But, if you don't destroy the Japanese industry, we're going to have to invade Japan. And how many Americans will be killed in an invasion of Japan? Five hundred thousand seems to be the lowest estimate. Some say a million. . . . We're at war with Japan. We were attacked by Japan. Do you want to kill Japanese, or would you rather have Americans killed?[81]

Haywood Hansell described his successor's predicament in early 1945 as follows: "The factor of time was taking on a new insistence. The invasion of the Japanese home islands—whose necessity had become an obsession with the Army planners—had been agreed upon. If air power was to end the war without a massive bloodletting on the ground, its application could not be delayed. A drastic reappraisal was in order. LeMay made it."[82]

American leaders knew as soon as it began that a war against Japan would be a long and costly affair. The nature of the fighting in the Pacific theater in 1942 and 1943 augmented this belief with the knowledge that Japan would fight to the bitter end, that defeating the Japanese would require an invasion of the home islands, and that this invasion could cost tens of thousands—if not hundreds of thousands—of American lives. Knowledge of the wood and paper construction of Japan's cities and their vulnerability to fire also spawned planning inside the AAF for an incendiary campaign. All of the pieces were in place for massive civilian victimization against Japan, which air planners had already recommended to begin in March 1945. The trigger was the defensive advantage in the Far East that made precision bombing costly and ineffective.

Alternative Explanations

Public Opinion and Electoral Accountability. Most Americans abhorred bombing civilians before the war, and lurid press descriptions of such attacks by Axis countries provoked widespread outrage. But Germany's invasion of Western Europe in spring 1940 helped spark a dramatic reversal in opinion on the subject. "By the time America entered World War II," writes historian George Hopkins, "public opinion had already solidified in favor of bombing Germany and Japan."[83] Some people felt that the military was overly timid in taking the war to the enemy civilian population.[84] "Even if Americans had known the exact results of bombing, it would not have made much difference," argues Conrad Crane. "Most families had experienced the deaths of loved ones, friends, or neighbors; if bombing enemy civilians would speed victory and save American lives, it had to be done."[85] In sum, according to John Dower, American airmen need not have worried about public censure for their actions:

> Although Allied military planners remained sensitive to the moral issue of bombing civilians (and to the possibility that reliance on obliteration bombing might provoke a public reaction detrimental to the postwar development of the air forces), no sustained protest ever materialized. The Allied air raids were widely accepted as just retribution as well as sound strategic policy, and the few critics who raised ethical and humanitarian questions about the heavy bombing of German cities were usually denounced as hopeless idealists, fools, or traitors. When Tokyo was incinerated, there was scarcely a murmur of protest on the home front. . . . Japan had merely reaped what it sowed.[86]

The American public overwhelmingly approved of firebombing on Japanese cities. In the immediate aftermath of Pearl Harbor, an opinion poll showed that 67 percent favored aerial bombardment of Japanese cities. Undermining the argument that deterrence can prevent resort to civilian victimization, another survey found that of the 59 percent who believed the United States should fight an "all-out" war against Japan, 84 percent approved of bombing Japanese cities even if it meant Axis retaliation against American cities.[87] An article in *Harper's* magazine summarized the prevailing view: "It seems brutal to be talking about burning homes. But we are engaged in a life and death struggle for national survival, and we are therefore justified in taking any action which will save the lives of American soldiers and sailors."[88] In short, as Dower puts it, "The overwhelming thrust of public opinion in the United Kingdom as well as the United States demanded, if not the extermination of the Japanese people, then most certainly the country's 'thoroughgoing defeat,'" even if this meant killing large numbers of Japanese civilians.[89]

To what extent did the American public's punitive attitudes toward Japan influence the decisions of U.S. officials regarding the use of force against Japanese civilians? Public attitudes were probably not the primary reason for the decision to target civilians in the Pacific War. As I have shown, civilian officials were only part of the story; two of the crucial decision-makers (Arnold and LeMay) were military men not subject to electoral pressures. The central civilian decision-maker, FDR, did worry about public attitudes to U.S. casualties and "had a horror of American troops landing again on the continent and becoming involved in . . . trench warfare with all its appalling losses." The president "also recognized the limits on American tolerance of sacrifices in another world war" and hoped that Soviet manpower in the European theater would carry the casualty burden. "No similar opportunity existed in the Pacific," however, "which only made the incentive to employ air power there more intense."[90]

Still, although the president often expressed his hope that bombing could limit U.S. casualties, he was by no means the driving force behind firebombing. Despite punitive public attitudes toward Japan, firebombing did not begin there until precision bombing failed, notwithstanding widespread knowledge of the probable effectiveness of fire attacks against Japan. Moreover, 1944 was an election year for Roosevelt: if public hatred of Japan was so widespread and demands to conserve on U.S. casualties were so important, why not initiate incendiary attacks on Japan in the midst of the campaign in autumn 1944 when it could have paid significant political dividends? It seems unlikely, therefore, that electoral politics were the critical factor in causing civilian victimization in 1945.

By contrast, there is little evidence that liberal norms played much of a role in restraining the bombing of Japanese civilians. Before the United States entered the war, the Roosevelt administration issued frequent proclamations denouncing indiscriminate bombardment of civilian populations. When war broke out in Europe in September 1939, for example, the president issued a plea to all sides to abstain from "the ruthless bombing from the air of civilians in unfortified centers of population [that] has sickened the hearts of every civilized man and woman, and has profoundly shocked the conscience of humanity."[91] The American public was also resolutely opposed to urban area bombing as "counter to American humanitarian ideals" in the 1930s.[92]

But when the United States entered the war, and especially when the costs of fighting began to mount, these idealistic declarations disappeared.

FDR, for example, eventually came to believe that the German people had to be taught a severe lesson: "We either have to castrate the German people or you have got to treat them in such manner so they can't just go on reproducing people who want to continue the way they have in the past."[93] As far as Japan was concerned, FDR was reported to be "simply delighted" in November 1940 at the prospect of using fire to obliterate Japanese cities and viewed the RAF's demolition of Hamburg as "'an impressive demonstration' of what America might achieve against Japan."[94] The president even approved a bizarre scheme that proposed to burn down Japanese cities by releasing swarms of bats equipped with tiny incendiary bombs.[95] In sum, as Roosevelt put it, "The Nazis and the Fascists have asked for it—and they are going to get it."[96]

The only civilian official on record as registering any objections to area bombing is Secretary of War Henry Stimson. After the press reported that the Allies had shifted to a policy of area bombing after the Dresden raid in February 1945, Stimson raised questions about the nature of American bombing there, but did not follow up. Later, Stimson attempted to hold the AAF to a policy of precision bombing in Japan, seemingly unaware that the policy had already changed to firebombing.[97] Finally, Stimson succeeded in having Kyoto removed from the target list for the atomic bombs. The secretary of war was no great humanitarian, however, as Barton Bernstein notes: "It was not that Stimson was trying to save Kyoto's citizens; rather, he was seeking to save its relics, lest the Japanese become embittered and later side with the Soviets."[98] Stimson also chaired the Interim Committee that recommended using the A-bomb without warning on a Japanese city.

A handful of military officers also expressed moral reservations about bombing civilians.[99] Some of this concern was indeed genuine, but much of it stemmed not from the belief that killing civilians was wrong, but rather that the time was not yet right to target noncombatants. General Ira Eaker's oft-quoted comment that "we should never allow the history of this war to convict us of throwing the strategic bomber at the man in the street" is frequently cited as an example of AAF moral opposition to bombing civilians (in this case German civilians). However, Eaker only opposed bombing civilians because he thought it was too early in the war to be effective. He continued: "I think there is a better way we can do our share toward the defeat of the enemy, but if we are to attack the civil population I am certain we should wait until its morale is much nearer [the] breaking point and until the weather favors the operation more than it will at any time in the winter or early spring."[100]

Much has also been made of Haywood Hansell's supposed principled opposition to urban incendiary bombing. Some historians have implied that Hansell's superiors removed him from command because he refused to conduct urban incendiary attacks.[101] There is little support for this view. First, although Hansell protested orders from Arnold to conduct experimental fire raids, as Thomas Searle points out, "For all his complaining, Hansell never even hinted at resigning or disobeying orders. If area bombing was what it took to stay in command, Hansell would have continued to do as much of it as Arnold told him to."[102] Second, despite his commitment to precision bombing, Hansell's forces did plenty of area bombing, including a night fire raid on Tokyo (November 29) before Arnold ordered him to experiment with incendiary tactics.[103] By contrast, there were several compelling reasons to replace Hansell with LeMay that had nothing to do with the incendiary issue: LeMay outranked Hansell, LeMay was a better commander, and Hansell's subordinates (and many of his superiors) did not care for him. Even some of his closest friends in the air force advocated his dismissal. Hansell's ouster, therefore, was caused by his poor performance, not his resistance to incendiary attack.

Racism: "Civilized" Americans, "Barbaric" Japanese. It is commonly argued that the AAF unleashed incendiaries and ultimately atomic bombs on Japan and not Germany because Americans held racist beliefs that the Japanese were subhuman vermin that needed to be exterminated. Put another way, the argument is that Americans viewed the Japanese as outside the realm of civilization and therefore unworthy of the protections owed to people from civilized countries. The identity of the Japanese as a barbaric race, therefore, meant that the United States was not bound by the laws of war in conducting the conflict in the Pacific. As President Truman put it in a letter defending the use of the first A-bomb, "When you have to deal with a beast you have to treat him as a beast. It is most regrettable but nevertheless true."[104]

There is plenty of evidence that racist stereotypes on both sides increased the ferocity of combat, and that the viciousness of the fighting further fed racist beliefs in the Pacific War.[105] The argument that racism was the determining factor in targeting civilians, however, is not convincing. For one, the very premise of this argument is flawed: the AAF did plenty of incendiary bombing of Germany, albeit mostly under cover of raids on railroad marshalling yards. The stereotype of Allied bombing in Germany is that while the British torched entire cities with incendiaries, the United States bombed only war production and industrial targets with high altitude, precision techniques. The reality, however, is that half of U.S. bombs were delivered by radar through clouds or bad weather, and accuracy for these was worse than that for British night bombing. The scholarly consensus on radar bombing is that it was the functional equivalent of British night area bombing.[106] American commanders acknowledged this fact by using incendiary-heavy bomb loads on radar-guided missions. American aircraft also launched almost seventy out-and-out area attacks. The key events that caused this shift in tactics were the disastrous daylight raids of August and October 1943, which demonstrated that the balance had shifted "away from the bomber and the offense to the fighter and defense."[107] Indeed, on close examination, the air campaigns in the two theaters look remarkably similar: a gradual transition toward less discriminate bombing owing to prevailing conditions and rising actual and potential costs.[108] Yet Americans were far more racist toward Japanese than toward Germans. Indeed, if racism was such a strong factor determining military operations, why did the AAF bother with a precision campaign at all in the Far East? Furthermore, the atomic bomb was initially developed to be used on Germany and would surely have been employed had it been ready in time.[109] Japan was the victim of bad timing, not racial identity.

The consensus among historians, moreover, is that racism did not cause the shift to firebombing in the Far East or the use of the atomic bombs.[110] A distinguished scholar of the role of race in the Pacific War, John Dower, argues that racism on both sides contributed to the brutality of the war by allowing soldiers to view their foes as less than human but does not contend that racism alone was the determining factor in targeting noncombatants: "Such dehumanization . . . surely *facilitated* the decisions to make civilian populations the targets of concentrated attack, whether by conventional or nuclear weapons."[111] Underlying racist beliefs—and race hatreds fanned by wartime atrocities—undoubtedly made the shift to targeting civilians easier (and allowed American airmen to be much more open about their tactics), but did not by themselves cause the change from precision to incendiary attack.

A more convincing answer is provided by the varying susceptibility of Japanese and German construction to fire. As discussed above, American planners recognized early on that incendiary bombs would be far more effective against wooden and paper Japanese construction than against the stone and brick German housing. In fact, American plans called for an eventual shift to firebombing against Japan. Japanese industry was also highly decentralized, rendering it relatively immune to concentrated high explosive strikes but vulnerable to fire. These conditions led American airmen to believe that incendiary attack would be more effective versus Japan than against Germany.

Organization Theory. Organizational culture arguments fail to account for the firebombing of Japan. As previously discussed, a belief in precision bombing permeated the AAF in the interwar years, and the air force's doctrine and plans called for the bombardment of specific objectives in the enemy's industrial economy, not overt attacks on civilians or civilian morale. In the Pacific, however, the known susceptibility of Japanese cities to fire and the possibility of bringing the war to an early conclusion quickly prompted air planners to contemplate torching entire towns. The airmen were still interested in crippling Japanese war production, but in Japan precision bombing was not the most efficient way to achieve this goal. The failure of precision tactics to achieve decisive results under Hansell and LeMay ensured a shift to incendiaries in defiance of the AAF's culture of precision.

By contrast, an argument can be made that parochial organizational interests were responsible for the AAF's turn to civilian victimization in World War II. Specifically, the air force's quest to become an independent service required that airpower contribute decisively to victory. As Thomas Searle puts it, "If USAAF strategic bombing could make a major contribution to the war effort, it would provide a powerful argument for the service autonomy U.S. airmen had sought for decades."[112] "The pressure on Arnold to prove the decisive nature of strategic bombing was intense," agrees John Ray Skates, "not only as a prerequisite for independence but also to justify the immense effort expended in manpower and money."[113] When faced with poor results from precision raids on Japanese industry, therefore, air force leaders turned to incendiary bombing as a means of making a contribution to the war effort, even if it violated their prewar doctrine.

The air force's pursuit of organizational independence clearly influenced some of the AAF's leading officers and thus played a role in contributing to the firebombing in Japan. America's air leaders needed palpable results to justify an independent service. But other air forces—the RAF and the Luftwaffe—that were already independent behaved in similar ways: both first attempted precision attack and later shifted to more indiscriminate tactics owing to ineffectiveness and high loss rates. For the parochial interests argument to be true, one would have to argue that the escalation to firebombing would not have occurred had the air force been independent. Moreover, the organizational argument implies that the failure of precision bombing was the key factor behind the shift to firebombing, but this ignores the AAF's extensive exploration of and planning for incendiary attack in the Pacific theater well before it suffered the loss of a single aircraft over Japan.

A slightly different take on the organizational argument places responsibility for the shift to firebombing on LeMay alone. Conrad Crane, for example, points out that LeMay had great autonomy in his command, was not a product of the ACTS precision doctrine school of thought, pioneered blind bombing methods in Europe, and led and ordered area raids in Europe and the Far East.[114] This argument, however, ultimately fails. Air planners were well aware of Japan's vulnerability to fire, and the plans for air attack on Japan called for eventual incendiary raids on urban areas. Even had Hansell remained in command, the shift in emphasis to firebombing would have come sooner or later.[115] Hansell himself points out in his memoirs that LeMay was not chiefly behind the shift to fire attack: "The change to area urban incendiary attack, when it finally came, can not be laid directly at General LeMay's door. Its initial support came from Twentieth Air Force Headquarters. And it had begun with the selection of urban targets, after a revised report on Far East economic objectives was written and issued in October 1944 by the Committee of Operations Analysts."[116]

GERMANY'S LUFTWAFFE: THE BATTLE OF BRITAIN AND THE BLITZ

The German strategic air offensive known as the Blitz was a campaign of night bombing that began in late September 1940 and concluded the following May. Its goal was to knock Britain out of the war by destroying key industrial objectives and terrorizing the population. The Blitz came on the heels of the Luftwaffe's costly failure to win air superiority in the summer of 1940 and prepare the way for Operation Sea Lion, the German invasion of Britain. Unable to drive English fighter defenses from the sky, and suffering heavy attrition, the Luftwaffe—contrary to its organizational precepts—shifted to night bombing and commenced an extended strategic campaign that took the lives of forty thousand civilians, about half of them in London.[117]

The Blitz unfolded in three phases.[118] In the first phase, lasting from mid September to mid November 1940, the primary target was London, which was hit with a raid of at least a hundred bombers on all but ten nights for a total of fifty-eight major strikes. Approximately thirteen thousand people were killed in this period in London. Phase two of the Blitz targeted British ports and war production in fourteen cities, beginning with the destruction of Coventry on the night of November 14 and lasting through mid February 1941. A pathfinder unit of German medium bombers using X-Gerät (System X)—a navigational aid consisting of a series of beams that steered the aircraft to the target and automatically released the bombs—guided the 449 bombers that struck Coventry that night.[119] The target folder for the mission specified the aiming points as seventeen aircraft and other armaments factories.[120] The raid badly damaged a total of twenty-one industrial sites, including twelve aircraft factories, and aircraft production suffered a major setback. As these targets were scattered throughout the city, harm to civilians was severe: 554 killed and 865 seriously hurt, with one-third of the city's houses left uninhabitable. Incendiaries comprised less than 10 percent of the bombs dropped on Coventry (881 canisters, nearly 32,000 individual munitions), but they started numerous fires that gutted the medieval center of the city.[121] Overall, the Luftwaffe carried out forty-eight raids during the second phase, dropping 10,500 tons of bombs.

In final phase of the Blitz, lasting from mid February until the termination of the campaign in mid May, Hitler directed the Luftwaffe to focus on ports in support of a blockade policy. Sixty-one large raids were launched in this three-month period, forty-six of them directed at ports such as Portsmouth, Plymouth, and Bristol. London was also struck seven times, raids that escalated in intensity as the campaign drew to a close. On April 16 and 19, Luftwaffe bombs killed more than a thousand people each night and wrecked a total of 148,000 houses; on May 10, 1,436 people died, the worst death toll of the campaign. This crescendo of violence, however, signaled an end to the Blitz. Substantial numbers of bombers had already been withdrawn to support the invasions of Greece and Yugoslavia, and with Operation Barbarossa looming, by late May only four groups of bombers (down from a high of forty-four) remained facing Britain.

Historians agree that although the Luftwaffe did not target civilian neighborhoods specifically, the targets they did choose—"factories, docks, the government quarter of Whitehall, and the economic and financial centre of the City of London"—made it "inevitable that a large proportion of the population would be killed and their houses destroyed," a development that Matthew Cooper argues German leaders "positively welcomed" "because of the impact they hoped it would have upon the British people."[122] According to Richard Overy, this target set exposed "the gradual abandonment of any pretence that civilians and civilian morale would not become targets."[123] "It cannot be denied," concludes Horst Boog, "that, in practice, the German air raids on Britain assumed an indiscriminate nature" judged by their results, "and that the terrorisation of the civilian population was accepted as a not unwelcome side-effect."[124]

Historians also agree that as bad as the destruction was in the winter of 1940–41, it could have been worse. Luftwaffe bomb loads, for example, consisted of a relatively low proportion of incendiary bombs. Between September 7, 1940, and May 10, 1941, Luftwaffe bombers dropped a total of 21,774 tons of bombs on London, only 2,633 tons (12 percent) of which were incendiaries. Against the whole of Britain in the same period, the Luftwaffe delivered 54,420 tons of bombs, with 7,920 tons (just under 15 percent) of this total consisting of firebombs.[125] If the Germans sought only to annihilate British civilians, their bomb loads would have included a higher ratio of incendiary bombs. Furthermore, the Luftwaffe had developed means of delivering bombs—such as *Knickebein* and X-Gerät—with decent accuracy. As Horst Boog argues, "Development of these navigation systems and automatic bomb-sights by the Luftwaffe would have made no sense had there been a decision to go for terror bombing of cities right from the beginning."[126]

In short, German bombers in the Blitz did not seek solely to kill civilians. The Luftwaffe hoped to demoralize the British population and support a policy of blockade (or possibly invasion in 1941) through the destruction of war production in British cities and concomitant civilian fatalities. Because the bombing offensive had to proceed at night to avoid untenable losses, however, and owing to the inability at that time to avoid hitting noncombatants when a military target was located in an urban area, civilian losses were high.

German Bombing Doctrine

Unlike air doctrine in the United States and Great Britain, which tilted heavily toward strategic bombing, German air doctrine in the interwar years remained fairly balanced between tactical and strategic missions. German fliers saw their role first and foremost as winning and maintaining air superiority, then as providing indirect support to advancing ground forces by bombing targets behind enemy lines and interdicting the supply and deployment of enemy forces (a mixture of close air support and operational interdiction missions), and finally as destroying the enemy's centers of power, namely his armaments production capability (strategic interdiction).[127] As R. J. Overy remarks, "The German air force became committed to limited strategic bombing" within the confines of the demands of the other armed services.[128] Conspicuously absent from this doctrine was the idea of bombing civilians to affect morale: "In fact," writes James Corum, "the Luftwaffe did not have a policy of terror bombing civilians as part of its doctrine prior to World War II."[129]

The Early Campaigns

Germany opened the set of conflicts we now call the Second World War with a series of victories stunning for their speed and audacity. First Poland, then Norway and Denmark, and finally France and the Low Countries fell before the Wehrmacht's onslaught. In each of these campaigns, airpower played a substantial role in subduing Germany's victims, but the impact of bombing on noncombatants corresponded to the ease or difficulty of the military situation. Against Poland, the Luftwaffe largely avoided civilians until the siege of Warsaw threatened to prolong the fighting and inflict heavy casualties on the army. Hitler could ill-afford the costly and protracted urban fighting it would have taken to subdue the 100,000 Polish defenders in the city, especially with his western frontier denuded of troops and defenseless in the face of a possible French invasion.[130] As the commander-in-chief of the German Army, General Walther von Brauchitsch, commented to his staff, "Every day of calm in the West is for me a gift from God."[131] In this atmosphere of strategic haste, and facing a costly, prolonged urban battle for Warsaw, the Wehrmacht and Luftwaffe together unleashed an intense bombardment on Warsaw in order to cow its inhabitants and defenders to surrender.[132] In the wake of this pummeling, in which about ten thousand civilians died, Polish forces in the city surrendered on September 28.[133]

German operations in the West in 1940, on the other hand, succeeded quickly without such complications, and thus the Luftwaffe largely stuck to its doctrine of providing close air support to the ground forces, operational interdiction, and limited strategic bombing of military targets. Operation *Weserubung,* for example, directed against Denmark and Norway in April 1940, achieved complete surprise: the Danes surrendered without a fight on the morning of the attack and the invading Germans occupied Norway's major cities and ports by the end of the first day.[134] The overwhelming victory the Germans achieved in the Battle of France—due in large part to careful strategic planning—again obviated the need for strategic bombing of civilian targets; the Luftwaffe thus concentrated on knocking out the enemy air forces and providing close air support to the advancing panzers.[135] The lone exception to this pattern—the bombing of Rotterdam—occurred when Dutch resistance—like at Warsaw—threatened to transform a quick German victory into a protracted siege.[136] Even here, however, the air attack proceeded by mistake as German and Dutch officers were negotiating terms.[137]

After finishing with France and the Low Countries, Hitler turned his attention to England. Hitler believed that the British would eventually seek terms from the Reich rather than fight on alone. As John Ray puts it, Hitler "was prepared to wait for Britain. He believed that sooner or later she would have to accept the reality of her position and sue for peace."[138] Until July 1940, therefore, the German strategy to defeat England was based on blockade (but not a starvation blockade), and German bombing in the early summer of 1940 concentrated on ports, military installations, and coastal shipping. Later, after Hitler ordered preparations for an invasion of Great Britain (Operation Sea Lion) on July 11, the Luftwaffe attempted to destroy the British fighter force to gain air superiority over the English Channel and southern England. The initial stages of this battle proved enormously costly to the Luftwaffe, which—in a last ditch effort to destroy RAF Fighter Command—pressed for massive attacks on London, heretofore prohibited by Hitler. Hitler vacated his ban on London in early September owing to British strikes on Berlin (probably calculated to relieve the pressure on RAF Fighter Command by provoking the Germans to retaliate with city bombing), and the Luftwaffe opened a new phase of the attack by launching large bomber raids against targets in London.[139] British fighters savaged these strikes, however, forcing the Luftwaffe to abandon daytime operations and continue its offensive against Britain at night.

Hitler's Beliefs and Luftwaffe Capabilities

Hitler's war directives and his conduct of the war up to the summer of 1940 indicated his inclination to limit the impact of the air war on civilians. As already indicated, the Luftwaffe lacked the ability and doctrine to prosecute extended campaigns of punishment bombing. Moreover, Hitler consciously limited German air strikes on cities in order to protect Germany from counterstrikes. "The German restraints in the campaign through the Low Countries and France," argues George Quester, "had demonstrated a continuing desire to impress distinctions on the Allies which would prevent a heavy assault on German cities." Hitler further hoped to convince Britain to make peace after the fall of France and hoped that "the possession of intact cities might make the British feel that they had more to gain by peace."[140]

Hitler's early war directives also show a clear desire to keep German bombers away from British cities. Directive No. 1 for the Conduct of the

War, issued on August 31, 1939, prohibited air attacks on the British main-
land.[141] War Directive No. 9, published on November 29, called for the destruction of the British war economy, but limited air operations to attacks
on shipping until Germany acquired bases closer to England.[142] OKW, the
military high command, similarly ordered that air operations against Britain should not be escalated until Germany was in possession of the channel
coast.[143] Only on May 24, 1940 (in Directive No. 13), did Hitler authorize
attacks on military targets in Britain itself.[144]

Hitler's reluctance to bomb Britain, while largely explained by deterrence
and his desire to reach an accommodation with the British, also stemmed
from his belief that airpower had a limited ability to achieve political goals
on its own. The Führer, for example, told his service chiefs that "a country
could not 'be brought to defeat by an air force,'" and predicted that a war
with Britain would be long and difficult.[145] Surprisingly, Luftwaffe generals
agreed with Hitler. A Luftwaffe study at the time of the Munich Crisis in
1938 argued that the German Air Force could achieve little in a potential
war against England and that to fight with the resources then at its disposal
appeared "fruitless."[146] Another study from 1939 accurately predicted the
likely course of an air offensive against Britain: operations staffers "held out
little hope of success in an onslaught against Britain's fighter force as a preliminary to a general attack at a later date. Conditions favoured the defence,
and it was considered that losses suffered by the attacking forces would
be prohibitively high."[147] The air force high command's view in May–June
1940 was that "with existing forces, the Luftwaffe on its own lacked the
necessary strength to gain a decisive victory over Britain."[148]

Phase One: *Kanalkampf*

This first phase of concerted air operations against Britain, often referred
to as the *Kanalkampf* (channel war), lasted for roughly six weeks starting
July 1, 1940, but achieved no decisive results. Luftwaffe chief Hermann
Göring, in his General Directions for the Operation of the Luftwaffe against
England issued on June 30, designated the destruction of Fighter Command
as the principal objective of the air campaign.[149] The Germans hoped that
strikes on British shipping and ports would draw English fighters into the
air where the Luftwaffe's elite single-engine fighter—the Bf 109—could destroy them.[150] Göring's order also "stressed that every effort should be made
to avoid unnecessary loss of life amongst the civil population."[151]

British fighters, however, assiduously avoided engaging their German
counterparts. Chief of Fighter Command Hugh Dowding knew that only
German bombers could destroy Britain's vital industries or Fighter Command's bases. As one RAF pilot later put it, "We RAF fighters were not
in the least interested in the German fighters—except insofar as they were
interested in us. Our job was defense. German fighters could do no harm

to Britain. German bombers with their deadly loads were the menace. Our orders were to seek them out and destroy them."[152]

The battle did not go well for the Luftwaffe. In the four weeks between July 10 and August 8, Luftwaffe bombers sank only 40,000 tons of British coastal shipping, a paltry 1 percent of the 4 million tons then operating. To destroy this meager tonnage, German aircraft suffered heavily. In five weeks of operations after July 1, Luftwaffe aircraft losses were nearly double those of Fighter Command, 279 against 142; 181 of the German losses were bombers.[153] Relative loss rates for the entire Battle of Britain are displayed in table 4.4.

Phase Two: *Adlerangriff*

Observing the evident failure of the *Kanalkampf* to destroy Fighter Command or isolate Britain from trade, Hitler issued Directive No. 16 calling for an invasion of Great Britain. To support Operation Sea Lion, Hitler authorized unlimited air and sea operations against Britain to begin anytime after August 5, with the proviso that London was to remain off limits.[154] Air superiority was vital to a cross-channel invasion, so the destruction of Fighter Command remained the central goal of air operations: "The English Air Force must be so reduced morally and physically that it is unable to deliver any significant attack against the German crossing."[155]

To achieve this goal, however, the new plan—designated *Adlerangriff* (Eagle Attack)—adopted a different means: attack British fighters not only in the air, but also on the ground through the destruction of airfields, radar stations, and related infrastructure in a thirteen-day offensive south and southeast of London.[156] To carry out this plan the Luftwaffe deployed almost 2,300 serviceable aircraft facing England: 963 fighters and 1,314 bombers (316 single-engine "Stukas" and 998 twin-engine aircraft of various makes). In the crucial category of single-engine fighters in the southern sector of operations (Fighter Command's 10 and 11 Groups), the Germans possessed a superiority of 702 Bf 109s to 312 British Hurricanes and Spitfires, more than a two to one advantage.[157]

Table 4.4. German and British aircraft lost in combat, July–September 1940

	July 1–August 8	August 13–18	August 24–September 6	September 7–15	September 16–30	Total
Germany	279	247	308	174	199	1,207
Britain	142	131	273	131	115	792

Source: Figures are from Matthew Cooper, *The German Air Force 1933–1945: An Anatomy of Failure* (London: Jane's Publishing, 1981), 129, 140, 141, 145, 154–55, 158.

A Disastrous Beginning. *Adlerangriff* opened disastrously for the Luftwaffe on August 13: the Germans lost 45 aircraft to Fighter Command's 13. Overall, the British emerged from the first week of *Adlerangriff* (August 13–18) with a significant edge over the Luftwaffe—131 British fighters lost to 247 German aircraft. Germany's medium bombers, the Ju 88 and the He 111, its primary dive bomber, the Ju 87 "Stuka," and its twin-engine fighter, the Bf 110, all turned out to be too slow and poorly maneuverable to escape from Britain's single-engine fighters, leaving only the single-engine Bf 109 as the equal of the British Hurricanes and Spitfires.

Two raids in particular devastated the German bomber force. First, on August 15 (known as "Black Thursday" to the Luftwaffe), British fighters annihilated unescorted German bombers and Bf 110s attacking northern Britain from Norway, shooting down twenty-two aircraft at no cost to themselves.[158] The results of this raid, according to Williamson Murray, "proved once and for all that unsupported daylight bomber operations against Britain were nearly impossible."[159] As a result, German Bf 109s had to escort the operations of every other type of aircraft (even the Bf 110, nominally a fighter) in addition to conducting their own attacks on Fighter Command.

Second, on August 18, German dive-bombers attacking RAF airfields in southern England suffered appalling losses with twenty-eight shot down, forcing Göring to withdraw the remaining Stukas from action the following day.[160] The Stukas, which had performed so well in Poland and France, were no match for determined fighter resistance and could not be escorted properly because of their slow cruising speed.

German losses, even more than those of Fighter Command, were unsustainable. The Luftwaffe lost 284 aircraft in the first week of *Adlerangriff*, 12.5 percent of those engaged in the battle.[161] During the month of August, total losses amounted to 774, a full 18.5 percent of the combat aircraft in the Luftwaffe inventory on August 1.[162]

The Battle Equalizes. Despite these heavy losses, German bombers continued to hammer RAF airfields and the battle began to equalize. In the second phase of *Adlerangriff* (August 24–September 6), the Germans nearly pulled even in the loss-exchange ratio, destroying 273 British fighters while losing 308 total aircraft (109 bombers). Overall, the British lost 657 fighters to all causes in the four weeks after August 8. Fighter Command's frontline strength remained about the same as it had at the commencement of the battle, but its reserves were dwindling. Moreover, Fighter Command began to experience a shortage of experienced pilots. Matthew Cooper argues that the Germans were four to five weeks away from attaining air superiority in early September, and Peter Townsend opines that "with the combined weight of its bombers and fighters, the Luftwaffe was gradually overpowering Fighter Command."[163]

The Germans, however, were running out of time. Shipping for the invasion was assembled, but Hitler repeatedly postponed the date, waiting for the Luftwaffe to knock out Fighter Command. But the pesky British showed no signs of cracking, and soon the Germans would face poor weather. With a sense of desperation, Luftwaffe leaders turned to London as the last remaining target that would draw out the British fighters where they could be destroyed. As Williamson Murray puts it, "The impact of losses over southern England combined with inclinations already present in Luftwaffe doctrine to induce a change in German air strategy early in September."[164] Hitler approved this target change on September 5, lifting his ban on bombing the British capital out of anger at Bomber Command raids on Berlin ordered by Churchill in retaliation for the accidental bombing of London by twelve German aircraft on the night of August 24. This mishap, of course, was made possible by the Luftwaffe's unsustainable daylight bomber losses over Britain, which forced the Germans to begin bombing at night. With Hitler now in the mood for reprisals, the Luftwaffe turned to round-the-clock bombing of military targets in London.

The Bombers Head for London. The new attacks commenced on September 7 with a strike on the docklands in London. For all of Hitler's bloodthirsty rhetoric about killing British civilians, the main objective of Luftwaffe attacks on London at this point was still to destroy the RAF, not terrorize the populace. Many civilians were indeed killed—1,000 on the night of September 7, 412 on September 8, 370 on September 9—but undermining morale was only a secondary goal.[165] General Albert Kesselring, commander of Luftflotte 2, "pressed for an all-out attack on the capital. Apart from its value as a target, chances were good that London's morale might crack."[166] Kesselring and others recommended attacks on residential neighborhoods, but Hitler would not allow it. Hitler rejected the intentional targeting of residential areas suggested to him by Luftwaffe chief of staff Hans Jeschonnek on September 14, for example, ordering that "although the target area has been extended, air raids on London will continue to be directed primarily against installations of military importance and vital facilities in the city, including train stations. Terror raids on purely residential areas should only be a last resort to exert pressure and, therefore, should not be used at this time."[167] The will of the populace might indeed break, but it would do so as a result of strikes on military targets, not from the all-out slaughter of civilians.

The German air fleets flying against Britain numbered 1,524 operational aircraft (772 of them bombers) on September 7, compared to 746 serviceable Hurricanes and Spitfires for Fighter Command.[168] Deceived by their own inflated kill estimates, however, Luftwaffe leaders convinced themselves that the RAF was on its last legs. The Germans, therefore, launched massive daylight raids totaling over thirteen hundred sorties on September 15 designed to deliver the coup de grâce to Fighter Command only to be stunned when the British met the raiders with huge clouds of fighters. The Luftwaffe was routed, its attacks broken up and its bombs dropped wildly at a cost of 56 aircraft to the RAF's 26.[169] This trend continued for the rest of the month until Göring terminated the daylight missions owing to unendurable losses: from September 16 to September 30 his forces had lost 199 aircraft, more than 13 percent of the aircraft available on the 7th.[170] Operation Sea Lion—postponed indefinitely by the Führer on September 17—was canceled for good on October 12.

Phase Three: The Blitz

The defensive advantage of fighters over bombers—even heavily escorted bombers—resulted in severe losses for the Luftwaffe and the failure of the daylight bombing of Britain in 1940. "The Luftwaffe simply could not sustain constant large-scale daytime bomber sorties," concludes Telford Taylor. "Fighter Command's defense was too fierce, and the strain and the losses suffered by the German crews too great."[171] Heavy casualties in the opening days of *Adlerangriff* prompted a partial shift to night bombing in late August, a shift consummated by the disastrous massed day raids of September. Although most historians give September 7 as the opening of the Blitz, this date actually marks the beginning of the final segment of *Adlerangriff*, when the goal was still the destruction of Fighter Command by large-scale attacks on London.[172] The failure of these raids to achieve their objective meant that Germany could not invade Britain in 1940. Hitler thus had only one weapon left in his arsenal, namely night bombardment of England's cities to destroy civilian morale: "It was hoped that a heavy bombardment would destroy its citizens' will to resist, and that this, together with the economic blockade, would induce the Government to sue for peace."[173] This strategy offered the possibility, however remote, of defeating Britain without an invasion while also lowering Luftwaffe bomber losses to an acceptable level.

Three factors were important in bringing about the gradual shift in German aerial operations from attrition and defeat of the RAF by day to destruction of British war industry and civilian morale by night. Probably the most important was the crippling losses sustained by the German bomber force. Already in the first week of *Adlerangriff*, the magnitude of the damage was so severe that Göring ordered that flight crews should consist of no more than one officer.[174] Göring also drastically increased the size of fighter escorts for bomber missions and withdrew the dive-bomber force. The shift to night bombing radically curtailed bomber losses: in the two months from September 7 to November 13, 1940, the Luftwaffe lost only 100 aircraft on night operations over Britain.[175] Fighter Command, so deadly in daylight, could do little by night, having few night fighters of indifferent quality. The Germans, notes Matthew Cooper, "soon realised that night attacks represented a safe way of proceeding with the war against Britain. . . . The Luftwaffe's bombers, which by day were so vulnerable, had, in the autumn of 1940, little to fear by night."[176] Yet the decrease in aircraft losses was not a victory for the Luftwaffe, as one historian notes: "Arguably the continued bombing campaign was actually an admission of defeat, a desperate alternative to the direct, annihilating contest with Fighter Command that, had the Luftwaffe emerged victorious, would have enabled it to rule the skies over England."[177]

Moreover, although Göring's generals believed they were destroying Britain's fighter force at a rapid pace, air superiority was not being gained quickly enough. Many Luftwaffe officers argued that only by attacking London could they force Fighter Command to commit its entire force where it could be destroyed. The first few weeks of the round-the-clock offensive versus London, therefore, supported the goal of knocking out the RAF. As is well known, of course, by turning the attack toward London, Göring provided battered Fighter Command with a much-needed breather from the strikes on its bases, and is widely regarded as the key blunder that lost Germany the battle.

Finally, there is the matter of the British raids on Berlin, which provoked Hitler into revoking the ban on bombing London. Most historians argue that Churchill ordered these missions hoping that Hitler would retaliate in kind against London, thus easing the pressure on a beleaguered Fighter Command—a rare example of a leader inviting strikes on his own *civilian* population to reduce his country's *military* losses.[178] Hitler did indeed send his bombers to London, but Churchill's provocation only quickened a decision that probably would have come sooner or later anyway owing to rising losses and Luftwaffe preferences.[179] Göring and his generals were already pressing for a decisive move against London to destroy the RAF independently of the pinprick Bomber Command raids on Berlin, and later hoped to knock Britain out of the war with airpower alone. Reprisal was undoubtedly a motive for sending the Luftwaffe's bombers against the British capital, but they would have gotten there eventually even without the attacks on Berlin.

Having failed to force Britain to come to terms with blockade, and with invasion rendered impossible by the failure to win air superiority, Hitler chose to continue the war against "perfidious Albion" with the only means at his disposal that was not prohibitively costly: night bombing. This is the conclusion reached by R. J. Overy:

> Thus when Göring turned the bombers against London in the Battle of Britain and the Blitz, it was not just out of the desire for reprisals against British raids on Germany, but because it was now hoped that, everything else having failed, *Terrorangriffe* would bring the British to their senses. The attacks were also combined with instructions to attack "the armaments industry (particularly air armament). The important harbours. London will be

attacked constantly night and day in order to destroy the city." The Blitz was an extension of this strategic aim, and was forced on the *Luftwaffe* because of the high combat attrition suffered through daylight raids. Thus gradually during the course of the Battle of Britain the German leadership began to move more towards the concept of a full strategic air offensive for the first time. This was not to be a limited strategic operation, but an offensive like that planned and prepared by the British: to bring the war to an end through the exercise of air power.[180]

Alternative Explanations

None of the alternative explanations for civilian victimization offer convincing accounts of the Blitz. I focus below on regime type and organizational theory, since I have uncovered no evidence that key German leaders viewed the British as barbarians.

Regime Type. The Blitz is superficially consistent with the norms version of the regime-type hypothesis: Nazi Germany was a dictatorship, and it victimized noncombatants. The details of the case, however, contradict both versions of the argument. Hitler repeatedly forbade his military commanders from striking directly at urban neighborhoods, restraint that is not attributable to liberal norms. In general, Hitler's directives and utterances portray him as viewing intentional attacks on civilians with airpower as a last resort, and his actions show that he used this instrument in a reprisal mode, attempting to punish and deter attacks on German cities.[181] Since Germany was not a liberal democracy, Hitler's restrained application of airpower versus civilians undermines the norms argument.

The case evidence also contradicts the institutions hypothesis. For a leader not subject to public recall, Hitler worried extensively about his popularity among the German people, suggesting that this concern is not peculiar to democratic leaders. In general, Hitler's regime was remarkably cost-sensitive, possibly because of its reluctance to mobilize German society for modern war. The Führer and his Wehrmacht developed a strategy and force structure designed to win lightning victories so as not to cause much displacement to the civilian economy. The war in Russia showed how ill-suited this military system was for a protracted war. This way of waging war also explains why Hitler was so quick to retaliate against Britain for air strikes on Berlin, which he believed would bring the war home to the civilian population, exactly what he was trying to prevent.

Organization Theory. Some scholars argue that German restraint in bombing Britain is explained by the "culture of land power" in Germany's armed forces and the Luftwaffe's orientation toward supporting the operations of the army rather than undertaking independent strategic operations. The culture of land power also shaped the Luftwaffe's capabilities, encouraging the development of medium and dive bombers but discouraging pursuit of a heavy bomber.[182] As a result, the Luftwaffe never acquired a four-engine bomber on par with the British Lancaster or the American B-17 or B-29. In sum, according to this view, "The Luftwaffe, like the army that fathered it, relied on furthering the land campaign and viewed the defeat of enemy forces, not the destruction of civilian morale, as the key to victory."[183]

The Luftwaffe's organizational culture—along with Hitler's skepticism of airpower and his preference for hitting military targets—helps explain the form the Blitz took, and the fact that it was not even worse. The argument, however, faces three anomalies. First, it maintains that the Luftwaffe's culture of ground support determined German restraint, but fails to acknowledge that Hitler—a civilian—was the key decision-maker. Although Hitler served in the army in World War I, it is not clear that Hitler's beliefs regarding the inefficacy of airpower to win wars on its own stemmed from his earlier immersion in the culture of land power or from some other cause.

Second, proponents of the cultural explanation contend that the Luftwaffe championed counterforce bombing and restraint with regard to noncombatants, but in fact several Luftwaffe generals—including Luftwaffe chief of staff Hans Jeschonnek and commander of Luftflotte 2 Albert Kesselring—became the most vocal advocates of bombing London as the Battle of Britain wore on.[184] Hitler—the civilian—consistently dismissed these calls and insisted on restraint, most likely because he still held out the faint hope that the British could be convinced to come to terms with Germany, and he did not wish to alienate them unduly by bombing civilians.

Finally, the cultural argument largely ignores the reality that the Luftwaffe actually engaged in a nine-month campaign of indiscriminate night bombing of British cities that killed forty thousand people. It may not have been as severe as that conducted later by Bomber Command against Germany, but the bombing was curtailed by Hitler's plan to invade the Soviet Union. A skeptic might respond that the cultural argument does not predict infinite restraint when that restraint is not reciprocated by the enemy. But this gets the timing backward: the Germans began their systematic campaign against British cities well before Bomber Command inflicted more than a handful of pinpricks on German cities. From the time Germany invaded Poland until the Battle of France, Bomber Command's operations consisted mostly of raids on naval vessels and dropping leaflets. Some limited bombing of German oil and rail targets began on May 15, 1940, but more effort was devoted to leafleting, mining the North Sea, and attacking German invasion barges, coastal shipping, and aircraft targets. After the Blitz was well underway, the Air Ministry designated oil as the primary target on October 30, with undermining civilian morale as a secondary objective. Of course, owing to the radical inaccuracy of British bombing, "the Germans were scarcely aware that their oil resources were supposed to have been the object of a systematic British assault."[185] Bomber Command launched its first explicit area raid on Mannheim in mid December, but this attack was ordered as a reprisal for the Luftwaffe's destruction of Coventry the previous month. It was not until July 9, 1941, that civilian morale rose to the top of the list of priorities, and only in 1942 did major urban area raids begin. Unless one is willing to ascribe the entirety of the Blitz to the largely symbolic Bomber Command reprisal attacks on Berlin in August 1940 and a handful of ineffective missions against industrial targets, the "Blitz as reprisal" argument is not credible. Indeed, the damage from the August 24 raid was so slight that German propaganda minister Josef Goebbels was forced to make it worse to gain any propaganda value from it. As one historian comments, "So feeble were the British efforts against German soil in the autumn of 1940 that Goebbels had to resort to faking British 'atrocities' to rouse the German public."[186]

The parochial organizational interest argument is even less persuasive because the Luftwaffe was already an independent military service. Even had bombing forced the British to seek an accommodation with Germany, the Luftwaffe would never have supplanted the army as the preeminent service.

THE evidence presented in this chapter supports the conclusion that escalating or expected military costs and desperation to achieve victory lead to civilian victimization. Against Japan, the high costs and poor performance of precision bombing—as well as the prospective costs to American troops of invading the Japanese home islands—influenced the decision to incinerate Japanese cities. Overwhelming majorities of the American public and U.S. political leaders approved of these policies in full knowledge of the price being paid by enemy civilians. Escalating costs to the Luftwaffe—and the faint hope that punishing bombardment of cities might vanquish British morale—also prompted the German Blitz.

Several distinguished scholars of airpower in World War II have noted that over the course of the conflict, existing moral constraints eroded until, by the end, few questioned the morality of obliterating more than one hundred thousand civilians with atomic weaponry. Richard Davis, for example, maintains that while American bombers over Germany tried to attack military objectives as much as they could, "the harsh realities of total war made it preferable to bomb something rather than nothing at all."[187] "Despite the poor accuracy of blind bombing," notes Gary Shandroff, "the proportion of radar missions continued to increase. It seemed logical to many in the Air Force that inaccurate bombing was better than no bombing at all."[188] Shandroff remarks that this shift in emphasis occurred "within a milieu dominated by one central theme: the drive to achieve military victory. When conflicting doctrines and policies clashed, they were judged by the pragmatic test of military efficacy and the degree to which they would contribute to victory. Moral and political considerations were secondary."[189] Finally, Barton Bernstein argues that the war caused a redefinition of morality that allowed Hiroshima and Nagasaki to occur, so that by 1945, "there were few moral restraints left in what had become virtually a total war. Even FDR's prewar concern for sparing enemy civilians had fallen by the wayside. In that new moral climate, any nation that had the A-bomb would probably have used it against enemy peoples. . . . America was not morally unique—just technologically exceptional. Only it had the bomb, and so only it used it."[190]

This chapter demonstrates the causal underpinnings of this erosion of moral restraint. Most governments began to fight by targeting military forces. But when victory appeared imperiled, or the costs of fighting became unacceptable, even societies that found bombing of civilians morally abhorrent—and military organizations that preferred precision bombing of military targets—turned to civilian victimization as a means to manage costs and produce victory by eroding enemy morale or undermining the adversary's ability to resist.

[5]

Guerrilla Warfare, Counterinsurgency, and Civilian Victimization

The Second Anglo-Boer War

Although uncommon in the dataset used for the statistical analysis in this book, guerrilla warfare is an important cause of civilian victimization.[1] In a study of mass killing since 1945, for example, Benjamin Valentino, Paul Huth, and Dylan Balch-Lindsay find that guerrilla wars in which the government faces a militarily threatening insurgency with widespread popular support are very likely to result in mass murder by the incumbents.[2] Furthermore, data compiled by Ivan Arreguín-Toft shows that strong actors are far more likely to use "barbarous" strategies that violate the laws of war and harm noncombatants when battling weak actors who employ guerrilla strategies.[3]

The statistical evidence is mixed, however, regarding the effect of regime type on the likelihood that states will victimize civilians as part of a counterinsurgency strategy. Valentino and his colleagues, for instance, find that democracy exerts a significant restraining effect on mass killing in military conflicts—the vast majority of which were guerrilla/civil wars—since World War II. In a limited study of twenty-five wars, Michael Engelhardt opines that the "literature confirms the assumption that nondemocratic regimes are free to use much harsher tactics in dealing with insurgency than are democratic regimes."[4] An analysis of Toft's data on strategic choice in asymmetric wars in the nineteenth and twentieth centuries, however, shows that democracies are not significantly less likely than autocracies to use barbarous strategies. Nor are democracies significantly less prone to victimize civilians in imperial and colonial wars.[5] Even Engelhardt notes that the examples of democratic successes in counterinsurgency—which they achieved without recourse to excessive brutality—occurred exclusively in low-cost wars (with a mean killed-in-action figure of 639, compared to an average of 14,508 fatalities in the democratic failures).[6] This fact undermines his claim that democracies are more humane in conducting counterinsurgency warfare; it simply shows that the enemies they faced in these wars were weak, and thus the conflicts were easily won without recourse to harsher measures.

In this chapter I argue that democracies historically have not been less prone than other types of regimes to use civilian victimization when combating guerrilla insurgencies in foreign lands. States fighting guerrilla insurgencies use violence against ordinary people as a means to defeat a rebellion. This violence generally takes two forms. In the first, belligerents employ targeted killings or indiscriminate reprisal massacres in order to convince the population to stop supporting a rebellion. In the second, belligerents simply try to make it impossible for people to help the insurgents by killing the population or otherwise removing it from the battle area.

The armies of democracies do not typically commit large-scale, face-to-face massacres. Democratic armies do commit atrocities, of course, but they tend to occur as unpremeditated revenge or reprisal measures rather than as part of a calculated, premeditated strategy. On the other hand, democracies are not shy about using targeted killings of known or suspected civilian supporters of insurgencies, such as during the Battle of the Casbah in Algeria or the Phoenix Program in Vietnam. The most common democratic counterinsurgency strategies, however, are those that seek to isolate the civilian population from the insurgents by concentrating the people in protected camps or villages. In this scenario, the incumbent does not intend to destroy the population per se; on the contrary, it would much rather control the people than kill them. Unfortunately, because the incumbent believes it cannot prevent the civilian population from helping the insurgents, it attempts to make it impossible for them to do so rather than trying to dissuade them. Democracies rarely kill these people outright; rather, they force thousands—sometimes millions—to move to fortified camps or communities that are rarely provided with adequate food, water, or medical care. Unsurprisingly—and quite forseeably—thousands die of disease, malnutrition, and hunger.

Through an in-depth examination of the Second Anglo-Boer War (1899–1902), I demonstrate in this chapter the causal link between the rising military costs and delayed victory stemming from a defender's choice of a guerrilla strategy and the choice to target noncombatants.

THE LOGIC OF CIVILIAN VICTIMIZATION
IN GUERRILLA WARS

In guerrilla wars, civilian victimization can help defeat an insurgency in two ways. First, incumbents target some noncombatants for violence in order to deter others from providing support to the enemy. The goal of this tactic is not to eliminate or destroy the population, but rather to convert it to one's cause by demonstrating that those (and/or their families) who aid the other side will meet an untimely and perhaps gruesome demise. Second, government forces sometimes dispense with selective uses of force entirely and try to separate the insurgents physically from their base of support in the population. In this scenario, incumbents either kill or relocate large numbers of civilians in order to make it physically impossible for insurgents to obtain food, shelter, recruits, or intelligence from the people.

A successful insurgency relies on a supportive population.[7] In addition to needing a favorable physical environment—such as mountainous, forested, or jungle-covered terrain, or a sanctuary in a neighboring country—guerrillas require a civilian population that acquiesces in their presence for two reasons. First, the people serve as another form of camouflage for the insurgents. Should superior government units deploy into a guerrilla-infested area, insurgents can simply stash their weapons and blend into the surrounding population. Second, a sympathetic populace provides the means of survival for a guerrilla force: food, shelter, intelligence on the whereabouts of the incumbent's forces, and military manpower. As Mao Zedong put it, the people are the water in which the fish—the guerrillas—swim.

The trouble with pursuing a "direct" strategy of battlefield victory against a guerrilla force is that it is difficult to distinguish between irregular forces and noncombatants. Finding the insurgents thus poses a serious problem: they tend to disappear when the government's army approaches, only to reappear when it moves on. Moreover, guerrillas avoid pitched battles on the strong actor's terms, striking only at times and places of their own choosing. In Vietnam, for instance, the Vietcong initiated more than 90 percent of the small-unit actions; American operations, by contrast, made contact with the enemy less than 1 percent of the time.[8] This means that as long as the guerrillas have sanctuaries and access to the population, defeating them will be a protracted process, raising the possibility that the strong actor will run out of patience and give up. This is why striking at insurgents via the population is so attractive to strong actors.

Civilian victimization as a counterinsurgency strategy takes the supposed strength of guerrilla warfare—the camouflage and support provided by the civilian population—and turns it into a deadly weakness. If the population is the water in which the guerrilla/fish swim, then counterinsurgency aims to "drain the sea," thereby exposing the fish for easy killing.[9] To achieve this separation of insurgents from civilians, incumbents have two options: (1) kill some or all of the civilians or (2) move them. Massacres—whether aimed only at known enemy supporters and their families on the one hand, or at entire villages where guerrillas are known to be active on the other—are supposed to deter people from providing aid and comfort to the enemy.[10] The logic of massacre is well illustrated by a report to the French Minister of War following the Setif massacre in Algeria in May 1945, during which

French settlers and military forces killed roughly three thousand Algerian Muslims in retaliation for an armed uprising in the town: "The real objectives of this military demonstration . . . were to . . . carry out an *operation of intimidation;* strike the imagination of the masses of Kabylie by a visible development of massive military means; constituting a deterrent to the intents of the nationalist agitators."[11] "Most people," notes Tom Marks, "sit on the sidelines" of a conflict until supporting one side or the other becomes in their interest. "Terror," Marks continues, "is but one tool for creating such an interest. . . . Providing it is not abused, then, terror, while it may alienate some, also fortifies others. At the margins, it can push an undecided group into support it would otherwise not give." Massacres by guerrillas follow the same logic. According to Stathis Kalyvas, for example, "Most victims of the summer 1997 massacres [in Algeria] were Islamist sympathizers who had either abandoned the rebels or were getting ready to. The rebels killed them to 'make an example' of them: to signal the cost of defection and thus deter it."[12]

The second option for cutting the link between insurgents and the population is to deny the rebels access to the people by relocating or concentrating the civilian population in protected areas. The goal of a policy of regroupment need not be to kill the population—although it certainly can be—but rather to reduce the insurgents' ability to fight and make them easier to destroy by removing all people from their operating areas, thus depriving the guerrillas of the food, shelter, and intelligence they need to survive. During the Second Italo-Sanusi War, for example, which was fought in Libya from 1923 to 1932, Italian commander Rodolfo Graziani emptied the sea, interning 80,000 to 100,000 people in concentration camps enclosed in barbed wire. "The colonialist goal was to separate the resistance from its social base," writes Ali Ahmida. "In taking this step," argues E. E. Evans-Pritchard, "the Italians were doing no more than others had done before them and have done after them, for an army fighting guerrillas is fighting an entire population."[13] Similarly, Guenter Lewy argues that "MACV [Military Assistance Command Vietnam] really believed . . . that forcible relocation of the civilian population would hasten the end of the war and was the most effective way of depriving the VC of supplies and manpower—the water in which they swam."[14] Evidence also suggests that much of the displacement of ethnic Albanians in Kosovo by Slobodan Milošević's security forces prior to the date of NATO's attack was as part of a counterinsurgency strategy directed against the Kosovo Liberation Army.[15]

If the government concludes that the civilian population, or some portion thereof, is irrevocably hostile, then a policy of mass murder may be substituted for one of removal. In this case, the resilience of the guerrillas or government forces in a certain area, or the strength of support for one side or the other among particular segments of the population, causes the enemy to equate combatants and noncombatants. In his account of the civil war in

El Salvador, for example, Mark Danner observes: "As the guerrillas were reduced to the status of terrorist delinquents, all civilians in certain zones were reduced to the status of *masas*, guerrilla supporters, and thus became [in the minds of army leaders] legitimate targets. North of the Torola [River], for example, it was believed that the civilians and the guerrillas were all mixed together, and were indistinguishable."[16] This belief helped produce a savage counterinsurgency campaign in northern El Salvador that culminated in a series of massacres, such as the one at El Mozote, that killed about 370 people. Similarly, the consistent support of the local population for the Sanusi rebels in Libya convinced the Italians that everyone was implacably hostile; there was no use trying to distinguish between the *sottomessi*—those who had supposedly submitted to Italian rule—and the *ribelli*—the rebels and their committed supporters. "In the end," writes Evans-Pritchard, "the Italians came to the conclusion that they could trust no Cyrenaican, least of all a Cyrenaican Bedouin. The hearts of all were with their fighting fellow countrymen and fellow Muslims."[17] The conviction that combatants and noncombatants were inseparable in Cyrenaica—indeed, that they were one and the same—set the stage for the incarceration of the entire population of northern Cyrenaica by the Italians in the war's later stages. Finally, when an insurgency draws most of its support from a single ethnic group, as in Burundi and Rwanda, members of that group may be targeted for killing on a genocidal scale.

THE SECOND ANGLO-BOER WAR

Great Britain and the Boer Republics of the Transvaal and the Orange Free State went to war on October 11, 1899. British officials expected a typically easy victory over another backward opponent, but the war turned out to be anything but quick and decisive. Facing imminent defeat at British hands in mid 1900, the Boers decided to continue the war in guerrilla fashion rather than submit to British demands and lose their independence. In retaliation, the British Army—first under Lord Roberts, and then under Lord Kitchener, the hero of Khartoum two years earlier—adopted a scorched-earth policy, burning down the farms of all those who supported the Boer cause and forcing Boer women and children into concentration camps. By the time the war was over, almost twenty-eight thousand Boer civilians had died in the camps, 79 percent of whom were children under the age of sixteen. Overall, including native African fatalities, as many as forty-six thousand noncombatants died in the British concentration camps, nearly double the number of military fatalities caused by the war.

The bulk of the civilian fatalities in the Boer War stemmed from the British policy of confining Boer and African noncombatants to concentration camps. Conditions in the South African camps were appalling, especially in 1900–1901. Tents were overcrowded; inhabitants did not receive soap as part of their rations; water was insufficient in quantity and of dubious quality; fuel for cooking was scanty; and food rations were at the starvation level.[18] The number of medical personnel was inadequate; in fact, of the 94 doctors in the camp system in February 1901, half had quit or been sacked a year later, as had 85 out of 217 nurses.[19] Moreover, as Thomas Pakenham notes, "undesirables" whose menfolk remained at large with the Boer commandos received a smaller ration than those who had surrendered to the British. At first these unfortunates were allotted no meat at all. "Even after rations were improved" in March 1901, however, "they still remained extremely low. There were no vegetables, nor jam; no fresh milk for babies and children; just a pound of meal and about half a pound of meat a day, with some scrapings of sugar and coffee; much worse than the diet of the barrack room, or the official diet of the troops on campaign; a diet quite poor enough to allow the rapid spread of disease."[20] Camps were often poorly sited, being vulnerable to the elements, and camp commandants gave little thought to sanitary facilities. In Bethulie, for example, a camp in the Orange Free State, "the smell from the latrines was appalling, and as a result sicknesses broke out because of fouling on the ground and the insufficiency of lavatory facilities." The water supply for the detainees was also contaminated with human waste.[21]

As a result of these conditions, the death rate in the camps shot up as the number of people confined in them increased (see tables 5.1 and 5.2).[22] Fatalities in the camp system, which numbered 550 in May 1901, tripled to 1,675 by July, and then doubled again by October, reaching 3,205 in that month (a fatality rate of 344 per 1,000 internees per year, equal to the death rate for plague).[23]

Table 5.1. Boer and African civilian fatalities in the concentration camps

	Boers	*Africans*
Total number incarcerated	160,000	130,000
Fatalities	27,927	18,003
Percentage of fatalities under age 16	79	81
Percentage of fatalities female or under age 16	94	NA
Fatalities as percentage of total number incarcerated	17	14

Sources: Figures for total number of Boers incarcerated are from André Wessels, "Afrikaners at War," in *The Boer War: Direction, Experience and Image*, ed. John Gooch (London: Frank Cass, 2000), 102. The figure for Boer civilian fatalities, and percentage of fatalities accounted for by women and children of both races is from Fransjohan Pretorius, "The Anglo-Boer War: An Overview," in *Scorched Earth*, ed. Fransjohan Pretorius (Cape Town: Human & Rousseau, 2001), 21. The figure for African fatalities is from Stowell V. Kessler, "The Black and Coloured Concentration Camps," in *Scorched Earth*, 148.

Table 5.2. Concentration camp death tolls by month and race

Month	White deaths	Black deaths
May 1901	550	NA
June	782	261
July	1,675	250
August	2,666	575
September	2,752	728
October	3,205	1,327
November	2,807	2,312
December	2,380	2,831
January 1902	1,805	2,534
February	628	1,466
March	402	972
April	298	630
May	196	523

Sources: Figures for white fatalities for May–July 1901 are from Thomas Pakenham, *The Boer War* (New York: Post Road Press, 1979), 540; for August–October 1901, Fransjohan Pretorius, "The Fate of the Boer Women and Children," in *Scorched Earth*, ed. Fransjohan Pretorius (Cape Town: Human & Rousseau, 2001), 44; for November 1901–February 1902, Byron Farwell, *The Great Boer War* (Hertfordshire: Wordsworth Editions, 1999), 408; for March–May 1902, Pretorius, "Fate of the Boer Women and Children," 49. Figures for black fatalities are from J. S. Mohlamme, "African Refugee Camps in the Boer Republics," in *Scorched Earth*, 120.

Kitchener was uninterested in the alarming increase in mortality: "Kitchener no more desired the death of women and children in the camps than of the wounded Dervishes after Omdurman, or of his own soldiers in the typhoid-stricken hospitals of Bloemfontein. He was simply not interested. What possessed him was a passion to win the war quickly, and to that he was prepared to sacrifice most things, and most people, other than his own small 'band of boys,' to whom he was invariably loyal, whatever their blunders."[24] What concerned the British commander-in-chief was crushing Boer resistance in the quickest, most efficient way possible. If ending the war quickly and preserving the lives of his troops required that Boer families suffer, then so be it.

Proof that the fatalities in the camps were not due to conditions beyond British control came when the army finally transferred control of the system to the civilian administration under High Commissioner Sir Alfred Milner in November 1901. Although he was one of those most responsible for the war's outbreak, throughout the conflict Milner advocated a more humane approach to fighting it, arguing that British troops should clear districts of rebels and then occupy them, rather than sending flying columns up and down the veldt chasing the commandos and burning everything in sight.[25] Once he assumed responsibility for running the camps, the mortality in them dropped precipitously; only 196 people died in the concentration camps during the last month of the war.

The confinement of Africans to concentration camps—and their deaths in large numbers—followed a similar logic and trajectory as that of the white Boers, if delayed a few months because overpopulation occurred earlier in the white camps than in the black camps. Although British apologists have claimed that the Africans were interned for humanitarian reasons and for their own safety, this contention obscures the truth:

> The reason that the British Army established the black concentration camps was for the same basic reason that the white concentration camps were established. And that reason was a military strategy based on an antiguerrilla warfare master plan that consisted of three chess-game-like interlocking pieces: (1) blockhouses and interconnecting barbed wire squares; (2) black and white concentration camps, and (3) massive sweeps by the British flying columns . . . the prevention of logistical and intelligence support to the Boer commandos was the primary reason for their [whites and blacks] being swept off the Boer farms into the concentration camps.[26]

Native camps suffered from even worse neglect than those that housed whites: they often lacked latrines, blacks had to work for (and in some cases also pay for) their rations, and the British provided medical care only if illness threatened the labor supply or the health of the army or the white settler community.[27] The leading study of the black concentration camps in the Boer War has documented eighteen thousand fatalities, and conservatively estimates that a minimum of twenty thousand deaths actually occurred.[28] The study concludes: "Based on the experience with the black and white concentration camps from September 1900 until June 1901, and the high death rates in those camps which were much better equipped, the British Army must have known that there was a high risk of the thousands of deaths that followed. As long as these camps were no threat to the military or the white camps or communities, adequate medical intervention was not undertaken."[29]

Outbreak and Course of the War

Ever since General Sir George Colley's ignominious defeat at Majuba Hill in the First Anglo-Boer War, the British had been itching for a rematch.[30] The discovery of immense gold deposits in Boer territory in 1886 did nothing to dampen British ardor, and political conditions in the Transvaal by the mid 1890s appeared to provide the needed pretext for intervention.[31] By this time the non-Boer population (or *Uitlanders*, as the Boers called them) of the South African Republic outnumbered the Boers, an unpleasant reality that had forced Transvaal president Paul Kruger to tinker with the electoral rules to preserve Boer rule.[32] The embarrassment of the ill-fated Jameson Raid notwithstanding, Britain's designs on South Africa persisted.[33] Negotiations between Sir Alfred Milner and Kruger at Bloemfontein from May 31–June 6, 1899—despite concessions on the political rights of the *Uitlanders* by Kruger—brought the two sides no closer to an agreement. The Transvaalers eventually rescinded their Bloemfontein concessions, and both sides prepared for war. British troop reinforcements began to flow to South Africa while the Transvaal activated its defensive alliance with the Orange Free State and both Boer republics mobilized their citizen armies.

Balance of Forces. At the outset of the fighting, as shown in table 5.3, the Boers outnumbered British forces in the region by a margin of three-to-one.[34] British forces in Natal, moreover, were dangerously divided into two forward garrisons at Dundee and Ladysmith where they were vulnerable to encirclement if the Boers invaded the province. The combined regular armies of the Orange Free State and the Transvaal, meanwhile, numbered forty thousand in peacetime, but by October approximately fifty-five thousand to sixty thousand men were available for service, thirty five thousand to forty-two thousand of whom were deployed along the borders of the two republics.[35] After the Jameson Raid exposed the poor military preparedness of his state, Kruger rearmed his citizen soldiers (known as burghers) by procuring thirty-seven thousand German-made Mauser rifles. The Transvaalers also acquired 75mm and 155mm artillery pieces from Creusot in France as well as 75mm field guns and 120mm howitzers from Krupp's in Germany.[36]

Table 5.3. Manpower and fatalities of the Second Anglo-Boer War

	British	Boers
Manpower at start of war	20,000	55–60,000
Fielded forces, end 1900	200,000	20,000
Total manpower employed	478,435	87,365
Military fatalities	21,942	6,189
Civilian fatalities	NA	27,927
Total war deaths	21,942	34,116

Sources: Figures for initial British and Boer troop strengths are from Bill Nasson, *The South African War 1899–1902* (London: Arnold, 1999), 61, 68. Figures for fielded forces at the end of 1900 and total Boer manpower employed (which included 2,120 foreign volunteers and 13,300 Boers from Cape Colony and Natal) are from Thomas Pakenham, *The Boer War* (New York: Post Road Press, 1979), 525, 607. Figures for total British manpower employed, military fatalities, civilian fatalities, and total war deaths are from Fransjohan Pretorius, "The Anglo-Boer War: An Overview," in *Scorched Earth*, ed. Fransjohan Pretorius (Cape Town: Human & Rousseau, 2001), 21. British manpower included 30,000 black soldiers, and British fatalities are broken down as follows: 5,774 killed in action, 2,918 died of wounds, and 13,250 died of illness.

Phase One: The Conventional War. The Boers capitalized on their initial military advantage by launching an invasion of Natal in the east and Cape Colony in the west, hoping that early defeats would discourage the British and make them amenable to a negotiated settlement. The Boers in fact won a series of quick victories but could not defeat the British decisively.[37] According to one historian of the war, "Given the balance at the outset, it was not altogether surprising that the war should have gone badly for the British; the Boers had the troops, the equipment, the field intelligence, the mobility, and the armaments to shake their enemy hard."[38] By choosing to wage siege warfare, however, and failing to seize critical rail junctions in Cape Colony or ports like Durban, the Boers ceded the initiative to their rapidly reinforcing opponents.

The British wasted little time in striking back. Throughout October, British troops poured into South Africa, but the first British counteroffensive in December failed utterly to obtain its objectives and suffered heavy casualties at the hands of the Boer commandos.[39] "Black Week"—as these British defeats became popularly known—prompted the War Office to sack Redvers Buller as commander-in-chief and replace him with Field Marshal Lord Frederick Roberts, assisted by Lord Kitchener as chief of staff. With new leadership and a flood of new troops, the tide began to turn in Britain's favor.[40] Piet Cronjé's defeat and surrender of four thousand men (roughly 10 percent of the total Boer army) at Paardeberg in late February 1900 devastated the Boer cause and precipitated a general retreat. One after another the key Boer towns fell: Roberts took Bloemfontein, the capital of the Orange Free State, on March 13, and Johannesburg and Pretoria (the Transvaal capital) fell on May 31 and June 5, respectively. The war appeared to be over, as eight thousand Transvaal burghers surrendered by the end of June, joining six thousand of their Free State brethren who likewise quit the war.[41] On September 1 Roberts annexed the South African Republic to Britain, then turned the situation over to his deputy Kitchener and returned to Britain on November 28.

Phase Two: The Guerrilla War. The Boer defeats in February swept aside older generals like Cronjé and Joubert and brought to prominence a younger, more dynamic generation of leaders, including Louis Botha, Koos de la Rey, and Christiaan de Wet. At a war council on March 20, 1900, Boer commanders decided to continue the war, but de Wet in particular "urged the general abandonment of burdening wagon laagers which stunted speed, stifled flexibility, and offered too obvious a target for enemy guns."[42] Henceforth the Boer commandos would travel light and capitalize on their mobility and elusiveness to strike at isolated British outposts and lines of communication. De Wet previewed this campaign in mid February by ambushing part of Roberts's supply column of two hundred wagons and three thousand oxen at Waterval Drift. The British steamroller depended on a lengthy logistical chain for supplies of food and ammunition.

As British forces used their superior numbers to overwhelm the defensive advantage of entrenchments and well-aimed rifle fire, the Boers increasingly abandoned set-piece confrontations with the British, breaking up into smaller units and mounting hit-and-run operations on the supply lines of Roberts's army. De Wet scored a series of major successes in late March and early April against British installations and columns, but it was his attack on Roodewal station on June 7 that prompted Roberts—realizing the threat to his lines of communication—to announce that houses in the vicinity of Boer attacks on rail and telegraph lines would be burned in retaliation. Furthermore, the British began to confiscate the property of Boer men who served as commandos and force their families out "destitute and homeless."[43]

The last pitched battle of the war was fought at Bergendal in late August. Possessing a four-to-one numerical advantage, British forces under Buller repeatedly smashed the Boer line until it finally cracked and the burghers took flight. This defeat confirmed to the Boer generals that only guerrilla tactics could persuade the British to come to terms: "These generals still clung to the hope that by prolonging hostilities they might sap Britain sufficiently to bring about an end to the war by negotiation, not by their having to succumb to a clear-cut imperial victory."[44]

The First British Reaction: Farm Burning

Defensive advantage was the hallmark of the Boer War in each of its phases. The Boer sieges of Ladysmith, Kimberley, and Mafeking, for example, failed because the attackers could not afford to risk the costs of assaulting the towns, choosing instead to induce them to surrender via starvation and half-hearted bombardment. Later, the British reverses of Black Week were caused by the advantage that accrued to concealed defenders armed with accurate, rapid-firing small arms. As Thomas Pakenham describes it, "In the new-style war pioneered by the Boers—long-range, smokeless, rapid-firing rifles plus trenches—the balance of advantage, as we have seen, had tilted dramatically to the side of the defenders. New, more subtle methods of attack were needed, as well as greater numerical superiority."[45] This defensive advantage—which cost the British dearly in their first counteroffensive—did not immediately spawn a policy of civilian victimization because the British were as yet outside the territory of the Boer republics. When British troops finally penetrated Boer territory, however, overwhelming with manpower the advantages of terrain and technology enjoyed by the Boers, not only was there "little effective check on the natural tendency of an army to loot and destroy 'enemy' property," but as the Boer commandos refused to come to terms and instead took to the veldt to wage guerrilla war, scorched earth soon became official policy.[46]

Farm Burning Initiated. The first British response to the budding guerrilla campaign was to institute a policy of destroying the property of Boer men found to be on commando. On assuming command, Roberts initially pursued a conciliatory policy toward Boer combatants, promising in a proclamation dated February 17, 1900, that those who surrendered "will not be made to suffer in their persons or property on account of their having taken up arms in obedience to the order of their Government."[47] Roberts repeated this offer on March 15, two days after occupying the capital of the Orange Free State and still maintained as late as the end of May that commandos who capitulated would be allowed to return home.[48] The British press, however, roundly criticized Roberts's amnesty policy as overly lenient; even members of the government began pushing for a harsher policy toward Boer noncombatants. Lord Lansdowne, in early 1900 still the secretary of state for war (he would shortly become foreign secretary) and an early exponent of a moderate policy, urged his military commander to adopt a sterner attitude in May: "I think you were right to begin by showing great leniency. The impression created was good on this side and probably on yours except among the most violent partisans. But experience has shown that your confidence has been grossly abused and you will be supported if you insist on thorough going measures for disarming the suspect part of the population and if you inflict stern retribution where unfair advantage has been taken of your clemency."[49]

As the carrot of amnesty had little effect, and the Boers refused to capitulate even as the British captured their major towns, Roberts turned to the stick, issuing two further proclamations in quick succession. The first, published on June 1, threatened "all inhabitants . . . who after 14 days from the date of this Proclamation . . . may be found in arms against Her Majesty within the said colony, that they will be liable to be dealt with as rebels and to suffer in person and property accordingly."[50] Two weeks later, Roberts threatened to take residents prisoner and burn their houses in areas where acts of sabotage were committed against British lines of communication.[51] "It was a sign, officially," notes Owen Coetzer, "for an orgy of farm burning."[52] As General Methuen commented in 1901, "It became the custom first of all to burn farms from which a treacherous attack was made upon our troops, then to burn all the farms within a radius of ten miles from any point on the railway at which an attack was made by the enemy, then to confiscate or burn anything which was the property of any Boer fighting for his country."[53]

Coercion by Punishment. Two logics underpinned the new policy of devastation. The first logic was one of deterrence and coercion. According to Pakenham, "The aim of farm burning was strictly military: to make an example of certain families, and so deter the others from aiding De Wet and the guerrillas."[54] The British hoped that by destroying the homes and farms of families known or suspected of providing assistance to the insurgents, the remainder would withhold their support for fear of the consequences of being caught in the act. As Roberts described his policy in September 1900, "I am not in favor of lessening the punishment laid down for any damage done to our railway and telegraph lines. Unless the people generally are made to suffer for misdeeds of those in arms against us the war will never end."[55]

As the year progressed and the farm-burning policy failed to curb Boer guerrilla activities, Roberts began to conceive of his strategy as that of a classic coercion-by-punishment campaign: a means to coerce the commandos into surrendering by inflicting suffering on their families. According to S. B. Spies, "The policy of clearing the country also came to have a further object: to put pressure on the Boers in the field to surrender, by subjecting their dependents to certain hardships."[56] "The more difficulty the people experience about food," Roberts argued in September, "the sooner will the war be ended."[57] British officers putting this policy into practice in the veldt apparently got the message: as one wrote to another, "I gather that Lord Roberts decides to treat the remnant of the burgher forces as brigands and to devastate the country of supplies and to use the consequent starvation as a lever to bring the recalcitrant fanatics to their senses."[58] Government officials in London explicitly approved of this rationale. Prime Minister Salisbury, in one of his few direct comments on the war, called for a harsher policy in a letter to the war minister in December 1900: "I do not like this protection of isolated hills. I should prefer to see a complete protection of lines and bridges; and then you ought to be able to destroy food with flying columns of considerable strength. You will not conquer these people until you have starved them out."[59]

Interdiction. Increasingly, however, the British tended to view all Boer civilians as active or potential guerrilla supporters: "To the British every farm was an outpost; every Boer a spy."[60] The second logic of devastation, therefore, began to come to the fore: to make it impossible for the rebels to live off the land. If Boer civilians could not be deterred from aiding their menfolk, and the commandos could not be coerced by the suffering of their families, then the noncombatant population would have to be prevented physically from aiding the rebels.

The British first tried to turn the Boer republics into a barren landscape incapable of supporting human life. As described by Pakenham, "Farm burning was designed to make guerrilla war impossible, and in certain areas it had already begun to achieve this. The Magalies valley was becoming a blackened desert, useless as a base for De la Rey's guerrillas, so efficient were Clements's columns at burning grain, seizing stock and trampling crops."[61] Kitchener instructed his commanders in the field on August 25 to see to it that "the country is so denuded of forage and supplies that no means of subsistence is left for any commando attempting to make incursions."[62]

"According to this order," writes Spies, "clearing the country was not intended as a punishment for transgressions committed by the inhabitants. Its clearly enunciated aim was to prevent commandos from existing in the districts so cleared."[63]

The testimony of numerous war correspondents and British soldiers confirms the extent of the devastation. "Along the line of march," wrote the *Cape Times* correspondent, "General Campbell has practically denuded the country of livestock and grain stores, whilst the sight of burning farmhouses and farm property is of daily occurrence."[64] One British officer recorded in September 1900 that "the various columns that are now marching about the country are carrying on the work of destruction pretty indiscriminately, and we have burnt and destroyed by now many scores of farms. Ruin, with great hardships and want, which may ultimately border on starvation, must be the result to many families. . . . Our troops are everywhere at work burning and laying waste, and enormous reserves of famine and misery are being laid up for these countries in the future."[65] British columns even began torching entire villages and towns for alleged complicity with Boer commandos.[66] Overall, British forces burnt in excess of thirty thousand Boer farms and forty towns over the course of the conflict, and killed or confiscated millions of head of livestock.[67]

Results of the Scorched Earth Campaign. In the short term, these severe policies undercut British objectives as much as they aided them. Nearly twenty thousand Boer commandos surrendered in mid 1900, but farm burning undoubtedly caused an unknown number to remain in—or return to—the field. In the opinion of many British officers, the scorched earth strategy was counterproductive and prolonged the war: as one officer wrote, "The Burgher out on Commando is bound always to his farm . . . by burning it and sending his family packing, we are only making him a roving desperado, consumed with hatred."[68] Other officers noted that " 'excessive' destructiveness would only end up benefitting the enemy cause by keeping combatants in the field . . . because they no longer had homesteads and a fixed family to which to go."[69] Many Boer men probably believed that the British would destroy their property no matter what they did, so they might as well fight. The British Army's reign of fire, therefore, breathed renewed life into the flagging Boer cause: eight thousand or nine thousand commandos were back in the field by October 1900.[70]

Over the longer term, however, the wholesale destruction visited on the veldt paid handsome dividends. The farm-burning policy without question deeply embittered the Boers against the British, but it clearly diminished their capability to continue fighting. As historian Byron Farwell remarks, "It [farm burning] did not lessen their will to resist, only their means for doing so." Farwell elaborates: "Kitchener's policy of deliberate wholesale destruction was intended to deprive the guerrillas of supplies, and in this he was successful. Even De Wet, ever scornful of British tactics, admitted that 'had not the English burnt the corn by the thousand sacks, the war could have been continued.' "[71] In sum, therefore, farm burning, while provoking increased Boer resistance in the short term, played a significant role in defeating the commandos in the long run. The most authoritative study of the impact of the war on noncombatants supports this conclusion, finding that "considerations which flowed out of the British policy of clearing the country of supplies played an important part in swaying the Boer scales in favour of peace."[72]

The Second British Response: Concentration Camps

The British strategy of farm burning gave rise to the policy of confining Boer civilians to camps in order to prevent them from providing aid and comfort to the commandos. The concentration-camp system apparently began as a means to cope with the increasing numbers of Boer women and children being rendered homeless as the British Army burned down their houses. Although there was some talk of forcing the Boer commandos to care for these unfortunates, and Roberts did send twenty-five hundred civilians to the Boer lines in eastern Transvaal in July 1900, British commanders realized something had to be done with these people lest they starve right there on the veldt.[73]

Here lies the terrible irony of the concentration camps: these compounds, which ended up killing so many innocents, were founded at least partially for a humanitarian purpose. According to Emily Hobhouse, who became an outspoken critic of the camps, "Humanity forbade, at this stage a continuance of the practice of their [Boer women and children] being left outside their ruined houses, and so it came to pass that they were brought in by convoys and placed in small camps which had been established for refugees."[74] Of course, as Coetzer points out, the British themselves caused the calamity they sought to remedy: "It was Britain's 'humanitarian desire' to safeguard the women and children which brought about the establishment of the camps. That they (Britain) had in the first place been responsible for the destruction of the farms escaped them entirely."[75]

The Military Rationale for the Camps. Although the humanitarian impulse that helped spawn the camps is admirable, it was accompanied and soon superseded by a military rationale. "The concentration camps were, in fact, established for military reasons" to deny supplies to the Boers, according to Spies. "A further military consideration governing the policy of clearing the population into concentration camps was the belief that if the women were taken away from their homes, men on commando would surrender so that they could join them in the camps."[76] The first camps to accommodate the displaced Boer women and children—many of whom did not consent to their confinement (which renders the term "refugee" camp used by the British a misnomer)—were established at Bloemfontein and Pretoria in September 1900. Pakenham writes that the population of these and other camps began to balloon in early 1901 when Kitchener launched a series of drives "to flush out the guerrillas . . . and to sweep the country bare of everything that could give sustenance to the guerrillas: not only horses, but cattle, sheep, women, and children."[77] The "first priority" of this roundup of "undesirables"—as the dependents of Boer combatants were known—was to "prevent the guerrillas being helped by civilians": "Kitchener felt that once the Boer women and children were gathered in camps the burghers on commando would no longer be able to get food from the women on the farms. He also believed that the burghers would lay down their arms in order to be reunited with their families."[78] This sweep was largely completed by autumn 1901, by which time thirty-four camps held about 110,000 Boer civilians.[79] It should be noted that Kitchener informed the government of his intentions in December 1900: "The Cabinet fully agreed with the proposed policy and [British High Commissioner in South Africa] Milner did not at the time or shortly after the inception of the scheme raise any objection."[80]

In choosing to incarcerate Boer women and children, Roberts and Kitchener seized on the example provided by Spanish General Valeriano Weyler in putting down the Cuban insurrection of 1895–98.[81] Weyler was widely condemned during that conflict for herding Cuba's rural inhabitants into camps (known as *reconcentrados*) and then systematically devastating the countryside to deprive the rebels of recruits and supplies.[82] The inadequate provisioning and deficient sanitation of the *reconcentrados*, however, made them breeding grounds for disease, which eventually killed between 100,000 and 300,000 Cuban civilians.[83] According to Stanley Payne, "Most of the suffering in the *reconcentraciones* was caused by the Army's inability to care for the needs of the relocated population rather than by a Spanish policy of violence or cruelty."[84] The British surely knew of Weyler's techniques and their deadly outcome, since he was widely castigated at the time in the press. As the war dragged on in South Africa, though, some London newspapers began to press for the "Weyler method" to be applied to the Boers.[85]

In combination, the three aspects of British counterinsurgency strategy proved effective: obliterating Boer sources of supply through farm burning, crop destruction, and killing of livestock; preventing the sympathetic Boer civilians from helping the rebels by removing the population to concentration camps; and driving the Boer commandos against blockhouse and barbed-wire barriers with flying columns. British columns swept the country clean of anything that could support human life, and "by constricting available territory and penning in the enemy Kitchener gradually countered the Boers' evasive warfare."[86] Moreover, the "high civilian mortality" in the concentration camps had a "devastating impact . . . on the morale of republican leadership . . . it seemed to be threatening the very reproductive future of the Boer people."[87] These factors—supplemented by a growing threat from their African neighbors, no hope of a rising by the Cape Boers, and a growing number (over five thousand) of Boer converts to the British cause—convinced the twenty thousand so-called "bitter-enders" that the war must end.

The Impact of Liberalism and Democracy

The origins and conduct of the war in South Africa had a decidedly non-liberal flavor. Liberal wars are supposed to be fought in self-defense only or to promote liberal democracy abroad.[88] Britain's war against the Orange Free State and the Transvaal possessed neither of these qualities. Although the Boers technically initiated hostilities, the war was clearly engineered by the British—in the person of Alfred Milner—to gain unfettered access to the bountiful mineral resources in the South African Republic and to impose Britain's "imperial political supremacy" in the region.[89] Milner found a convenient pretext in the disenfranchisement of the British settler population, but this issue was merely a legitimatizing instrument with which to advance ulterior interests.

The onset of this illiberal war in South Africa was greeted by an outburst of patriotic fervor in Great Britain and not a few bloodthirsty calls for the extermination of the Boers as "a plague-infected rat."[90] Although opposition to the war existed, according to Bill Nasson, "Once hostilities had got under way, and particularly after the dispiriting early British reverses, anti-war or equivocal Liberal, Labour, trade union, and socialist positions split, and minority opposition to the war became ever more marginal and muted; there continued to be such radical voices, but they were few and diminishing. While the issues of the war may have meant precious little, if anything, to working-class people, its rights and wrongs were quite secondary to the need that it be won."[91] Jane Waterston, a physician who would later serve on the commission charged with investigating conditions in the concentration camps, expressed the standard national partiality when she wrote:

> Judging by some of the hysterical whining going on in England at the present time, it would seem as if we might neglect or half-starve our faithful soldiers, and keep our civilian population eating their hearts out here as long as we fed and pampered people who have not even the grace to say thank you for the care bestowed upon them. At present there is the danger that the Boers will waken up to have a care for their womenfolk and will go on fighting for some time, so as to keep them in comfortable winter quarters at our expense, and thus our women and children will lose a few more of their husbands and fathers.[92]

The early defeats and hardships suffered by British forces galvanized British public opinion in favor of the war and elevated victory—and the preservation of British lives—above humane conduct toward Boer civilians.

The elections in the autumn of 1900 provide a fine illustration of the indifference to the miseries of Boer civilians displayed by even the liberal segment of the British political spectrum. The Conservative government of Salisbury conducted the campaign as a referendum on the government's conduct of the war and tarred all criticism as unpatriotic and "pro-Boer." Roberts's farm-burning policy had been in effect for several months, with results widely reported in the British press, but inexplicably, "The Liberals made almost no references to the drastic methods which Roberts had begun to adopt in an effort to end the war . . . it is odd, considering the political storm that would soon burst over the government's head because of farm burning, how meekly the Liberals accepted the policy at the time."[93] Unsurprisingly, the Conservatives trounced the opposition in the so-called "Khaki" elections, earning an iron-clad majority of 134 seats over the combination of the Liberals and Irish Nationalists.

Enter Emily Hobhouse. Prominent Liberals, such as Henry Campbell-Bannerman and David Lloyd George, would later use the results of Emily Hobhouse's reports of terrible suffering and death in the concentration camps to condemn the government's conduct of the war as "methods of barbarism."[94] Hobhouse, described by Pakenham as a "dumpy, forty-one-year-old spinster from Cornwall" and by Kitchener as "that bloody woman," visited the camps in early 1901 as part of her work for the South African Women and Children Distress Fund.[95] She, more than anyone else, was responsible for publicizing the squalid conditions and startlingly high death rates in the camps. Hobhouse briefed Campbell-Bannerman on her return to London, and he and Lloyd George led the Liberals in denouncing the government in the House of Commons. Secretary for War St. John Brodrick steadfastly denied the opposition's charges, averring that "the policy of sweeping the country had been forced on them by the guerrillas" and downplaying the severity of health and sanitation problems in the camps.[96] His cause was assisted by the fact that Kitchener kept a tight lid on the mortality figures, and a motion against the government by David Lloyd George was easily defeated in June 1901. By the time these alarming figures were revealed in August, the House was about to leave for its five-month recess; "no one bothered Brodrick with further questions about the camps."[97] Regarding the June debate in the Commons, Hobhouse wrote:

> Very clearly in my remembrance of that debate stands out Mr. Herbert Lewis's attempt to fix the attention of the House on the humanitarian side of

the question. The House was unsympathetic, and neither knew nor cared to hear. Humanity was appealed to in vain, and Mr. Lewis was literally howled down by continual noise and wearied shouts of "Divide" from the crowded Ministerial benches. The picture thus exhibited of callousness and impatience, not willing even to listen to sufferings innocently endured, contrasted badly with scenes fresh in my mind in South Africa. In common with the Boer women, I had felt sure that English humanity would not fail to respond instantly if the facts were clearly understood. I was wrong; no barbarisms in South Africa could equal the cold cruelty of that indifferent House.[98]

The government sought to forestall further meddling by Hobhouse in South Africa by appointing a Ladies Committee to report on conditions in the camps—a commission composed of women sympathetic to the war that would presumably be easier to control than a free-lancing activist.[99] Unfortunately for the government, the Fawcett Commission, named for its chairwoman Millicent Fawcett, largely confirmed Hobhouse's accusations. As Fawcett made clear in her report to Milner in December 1901, "The deaths were *not* simply the result of circumstances beyond the control of the British . . . the Fawcett Commission pointed a feminine finger at the military (and, of course, male) red tape in which the camps had been trussed: the spread of the epidemics should have been foreseen; elementary rules of sanitation should not have been forgotten; vegetables should have been provided; doctors and nurses should have been rushed to the scene from England when the epidemics first broke out."[100] Meanwhile, Kitchener had finally turned over control of all of the camps to Milner's civilian administration, and the government, catching the scent of a scandal in the air, directed him to take steps to curb the death rate.[101]

Implications. The Hobhouse scandal has several implications. First, in a partial vindication for the liberal-norms argument, the British government feared that the high death rates among Boer women and children in the concentration camps would bring domestic consequences, which led them to improve the conditions in the camps, reforms that drastically reduced the number of deaths. Liberal norms, therefore, backed by the threat of a political setback for the government in Parliament, helped moderate the abuse of noncombatants in South Africa.[102] But this same combination of norms and institutions could not deter or prevent civilian victimization from occurring in the first place. Moreover, by the time the government moderated its policy, the war was well in hand and thus improving conditions in the camps did not compromise military effectiveness.

Second, the Boer War demonstrates that publics in liberal states take on decidedly nonliberal attitudes toward enemies during war. The British public lined up in patriotic fashion behind the war effort, and although calls for harsh treatment of Boer civilians were exceptional, no broad-based public protest ever emerged over the concentration camp death rates.[103] Milner's statement in December 1901 that "the continuance of the present state of affairs [i.e., the high death rate in the camps] for another two or three months will undoubtedly blow us all out of the water" indicates that government officials feared a public backlash against the harsh policy they had implemented toward Boer civilians.[104] But Hobhouse's depiction of British public opinion shows that the government need not have worried:

> But in spite of the Blue Books, debates, and publication of facts, ignorance still prevailed about the Boer women and children, only it was now a willful ignorance. . . . In a word, the majority did not heed or did not care, while others were glad to avail themselves of the new reasons given for the origin of the camps by Mr. Chamberlain in the House of Commons [on January 19, 1902]. He assured the country that the "whole responsibility for such misery as has been caused rested upon the shoulders of the Boer Commandant."[105]

Finally, the Hobhouse scandal and its outcome imply that civilian victimization by democracies may be easier to control—if not prevent—in wars in which the state's survival is not at stake or where participation in the conflict is seen as voluntary or optional. Starving German civilians in World War I, or bombing Germans and Japanese in World War II needed little justification as British and American publics recognized (or were persuaded of) the direness of the threat those states represented. Liberal democratic governments seem to worry more about the attitudes of their domestic publics toward strategies that harm or target civilians in conflicts where the connection between the war and the state's security is less apparent, such as the United States in Vietnam. This concern does not always stop large numbers of non-combatants from being killed—nor is it even based in the public's actual views, which tend to be quite permissive when it comes to killing enemy civilians. Democracies, however, may be more vulnerable to what have been labeled "hypocrisy costs": reputational costs imposed by other actors—such as states or nongovernmental organizations—when liberal states violate the norms they otherwise live by and try to impose on others, of which the norm against killing noncombatants is particularly prominent.[106] Ironically, therefore, the globalization of liberal human rights norms can create international costs (rather than domestic ones) for targeting civilians that could mitigate the damage done in relatively minor wars.[107]

Other Alternative Explanations

Comparing the conduct of the Boer War to another British war fought in southern Africa—the Zulu War of 1879—largely contradicts the predictions of the identity theory, which posits that civilian victimization should be restricted to those wars in which one or more of the belligerents views its opponent as a "barbarian" or "savage" society. Colonial wars should be easy cases for the identity argument: civilized European powers confronted and conquered groups they considered to be racially inferior. However, European states' treatment of noncombatants in these wars seems to vary more with the type of resistance offered—and hence the cost and difficulty of achieving military victory—than with the identity of the opponent.[108] Britons may have viewed the Boers as rough and lacking in civilization, but at least they were white and descended from Europeans. The Zulus, on the other hand, were seen as a barbarous, warlike, African race; British propaganda about them was filled with blood-curdling imagery and reflected the widespread view that the Zulus were innately aggressive. A favorite refrain of British observers was that the ferocity of Zulu warriors in battle was due to sexual frustration, as the king did not allow his troops to marry until after they had been released from active duty. This led Sir Bartle Frere, Britain's South African emissary, to refer to them as "celibate man-slaying gladiators."[109] Yet maltreatment of civilians was far more pervasive in the war against the Boers—a costly, protracted, frustrating, guerrilla conflict—than in the relatively short and easy war against the Zulus. In the Boer War, both whites and blacks alike were swept from the veldt for the same reason: to prevent the Boer commandos from obtaining supplies. Large numbers of civilians of both races died in the camps. On balance, the British were probably more negligent in their operation of the African camps—demonstrating a racist bias—but even there the death rates declined in the last few months of the war.

On the whole, therefore, this pair of cases casts doubt on the thesis that the opponent's identity has an independent causal effect on the likelihood that its civilians will be targeted. More plausible is the argument that conflicts of interest cause perceptions of the other's identity to be redefined. The more severe the conflict—measured in this book by the costliness of the war—the more likely that the enemy will come to be viewed as evil or barbarous.

THE Second Anglo-Boer War demonstrates how the escalating costs of fighting and the inability to defeat guerrilla insurgencies with conventional tactics provoke belligerents to take action against the civilian population. In guerrilla conflicts, the ties between insurgents and civilians are especially intimate, since the former depend on the latter directly for food, shelter, intelligence, and manpower. These ties give the army incentives to cut those ties, either by using violence to intimidate and deter noncombatants from providing support to the rebels, or by "draining the sea": removing civilians from the theater of battle and thereby preventing the insurgents from obtaining any supplies. Kalyvas hypothesizes that incumbent violence is usually indiscriminate at first because the government lacks information on who is supporting the rebels, and thus lashes out blindly. This tends to be ineffective because it drives the uncommitted into the rebel camp simply out of the instinct for self-preservation. Over time, however, as the army obtains better information on the precise identity of defectors, violence becomes increasingly discriminate and effective, since it targets the guilty, thereby removing actual supporters and having a better deterrent effect.[110]

The evidence in this chapter has demonstrated the opposite trend: the British were never able to penetrate the civilian support network of the Boers, and thus could not gain the information necessary to shift to more discriminate violence. British leaders became increasingly convinced that the entire population was in league with the rebels and eventually concluded that the only way to defeat the rebels was to target all civilians. This strategy proved effective because the Boers were uniquely vulnerable: the population from which they drew their support was quite small and geographically concentrated. This allowed the British to sweep them into camps, deprive the rebels of supplies, and use the suffering of civilians to coerce the insurgents to quit. Under certain conditions, therefore, the scope of civilian victimization in guerrilla wars can expand rather than contract and prove not only more deadly, but effective as well.

[6]

Territorial Annexation and Civilian Victimization

The Founding of the State of Israel, 1947–49

The bulk of this book has been devoted to delineating the desperation causal mechanism for civilian victimization. This chapter, however, turns to the second causal mechanism: territorial annexation. The desperation logic makes no assumptions about belligerents' war aims and ascribes the occurrence of civilian victimization solely to battlefield events that take place after the war has begun: failure to win a quick and decisive victory, higher than anticipated costs of fighting, or the failure of particular counterforce strategies. Civilian victimization is adopted as a means to coerce the enemy—whether it be a state or a rebel force—to capitulate.

In the territorial mechanism, by contrast, at least one of the belligerents intends to conquer and annex territory from its adversary. This war aim tends to produce a form of civilian victimization different than that found in wars of attrition, that is, violence not to coerce the enemy to quit the war but violence meant to terrorize a population into flight. In other words, wars of territorial annexation produce cleansing because invaders often conclude that the population living in the conquered territory—which usually shares the national identity of the adversary—cannot be trusted and represents a threat. Belligerents tend to reach this conclusion under two sets of conditions: either when a conflict erupts between two intermingled populations, or when one belligerent attempts to annex territory where many of the inhabitants are of a different ethnicity or nationality. Cleansing is likely in these types of cases because belligerents perceive the other group's civilians as representing a security threat. Not only do enemy civilians embody a potential fifth column, but they may also be the objects of rescue attempts by fellow group members located in nearby regions.

The basic argument of this chapter, therefore, is that when war breaks out between intermingled antagonists, or when a belligerent seeks to conquer territory but fears that the population will rebel and pose a permanent threat to its control over the area, a strategy of civilian victimization designed to eradicate that group is the likely outcome. Conversely, when an invader perceives little or no threat from a particular group, such as when group members share substantial traits (religion, language, or other characteristics) in common with the conqueror, the invading force will employ strategies of assimilation rather than eradication.

This chapter examines territorial annexation arguments in the context of the Palestine War of 1947–49, particularly the origins of the Palestinian refugee problem. The historical record is clear: before the war top Jewish leaders viewed the creation of a Jewish state in part of Palestine via partition as a first step toward acquiring the remainder of the country. Furthermore, although there was no explicit, formally enunciated policy of expulsion at the war's outset, there was an informal understanding among Jewish political leaders and military commanders based on Zionist ideology and the role of "transfer" in Zionist thinking that an Israel with as few Arabs as possible was preferred. The evidence indicates that future Israeli prime minister David Ben-Gurion was unequivocal on this matter, but that he refrained from issuing written orders that would leave a paper trail. Jewish military plans, most notably Plan D, specifically endorsed reprisals against civilians and the leveling of villages and ejection of villagers who resisted Jewish occupation. Moreover, as the war progressed, and the Zionist dream of a homogeneous Jewish state in Palestine seemed as if it might become a reality, forcible expulsion became an increasingly explicit policy. This policy was not always carried out in a uniform fashion in the field, but banishment of the Palestinians grew more prevalent later in the war. Finally, Jewish forces exploited the fear induced in the Arab population by a number of prominent massacres, such as those at Deir Yassin and Lydda and Ramle, to frighten the Arab masses into flight. In short, if expulsion was not Zionist policy at the outset, it became such over time, and at the heart of this strategy was the fear that leaving the Arab population in place would pose a permanent danger of a fifth column in the Israeli rear.

After a brief section that elaborates the logic of territorial annexation and civilian victimization, and which gives examples from other cases, I turn to the Palestine case. I first outline the causes and history of the war. I then review the territorial objectives of Zionism and the history of Zionist thinking on the subject of transferring the Arabs of Palestine to other areas of the Arab world. The evidence shows that Jewish leaders hoped to obtain all of Palestine for the Jewish state and saw partition as a first step toward this goal. Moreover, transfer was inherent in Zionist ideology from the beginning, and over time most leading Zionists came to accept the necessity of displacing the Arabs as essential for the survival of the Jewish state. Third, I examine the implications of the Yishuv's military plans—particularly Plan D—for Palestinian civilians. Was Plan D a blueprint for the expulsion of the Arab population? Did it provide a warrant for the wholesale destruction and emptying of Palestinian villages? I examine the Arab flight from Haifa to discern Zionist policy toward the Palestinians in this phase of the war. Fourth, I use the massacre and expulsions from Lydda and Ramle, and Operation Hiram in central Galilee to illustrate the increasingly open and deliberate nature of violence and expulsions as the war progressed. Finally, I examine the effect of Israel's democratic regime type, perceptions of Arab identity, and the organizational culture of Jewish military forces on civilian victimization. I also highlight the contribution of desperation in causing the shift from a defensive to an offensive strategy in 1948. I argue that the underlying desire on the part of Zionist leaders for a Palestine without Arabs, combined with the desperate military position the Yishuv faced in early 1948, produced an increasingly open policy of expulsion of the Arab population.

TERRITORIAL ANNEXATION AND CIVILIAN VICTIMIZATION

The reasons why the goal of annexing territory can lead to civilian victimization are amply demonstrated by the war in Bosnia from 1992 to 1995. In 1992, the declaration of independence by Bosnia's Muslim-led government from Yugoslavia triggered a countersecession by Bosnia's Serbian community. The Bosnian Serbs hoped to carve out a state for themselves in the eastern parts of Bosnia adjacent to Serbia and extending into Serb-inhabited areas in the northwest of the country. Eastern Bosnia, however, was heavily populated by Bosnian Muslims. The Serb leadership knew that a substantial Muslim population represented an obstacle to a Serb state and a threat to its survival, since in a war for secession against the government, local Muslims would constitute a "fifth column" who could attack Serb forces from the rear.[1] Bosnian Serb militias, therefore, backed by units of the Serb-dominated Yugoslav National Army, terrorized the Muslim population in the towns along the Drina River in the conflict's early phases in an effort to drive them out of territory the Serbs claimed as their own.[2]

The source of this fear of subversion is that civilians share a common identity with the enemy, whether the foe is a state, an ethno-religious group, or an ideological faction, and belligerents assume that because of this shared identification, civilians will at least sympathize with the enemy and possibly even support it militarily. This is the same logic that leads to severe, exterminationist-type violence in guerrilla conflicts: the government or the rebel group concludes that the entire civilian population supports the enemy and thus there is no point in distinguishing between combatants and noncombatants. But it is not the same as the barbaric identity argument, which posits that the enemy must be viewed as savage or uncivilized for civilian victimization to occur. In most interstate wars, the common identity in question is nationality or ethnicity, but this need not always be the case. When the Spanish Civil War—an ideological conflict—broke out in 1936, for instance, loyalists of the Republic and the Nationalists were highly inter- mingled and became trapped in zones controlled by the enemy. According to one historian, "Throughout Nationalist Spain, all Masons, all members of Popular Front parties, all members of trade unions and, in many areas, everyone who had voted for the Popular Front in the elections of February were arrested and many of these were shot." Meanwhile, in Republican- held areas, "All who could conceivably be suspected of sympathy for the Nationalist rising were in danger."[3] Membership in the upper class, bour- geoisie, or a Catholic political party was often enough to be a death warrant. Republicans also targeted the Roman Catholic clergy because the church supported the Nationalists, and priests were viewed as an enemy within.[4]

The most common scenario in interstate wars, however, is when one country attempts to wrest possession of a particular piece of territory away from another state. Typically, the population of the area in question is split between nationals of the current possessor and the challenger or, in a few cases, the area is inhabited by people that—although identified with nei- ther side—each party claims are "lapsed" members of its own group. An example of the former is the Greek invasion of western Asia Minor in 1919, an area of heavy Greek settlement claimed by the Greek government. After landing in Smyrna on the coast, the Greek Army advanced eastward into Anatolia, "massacring, burning, pillaging and raping as they went," driv- ing Turkish civilians out of the areas in which the Greek population was concentrated.[5] According to a British commission that investigated Greek conduct in the area, "There is a systematic plan of destruction and extinc- tion of the Moslem population."[6] The Turks, for their part, accepted the "principle of expelling large portions of Greeks as an alien and intractably hostile nation within Turkey."[7] When the tide of battle turned in 1922, the Turkish Army returned the favor in a campaign that culminated in the mas- sacre and burning of Smyrna (now Izmir), ending the Greek presence in Asia Minor.[8]

Prussia's claim to Alsace-Lorraine in the Franco-Prussian War, on the other hand, resulted in a very different outcome. Alsace was formerly part of the Holy Roman Empire until King Louis XIV annexed it to France in the late seventeenth century. It was widely believed in Prussia that the popu- lation of the two provinces was German at heart. Heinrich von Treitschke expressed the prevailing view when he wrote in 1870 that Alsace and Lorraine "are ours by the right of the sword. . . . At all times the subjec- tion of a German race to France has been an unhealthy thing; today it is an offense against the reason of History—a vassalship of free men to half- educated barbarians."[9] This belief in the fundamentally German nature of the disputed provinces' population led Prussia to prefer a policy of assimi- lation rather than expulsion.[10] In a similar vein, Bulgaria treated the two types of Muslims it acquired in the First Balkan War differently, depending on how susceptible to assimilation each group was thought to be. Muslim ethnic Turks—viewed as part and parcel of the enemy—were attacked and expelled, whereas Bulgarian-speaking Muslims—known as *pomaks*—were thought to be less resistant to integration and thus for the most part allowed to remain. Bulgaria instead tried to convert the *pomaks* to Christianity and assimilate them into Bulgarian society.[11]

Because the intention to annex an adversary's territory is both a reason to go to war and a reason to target civilians in war—and thus the likelihood of the latter depends on the former—it matters whether certain types of states are more likely to engage in territorial aggrandizement than others. One might hypothesize that nondemocracies would be more likely to seek territorial aggrandizement than democracies, which tend to be more satisfied with the status quo. In interstate wars, however, controlling for the number of each regime type in the dataset, there is virtually no difference in the rates at which democracies and nondemocracies engage in wars to permanently seize territory from a neighboring state.[12] As table 6.1 shows, moreover, the relative rates at which the two regime types target noncombatants in wars of territorial annexation are almost identical: 83 percent for democracies versus 81 percent for autocracies.[13] Although the absolute number of cases is small, when democracies do fight wars to annex territory, they tend to behave much like their autocratic counterparts.[14]

An excellent example of this similarity in behavior is provided by the Balkan Wars of 1912–13. Each member of the Balkan League—Serbia, Montenegro, Bulgaria, and Greece (three autocracies and a democracy)—hoped to make territorial gains in Europe at the expense of the Ottoman Empire, weakened by years of internal decay and distracted by its war with Italy in Libya. Considerable numbers of Turks lived in the empire's European lands, however, and they would have to be removed to ensure the security and permanence of conquest. The Balkan states, therefore, mainly victimized Turkish villagers in the first war, but when the former allies turned on each other in 1913, each sought to drive its adversary's population out of the lands it hoped to control. The Carnegie Commission sent to investigate the conduct of the Balkan Wars, for example, reported that immediately on the outbreak of the first war, Bulgarian troops and irregulars—in what the commission called "national tactics"—burned Muslim villages, massacred civilians, and destroyed cultural institutions. Bulgaria's allies behaved similarly toward the Turks. In the second war the Balkan states fell to quarrelling over the spoils and Bulgaria got the worst of it. Democratic Greece was one of the worst perpetrators of civilian victimization, producing graphic propaganda inciting violence against Bulgarians and sanctioning a strategy of cleansing to clear newly acquired land of Bulgarian civilians. Captured letters authored by Greek soldiers tell the story: "We burn all the Bulgarian villages that we occupy, and kill all the Bulgarians that fall into our hands. . . . The Greek army sets fire to all the

Table 6.1. Civilian victimization as a function of territorial annexation: democracies vs. autocracies

		Democracy		
		Yes	No	Total
Civilian victimization	Yes	5 83.3%	22 81.5%	27 81.8%
	No	1 16.7%	5 18.5%	6 18.2%
	Total	6 100.0%	27 100.0%	33 100.0%

Pearson Chi^2(1) = 0.0113   Pr = 0.92

villages where there are Bulgarians and massacres all it meets. It is impossible to describe what happens." As the Carnegie Commission summarizes, "The inference is irresistible . . . the Greeks were resolved to have no Bulgarian subjects."[15]

ROOTS AND COURSE OF THE CONFLICT IN PALESTINE

On November 29, 1947, the UN General Assembly voted in favor of partitioning Britain's Palestine Mandate into a Jewish state and an Arab state. The roots of the conflict in Palestine lay in Jewish immigration and the two groups' incompatible nationalisms. The Jewish community—known as the Yishuv—composed a scant 6 percent of Palestine's population in 1880, but by 1947 had grown to about one-third.[16] Jewish immigration and Zionist national aspirations proved a volatile mix with the attitudes of the Palestinian Arabs, who never accepted the idea of any type of Jewish polity in their midst. The Arabs called instead for the British—who administered Palestine as a League of Nations Mandate after World War I—to grant independence to the Mandate and its Arab majority. This fundamental conflict led increasingly to violence between Arabs and Jews—in April 1920 (9 dead), May 1921 (nearly 100), and August 1929 (249).[17] The Shaw Commission, appointed to investigate the 1929 violence, highlighted the tensions caused by the Jewish influx to Palestine, concluding that the "Arabs have come to see in Jewish immigration not only a menace to their livelihood, but a possible overlord of the future."[18] Later, fears of becoming a minority in Palestine owing to the upsurge in Jewish immigration in the mid 1930s helped set off the Arab Revolt against British rule from 1936 to 1939 in which five thousand Arabs died.[19]

The partition plan drawn up by the UN Special Commission on Palestine (UNSCOP) and approved in 1947 suffered from three serious flaws that contributed to the outbreak of conflict. First, unlike the proposal recommended by the Peel Commission a decade earlier, UNSCOP's plan failed to provide for the separation of Arabs and Jews. In fact, even though nearly the entire Jewish community in Palestine (500,000) was to be concentrated in the Jewish state, this state would also contain 400,000 Arabs.[20] Second, the plan's authors disregarded future defensibility when they drew the two states' boundaries. As historian Avi Shlaim has pointed out, "The borders of these two oddly shaped states, resembling two fighting serpents, were a strategic nightmare."[21] Third, the division of land proposed in the partition plan was inequitable: the Jewish state included 56 percent of Palestine (5,893 square miles) at a time when Jews owned about 6 percent of the land, and only 10 percent within the territories that would comprise the Jewish state.[22]

Although the Jewish Agency accepted the proposed partition and Jews everywhere celebrated the creation of a Jewish state, the Palestinian Arabs angrily rejected partition and lashed out at their Jewish neighbors: Arab riots in the first week after the partition vote killed about forty Jews. The key difference this time was that there would be no consistent British response to keep a lid on the violence: the British declined to remain in Palestine to implement the partition and instead prepared to depart when the Mandate expired in May 1948.

The ensuing conflict consisted of two separate wars. The first was a communal war between Jewish forces numbering about fifteen thousand— mainly the Haganah, supplemented by the two thousand to three thousand members of Irgun Z'vai Leumi (IZL) and three hundred to five hundred fighters from Lohamei Herut Yisrael (LHI), two Jewish dissident organizations—and Arab irregulars perhaps a few thousand strong.[23] The only organized Arab opposition was the four-thousand-man Arab Liberation Army (ALA) under Fawzi al-Qawuqji, but this unit did not fully join the fighting until May 1948. Most Arab forces were village militia that fought locally. This civil conflict—after some early reverses—resulted in a decisive Jewish victory in April 1948. Plan D, the Haganah offensive that opened on April 2, temporarily broke the Arabs' stranglehold on Jerusalem, enabling several convoys to reach the beleaguered Jewish population there. Elsewhere, the Haganah captured all of the Arab villages and towns within the Jewish state's UNSCOP borders, including Haifa on the coast and the major towns of the eastern Galilee like Safed, Tiberias, and Beisan, as well as a few outside of those borders in territory awarded to the Palestinian state by UNSCOP, such as Jaffa and Acre. Armed Palestinian resistance collapsed as a result of these defeats, and the flight of the Palestinian Arabs—already underway—accelerated.

The second war began when the armies of Lebanon, Syria, Iraq, Transjordan, and Egypt attacked in response to Israel's declaration of independence on May 14, 1948. This conflict unfolded in four distinct phases, punctuated by cease-fires, extending until January 7, 1949. Arab regular forces initially comprised about 28,000 troops, supplemented by the remainder of the Arab Liberation Army, compared to Israeli forces numbering about 38,000. As the war continued, Israel's manpower edge increased: 65,000 Israelis versus 40,000 Arabs in mid July, and 115,000 Israeli soldiers versus 55,000 Arab troops in early 1949.[24] Initially, the Arab armies held the upper hand, making progress on all fronts, but were unable to break through the Israeli defenses decisively. The Haganah, renamed the Israel Defense Forces (IDF), suffered its worst defeats at the hands of the Arab Legion in and around Jerusalem, losing the Jewish Quarter in the Old City on May 28, but after the war's second phase (July 8–18), a truce prevailed between the IDF and the legion on the central front.[25] The IDF henceforth concentrated its energies on ejecting the Egyptians and Syrians from the country, which it achieved in the war's third and fourth phases, fought in October 1948 and late December–early January 1949, respectively.

As a result of the war, Israel obtained all of the territory destined for UNSCOP's Jewish state as well as twenty-five hundred square miles of territory designated for the Palestinian state. Transjordan annexed the remaining twenty-two hundred square miles (the West Bank). Israel's armed forces destroyed 418 Arab villages, and only 133,000 Arabs remained within Israel's borders; the remaining 500,000–750,000 became refugees. The reasons for their flight have been disputed ever since.[26]

There is no precise estimate of the number of Arab civilian fatalities resulting from the war or from Jewish attacks and expulsions in particular, although the number is probably a few thousand. The figure for civilian deaths on the Jewish side is 1,162.[27] At least thirty-one massacres were committed by Jewish forces, but there was also widespread use of indiscriminate artillery and mortar fire. Civilians were intentionally targeted, however, increasingly so as the war continued, but this case is on the mild end of the civilian victimization spectrum. One reason is that the Arab population—especially early in the war—often fled the fighting relatively easily. Many well-to-do city-dwellers abandoned their homes in the first month or two. This uncoerced flight reflects the weak cohesion of Palestinian Arab society in 1947, as well as the tendency of the Arabs to leave temporarily when fighting flared up only to return later.[28] As Palestinians came to understand that Israel would not permit them to return, they increasingly stood their ground, and massacres became more frequent.

OF TERRITORY AND TRANSFER

This section elaborates the territorial ambitions of key Zionist decision-makers before the war as well as their beliefs about the legitimacy and necessity of removing the Arab population from a prospective Jewish state.

Although Zionist leaders accepted partition in 1947, this did not mean that they viewed the establishment of a Jewish state in part of Palestine as the end of the Zionist project. Rather, they viewed it as a stage on the way to the fulfillment of Zionism, which was to redeem the whole land of Israel. Thus, Zionist leaders had a clear interest in territorial expansion before the war. Furthermore, there was nearly unanimous support among major Zionist figures—ranging from the founder of the Zionist movement, Theodor Herzl, to the first Israeli prime minister, David Ben-Gurion—for "transferring" the Palestinian Arabs out of Palestine—a polite word for expelling them. Finally, the reason Zionist thinkers viewed expulsion as necessary was the security threat a large Palestinian population would represent to the survival of a Jewish state.

Zionism's Territorial Ambitions

When the United Nations voted to partition Palestine in 1947, Jewish leaders accepted the decision whereas the Arabs rejected it. This acceptance, however, did not mean that the Jews were content with the portion of Palestine they received, or viewed it as the fulfillment of Zionism. On the contrary, already ten years before the UN partition plan, Ben-Gurion conceived of a Jewish state in part of Palestine as "not the end, but only the beginning . . . [a] powerful boost to our historic efforts to redeem the country in its entirety." Ben-Gurion viewed the founding of a state as "an important and decisive *stage* in the realization of Zionism," but not the final stage.[29] He knew that the slice of Palestine the Yishuv would probably be awarded in any partition arrangement would never be sufficient to hold the millions of Jews who were likely to immigrate to the new state. Thus, once a state was established, the first stage would comprise "the period of building and laying foundations" in preparation for the second stage, "the period of expansion." This growth into the remainder of Palestine, according to Ben-Gurion, would be made possible by the future Jewish state's military power, which meant that "we won't be constrained from settling in the rest of the country, either by mutual agreement and understanding with our Arab neighbors, or by some other way."[30] Ben-Gurion clarified that this "other way" would be by armed force in remarks he made to the Zionist Executive: "After the formation of a large army in the wake of the establishment of the state, *we will abolish partition and expand to the whole of Palestine.*"[31] "The acceptance of partition," Ben-Gurion noted, "does not commit us to renounce Transjordan. . . . We shall accept a state in the boundaries fixed today—but the boundaries of Zionist aspirations are the concern of the Jewish people and no external factor will be able to limit them."[32] Ben-Gurion perceived the potential for a state in part of Palestine, therefore, as "a nearly decisive initial stage in our complete redemption and an unequaled lever for *the gradual conquest* of all of Palestine."[33]

Nor was Ben-Gurion the sole exponent of this view. Chaim Weizmann—at the time president of the Zionist Organization and the Jewish Agency Executive (JAE)—and Moshe Shertok—a member of the JAE—similarly viewed the Peel Commission's 1937 partition plan as a stage in the development of a Jewish state to include all of Palestine. Weizmann went so far as to inform the British high commissioner, Arthur Wauchope, "We shall expand in the whole country in the course of time . . . this is only an arrangement for the next 25 to 30 years."[34]

The Zionist commitment to a Jewish state in the entirety of Palestine continued into the 1940s. The Biltmore Program of 1942, for example, which became the official policy of the Zionist movement, called for Palestine to "be established as a Jewish commonwealth." Ben-Gurion was careful to point out that by Palestine, the Biltmore Program meant all of Palestine, "*not as a Jewish state in Palestine but Palestine as a Jewish state.*"[35] Similarly, Zionist acceptance of the UN partition plan did not signal an end to the movement's territorial ambitions. Ben-Gurion, for example, rejected several fundamental aspects of the UNSCOP plan—such as the proposed borders and the establishment of an Arab state—and noted that "arrangements are never final, 'not with regard to the regime, not with regard to borders, and not with regard to international agreements.'"[36] Israel Galili, head of the Haganah National Command, was even more direct in an address in April 1948: "The Jews' assent to the General Assembly's resolution does not signify acquiescence to partition. . . . The fullness of our strength shall determine the territorial limits of our independence in *Eretz-Yisra'el*. The political boundaries will correspond in extent to the land wrested from the enemy."[37]

None of this evidence regarding Zionist ambitions to establish a Jewish state in all of Palestine should be interpreted as meaning that Zionist leaders had a plan to conquer the entire region by force of arms. On the contrary, the Jewish side celebrated the partition resolution and agreed to cooperate with UN authorities in implementing the plan. It merely shows that in the years preceding partition, mainstream Zionism aspired to redeem all of Palestine and viewed a Jewish state in part of the region as a springboard from which to expand. Zionists, in short, hoped to settle in and annex—peacefully or by force—the rest of Palestine in the future.

Zionism and Transfer

It is now well-known that leading Zionists accepted that establishing a Jewish state in Palestine meant displacing the resident Arab population.[38] Early Zionists tended to gloss over or ignore entirely the reality that Palestine was not an empty vessel, but was actually inhabited by an Arab population sure to dispute a Jewish claim to the region. Herzl himself, while not ignorant of the presence of a substantial native population, did not conceive of the Palestinian Arabs as a cohesive political community with rights over the land they occupied. He thought that the Arabs might allow the Zionists to expropriate their lands because of the economic benefits they would receive from a large Jewish presence in Palestine. Herzl, although never calling openly for the transfer of the Arabs, clearly found a Palestine empty of Arabs an appealing thought, as a diary entry from 1895 demonstrates: "We must expropriate gently. . . . We shall try to spirit the penniless population across the border by procuring employment for it in the transit countries, while denying it any employment in our country. . . . Both the process of expropriation and the removal of the poor must be carried out discreetly and circumspectly."[39]

Openly advocating such a policy was risky, however, both because it increased Arab hostility and suspicion, and because during the mandate period, British authorities—although they intermittently supported Zionist aspirations—never committed to expropriating the Arabs or turning them out of their homes. Public Zionist rhetoric, therefore, remained muted on the question of transfer: "The Zionist public catechism, at the turn of the century, and well into the 1940s, remained that there was room enough in Palestine for both peoples. . . . There was no need for a transfer of the Arabs and on no account must the idea be incorporated in the movement's ideological-political platform."[40] Nevertheless, prominent Zionists continued to voice support for the idea: Chaim Weizmann, for example, proposed a transfer scheme to British colonial authorities in 1930. Similarly, Menahem Ussishkin, chairman of the Jewish National Fund, told reporters in April 1930: "We must continually raise the demand that our land be returned to our possession. . . . If there are other inhabitants there, they must be transferred to some other place. We must take over the land. We have a greater and nobler ideal than preserving several hundred thousands of Arab fellahin."[41]

The Zionist debate over the Peel Commission Report of July 1937—which recommended population transfers as part of a partition plan—reveals the extent of support among Zionist leaders for wholesale and compulsory transfer as the solution to the Yishuv's demographic problem. Although the recommendation to partition Palestine was contested and ultimately rejected by Ihud Po'alei Tzion (the governing body of the most prominent Zionist world labor movement) and the Twentieth Zionist Congress, support for transfer in both of these fora was enthusiastic and widespread.[42] The question was not the morality of transfer, but the practicality of removing the Arabs from a Jewish state.

Key Zionist leaders expressed strong support for the Peel recommendation to deport 225,000 Arabs from the proposed Jewish state. In a private letter written shortly after the Peel Commission issued its findings, Ben-Gurion argued strongly for transfer, by force if necessary: "We must expel Arabs and take their places . . . and if we have to use force—not to dispossess the Arabs of the Negev and Transjordan, but to guarantee our own right to settle in those places—then we have force at our disposal."[43] At a JAE meeting in

June 1938 where the issue was discussed extensively, almost every member voiced their support for transferring the Arabs out of the Jewish state: "There was a virtual pro-transfer consensus among the JAE members; all preferred a 'voluntary' transfer; but most were also agreeable to a compulsory transfer, preferring, of course, that the British rather than the Yishuv carry it out."[44] Ben-Gurion summed up the attitudes of his fellows when he said: "I support compulsory transfer. I do not see anything immoral in it."[45]

Transfer continued to gain momentum in the 1940s even in the wake of Britain's renunciation of partition in the Woodhead Commission report and the 1939 White Paper. Yosef Weitz, for example, director of the Jewish National Fund's Lands Department, disclosed the following thoughts in his diary in late 1940:

> It must be clear that there is no room in the country for both peoples.... If the Arabs leave it, the country will become wide and spacious for us.... The only solution [after World War II ends] is a Land of Israel, at least a western Land of Israel [i.e., Palestine], without Arabs. There is no room here for compromises.... There is no way but to transfer the Arabs from here to the neighboring countries, to transfer all of them, save perhaps for [the mainly Christian Arabs of] Bethlehem, Nazareth and old Jerusalem. Not one village must be left, not one [bedouin] tribe. The transfer must be directed at Iraq, Syria and even Transjordan. For this goal funds will be found.... And only after this transfer will the country be able to absorb millions of our brothers and the Jewish problem [in Europe] will cease to exist. There is no other solution.[46]

At another JAE debate on the merits of transfer in May 1944, the director of the Jewish Agency's Immigration Department, Eliahu Dobkin, stated: "There will be in the country a large [Arab] minority and it must be ejected," a sentiment echoed by the rest of those present.[47] Statistician Roberto Bachi pointed out in a study in December 1944 that the Palestinian Arabs' rate of natural increase rendered their transfer out of the Jewish state absolutely necessary: even with the massive Jewish immigration (200,000 per year) needed to give the Jews a majority of the population in Palestine, the Arabs would soon again outnumber the Jews because of their higher birthrate.[48] That those involved understood that transfer would likely involve violence is made clear by an October 1941 Ben-Gurion memo, "Outlines of Zionist Policy," in which he wrote: "Complete transfer without compulsion—and ruthless compulsion at that—is hardly imaginable."[49]

Transfer as a Solution to the Arab Fifth Column

The idea of transfer was "deeply rooted in Zionist ideology" and over time came to be accepted by all leading Zionist figures.[50] The reason is clear: the Jews would soon be outnumbered in their own country if the Arabs were allowed to stay. Not only would the Arab population pose a permanent security threat; their presence could be used as leverage to pry apart the Jewish state, much as Hitler sliced off the Sudetenland from Czechoslovakia in 1938.[51] Consider the words of JAE member Avraham Ussishkin uttered in 1938: "We cannot start the Jewish state with . . . half the population being Arab. . . . Such a state cannot survive even half an hour. It [i.e., transfer] is the most moral thing to do. . . . I am ready to come and defend . . . it before the Almighty."[52] Berl Katznelson, a leader of the Mapai Party, agreed: "There is the question of how the army, the police and the civil service will function and how a state can be run if part of its population is disloyal."[53]

In late 1947, Ben-Gurion demonstrated an appreciation for the security problem posed by the Palestinian population as war loomed between the two communities. Ben-Gurion argued in November that because the Arabs would represent a "Fifth Column," as many of them as possible should be given citizenship in the Palestinian Arab state envisioned by the UN's 1947 partition plan so that they could be expelled in the event of hostilities rather than merely imprisoned.[54] A month later, Ben-Gurion laid out the problem of a large Arab minority explicitly: "In the area allotted to the Jewish state there are not more than 520,000 Jews and about 350,000 non-Jews, mostly Arabs. . . . Such a composition does not provide a *stable basis for a Jewish state*. This fact must be seen in all of its clarity and acuteness. Such a composition does not even give us absolute assurance that control will remain in the hands of the Jewish majority."[55]

In short, Zionist leaders viewed a substantial Arab population in a Jewish state as a security threat and embraced transfer as the solution. According to Morris, the leaders of the Yishuv "were justified in seeing the future minority as a great danger to the prospective Jewish state—a fifth political, or even military, column. The transfer idea . . . was viewed by the majority of the Yishuv leaders in those days as the best solution to the problem."[56] The Arab violence of the 1920s and 1930s only highlighted the threat because it "demonstrated that a disaffected, hostile Arab majority or large minority would inevitably struggle against the very existence of the Jewish state to which it was consigned, subverting and destabilising it from the start."[57] Morris, who in his earlier work downplayed the link between transfer thinking and the origins of the Palestinian refugee crisis, conceded in 2001 that Zionist leaders understood in 1948 that "transfer was what the Jewish state's survival and future well-being demanded . . . expulsion was in the air in the war of 1948."[58] As Nur Masalha puts it, "There was nothing new about this approach of 'forcible transfer,' nor did it emerge out of the blue merely as a result of the outbreak of hostilities in 1948."[59]

Again, none of this means there was a "master plan" calling for the expulsion of the Arabs and conquest of all of Palestine. First of all, Zionist forces were initially on the defensive and did not possess the capability to expel many Arabs. Furthermore, as I argue more extensively below, Jewish forces turned to expulsions and destruction of villages only as their military circumstances grew more precarious in early 1948. Moreover, no one has yet discovered documentary evidence of a blanket policy of expulsion before the war by the Yishuv. Still, the gap between Morris and his critics has narrowed considerably, as evidenced by Morris's statement in *The Birth of the Palestinian Refugee Problem Revisited* that "the displacement of Arabs from Palestine or from the areas of Palestine that would become the Jewish State was inherent in Zionist ideology and, in microcosm, in Zionist praxis from the start of the enterprise."[60]

Plan D and the Shift from Defense to Offense

Despite the widespread belief in transfer among leading Zionists before the war, the Yishuv began the war on the defensive and did not have a master plan calling for the expulsion of the Palestinian Arab population from within the boundaries of the UNSCOP-designated Jewish state. From December 1947 to March 1948 the Haganah pursued a defensive strategy that largely eschewed targeting Arab civilians in order to avoid escalating the conflict. This strategy reflected the belief that the Arab response could be controlled and partition carried out. The dispersed nature of Jewish settlement also rendered the Yishuv vulnerable to Arab attack, and Ben-Gurion and other Zionist leaders sought to limit Haganah attacks so to avert driving the bulk of the Arab population into active hostilities. This defensive strategy, however, grew unsustainable in March 1948 as Arab militias ambushed Jewish convoys on the roads and threatened to isolate and dismember the Yishuv's separate pieces.

In the face of this overwhelming military threat, Jewish leaders shifted from defense to offense by adopting Plan D, which sought to eliminate Arab enclaves within Jewish-inhabited areas and join these districts together by removing Arabs from the territory in between. Realizing their peril, Ben-Gurion and the Yishuv's other leaders for the first time adopted a *policy* that called for the destruction of Arab villages and the expulsion of their inhabitants. Haganah forces used indiscriminate artillery and aerial bombardment to terrorize Arab townspeople and villagers to flee, committed massacres, such as at Abu Shusha (southeast of Ramle) and Tantura (south of Haifa), and tolerated and exploited massacres perpetrated by allied Jewish militias at places like Deir Yassin.[61] Plan D, in short, marks the decisive change in Jewish military strategy from a defensive policy designed to hold on in the face of Arab attacks and to keep the conflict limited, to an offensive policy of targeted violence and indiscriminate terror tactics designed purposefully to rid the country of Arabs in order to reduce the threat to the Jewish State's survival posed by the Arab fifth column.

The Defensive: December 1947–March 1948

The Haganah began the war with a defensive strategy that tried to avoid targeting civilians, destroyed few Arab villages, and generally sought to limit the growing conflict. As shown above, there is no question that Jewish leaders desired a Jewish state free of Arabs. While this was an appealing vision, however, the Zionist dream was not reflected in official Yishuv policy: "The overarching, general assumption . . . during the war's first weeks was that the emergent Jewish State would come to life with a large Arab minority."[62]

This assumption was reflected in the war plans that guided the Haganah's military strategy in the first weeks of the conflict, which had no offensive objectives. As Morris describes them, these plans called for "Haganah retaliatory strikes against Arab perpetrators or potential perpetrators and against Arab targets identical to those attacked by Arab terrorists, such as road traffic." In other words, the strategy was a tit-for-tat policy of reprisal aimed at Arab combatants and the same types of targets the Arabs attacked. The Yishuv leadership was deterred from implementing harsher measures by the fear that doing so would push uncommitted Arabs into the hostile camp and end up worsening the Yishuv's military position. The goal was to be "strong enough to quell local unrest, but restricted enough not to bring into the cycle of violence those Palestinians who remained out of it at this stage." Ben-Gurion opposed indiscriminate killing of civilians as a means of reprisal, advocating instead destruction of property as a deterrent to further attacks. Israel Galili argued that the Jewish military was a moral force and that adherence to moral values could not be disregarded: "The Haganah is not built for aggression, it does not wish to enslave, it values human life, it wants to hit only those who are guilty, it does not want to ignite, but to douse out flames." The policy and the reasons for it are summarized in a memo circulated by one of the Haganah's brigades: "We must avoid as far as possible killing plain civilians . . . and to make an effort as far as possible to always hit the criminals themselves, the bearer of arms, those who carry out the attacks. . . . We do not want to spread the disturbances and to unite the Arab public . . . around the Mufti and his gangs. Any indiscriminate massacre of Arab civilians causes the consolidation of the Arab masses around the inciters."[63] Other factors that kept the Haganah response limited were fear of unfavorable international reaction to excessive violence, particularly British intervention.

By the second week of December, however, as Jewish losses mounted and it became apparent to all that this was not just another minor outbreak of anti-Jewish hostility but in fact a real war, Haganah strategy became more aggressive, but still somewhat restrained in its conduct toward Arab civilians. Orders to local Haganah units, for example, demonstrated a greater willingness to accept civilian casualties in the course of strikes on Arab vehicles. Jewish retaliatory strikes were aimed at militia units but also the villages in which they were based, and included killing not only armed combatants, but also unarmed men and the demolition of homes. As the situation deteriorated further in early 1948, according to David Tal, Jewish forces grew increasingly brutal, and "it seemed that any operational and moral restrictions that the Hagana had practiced hitherto had been abandoned, as it indiscriminately hit anyone present during reprisal attacks."[64] As Yishuv military leaders apprehended the nature of the threat they faced, Jewish military losses escalated, and the situation became increasingly dire, the level of violence perpetrated by the Haganah increased.

Military Crisis of March 1948

After four months of war, the Haganah's defensive strategy was failing. Despite its numerical advantage over the ALA and associated local Arab militias, the Haganah was severely handicapped by the geographic dispersal of Jewish areas of settlement. Although the Jews comprised one-third of Palestine's population in 1948, they were not geographically concentrated in one region. The only contiguous stretch of Jewish-majority territory was the coastal plain stretching from Tel Aviv to Haifa. Districts in which Arabs comprised overwhelming majorities separated the subdistricts that contained the main areas of Jewish settlement—Jerusalem, Jaffa, Haifa, and Tiberias. Of these areas, moreover, only in Jaffa district did Jews constitute an actual majority of the population; most major towns and cities (Tel Aviv excepted) were populated by both Jews and Arabs living in close proximity, with the latter often in the majority.[65]

The key battles, therefore, were waged for the roads linking these areas, almost all of which passed through hostile areas or near Arab villages. Rather than engage in open confrontations with the Haganah, the Arabs blocked the roads and attacked Jewish convoys, a tactic that gave them the upper hand in the conflict by March 1948. In the last week of March, for example, Arab forces ambushed and wiped out three major Jewish convoys, killing one hundred Haganah fighters and destroying most of the Haganah's armored trucks. Combined with the impending British withdrawal and the possibility of an attack by the neighboring Arab states, the "convoys' crisis" created the perception among top Jewish leaders that the "Yishuv was struggling for its life; an invasion by the Arab states could deliver the *coup de grace.*"[66]

The perception of crisis and imminent threat in March 1948 led to a radical change in strategy from a defensive orientation of reprisal, conflict limitation, and restricted impact on civilians to an offensive policy designed explicitly to eliminate the Arab population from the Jewish State. Jewish forces needed to purge the Arab presence within Jewish areas and link these areas by eliminating the intervening Arab enclaves.[67]

The new policy was enunciated in Plan D. The introduction to Plan D describes its goals as follows: "The objective of this plan is to gain control of the areas of the Hebrew state and defend its borders. It also aims at gaining control of the areas of Jewish settlement and concentration which are located outside the borders [of the Hebrew state] against regular, semi-regular, and small forces operating from bases outside or inside the state."[68] The plan also called for "operations against enemy population centers located inside or near our defensive system in order to prevent them from being used as bases by an active armed force." These operations were to consist of two types: "Destruction of villages (setting fire to, blowing up, and planting mines in the debris), especially those population centers which are difficult to control continuously" and "mounting combing and control operations according to the following guidelines: encirclement of the village and conducting a search inside it. In the event of resistance, the armed force must be wiped out and the population must be expelled outside the borders of the state. . . . In the absence of resistance, garrison troops will enter the village and take up positions in it or in locations which enable complete tactical control."[69]

The security situation facing the Yishuv in March 1948 clearly drove this new plan. According to Morris,

> The battle against the militias and foreign irregulars had first to be won if there was to be a chance of defeating the invading armies. To win the battle of the roads, the Haganah had to pacify the villages and towns that dominated them and served as bases of belligerency: Pacification meant the villages' surrender or depopulation and destruction. The essence of the plan was the clearing of hostile and potentially hostile forces out of the interior of the territory of the prospective Jewish State, establishing territorial continuity between the major concentrations of Jewish population and securing the future State's borders before, and in anticipation of, the invasion.[70]

Given that "the Haganah regarded almost all the villages as actively or potentially hostile," Plan D anticipated the wholesale expulsion of the Arab population in or near the boundaries of the Jewish State. Villages had to be destroyed rather than simply evacuated because if their homes still stood, Arab villagers might return to them and pose a renewed threat.[71]

Implementation of Plan D

The facts on the ground and the documentary record show that the Haganah and the Jewish militias from early April initiated a campaign of forced expulsion and village destruction that involved outright massacres as well as indiscriminate bombardment to induce panic and flight among Arab civilians. "During 4–9 April," writes Morris,

Ben-Gurion and the HGS, under the impact of the dire situation of Jewish Jerusalem and the ALA attack on Mishmar Ha'emek, and under pressure from settlements and local commanders, decided, in conformity with the general guidelines of Plan D, to clear out and destroy the clusters of hostile or potentially hostile villages dominating vital axes . . . a policy of clearing out Arab communities sitting astride or near vital routes and along some borders was instituted. Orders went out from HGS to the relevant units to drive out and, if necessary, expel the remaining communities along the Tel Aviv-Haifa axis, the Jenin-Haifa road (around Mishmar Ha'emek) and along the Jerusalem-Tel Aviv road.

During the crucial April-June time period, "Most communities attacked were evacuated and where no spontaneous evacuation occurred, communities more often than not were expelled. Throughout, Arabs who had fled were prevented from returning to their homes." Specific orders were issued to brigade commanders: each "received a list of the villages or neighbourhoods that had to be occupied, destroyed and their inhabitants expelled, with exact dates."[72]

The typical method of attack involved indiscriminate mortaring of Arab towns and villages to terrorize the inhabitants into surrender or flight. The decisive act that caused the remaining disheartened Arabs of Haifa to flee, for example, was the Haganah mortaring of the crowded market square on April 21–22. In Jaffa, IZL pummeled the town for three days with twenty tons of mortar rounds designed—according to IZL's head of operations—"to prevent constant military traffic in the city, to break the spirit of the enemy troops, [and] to cause chaos among the civilian population in order to create a mass flight." Indiscriminate mortar fire also helped trigger mass panic in Jewish attacks on Tiberias, Safed, and Beisan, as well as numerous villages in operations launched under Plan D, such as Yiftah in eastern Galilee and Lightning in the south.[73]

As Plan D unfolded in April and May 1948, orders to expel Arabs and destroy their homes became commonplace. Ben-Gurion first ordered the expulsion of Arabs from a whole area of the country in the context of the battle for Mishmar Ha'emek—the besieged kibbutz between Haifa and Jenin—in early April, but the rhetoric of elimination permeates the operational orders from this period. Haganah units participating in Operation Nashon along the Tel Aviv-Jerusalem road, for example, received orders calling for the "liquidation," "annihilation," and "destruction" of villages. The objective of Operation Lightning was "to deny the enemy a base for future operations . . . by creating general panic and breaking his morale. The aim is to force the Arab inhabitants 'to move.'" The operational order for the Giv'ati Brigade's attack on Sawafir al Sharquiyya and Sawafir al Gharbiyya instructed units "to expel the enemy from the villages . . . to clean the front line. . . . To conquer the villages, to cleanse them of inhabitants (women and children should [also] be expelled), to take several prisoners . . . [and] to burn the greatest possible number of houses." When about a thousand Arab villagers remained in Beisan after the Haganah assault and conquest of the town in mid May, Haganah officers—who viewed this concentration of Arab civilians so close to the front lines as a security threat—sought and received approval to expel them: "There was a danger that the inhabitants would revolt in the rear, when they felt a change in the military situation in favour of the [Arab] invaders, [so within days] an order was given to evict the inhabitants from the city." By the end of May, according to David Yizhar, one of the authors of the history of the Golani Brigade in the 1948 war, "For the first time . . . the Beit Shean Valley had become a purely Jewish valley."[74]

Increasingly, as the Haganah implemented Plan D, the "provision to leave intact nonresisting villages was superceded by the decision to destroy villages in strategic areas or along crucial routes regardless of whether or not they were resisting" Haganah conquest because villages left standing could quickly revert to enemy control.[75] "If, at the start of the war," writes Morris,

> the Yishuv had been (reluctantly) willing to countenance a Jewish State with a large, peaceful Arab minority, by April the Haganah's thinking had radically changed: The toll on Jewish life and security in the battle of the roads and the dire prospect of pan-Arab invasion had left the Yishuv with very narrow margins of safety. It could not afford to leave pockets of actively or potentially hostile Arabs behind its lines . . . the Yishuv faced, and knew it faced, a life and death struggle. The gloves had to be, and were, taken off.[76]

In addition to deaths inflicted by indiscriminate mortaring of civilian areas, Jewish forces committed more than a few atrocities and massacres in the implementation of Plan D to help speed the population on its way. At Abu Shusha, southeast of Ramle, Giv'ati Brigade troops killed between thirty and seventy civilians in their assault in mid May. In preparation for the final attack on Safad, the Palmah conquered the village of 'Ein al Zeitun on May 1 and executed dozens of prisoners a day or two later. In Jaffa, IZL or Haganah men executed fifteen Arabs in mid May after the fall of the town.[77]

The most famous massacre committed under the aegis of Plan D, however—perpetrated by IZL and LHI—occurred in the Arab village of Deir Yassin, a town of about 750 inhabitants located east of Qastal and just south of the Tel Aviv-Jerusalem highway. The available evidence indicates that the operation against Deir Yassin was intended to expel the town's Arab residents but, in the face of unexpected resistance and mounting attacker casualties, devolved into massacre. According to one historian of the incident, "Although massacre of civilians was not the main or original purpose of the Deir Yassin operation, the atrocities did not result purely from 'heat of battle.' Massacre was discussed in advance, not restrained when it erupted, and later pursued with organized deliberation, impunity,

and brutality."[78] The attack was conducted with the approval and cooperation of the Haganah, but neither the mainstream Jewish military nor the
Jewish Agency directed the revisionist militias to murder the townspeople.
The Jewish Agency issued a statement disavowing the massacre, but no
one was ever detained or prosecuted for the outrages committed there, and
the Haganah benefited from the fear which Deir Yassin imbued in the Arab
population. Indeed, Israeli intelligence viewed the atrocity as a "decisive
accelerating factor" in promoting the flight of the Arab population.[79] In the
opinion of historian Avi Shlaim, "More than any other single event, it [Deir
Yassin] was responsible for breaking the spirit of the civilian population
and setting in motion the mass exodus of Arabs from Palestine."[80]

Plan D in Action: The Arab Flight from Haifa

The battle for Haifa will suffice to show the nature of Jewish military operations during Plan D and their impact on the Arab population. The Haganah assault on Haifa, which commenced on April 21, was similar in spirit
and execution to other attacks conducted under the aegis of Plan D. The
battle began when the British commander in the area, Major General Hugh
Stockwell, fearing a serious fight between Arab and Jewish forces in Haifa,
pulled his troops out from in between the two belligerents. Observing the
British redeployment, officers of the Carmeli Brigade decided to launch an
offensive, Operation Passover Cleansing, aimed at "breaking the enemy."[81]
That the violent expulsion of the Arab population was likely the objective is
shown by the order issued to the troops: "Kill any Arab you encounter; torch
all inflammable objects and force doors open with explosives."[82]

Jewish political leaders did not order the cleansing of Haifa, but they
favored such an exodus and approved it retroactively. Yosef Weitz, for example, the head of the Jewish National Fund and an ardent supporter of
transfer, visited Haifa at the time of the Haganah assault. Weitz wrote the
following in his diary: "I think that this [flight-prone] state of mind [among
the Arabs] should be exploited, and [we should] press the other inhabitants
not to surrender [but to leave]." Apparently Weitz found much sympathy
for this view at Carmeli Brigade headquarters: "I was happy to hear from
him [Carmel's adjutant] that this line was being adopted by the [Haganah]
command, [that is] to frighten the Arabs so long as flight-inducing fear
was upon them."[83] Ben-Gurion, while professing to be puzzled by the Arab
flight from Haifa, declared it to be "a beautiful sight" in his visit to the
town on May 1, and commented, "Doesn't he have anything more important to do?" when observing the efforts of a local official to persuade the
Arabs to stay.[84]

In its attack on Arab Haifa, the Carmeli Brigade made liberal use of firepower, particularly indiscriminate mortar fire intended to panic the population into flight. The orders of one Carmeli battalion (the Twenty-second)

instructed the troops "'to kill every [adult male] Arab encountered' and to set alight with firebombs 'all objectives that can be set alight.'"[85] Arab civilians fled the eastern parts of Haifa during the night of April 21–22, and mortar fire and advancing infantry drove residents out of the central and downtown areas and down to the port, one of the few remaining areas held by the British. Jewish mortars again opened fire on the people milling around, using the bombardment to cause a collapse in civilian morale. According to the Haganah official history, "a great panic took hold. The multitude burst in the port, pushed aside the policemen, charged the boats and began fleeing the town."[86] Morris contends that Haganah commanders did not intend the bombardment to bring about the mass flight of the Arabs, but acknowledges that this was nonetheless the effect that it had: "Clearly the offensive, and especially the mortaring, precipitated the exodus."[87] Others are less charitable in their reading of Jewish intentions: "The commander of the Carmeli Brigade, Moshe Carmel, feared that many Arabs would remain in the city. Hence, he ordered that three-inch mortars be used to shell the Arab crowds on the market square. The crowd broke into the port, pushing aside the policemen who guarded the gate, stormed the boats and fled the city. The whole day mortars continued to shell the city, even though the Arabs did not fight."[88] According to British troops who witnessed the scene,

> During the morning [the Jews], were continually shooting down on all Arabs who moved both in Wadi Nisnas and the Old City. This included completely indiscriminate and revolting machinegun fire, mortar fire and sniping on women and children . . . attempting to get out . . . through the gates into the docks . . . there was considerable congestion outside the East Gate [of the port] of hysterical and terrified Arab women and children and old people on whom the Jews opened up mercilessly with fire.[89]

In circumstances like these, and with the massacre at Deir Yassin less than two weeks old, the magnitude of the Arab flight from Haifa is not surprising. Fifteen thousand people escaped during the first two days of the Haganah attack alone.

Why was the Haganah so eager to see the Arabs of Haifa leave? The answer is provided by the military situation in the northern theater. The Yishuv expected an invasion by the Arab states, supplemented by ALA forces already in the vicinity. Having captured Haifa, the question of how to defend it against Arab attack became paramount. In this regard, Haifa with its Arab population in situ presented a problem that an all-Jewish Haifa did not: "Carmel's commanders were keenly aware that an exodus would solve the brigade's main problem—how to secure Jewish Haifa with very limited forces against attack by Arab forces from outside the town while having to deploy a large number of troops inside to guard against insurrection or attack by a large, potentially hostile Arab population." As Morris puts it, "It made simple military as well as political sense: Haifa without Arabs was more easily defended and less problematic than Haifa with a large minority."[90]

Most accounts of events in Haifa focus on the British-brokered negotiations between the town's Arab notables and local Jews and members of the Haganah command. These accounts suggest that Haifa's Jewish leaders (and British officers) were genuinely shocked when informed on the evening of April 22 that the Arabs wished to evacuate the town, and that Jewish mayor Shabtai Levy begged the Arabs to stay. This shock soon faded, however, as the benefits of Arab flight dawned on the city's Jewish leaders:

> The local Jewish civilian leadership initially sincerely wanted the Arabs to stay. . . . At the same time, the attitude of some of these local leaders radically changed as they took stock of the historic opportunity afforded by the exodus—to turn Haifa permanently into a Jewish city. As one knowledgeable Jewish observer put it a month later, "a different wind [began to] blow. It was good without Arabs, it was easier. Everything changed within a week."

In any event, Haifa's civilian elites had little ability to influence the course of events: "The offensive of 21–22 April had delivered the Arab neighbourhoods into Haganah hands, relegating the civil leaders to the sidelines and for almost a fortnight rendering them relatively ineffectual in all that concerned the treatment of the Arab population."[91]

Massacres and Expulsions in the Second Half of 1948

The implementation of Plan D succeeded in clearing much of the territory designated by UNSCOP as part of the Jewish State, but Egypt, Transjordan, Syria, Iraq, and Lebanon responded to Israel's declaration of independence on May 14 by invading. The Arab armies advanced on all fronts in the war's first phase and again imperiled the life of the Jewish community. The IDF took the offensive for the remaining three phases, driving out the Arab invaders and conquering large chunks of land assigned to the Arabs by UNSCOP. Again, as in April and May, a central feature of these military operations was the destruction of Arab villages and the expulsion of their inhabitants. Indeed, the IDF's conduct toward Arab civilians grew more brutal as the war went on, culminating in a spate of massacres in October in the Galilee.

This section examines two particular IDF operations, Dani in the center of the country and Hiram in the north. The evidence shows that Israel's political and military leaders endorsed a policy of expulsion of Arab noncombatants and that indiscriminate aerial and artillery bombardment as well as outright massacre played a central role in precipitating flight.

Lydda and Ramle

During the second phase of the interstate war in July 1948—the so-called "Ten Days"—the IDF launched Operation Dani, designed to relieve Jerusalem by securing the Tel Aviv-Jerusalem road. This entailed the conquest of Lydda and Ramle, two towns occupied by the Transjordanian Arab Legion a scant ten miles from Tel Aviv, as well as the area running from Latrun north to Ramallah. The presence of legion troops and Lydda and Ramle's location inside the area assigned to the Arab state by the UN partition plan allowed the residents to feel fairly safe, but in reality the IDF forces employed in the operation greatly outnumbered the legionnaires stationed in the two towns.[92]

Again, the preattack evidence is ambiguous regarding Israeli intentions toward the civilian inhabitants of Lydda and Ramle. Neither the plans for Operation Dani, nor the plans that preceded it contained any orders on the treatment of the fifty thousand to seventy thousand Arab residents, although orders for other operations in early July explicitly called for cleansing.[93] But Morris also observes that a "strong desire to see the population of the two towns flee already existed" among the officers charged with commanding the operation before it began, and that from the beginning of the assault during the night of July 9–10, "the operations against Lydda and Ramle were designed to induce civilian panic and flight—as a means of precipitating military collapse and possibly also as an end itself."[94] Further supporting this view is a message sent by Operation Dani headquarters to one of the brigades involved in the attack on July 10: "Flight from the town of Ramle of women, the old and children is to be facilitated. The [military age] males are to be detained."[95] Ben-Gurion himself was also reportedly obsessed with the threat posed by Lydda and Ramle to Jewish Jerusalem and Tel Aviv.[96]

The methods by which the offensive was executed also sustain the interpretation that the IDF brass sought to displace the inhabitants of Lydda and Ramle. The assault began with aerial bombardment designed to frighten the population, a new tool in the IDF arsenal. As Dani headquarters informed the IDF General Staff on July 10, "A general and serious [civilian] flight from Ramle" was underway. "There is great value in continuing the bombing."[97] Dani headquarters repeatedly radioed the General Staff to request further bombardment—including the use of incendiary bombs—owing to its impact on the population (especially in Ramle).[98] A Yiftah Brigade unit—the Eighty-ninth Battalion led by Moshe Dayan—also launched an armored raid into Lydda on the eleventh, "spraying machine-gun fire at anything that moved," an attack that killed and wounded as many as two hundred Arabs, many if not most of whom were noncombatants.[99]

Following the pullout of the Arab Legion company stationed in the town during the night of July 11–12, the leading citizens of Ramle agreed to surrender. The document guaranteed the safety of the population, and stipulated that all people except men of military age were free to leave. In Lydda, on the other hand, some legionnaires and Arab irregulars holed up in the police station, but otherwise there was no resistance as Israeli troops entered the town (although no surrender or cease-fire negotiations had taken place). On the morning of the twelfth, however, a few Arab Legion armored cars drove into Lydda, sparking a firefight in which some armed townspeople participated, possibly believing that the incursion represented the opening of a legion counterattack. IDF troops, numbering only three hundred or four hundred, were ordered to "shoot at 'any clear target' or, alternatively, at anyone 'seen on the streets'" in order to suppress the sniping. Morris describes what happened next:

> Some townspeople, shut up in their houses under curfew, took fright at the sounds of shooting outside, perhaps believing that a massacre was in progress. They rushed into the streets—and were cut down by Israeli fire. Some of the soldiers also fired and lobbed grenades into houses from which snipers were suspected to be operating. In the confusion, dozens of unarmed detainees in one mosque compound, the Dahaimash Mosque, in the town centre, were shot and killed. Apparently, some of them tried to break out and escape, perhaps fearing that they would be massacred. IDF troops threw grenades and apparently fired PIAT (bazooka) rockets into the compound.[100]

Approximately 250–400 people were killed in the massacre, and many others died after being expelled.[101] Two IDF soldiers died.

If a policy of expulsion had not already been formulated—and the prebattle attitudes of IDF commanders as well as their chosen methods of attack in the event indicate that such a strategy may have existed—the firefight in Lydda changed that. The brief battle underlined the tremendous danger of leaving substantial concentrations of Arabs intact behind the front lines:

> The unexpected outbreak of shooting [by snipers in Lydda] highlighted the simultaneous threats of a Transjordanian counterattack and of a mass uprising by a large Arab population behind the Israeli lines, as Allon's three brigades were busy pushing eastwards, towards their second stage goals, Latrun and the Ramallah ridge. This was the immediate problem. In the long term, the large hostile concentration of Arab population in Lydda and Ramle posed a constant threat to the heartland of the Jewish state—to Tel Aviv itself and to the road artery linking it to Jewish Jerusalem—as Ben-Gurion had put it six weeks before.[102]

Even some Israeli elites who opposed a general policy of Arab expulsion, such as Yitzhak Ben-Aharon, a leader of one wing of the Mapam Party, saw the necessity of driving out the inhabitants of Lydda and Ramle owing to the security threat they would always pose: "If there remains a large Arab center . . . there will always remain the problem of [Arab] attack [on Jews]. The problem of Ramle and Lydda stands, because the evil [i.e., an Arab attack from the two towns] could break out at any minute."[103] Creating a giant refugee flow also served an immediate military purpose by congesting the lines of a potential Arab Legion counterattack with fleeing Arab civilians.

The fate of Lydda and Ramle's inhabitants was decided by Ben-Gurion himself. As news of the sniping in Lydda came in to Dani headquarters, Yigal Allon asked what should be done with the Arabs. Ben-Gurion reportedly "responded with a dismissive, energetic gesture with his hand and said: 'Expel them.' "[104] Subsequently, orders were sent from headquarters to the Yiftah Brigade signed by Yitzhak Rabin, Dani's chief of operations, directing that Lydda's residents be expelled immediately.[105] A massive exodus from the two towns took place on July 12–13, an evacuation that the IDF made no pretense was voluntary, as IDF signals traffic spoke of "expelling the inhabitants" and the "eviction/evacuation of the inhabitants."[106] The expellees suffered from heat, lack of water, and hunger on the trek, and an undetermined number died.

Operation Hiram

Most of the fighting after the "Ten Days" occurred against the Egyptians in the south.[107] One exception, however, was Operation Hiram, meant to smash Qawuqji's ALA in the north-central Galilee, where it barred a linkup between the Jewish-held coastal areas in the west and Jewish areas north and south of the Sea of Galilee to the east. The offensive, which took place over the last four days of October, crushed the ALA, captured the rest of northern Palestine, and advanced into Lebanon up to the Litani River. At least half of the area's population of fifty thousand to sixty thousand fled to Lebanon.

The recent release of Haganah and IDF documents shows that there was in fact "a central directive by Northern Front to clear the conquered pocket of its Arab inhabitants," issued by General Moshe Carmel on the morning of October 31.[108] The order itself reads: "Do all in your power for a quick and immediate cleansing [*tihur*] of the conquered areas of all the hostile elements in line with the orders that have been issued[.] The inhabitants of the areas conquered should be assisted to leave."[109] Carmel issued this order during or shortly after a meeting with Ben-Gurion in Nazareth, indicating that the prime minister supported—or even authored—the expulsion order. Carmel restated the order ten days later, adding that a cordon sanitaire five kilometers deep along the Lebanese border was also to be cleared. According to Morris, "There can be no doubt that, in the circumstances, the brigade and district OCs understood Carmel's first order, of 31 October (and perhaps also his follow-up of 10 November), as a general directive to expel."[110]

Operation Hiram opened—as had Operation Yoav in the Negev two weeks earlier—with aerial bombing attacks on several villages by B-17s and C-47s.[111] The IDF tended to view Christian villages as less threatening than those populated by Muslims. Moreover, Muslim settlements usually fought, whereas Christians, Druze, and Circassians tended to submit peacefully and avoid involvement with the ALA. Thus, Muslims primarily incurred the wrath of IDF units and fled or were expelled, while non-Muslims were generally left alone.[112]

Hiram resulted in a spate of massacres at Saliha, Safsaf, Jish, Hule, Sa'sa, 'Arab al-Mawasi, Majd al Kurum, Deir al Asad, and 'Eilabun. "These atrocities," writes Morris, "mostly committed against Muslims, no doubt precipitated the flight of communities on the path of the IDF advance."[113] They also sparked several investigations into IDF conduct vis-à-vis Arab civilians. Ben-Gurion, however, who was delighted by the absence of Arabs on a trip in Galilee after Hiram, managed to impede and then later gain control of the investigations, which unsurprisingly resulted in no prosecutions. New orders were issued to the IDF regarding the treatment of Arab civilians, but the war was largely over and thus these rules had little practical effect.

The demographic incompleteness of Operation Hiram's results is not evidence of the absence of an expulsion policy, but rather of an expulsion policy implemented late in the offensive and in incomplete fashion. Moreover, for a variety of reasons many villagers in central Galilee did not readily flee their homes. The swiftness of the Israeli advance, ALA proscriptions against flight, and Lebanon's refusal to permit refugees to cross the border all played a role; many Arabs had probably also learned by now that running away meant permanent exile.[114] As a classified IDF report on the operation concluded, "It appears, therefore, that the Arab population in the Galilee by and large stayed put in its villages, despite the fact that our forces tried to throw it out, often using means which were illegal and not gentle."[115] These means included massacres of Arab villagers. There is no evidence to indicate that a specific policy of massacre was communicated from the Yishuv's political leadership to the fighting units. But, according to Morris, "two things indicate that at least some officers in the field understood Carmel's orders as an authorization to carry out murderous acts that would intimidate the population into flight: the pattern in the actions and their relative profusion; and the absence of any punishment of the perpetrators."[116]

ALTERNATIVE EXPLANATIONS

In this section I briefly consider the impact of Israel's regime type, perceptions of the identity of the Palestinian Arabs, organizational dynamics within the Israeli military, and desperation on the ethnic cleansing that occurred in 1948.

Regime Type

Let me first clarify the coding of Israel's regime type. Israel declared independence on May 14, 1948, having just survived a civil war and bracing for an invasion by five neighboring Arab states. I have coded Israel as a democracy from the date of its proclamation of statehood, making this one of the few cases of a democracy fighting a war of territorial aggrandizement. The Polity 4 dataset, the primary source for coding political regimes in international relations, gives Israel its highest possible democracy score in 1948. Michael Doyle, however, codes Israel as a liberal democracy starting in 1949, presumably because the new state did not hold its first elections until January 25, 1949. Why, then, do I code Israel as a democracy?

Observers are unanimous that although other representative institutions existed—such as the Va'ad Le'umi, or National Assembly—the Jewish Agency comprised a "quasi-government" or a "state within a state" under the British Mandate by the 1930s. One British observer noted in 1944 that the agency "was in some respects arrogating to itself the powers and status of an independent Jewish government."[117] Not only did the Jewish community have its own military force—the Haganah—Morris points out that it also had a "protogovernment—the Jewish Agency—with a cabinet (the Executive), a foreign ministry (the Political Department), a treasury (the Finance Department), and most other departments and agencies of government," including a school system, taxing authority, and agencies for settling new arrivals and purchasing and developing land.[118] The Council (legislative body) of the Jewish Agency was elected, half being selected by the World Zionist Organization and the other (non-Zionist) half being chosen from a variety of countries "in a manner best suited to local conditions."[119] The Council in turn selected the Executive, and the chairman of the Executive functioned like a prime minister. The president was more of a figurehead position, much as the president of Israel is today. In the late mandate period, these two positions were held by David Ben-Gurion and Chaim Weizmann, respectively. One Israeli historian dubbed this system essentially a self-governing democracy under the British Mandate, and Polity saw fit to label it as democratic from the moment of Israel's inception rather than waiting until after the 1949 elections.[120]

The ease of the transformation from Jewish Agency to government of Israel indicates just how isomorphic the two structures were. As independence neared, a multiparty committee from the Agency Executive and the Va'ad Le'umi appointed a thirty-seven-member People's Council drawn from Jewish political parties "according to their proportional political strength in the Yishuv." On independence, this body became the legislature of the Provisional Government, and the various departments, agencies, and bureaus that already existed melded into the new government ministries. "During its tenure, from May 14, 1948, until March 10, 1949, when the first constitutional government was officially installed, the Provisional Government evoked the broadest measure of national loyalty. No one questioned either its moral or legal authority."[121]

It is thus easy to see why Polity codes Israel as a democracy in 1948. The legislature, although not directly elected, was appointed by people who were elected, and was broadly representative of the political parties in the Yishuv. This government had a rudimentary parliamentary system, an army (that soon brought other armed Jewish groups under its control), established a supreme court, and enjoyed a high level of legitimacy among its people. In practice, Ben-Gurion, head of the Provisional Government, exercised a great deal of personal authority, but this is not enough to differentiate Israel from other democracies, where executives often wield expansive powers.

Did the democratic nature of the Israeli government have any effect one way or the other on civilian victimization? The main consequence that democratic politics seems to have had for Israeli policy toward Arab civilians during the war was to moderate it slightly owing to the presence of the Mapam Party in the ruling coalition. Mapam—the United Workers Party— was a socialist party to the left of Ben-Gurion's Mapai that advocated a classless society, equal rights for Arabs, and a binational state. Mapam ministers sometimes questioned or opposed what they perceived to be the government's policy of expulsion. In May 1948, for example, Bechor Shitrit, the minister of police and minority affairs, argued that Arabs displaced by the fighting should be allowed to return to their homes. Similarly, Shitrit and his Mapam colleagues in the cabinet opposed the destruction of Arab villages and the transfer of their inhabitants. Mapam ministers also demanded investigations into alleged IDF atrocities during Operation Hiram.[122]

In general, these Mapam interventions had little effect on policy; they just forced Ben-Gurion and the government to be more discreet in their anti-Arab activities. Mapam's intercessions did manage to save a few villages, but the vast majority attacked were evacuated and destroyed. Mapam's position, however, was compromised by the activities and attitudes of its own members. As Morris notes, although some officials and kibbutz members spoke out against village destruction, "The great majority of settlements and officials supported the destruction." Mapam's quandary is illustrated by the Operation Hiram atrocities: "The party faced its usual problem: Ideologically, it was motivated to lead the clamour; in practice, caution had to be exercised as its 'own' generals, party members Sadeh and Carmel, were involved if not implicated." These practical connections to actions the party ideologically opposed—as well a fundamental loyalty to the newfound state—limited Mapam's ability to intercede. Agriculture Minister Aharon Cisling, for example, charged in a cabinet meeting about the Hiram massacres on November 17 that "Jews too have committed Nazi acts," but then "agreed that outwardly Israel, to preserve its good name and image, must admit nothing." The government and the IDF stonewalled the investigations into the atrocities, and the only result was that new orders were issued to the IDF in mid December—when the war was nearly over—to respect civilian life. Thus, although the presence of Mapam in the governing coalition at times proved to be a "nettle in the garden," its objections were easily circumvented by Ben-Gurion and Mapai with the result that the expulsion of Arab civilians, destruction of villages, and prevention of refugee return went forward largely unhindered.[123]

Identity

Jewish leaders viewed themselves as superior to Arabs, but if anything this belief had the opposite effect of the one predicted by the barbaric identity hypothesis. In the midst of the Arab Revolt, for example, Ben-Gurion argued that the Arabs were trying to provoke the Jews to descend to their level and turn the "country red with blood." Ben-Gurion maintained that the Yishuv should respond with a policy of *havlaga* (restraint): "We are not Arabs, and others measure us by a different standard, which doesn't allow so much as a hairsbreadth of deviation . . . our instruments of war are different from those of the Arabs, and only our own instruments can guarantee our victory." Ben-Gurion's desire to displace the Palestinian Arabs was political, not emotional, motivated by the need to establish a viable Jewish state rather than perceptions of the Arabs as savages. As he wrote in his diary in 1936: "I have never felt hatred for Arabs, and their pranks have never stirred the desire for revenge in me. But I would welcome the destruction of Jaffa, port and city. Let it come; it would be for the better." He may very well have viewed the Arabs as "barbaric and mendacious," but these feelings were not the source of his policy toward them.[124]

Clearly, however, the Palestinian Arabs' identity affected Israel's treatment of them. The Jews viewed them as a fifth column because they shared the same Arab identity as the surrounding Arab states, which eventually invaded Israel in May 1948. This is not the same argument, however, as the identity hypothesis explored here: that civilians of another group are targeted because members of that group are viewed as barbarians. Surely many Zionist leaders viewed the Palestinians paternalistically or with contempt, but in the high level discussions of Zionist leaders over decades, there is not much rhetoric to support the argument that Arabs were victimized because Jews perceived them as barbaric savages.

Organization Theory

The parochial organizational interest argument can be quickly dismissed, as the Haganah (later IDF) was the only military service the nascent Israeli state possessed.[125] The organizational culture argument, however, does merit consideration, as leaders of the Haganah early in the war adhered to what might be considered a precursor to the later "purity of arms" doctrine. The Haganah General Staff, in the period December 1947–March 1948, "attempted to keep its units' operations as 'clean' as possible . . . orders were repeatedly sent out to all Haganah units to avoid killing women, children and old people. In its specific orders for each operation, the HGS almost always included instructions not to harm noncombatants."[126] The Haganah, at least according to these pronouncements, had a culture of restraint when it came to civilians, beliefs on which it acted when hostilities began in December 1947.

This culture began to decline in importance, however, as the violence of Haganah reprisals quickly escalated. In fact, it appears that a better explanation for Haganah restraint toward Arab civilians in the war's early months was the desire to prevent the conflict from spreading: "Our interest, if disturbances break out," wrote Galili, chief of the Haganah National Staff, "is that the aggression [i.e., violence] won't spread out over time and over a great deal of space. From this perspective, the most important defensive measure is where we are attacked, there to retaliate."[127] As described above, however, as Arab attacks became more widespread and the Jewish military position grew more precarious, any culture of restraint began to give way. By the time of Plan D, which entailed the destruction of villages and purposeful targeting of civilians, whatever culture of restraint existed in the Haganah had largely evaporated. The Jewish armed forces willingly executed the national policy of using violence to expel the Palestinian Arabs.

Deterrence and Desperation

As should be evident by now, deterrence and desperation played key roles in addition to the underlying Zionist desire to expand territorially in generating the outcome in 1948. When hostilities broke out in December 1947, Jewish leaders exercised restraint because they hoped to keep the conflict limited and wished to avoid provoking uninvolved Arabs from joining the fight. Despite possessing an edge in overall manpower, the Zionist military position was precarious owing to the dispersed nature of Jewish settlement in Palestine. This vulnerable position deterred the Zionist leadership from aggressively targeting the Arab population for fear of provoking potentially devastating counterattacks. Over time, however, as their military position worsened and casualties rose, Jewish leaders realized that victory and conquering Arab areas and expelling Arab civilians were deeply intertwined. In fact, they were one and the same. Winning the war required a general attack on Arab society, not just reprisals against Arab combatants. Only by removing the latent threat posed by the Arab population in the midst of the Yishuv could the Jews of Palestine obtain security. In this way, the strong prewar desire for a Palestine without Arabs aligned with the military needs of the moment to produce a policy of expulsion.

THIS chapter has argued that civilian victimization—in the form of cleansing—occurs when belligerents intend to conquer and annex territory inhabited by people they view as threatening or hostile. In the case of Palestine in 1947–48, the Yishuv implemented a policy of violence and expulsion against Palestinian Arabs because Jewish leaders believed that Arab villagers were a real or potential fifth column who threatened the existence of the Jewish state.

Three points bear emphasizing. First, Ben-Gurion and others did not view partition as the fulfillment of the Zionist ideal, but only a stage in the ultimate redemption of the entirety of Palestine as a Jewish state. They wanted to expand territorially, and this desire came increasingly to the fore as it became militarily possible.

Second, the idea of transferring—that is, expelling—the Arabs from Palestine did not occur to Jewish leaders de novo in 1948. Rather, transfer was an essential part of Zionism from Herzl forward, and support for transfer was nearly unanimous among Zionists from all points on the ideological spectrum. It would be inaccurate and ahistorical to claim that the rich history of transfer thinking did not deeply inform events as they unfolded in 1948. Indeed, the only reason that Arab villages interspersed with Jewish ones represented a security threat "resulted from the Zionist movement's ideological premise and political agenda, namely the establishment of an exclusivist state."[128] The prerequisite for the creation of a Jewish State was a permanent Jewish majority, and the closer to homogeneity the better.[129] A hostile Arab population within was doubly dangerous given the overwhelming hostile majority without.

Third, there was a decisive shift in Jewish military strategy at the end of March 1948 that came in response to the military predicament of the Yishuv, particularly the severe losses suffered in the battle for the roads. These setbacks apparently convinced Jewish leaders that they would lose the war by remaining on the defensive. The implementation of Plan D, originally scheduled for after the British completed their departure from the country, was pushed forward to early April with the goal of welding together the regions of Jewish settlement and subduing the Arab populations within and between those regions. This meant conquering and occupying Arab towns and villages, as well as leveling those villages (and expelling their inhabitants) from areas along sensitive lines of communication or if the settlements resisted (or were suspected of disloyalty). If Plan D was not the "master plan" for the expulsion of the Palestinians claimed by Walid Khalidi or Ilan Pappe, it certainly envisioned their forcible displacement on a large scale, a process facilitated by massacres and terror tactics such as aerial bombardment.

The fear of a substantial Arab fifth column also decisively influenced the decision to bar any return of Arab refugees after the war. According to the director of the IDF Intelligence Department, for example, "There is a serious danger [that returning villagers] will fortify themselves in their villages behind our front lines, and with the resumption of warfare, will constitute at least a [potential] fifth Column, if not active hostile concentrations."[130] Israeli leaders were well aware of the historic opportunity the Arab evacuation presented: the possibility of achieving a (nearly) homogeneous Jewish state was within their grasp.

That said, the Yishuv viewed Muslim Arabs as more threatening than Christian Arabs or Druze. The IDF expelled hardly any Druze even in one case in which the Druze resisted. Druze were allowed to remain in mixed villages from which Muslims and/or Christians were removed.[131] The preferential treatment afforded the Druze (and some Christian Arabs) by the IDF highlights a larger point: whether or not a particular group is attacked in a war like the one between the Jews and Arabs in 1948 depends on the threat the attacker perceives that group presents and thus the potential costs of occupying the territory. Ethnic or national identity is often the proxy used for threat. The Zionists perceived their dispute to be primarily with the Muslim Arabs of Palestine, and viewed Christian Arabs and Druze as less threatening. Not all wars of territorial expansion, therefore, will necessarily be accompanied by brutality and expulsions; it depends on how the invader views the reliability of the newly subjected population.

[7]

Negative Cases

Why Civilian Victimization Doesn't Happen

In the past four chapters I have presented evidence to support the claim that desperation—to win and to save the lives of one's own soldiers—and the intention to conquer and annex territory cause civilian victimization. These case studies have shown, for example, that democracies and nondemocracies each target civilians when these factors are present. Moreover, states from similar and disparate cultural backgrounds have attacked each other's noncombatant populations, indicating that the perception of "barbarity" is not the key factor. Finally, military organizations with and without "punishment" cultures, and services seeking organizational independence and those already established as separate armed services, have behaved similarly when faced with desperate circumstances.

The analysis thus far has focused on cases in which civilian victimization occurred and sought to explain why it happened. An equally important task, however, is to examine cases where civilian victimization did not occur and ask: Why was it absent? Were desperation and the desire to annex territory also absent? If my theory is right, short, victorious wars that cost little in the way of casualties should not be accompanied by civilian victimization, unless the victor intends to annex the loser's land and perceives a threat from the local population.

This chapter provides an overview of a variety of negative cases before turning to a case study of U.S. decision-making in the 1991 Persian Gulf War. The details of this case confirm that President Bush and his key military advisers came to expect a short, victorious war with limited American casualties. Civilians were not targeted intentionally, in line with American values and the low costs of military operations, which provided no reason to escalate.

Other aspects of this case give some cause for unease, however. First, although it was technically not a case of civilian victimization, U.S. targeting of Iraqi electrical systems led to substantial civilian deaths after the war, owing to disease caused by contaminated water. These deaths were not purposefully inflicted, but they were not wholly collateral either since the intent of the United States was to "pressure" the civilian population to depose Saddam Hussein. This incident highlights the fine line between making noncombatants uncomfortable versus killing them, and also how abiding by the rules of war does not always reduce the number of civilian casualties.

Second, the U.S. resort to economic sanctions—though mostly before and after the actual war—did target Iraqi civilians. American leaders, anxious to avoid the costs of battle, implemented a blockade of Iraq, embargoing all foodstuffs before the war and to a lesser degree afterward. The immediacy with which the United States decided to deny food to the Iraqi population suggests that the concern that democracies increasingly show for protecting civilians from direct attack does not extend to less overt forms of harm, and that democracies continue to accept the deaths of enemy civilians as a means to protect the lives of their own soldiers.

The chapter closes with a brief examination of the 2003 Iraq War and the Iraqi insurgency, arguing that although the war against the insurgents has become protracted, several factors—such as the historically low fatality rates suffered by U.S. forces, the U.S. goal of stabilization and withdrawal rather than inflicting decisive defeat on the rebels, and possibly the organizational culture of the military—has so far averted civilian victimization.

Negative Cases: An Overview

A few of these negative cases have already been mentioned in passing. Germany's campaigns in Western Europe in 1940, for example, resulted in quick and decisive victories, and were generally characterized by little loss of civilian life. Only when stymied by the Royal Air Force in the Battle of Britain did the Germans strike at the civilian population in the hope that bombing would bring the British to their senses. Germany's attack on Poland in 1939, however, appears at first glance to contradict the argument, as civilian victimization took place in a war that lasted less than a month. A closer look reveals that in spite of the war's brevity, both factors that trigger civilian victimization were present. At a time when Germany had few units to ward off France in the west, Polish resistance in Warsaw threatened to bog down German forces in a protracted siege. Hitler authorized air and artillery strikes on the capital, hoping to demoralize the defenders and bring about an early surrender. Moreover, Poland was destined to be annexed to the

Reich, and Hitler moved quickly to target Polish civic leaders, intelligentsia, as well as some Jews to decapitate potential resistance.[1]

Colonial Wars

British colonial wars provide another set of negative cases. The British Army triumphed easily in many of these conflicts when their tribal opponents attempted to confront superior British firepower and discipline in open battle. Perhaps the most famous confrontation of this type was the Battle of Omdurman in 1898, where British forces under Lord Kitchener slew nearly eleven thousand of the Mahdi's Dervishes at a cost of only forty-nine fatalities on their own side.[2] British wars in the 1840s against the Sikhs— who possessed a conventional army and fought set-piece battles—ended with similar, if slightly less lopsided, outcomes. Another good example is the Zulu War of 1879. After an early reverse at Isandlwana, British forces won a quick and decisive victory over the Zulus, who contributed to their own defeat by repeatedly confronting the redcoats' massed firepower in the open with frontal attacks. According to one assessment, the reason the Zulus lost was "because of the superior military technology and vast forces their attackers could bring against them at that time."[3] Civilian victimization was largely absent from the Zulu War because the Zulu style of fighting played to British strengths; there was no need to apply coercion to the civilian population when the war could be won so quickly by fighting battles.

As noted in chapter 5, guerrilla wars frequently lead to civilian victimization by incumbents and insurgents, but this is not an iron law. The British in Malaya, for example, managed to suppress a Maoist rebellion by the Malayan Races Liberation Army (MRLA), which—the inclusive name notwithstanding—was composed predominantly of ethnic Chinese and drew its support from the small Chinese community on the peninsula. The MRLA, however, was not popular within this community and as a result never exceeded a few thousand combatants who lacked heavy weapons of any sort. That the MRLA did not represent a major threat to British control in Malaya is exemplified by the fact that the MRLA was able to inflict only 1,865 fatalities on the security forces between 1948 and 1960.[4] Moreover, the MRLA's diminutive support base was vulnerable to interdiction, and the British adopted a strategy of severing the rebels' links with the population. First, the bulk of the Chinese community was relocated to "New Villages" where it could be protected from the insurgents and organized to defend itself. Second, British forces specifically targeted the rebels' food supply by seizing their sources of rice in the towns and destroying their jungle gardens. Lacking much civilian support to begin with, and with its source of supplies cut off, the insurgency eventually dwindled and sputtered out. Since the Malayan Chinese were not eager to support the rebellion, the task for the British was to protect them from the rebels; targeting civilians was unnecessary and would have been counterproductive, driving them into the arms of the rebels for their own survival.

Interstate Wars

Several interstate wars since World War II support the contention that states tend to abjure targeting civilians when they are able to win wars quickly and at low cost. China, for example, has fought three limited wars since Korea—one against India in 1962, and two against Vietnam in 1979 and 1987—and has not targeted civilians in any of them. In the 1962 border dispute with India, Chinese troops routed ill-prepared Indian defenders, but then declared a unilateral cease-fire and withdrew, inflicting little damage on civilian life.[5] China's three-week-long punitive expedition into northern Vietnam in 1979 was far more destructive and resulted in a larger number of battle deaths, but again did not intentionally target noncombatants (although much civilian property was destroyed).[6] The 1982 Falklands War between Britain and Argentina, too, remained limited in scope, duration, and intensity, as did the Kargil War between India and Pakistan in 1999.

One factor that several of these conflicts have in common is the remote location of the hostilities, which helped to limit the impact of the fighting on the population. The Falklands War, for example, was largely an air and naval affair fought in the waters surrounding the Falkland Islands. The ground combat after the British landings there occurred amidst a civilian population of less than two thousand.[7] A total of three civilians were killed by an errant British shell.[8] Similarly, the Kargil conflict—initiated by Pakistan's infiltration of troops across the Line of Control in Kashmir in spring 1999—was fought high in the Himalayas at elevations exceeding fifteen thousand feet. Some of the Pakistanis' lodgments overlooked Highway 1A on the Indian side of the line, and Pakistani artillery shelled the town of Kargil, blowing up an Indian ammunition dump nearby.[9] Indian accounts, however, mention no civilian casualties, and none of the actual combat took place in or near inhabited areas.

Another factor that can limit civilian victimization, even in protracted wars of attrition, is when the belligerents possess limited capabilities to harm the adversary's population. In the war between Ethiopia and Eritrea from 1998 to 2000, for example, estimates of battle deaths range as high as 100,000.[10] The conflict was likened to World War I on the Western Front because it was characterized by trench warfare and human-wave attacks. Despite these massive human costs, however, neither side resorted to extended strategies of targeting noncombatants. The reason is that when it came to air raids and mistreatment of enemy nationals living on its own soil, each belligerent faced retaliation by the other side. Given the limited damage that such attacks afforded, the two countries were able to agree to a moratorium on air strikes against civilians and never resorted to killing enemy nationals. Furthermore, both parties were minor powers, which made them more susceptible to persuasion and mediation of great powers, particularly the United States.

The Ethiopian-Eritrean War affected civilians in three ways, none of which rose to the level of civilian victimization. First, the fighting caused hundreds of thousands of people on both sides of the border to flee the battle area. One study reports that by March 1999, the conflict had displaced as many as 800,000 people, not surprising given that the front line was a thousand kilometers long.[11] There is no evidence, however, that either side intentionally targeted noncombatants in order to cause this flight.

Second, the Ethiopian government expelled more than sixty-seven thousand Eritreans living in Ethiopia—many of whom were Ethiopian citizens—claiming that they were spies who represented a threat to national security.[12] Although such expulsions were undoubtedly illegal and a flagrant violation of human rights—most expellees were not allowed to challenge their deportation nor take any of their belongings—those banished were not killed or treated in such a way that large-scale deaths could be expected. As many as forty thousand Ethiopians also left Eritrea, but most of these departures seem to have been voluntary rather than coerced. As Amnesty International concluded in 1999, "There have been mass expulsions in cruel and inhuman conditions of Eritreans from Ethiopia. The Eritrean security forces ill-treated some Ethiopians but there was no evidence found of a systematic policy in Eritrea of deliberate or widespread ill-treatment of Ethiopians."[13]

Finally, both sides conducted a handful of air strikes—especially at the beginning of the war—on urban areas. On June 5, 1998, for example, Ethiopian MiG jets bombed and strafed Asmara airport—clearly a military target—killing one and wounding five.[14] In retaliation, Eritrean aircraft bombed targets in Mekele, the regional capital of Tigray. The Eritreans apparently hit a school, however, killing 47 people and wounding 153.[15] Ethiopian jets then attacked Asmara airport again the next day, while the Eritreans struck the town of Adigrat on the eleventh. In response to this escalation of the war, U.S. president Bill Clinton intervened and helped negotiate an "air cease-fire" between the two belligerents. While both sides imported aircraft during the extended cease-fire from June 1998 to February 1999, and Ethiopia used its jets in support of its ground forces and to bomb a few military targets, further attacks against civilians failed to materialize.[16]

This restrained treatment of noncombatants in a war of attrition is explained by each side's lack of capability. Both Eritrea and Ethiopia had only a handful of jet fighter aircraft, pilots of indifferent quality, and no bombers. The amount of damage that each could inflict on noncombatants, therefore, was small. The costs—both in downed aircraft and lost international support—would be large, however, which meant that launching sustained bombing of civilians was simply not feasible or cost-effective. Given that bombing civilians conferred little military advantage, it was relatively easy for third parties to work out a cease-fire, which redirected air operations toward the immediate battle area or military targets.

Wars that end quickly and with relatively little bloodshed tend to spare noncombatants; belligerents may avoid civilian victimization even in some protracted wars of attrition when they are unable to inflict much damage on the adversary's civilian population and doing so is not worth the cost of the retaliation it would trigger. Below I present a detailed analysis of one case in which the attacker anticipated a quick and decisive victory and refrained from targeting civilians: the United States in the 1991 Persian Gulf War. I show that the shift in strategy from a one-corps frontal attack to a two-corps flanking maneuver caused U.S. leaders to grow optimistic that the Iraqis could be ejected from Kuwait speedily and with few U.S. casualties.

THE PERSIAN GULF WAR

The U.S.–led coalition refrained from serious direct attacks on civilians in the Persian Gulf War, I argue, because American political and military leaders expected—correctly, it turned out—a relatively low-cost war.[17] Coalition members lost a mere thirty-eight aircraft in the course of six weeks, and the ground war that routed the Iraqi Army lasted only a hundred hours. The U.S. military as a whole suffered a total of 147 fatalities during the course of the war; only 63 of these were inflicted on ground forces by enemy fire.[18] President Bush then called a halt to offensive operations rather than risk higher casualties and a collapse of the coalition by seeking Saddam Hussein's ouster.

The Ground Plan

The original American force deployed to the Persian Gulf in autumn 1990 to defend Saudi Arabia from an Iraqi invasion (Operation Desert Shield) was insufficient to eject Saddam Hussein's army from Kuwait.[19] With the forces available, the best that General H. Norman Schwarzkopf's Central Command (CENTCOM) planners could come up with was a frontal assault into the teeth of the Iraqi defenses. As Schwarzkopf commented in his memoirs, "I actually had asked my planners [in early August] to look into conducting an offensive using only the forces we were sending for Desert Shield. They'd studied the problem and come back with, 'It can't be done.' "[20] The CENTCOM team briefed the frontal attack strategy in Washington at the Pentagon and the White House on October 10–11, estimating a total of ten thousand American casualties (fifteen hundred dead).[21] CENTCOM's plan went over like a lead zeppelin in Washington, derisively dubbed the "high diddle diddle up-the-middle plan" and earning Schwarzkopf unflattering comparisons to General George McClellan, the reluctant warrior of the Civil War.[22]

Spurred on by dissatisfaction with CENTCOM's efforts, Defense Secretary Dick Cheney and chairman of the Joint Chiefs of Staff General Colin Powell each put together their own separate planning efforts. Cheney's plan called for American ground forces to seize territory in the far west of Iraq where they could simultaneously threaten Baghdad, suppress the Scud missile threat to Israel, and use the land as a bargaining chip to trade for Saddam's withdrawal from Kuwait.[23] Powell, on the other hand, preferred to use decisive force to attack around the exposed western flank of the Iraqi forces. Powell pushed his conception, which would require an additional army corps, when he visited Schwarzkopf in Riyadh in late October. Upon his return to Washington at the end of the month, Powell found the president ready to provide the forces necessary to do the job. The decision to reinforce U.S. forces in the gulf, announced by Bush on November 8, eventually brought U.S. strength in theater to more than 454,000 by the start of the air campaign and over 541,000 for the ground campaign.[24] America's coalition allies committed about 200,000 troops, bringing the total coalition force to almost three-quarters of a million personnel.[25] American ground forces alone accounted for almost twenty-two hundred tanks, 80 to 90 percent of which were M1A1s, while other coalition members contributed about twelve hundred tanks.[26]

The plan for the ground offensive as finally conceived consisted of two elements. First, two U.S. Marine divisions along the coast would launch an attack directly into the Iraqi defense lines in the direction of Kuwait City. This attack, along with the threat of amphibious landings by marines floating offshore, was intended to fix the Iraqis in place and draw in their mobile reserves, including the elite Republican Guard divisions. Second, the army's Seventh and Eighteenth corps, secretly redeployed far to the west during the air campaign, would sweep out of the desert, take the Iraqis in the flank, and cut off their line of retreat across the Euphrates River.

The Air Plan

The air campaign in the Persian Gulf War was divided into two parts: a strategic decapitation campaign directed against Saddam Hussein's regime in Baghdad, and a close air support denial campaign aimed at Iraqi ground forces in the Kuwaiti theater of operations (KTO). The initial conception for the use of air power, however, omitted the latter part entirely and focused solely on paralyzing the Iraqi regime by destroying its instruments of coercion, interdicting its ability to control its forces in the field, and perhaps even killing Saddam himself or facilitating his overthrow. The denial portion of the campaign was only added later as the plan expanded, went through several iterations, and army officers like Powell and Schwarzkopf exerted their influence.

The strategic part of the campaign was initially designed by Colonel John A. Warden III, the deputy director of plans for warfighting concepts, and reflected his vision of "the modern battlefield as a dartboard."[27] This dartboard modeled an enemy's centers of gravity—which together constituted its warfighting capability—as a set of five rings moving outward from the bull's-eye in decreasing degrees of importance. These five rings in turn translated in the Instant Thunder plan into twelve target categories.[28] In the center of the board sat the most important center of gravity, the enemy leadership and the assets that allowed it to command, control, and communicate with its military forces in the field. Destroying the targets in this ring would cause the enemy regime to collapse and its war effort to founder. The target categories in the bull's-eye consisted of telecommunications/command, control, and communications, and national leadership facilities, such as Saddam's presidential palaces.

The second ring on the dartboard contained the adversary's war-related production and economic infrastructure. Specific target categories here included electric power, oil refineries and storage, weapons of mass destruction, and general military research, production, and storage. Next came the transportation network, destruction of which would handicap the enemy's ability to move and supply his troops. Targets in this group included Iraq's railways and key bridges. Inside the fourth ring lay the civilian population and its means of sustenance, while the last ring consisted of the enemy's actual military forces. The only target category falling in the outer two rings was Saddam's short-range ballistic missile capability (Scuds); the civilian population was not directly targeted. The number of individual aim points associated with these target categories increased by almost an order of magnitude from the inception of Instant Thunder to the end of the war, from 84 in August 1990 to 772 in late February.[29]

The central idea of Warden's conception, as with all strategic bombing, was to go straight to the heart of an enemy society and destroy the vital targets that would lead to its collapse. What was new about Warden's plan, however, was its emphasis on targeting leadership, a focus made possible by the revolution in accuracy produced by precision-guided munitions (PGMs). Indeed, despite their coyness about it afterward, U.S. air planners hoped to kill Saddam Hussein and actively pursued this objective during the war.[30] The advent of PGMs allowed airmen to destroy important urban targets without also inflicting enormous damage on the surrounding civilian population. In fact, the marriage of PGMs with Stealth technology in the form of the F-117 fighter finally made it possible to implement the strategy originally envisioned by American air planners in AWPD-1 before World War II. According to former air force chief of staff General Michael

Dugan, "Desert Storm was . . . a vindication of the old concept of precision bombing. . . . The technology finally caught up with the doctrine."[31]

Warden had previously developed his ideas in a book, and so when called on by CENTCOM in early August to design an air campaign to drive the Iraqis from Kuwait, he and his colleagues quickly put together a plan and briefed Schwarzkopf and Powell on August 10–11. In a nutshell, Warden proposed to go after the three innermost rings: leadership, economic infrastructure, and lines of communication. "The political objective of these strikes," observe Michael Gordon and Bernard Trainor, "would be to make it impossible for Saddam Hussein to run his country and to drive a wedge between the Iraqi leadership and the Iraqi people by bringing home the costs of the war. The military objective would be to knock out that portion of the national infrastructure that was essential for the war effort."[32] Pape puts it more bluntly: "Instant Thunder sought to kill, overthrow, or isolate Saddam Hussein and his regime or to use the threat of these events to compel Saddam to withdraw from Kuwait."[33] Warden's original plan contained no provision for attacking Iraqi ground forces for the simple reason that he did not believe such attacks would be necessary.

Warden's belief that airpower alone could persuade Saddam to pull his army out of Kuwait was not shared by Powell, who was convinced a ground campaign would be necessary and wanted to inflict maximum damage on Saddam's army. As Powell told Warden in August 1990, "I won't be happy until I see his tanks destroyed. I want to leave their tanks as smoking kilometer fence posts all the way back to Baghdad."[34] Nor was Schwarzkopf sold on the idea that Iraq would collapse from strategic attacks only. He wanted to inflict heavy attrition on the Iraqi Army in the KTO, and particularly on Saddam's elite units in order to ease the way for the coalition ground attack: "We need to destroy—not attack, not damage, not surround—I want you to *destroy* the Republican Guard."[35] It was to accommodate these preferences that U.S. planners revised the air campaign to include a major effort against Iraqi ground forces.

Although Instant Thunder aimed to achieve its effects primarily by targeting Saddam Hussein and his instruments of control, bombing was also intended to influence the morale of the Iraqi civilian population. By showing them that U.S. airpower could strike anywhere at any time, and that the regime could not protect its citizens, the designers of Instant Thunder hoped to impress on ordinary Iraqis the "bankruptcy and impotence of the Saddam Hussein regime."[36] Furthermore, wrecking the country's economic infrastructure would "convince the Iraqi populace that a bright economic and political future would result from the replacement of the Saddam Hussein regime."[37] In fact, air planners believed that Instant Thunder might encourage Iraqis to dispose of Saddam. As Daniel Kuehl argues, "Planners hoped that demonstrating Saddam Hussein's inability to prevent coalition aircraft from 'turning out the lights' in Baghdad and denying electricity, the sinews of modern society, to the populace would cause civil unrest and weaken the regime's stability."[38]

Several air force officers and planners confirmed after the war that a goal of Instant Thunder was to lower civilian morale in the short term and gain leverage over Iraq in the long term. General Charles Horner, for example, commander of CENTCOM's air armada during the war, commented that a "side benefit" of the strategic air campaign was "the psychological effect on ordinary Iraqi citizens of having their lights go out." One air planner voiced the hope that the bombing would induce a coup or popular revolt: "Big picture, we wanted to let people know, 'Get rid of this guy and we'll be more than happy to assist in rebuilding. We're not going to tolerate Saddam Hussein or his regime. Fix that, and we'll fix your electricity.'" Finally, Warden argued that knocking out the power created leverage for the coalition should Saddam survive the war because it could offer to restore electricity in exchange for Iraqi concessions.[39]

It is important to recognize, however, that although U.S. military planners intended to influence civilian morale with the instrument of air strikes, they never targeted civilians themselves for attack.

Growing Optimism

Despite dire predictions of high American casualties by a variety of pundits as well as the director of the CIA, both the military and the Bush administration became increasingly optimistic that the United States could win a quick victory at low cost.[40] Colin Powell, for example, recounted in his memoirs a conversation he had with Bush and Cheney at Camp David on Christmas Eve:

> I completely rejected the highest [casualty] estimates. They were extrapolated from old war game formulas in which the U.S. and Soviet armies would grind each other down in Europe. That was not our strategy. First, we planned to punish the Iraqi ground forces with an air offensive of an intensity the world had never witnessed. The air war was to be followed by a ground campaign employing not World War I–style infantry charges but swift, heavily armored units engaged in the left hook around the Iraqis' lightly defended Western flank. I resisted giving anything as slippery as casualty estimates to the President, and so far had managed to avoid specifics. But, when pressed to the wall, I finally came in below even Schwarzkopf's estimate, at three thousand killed, wounded and missing.[41]

At the beginning of Instant Thunder, computer models estimated likely American casualties (defined as killed and wounded) at about five thousand in a six-week ground campaign.[42] As coalition airpower pounded away at Iraqi forces in the KTO, however, U.S. casualty projections continued to decline. On the eve of the ground war, according to Lawrence Freedman and

Efraim Karsh "the expectation was a week if the Republican Guard was bold enough to come out to fight, a little longer if they kept their heads down."[43] Bob Woodward, although correctly emphasizing the uncertainty inherent in such estimates, reports that "some of the senior officers on the Joint Staff had confidentially estimated that the killed in action on the American side would be about 1,000."[44]

President George Bush, the man who mattered most, also believed U.S. casualties would be light. As early as his trip to the gulf at Thanksgiving, Bush thought the Iraqis could be defeated quickly and with a minimum of American deaths. After being briefed on the battle plan by Schwarzkopf, Bush remarked: "From the presentation, and what I was hearing back in Washington, the military seemed confident that any war would be a short one. . . . On this trip I became convinced we could knock out the Iraqis early; certainly he [Schwarzkopf] felt we would."[45] Later, during the air campaign, the president reiterated his confident view: "I did not believe that Iraq's army had the ability to inflict as much damage as Saddam, or our critics, seemed to think it could. Briefing after briefing had convinced me that we could do the job fast and with minimum coalition casualties. . . . I had no fear of making the decision to go. I was resigned to it. I knew there would be lives lost on both sides, too many, but I was convinced we would move fast, catch the Iraqis off guard, and have the job done in less than a week."[46] Further evidence on the president's attitude is provided by the fact that as the air strikes rolled on without prompting major concessions by Saddam, Bush was anxious to get the ground war started rather than seeking to delay it.[47]

Reasons for Optimism

The most important reason for the change in outlook is that U.S. planners had devised a clever strategy that—if well executed—could result in the complete collapse and destruction of Iraqi forces in the KTO. The transformation of the one-corps "high diddle diddle up-the-middle" plan—an attrition strategy—into the sweeping two-corps western flank attack increased the likelihood of achieving a quick and decisive victory. The Iraqi Army's deployment, with the bulk of its forces in forward, static positions, enhanced the probability that the coalition attack would succeed. By taking the mailed fist of their striking force well out to the west, coalition ground commanders maximized their chance of cutting off the Iraqi forces' line of retreat, encircling them, and destroying them, including the Republican Guard. Moreover, the flanking attack guaranteed that the coalition would possess an overwhelming numerical superiority at the point of attack, rendering theaterwide numbers of less importance. The plan as executed did not fully succeed, since the marines' fixing attack—rather than holding the

Iraqis in place and drawing in their reserves—quickly penetrated the Iraqi defenses and reached Kuwait City in two days, which put the left hook behind schedule and allowed some enemy units to escape. Still, the ground plan stood a good chance of defeating the Iraqi Army decisively with relatively low losses to coalition ground troops.

Two other factors also helped tip the balance in favor of the coalition. First, the vast American buildup and attrition of Iraqi forces by coalition airpower brought the coalition to parity with the Iraqis on paper, and superiority over them in fact.[48] The original conception of the air campaign focused on targets at the core of Iraqi power, but the plan that was actually implemented dedicated the bulk of air strikes to Iraq's fielded military forces. "A specific objective of the air campaign," according to Gulf War Air Power Survey (GWAPS), "was the decrease in combat effectiveness of the Iraqi Army by 50 percent," a goal which U.S. airpower began to pursue in earnest after January 26. In all, about 55 percent of coalition air strikes fell on Iraqi ground forces in the KTO.[49]

The level of destruction inflicted by the bombing is disputed, but since our concern is with what decision-makers believed at the time, it is appropriate to focus on estimates made before the ground war commenced. CENTCOM, for example, estimated that the Iraqis had 4,280 tanks and 540,000 men deployed in the KTO at the start of the air campaign in mid January. By February 23, owing to destruction imposed by airpower, CENTCOM put these figures at 2,592 and 450,000 respectively.[50] In reality, the number of Iraqi troops in theater at the start of the ground war was probably about half this size owing to high rates of desertion.[51] Total coalition forces at this time, as noted above, numbered nearly 750,000 and 3,400 tanks, which significantly outnumbered even CENTCOM's inflated estimate of Iraqi strength.[52] In actuality, the coalition probably had two to three times as many ground troops in the KTO as did the Iraqi Army.[53]

Second, the coalition also held serious qualitative advantages. The standard American tank, for example—the M1A1—substantially outgunned and outranged the T-72, the best tank in the Iraqi arsenal.[54] Most Iraqi divisions, however, did not even have T-72s, which were confined to the three heavy Republican Guard divisions. The only Iraqi formations that approached the quality of coalition units were the Republican Guard divisions, but they still did not possess the level of training and professionalism of the Western armies.[55] Moreover, the quality of Iraq's regular army divisions was much worse. According to one study, the heavy divisions of the regular army "were inferior to the Republican Guard and substantially inferior to their U.S. and British counterparts," while the frontline infantry divisions, which composed the bulk of Iraqi manpower (there were thirty-four of them deployed in Kuwait), "were drawn predominantly from Iraq's rebellious Kurdish and Shi'a populations, who generally opposed Saddam's Ba'th

Party."[56] The coalition, therefore, was qualitatively superior to the Iraqis in terms of troops and equipment.

Impact of the War on Civilians

The aspect of the war that had the greatest impact on Iraqi civilians was the strategic air campaign, Instant Thunder, which opened with F-117 and cruise missile strikes on targets in Baghdad in the early hours of January 17, 1991. Over the next forty-three days, coalition forces delivered 88,500 tons of bombs and conducted more than 41,000 strikes against targets in Iraq and the KTO.[57] More than half of these strikes were directed at Iraqi ground forces in the KTO, while 15 percent of them aimed at the eight categories in the strategic target set.[58] Leadership and command, control, and communications targets absorbed nearly 1,700 strikes, electric power generation facilities were hit 345 times, while oil storage and refining attracted 539 strikes. For all of this sound and fury, relatively few bombs actually hit Baghdad. As William Arkin has pointed out, only 330 bombs (including cruise missiles) totaling a mere 287 tons fell on the Iraqi capital during the entire war.[59]

The United States never targeted civilians themselves during the air campaign, and the ground war was fought in the desert away from populated areas. This does not mean, however, that U.S. bombs did not kill Iraqi civilians. Several incidents of weapons going astray into markets or civilian neighborhoods led to the deaths of scores of noncombatants in each case.[60] Civilian vehicles were also mistakenly bombed or strafed on occasion.[61] The most memorable—and deadly—of these incidents was the bombing by two F-117s of the al-Firdos bunker in the early morning hours of February 13, killing between two hundred and three hundred civilians. Originally built during the Iran-Iraq War as an air raid shelter, the facility was upgraded in 1985 and became an emergency headquarters for Iraqi officials. It contained some telecommunications equipment, but nothing terribly sophisticated. American intelligence concluded that the bunker had been activated as an Iraqi command and control center, but unbeknownst to CENTCOM al-Firdos instead sheltered hundreds of civilians. After the bunker was hit, Baghdad was temporarily placed off limits to further air strikes and hitting targets in the capital was made subject to approval by Washington. This reflected not only humanitarian concerns, but also the political reality that "a few more strikes like that at Al Firdos and the coalition would be undone."[62] Overall, the number of Iraqi civilians killed directly by coalition bombs is estimated to be about three thousand.[63]

In sum, the United States refrained from civilian victimization in the Persian Gulf War because U.S. leaders anticipated scoring a quick and decisive victory over Saddam Hussein, a belief that was validated by events. The air campaign began—as bombing campaigns usually do—by hitting military targets, and the low costs suffered by U.S. aircraft and ground troops gave leaders no reason to deviate from this plan.

Alternative Explanations

Regime Type. Explanations based on regime type yield contradictory predictions in this case. On the one hand, it could be argued that U.S. leaders, imbued with liberal norms regarding the sanctity of innocent life, were repulsed by the idea of bombing civilians. According to GWAPS, for example, the authoritative account of air planning, operations, and effectiveness in the conflict with Iraq,

> Of the five broad components of national power, only the Iraqi population was not made a direct target of bombing. From President George Bush on down, there was widespread agreement from the outset of the planning process that directly attacking the people of Iraq or their food supply was neither compatible with U.S. objectives nor morally acceptable to the American people, whose support was felt, in light of the Vietnam experience, to be essential to the war effort. Thus, the Coalition's "targeting" of the will of Iraq's civilian population was limited, for the very best of reasons, to psychological operations and indirect effects stemming from the bombing of other core target categories.[64]

Public opinion polling, by contrast, tends to support the view that the American people cared little about the lives of Iraqi civilians. Polls taken during the air war indicated that most Americans did not think that the United States should avoid bombing certain targets because of the possibility that Iraqi civilians would be killed, and about two-thirds believed the United States was "making enough of an effort to avoid bombing civilian areas in Iraq."[65] Moreover, more than 80 percent of Americans felt that the al-Firdos bunker was a legitimate military target, and two-thirds held Saddam Hussein responsible for the deaths that occurred in that incident.[66] This episode prompted an international outcry and caused the Bush administration to worry about the stability of the coalition, but there was no domestic backlash. As John Mueller put it in his study of public opinion and the Gulf War, "The public's view of Iraqi civilian deaths and its unalarmed reaction to the bombing of the Baghdad air raid shelter during the war . . . indicate that the American people were quite insensitive to Iraqi casualties, even though they appear to have harbored little ill will toward the Iraqi people."[67] There is thus little reason to suppose that the Bush administration would have been punished by the electorate for killing Iraqi civilians. Bush actually expressed significant anxiety regarding his future in office if the United States did not win the war: "I'll prevail or I'll be impeached."[68] This imperative for victory, according to accountability arguments, translates into a no-holds-barred approach to warfighting: if civilians have to die for victory (and the incumbent's political future) to be secured, so be it. Yet the United States did not wage an all-out war against Iraq; in fact, despite the rout of the Iraqi ground forces in Kuwait, U.S. policymakers refused to expand their war aims and head for Baghdad to topple Saddam Hussein.

Identity. This case undermines the identity argument because the cultural differences between the United States and Iraq did not spur the victimization of civilians. President Bush also repeatedly demonized Saddam Hussein as another Adolf Hitler: a brutal dictator who had to be faced down or else he would continue his aggressive behavior. Bush's depiction of Hussein as another Hitler and his comparison of Iraq's conquest of Kuwait as another Munich helped rally the American public behind deploying troops to Saudi Arabia, but Bush sincerely seemed to believe it.[69] If Saddam was Hitler, however, what did that make the Iraqi people? Yet despite Bush's inflammatory statements, most Americans did not call for harsher treatment of Iraq, and the United States instituted no policy of civilian victimization.

Organization Theory. The organizational culture argument in this case would be that civilian victimization was absent because the U.S. Air Force had a culture of precision strategic bombing. This conjecture is hard to sustain in view of the facts. John Warden, the initial and primary architect of Instant Thunder, received the assignment only because his boss—a strong advocate of using airpower to interdict the enemy's ground forces—was on leave when the Iraqis invaded Kuwait. Warden, who was "passionate about strategic bombing to the point of zealotry" but whose views were not in the air force mainstream, happened to be at the right place at the right time.[70] CENTCOM's air commander, Charles Horner, reportedly threw a draft of Warden's briefing against the wall—not once, but twice—when he first read it in mid August 1990. Some of Horner's pique is explained by his resentment of meddling by armchair strategists from Washington, but substantively he simply disagreed with Warden's argument that Iraq's army could be driven from Kuwait by bombing targets in Baghdad. Horner was far more concerned with how to stop a potential Iraqi invasion of Saudi Arabia than with esoteric theories about decapitating the Iraqi regime. Indeed, the air plan that was eventually implemented—which sent more than half of its attack sorties against Iraqi forces in the KTO—bore little resemblance to Warden's original conception. The point is that there was hardly unanimity inside the air force on the correct way to wage an air campaign against Iraq. Warden was a fringe figure, and it was sheer coincidence that his office—and not Tactical Air Command, for example—was asked to develop the plan. In short, although the Warden decapitation model has since been adopted as one of the air force's primary strategic bombing strategies, this was not the case before the Persian Gulf War.

The parochial organizational interest hypothesis is upheld in its most basic form: advocates of strategic bombing inside the air force argued that bombing Baghdad would win the war by itself, obviating the need for a ground war. The failure of strategic bombing to produce concessions, however, did not lead to escalation against civilians in an attempt to boost the air force's organizational fortunes. If anything, after the bombing of al-Firdos, the opposite occurred, as hardly any bombs hit Baghdad after that incident. Organizational advancement, therefore, cannot be said to have made much of an impact on bombing policy.

The Bombing Norm. A final explanation worth examining is the argument that U.S. restraint in the Gulf War was attributable to the spread of human rights norms globally, specifically the recovery and expansion of the norm against bombing noncombatants. A leading study, for example, argues that "the bombing norm has slowly recovered from the catastrophe of World War II. While far from absolute, the reborn norm has in recent decades engendered a sensitivity to noncombatant casualties that not only constrains states from targeting civilian populations per se but also creates pressures to minimize incidental casualties in general."[71] Another analyst of airpower concludes that "it is highly unlikely that advanced powers will again resort to the wholesale devastation of cities and towns, whether to shatter enemy morale or as a by-product of efforts to hit other target systems, such as railroad yards or factories."[72]

It is true that the norm against bombing civilians has become much stronger and more widely accepted. Aside from revulsion at the infernos of World War II, swiftly advancing technology has played a key role in promoting the norm. "In other words," as Ward Thomas notes, "by making it easier to 'be good' . . . technology has also created *pressure* to be good by removing a possible excuse for being bad."[73] Of course, the U.S. Air Force has always wanted to bomb precisely but was not able to do so in the past. This indicates not so much a change in preferences (induced by norms) but rather a change in capability. The bombing norm argument also misunderstands the progression of most bombing campaigns, which typically start by targeting counterforce objectives before escalating to civilians owing to high losses or failure to coerce the enemy. When a war is won quickly and decisively at extremely low cost, therefore, bombing simply has no time or reason to escalate. In the Persian Gulf War, targets were being destroyed, aircraft losses were miniscule, and the war lasted a few weeks. In such circumstances, there is little reason to deviate from attacking military targets.

Indirect Effects of Bombing and Sanctions on Civilians

Although they did not produce civilian victimization as I have defined it, or large numbers of directly inflicted civilian fatalities, U.S. strategies in the Persian Gulf War nevertheless resulted in large numbers of noncombatant deaths that would not have otherwise occurred. Two factors contributed to this outcome: the U.S. bombing of Iraqi infrastructure—particularly electric power facilities—during Instant Thunder, and the UN-imposed economic sanctions on Iraq beginning in August 1990 and continuing until the overthrow of Saddam Hussein in 2003. These two strategies each served to undermine the health of the Iraqi population, resulting in increased civilian mortality from preventable disease and illness. Policies such as these—that harm civilians but in an indirect manner with diffuse responsibility—may be the civilian victimization of the future for democracies.

Bombing of Infrastructure. The story of civilian suffering unfortunately did not end when the guns fell silent in late February 1991. Although actual bombs killed only a few thousand Iraqis in the strategic air campaign, far more died from the indirect consequences of American air attacks on the country's electrical power systems. Air planners believed that disabling the electric grid and turning out the lights would "depress the morale of the Iraqi people in ways that might serve to loosen Saddam Hussein's political grip on the country."[74] Twenty-five large generating facilities and more than 140 transformer stations supplied Iraq's electricity. Most of the strikes on this system occurred at the outset of the air campaign. In the first two days of the war, 11 power plants and 7 transformer stations were struck. Eventually, bombs fell on a total of 18 plants and 9 transformers. Overall, coalition forces struck Iraqi electric targets 345 times, rendering 88 percent of the system damaged or inoperative.[75] A postwar survey of 21 sites showed that most were hit multiple times, with many suffering extensive damage and some completely destroyed.[76]

The strikes on electric power were intended to have a bloodless psychological effect on the Iraqi citizenry, but several postwar studies showed that turning off the power resulted in significant mortality among civilians, especially the very young and the elderly. The death toll has been put as high as 111,000.[77] All of Iraq's water purification facilities and sewage treatment plants relied on electricity; when power failed as a consequence of the war's opening salvos, the electric pumping stations in the water and sewage systems also failed.[78] The inability to clean the water supply and get it to the citizenry was bad enough, but the sewage system breakdown exacerbated the problem by causing untreated sewage to flow into rivers used for bathing and drinking water. According to Rick Atkinson, "Without power, Baghdad's two sewage-treatment plants no longer functioned, and millions of gallons of raw waste poured into the Tigris. Despite the filth and a shortage of fuel for boiling tainted water, the river served as both communal well and public bath."[79]

The contamination of the water supply in Iraq caused by the lack of electricity in turn led to increased rates of disease. Those most vulnerable to waterborne illnesses—young children and the elderly—suffered the most. One group of analysts reports the results: "Our data demonstrate the link between the events that occurred in 1991 (war, civilian uprising, and economic embargo) and the subsequent increase in mortality. The destruction of the supply of electric power at the beginning of the war, with the subsequent disruption of the electricity-dependent water and sewage systems, was probably responsible for the reported epidemics of gastrointestinal and other infections."[80] A Defense Intelligence Agency (DIA) document from March 1991 noted that the health problems plaguing Iraq were "attributable to the breakdown of normal preventive medicine, waste disposal, water purification and distribution, electricity, and transportation." The document also judged that "communicable diseases in Baghdad are more widespread than usually observed during this time of the year and are linked to the poor sanitary conditions (contaminated water supplies and improper sewage disposal) resulting from the war."[81] These systemic breakdowns and unsanitary conditions, of course, resulted from U.S. bombing.

These deaths do not comprise civilian victimization as I define it, as the effects of cutting electricity were apparently unforeseen, but this episode highlights the risks of pressuring the civilian population through indirect attacks on infrastructure.[82] Prevalent since Vietnam, this "punishment light" strategy is "bombing that makes civilians as miserable as possible without actually killing them."[83] The difficulty with such a policy, of course, is that there is a thin line between causing civilians discomfort and doing things that maim or kill them. As William Arkin put it, "You can't separate neat and clean bombing from postwar deaths. People just died in a different way because of the efficiency of the attacks."[84] The effort to remain within the laws of war but also target civilian morale does not always result in a lower overall death toll.

Sanctions of Mass Destruction? The bombing of Iraqi infrastructure in Instant Thunder had an interactive effect with the economic sanctions that were slapped on Iraq by the UN Security Council (UNSC) in the days following the invasion of Kuwait in August 1990. Technically, the sanctions on Iraq fall outside the purview of this book, since they were initiated by countries that were not at war with Iraq and were actually viewed as an alternative to the use of force to compel Saddam Hussein to abandon Kuwait. Sanctions also continued for more than a decade after the war ended, although their goals shifted from coercing Iraqi forces to leave Kuwait (accomplished during the war) to compelling the Iraqi regime to comply with a variety of other demands, mainly the dismantling of Iraq's weapons of mass destruction programs, recognition of Kuwait's sovereignty, and agreement to pay war reparations. Nevertheless, the major impact that sanctions have had on the health of Iraqi civilians merits discussion.

Sanctions, like coercion in general, are a means of achieving states' objectives on the cheap. When Iraqi forces rolled across the border into Kuwait, the United States and its allies had few military forces in the region and no way to force Saddam to reverse course. Indeed, the main concern of U.S. policymakers in the summer and early fall of 1990 was defensive: to prevent Iraq from overrunning Saudi Arabia. Only later did President Bush decide to use force to eject Saddam's army from Kuwait. The United States turned to sanctions as a cheap alternative that would raise the costs to Iraq of seizing Kuwait and convince Saddam to withdraw.

The sanctions applied to Iraq were the most comprehensive in the history of the United Nations, the first time that body had imposed mandatory sanctions on a country since it levied them on Southern Rhodesia in the 1960s. The sanctions forbade all trade with Iraq; banned the sale of oil, Iraq's only major export; established a naval blockade and severed all air links with Iraq; froze Iraq's financial assets abroad; and prohibited any arms sales to Saddam Hussein's regime. Resolution 661 permitted Iraq to import medical supplies and "in humanitarian circumstances, foodstuffs."[85] Officially, anyway, the blockade made exceptions for food, but in practice Iraqi food imports were soon being interdicted. Comments by U.S. officials indicated that they intended to cut off all imports and exports, including food.[86] The blockade was extremely effective judged by its impact on Iraqi trade: director of the CIA William Webster reported to Congress in early December 1990 that 90 percent of Iraq's imports and 97 percent of its exports had been stopped.[87]

Sanctions also cut off Iraq's ability to obtain parts and chemicals for its water treatment system even though it was known that this could lead to serious health problems. Before the war Iraq depended on these imports—particularly of chlorine—to purify its water supply, much of which is high in salinity. According to a report written by the DIA in January 1991, "Iraq's rivers also contain biological materials, pollutants, and are laden with bacteria. Unless the water is purified with chlorine epidemics of such diseases as cholera, hepatitis, and typhoid could occur." As the report concluded, "Failing to secure supplies will result in a shortage of pure drinking water for much of the population. This could lead to increased incidences, if not epidemics, of disease."[88]

Moreover, what exactly comprised "humanitarian circumstances" quickly became the subject of debate in the Sanctions Committee, the body established by the Security Council to oversee the embargo. Some states maintained that such circumstances prevailed at the first signs of food deprivation, whereas others—the United States and Britain among them—argued

[228]

that Iraq should be denied food until famine conditions took hold.[89] In practical terms, the prohibition on the sale of Iraqi oil deprived a country that imported 75 percent of its food supply of 95 percent of its revenue. The freezing of Iraqi assets overseas further denied to Iraq sources of foreign exchange. Iraq would soon be unable to purchase foodstuffs even if "humanitarian circumstances" were deemed to exist.

In the few months that the embargo was in place before the war started, Iraq experienced shortages of certain commodities like meat, flour, sugar, and cooking oil, which caused prices to rise dramatically but did not lead to anything approaching famine.[90] Indeed, the successful Iraqi wheat harvest in 1990—four times the yield of the previous year—was one of the factors that convinced the CIA that sanctions would not produce Iraqi concessions in the short-to-medium term. Still, there was a fundamental tension at the heart of the sanctions policy, between the wish to use civilian deprivation as a tool to coerce Saddam while also appearing to act humanely. One UN diplomat phrased the dilemma as follows: "The sanctions weapon when applied to food is a double-edged sword. We want Iraq to hurt, but cannot be seen to use famine to bring the country down."[91]

Despite the rout of the Iraqi Army from Kuwait, UN sanctions on Iraq did not end. The Security Council imposed a host of new conditions for the lifting of sanctions, among them the payment of reparations, recognition of the border with Kuwait, renunciation of weapons of mass destruction, and an inspections regime to discover and dismantle Iraq's WMD programs. The Bush and Clinton administrations, however, were quite explicit that sanctions would never be lifted until Saddam was removed from power, thereby giving Saddam little incentive to cooperate.[92] Robert Gates, for example, at the time the nominee to direct the CIA, commented that "Iraqis will pay the price while he is in power. All possible sanctions will be maintained until he is gone. Any easing of sanctions will be considered only when there is a new government."[93] Resolution 687 (April 1991) continued the embargo on trade with Iraq, but Article 20 ended the food blockade, allowing Iraq to notify the Sanctions Committee of its food purchases under the "simplified and accelerated 'no-objection' procedure." The terms of the resolution also permitted Iraq to import "materials and supplies for essential civilian needs."[94] Since Iraq was still not allowed to sell any oil, however, these exemptions were largely meaningless because Iraq had no income with which to purchase these supplies.

As reports emerged of the humanitarian catastrophe unfolding in Iraq, the United States faced another dilemma: how to keep the pressure on Iraq without leaving itself open to the accusation that it was starving innocent civilians? The answer suggested was the oil-for-food program: allow Iraq to sell limited amounts of oil to pay for its humanitarian needs. UNSC Resolutions 706 and 712 (August and September 1991) permitted Iraq to sell $1.6 billion worth of oil every six months, to be deposited in a UN escrow account and used to buy supplies for the civilian population. The details of these resolutions, however, cloud the picture of enlightened humanitarian relief. A UN report on humanitarian conditions in Iraq estimated that the cost of restoring the country's infrastructure to prewar levels would be $22 billion. The report also suggested that Iraq should be allowed to sell $2.65 billion worth of oil every four months. The UNSC resolutions, though, set the limit at $1.6 billion every six months, but not all of this total would be available for humanitarian relief. After deducting sums for reparations and funding the UN inspections teams, the amount left over to purchase food and medicine was $930 million. These funds would be placed in an account controlled by the UN, not an Iraqi government account. The Iraqis perceived this arrangement as an unacceptable infringement on their sovereignty and rejected the resolutions.[95] Not until 1996 did Saddam Hussein's government accept a revised version of oil-for-food proposed in UNSC Resolution 986 that allowed Iraq to sell $2 billion of oil every six months to raise money for humanitarian goods (after deductions, $1.3 billion was available for purchases).

United States government officials commonly argued that Saddam was responsible for any ill effects of sanctions on the Iraqi people because he refused to accept the original oil-for-food deal as contained in Resolutions 706 and 712 in 1991. Several pieces of evidence show this position to be somewhat disingenuous. First, the amount of money allocated for Iraqi relief, as just shown, was inadequate. Second, UN officials were reportedly convinced "that the US intention was to present Saddam Hussein with so unattractive a package that Iraq would reject it and thus take on the blame, at least in Western eyes, for continued civilian suffering." A Bush administration official told the *New York Times* that Resolution 706 was "a good way to maintain the bulk of sanctions and not be on the wrong side of a potentially emotional issue." American leaders appeared to be interested principally in maintaining sanctions at all costs, and secondarily to avoid being "embarrassed by the scale of civilian suffering" in Iraq.[96]

Third, before and after the inauguration of the oil-for-food program, the United States vetoed almost every Iraqi application to import goods to repair its devastated infrastructure on the grounds that such commodities were "dual use," that is, usable for both military and civilian purposes. In the postwar period, Iraq's most important problem—other than food shortages leading to chronic malnutrition (especially in children)—was the decrepit state of the country's electricity-generating facilities and its water and sewage treatment plants. To restore these services, the Iraqis needed to import equipment and chemicals, but the United States "took the view that all infrastructure was dual use" and thus blocked Iraq from importing supplies related to these key sectors, particularly electricity. Through mid 2002, the United States had held up $5 billion worth of goods, "equal to one-quarter of all the humanitarian goods delivered to Iraq over the entire history of the Oil-for-Food program up to that point."[97]

That a humanitarian disaster has occurred in Iraq since 1991 is "evident and undeniable"; the scale of this disaster, however—and who is responsible for it—is hotly disputed. Critics of sanctions began citing the figures of 500,000 excess deaths in the mid 1990s, claims that subsequently rose as high as 2 million.[98] Scientific assessments are more measured, but still chilling. UNICEF, for example, concluded in 1999 that "if the substantial reduction in child mortality throughout Iraq during the 1980s had continued through the 1990s, there would have been half a million fewer deaths of children under-five in the country as a whole during the eight year period 1991 to 1998."[99] Richard Garfield, a public health scholar, estimated excess deaths of Iraqi children from August 1991 to March 1998 to be at least 100,000, and more likely 227,000, with three-quarters of these fatalities associated with sanctions.[100] Garfield's most likely estimate implies a death rate of 1,850 children per month and 60 per day.[101]

The question of responsibility is highly polarized, with some accusing the United States of perpetrating genocide while others fix the blame entirely on Saddam Hussein for failing to take advantage of opportunities to obtain foodstuffs for his people. Neither of these extreme views withstands careful scrutiny. Saddam clearly bears a large measure of responsibility. He rejected the original oil-for-food proposal for several years—flawed though it was—because of the infringement on Iraqi sovereignty it entailed, but Iraqi sovereignty was already heavily curtailed by UN inspections. Moreover, the UN often had to push Iraq to purchase more food and larger amounts of certain types of food—such as high protein biscuits good for nursing mothers and small children. Finally, Saddam manipulated the distribution of food inside the country: health, water, and sanitation conditions tended to be worse in the southern, Shi'a-dominated provinces than in Baghdad and other Sunni Arab areas.[102]

Saddam's manipulations, however, do not let the United States and its allies off the hook. Although the text of Resolution 661 allowed a somewhat ambiguous exception for food, the way in which the embargo was implemented in August 1990 targeted civilians by stopping all food imports to Iraq. After the war in 1991, the UNSC lifted the food blockade knowing that Iraq had no source of income with which to buy any foodstuffs. Later that year, U.S. officials helped craft an oil-for-food resolution at least partially for public relations rather than humanitarian purposes, hedging it with conditions that Saddam could be expected to reject, thus shifting the onus for civilian suffering in Iraq to him. United States representatives on the Sanctions Committee took a hard line on dual-use goods, proscribing many seemingly innocuous items but also goods that would help Iraq with its electrical, water, and sewage problems, leaving the country unable to recover from wartime destruction. Implementation of oil-for-food, however, clearly improved the situation in Iraq, increasing the calorie level in the Iraqi diet and reducing mortality rates. Yet it is hard to disagree with the assessment of John and Karl Mueller: "While the impact of sanctions on the Iraqi people—Saddam's hostages, in effect—may ultimately be his fault, they are also a predictable, and arguably inevitable, consequence of the sanctions policy. If sanctions had not been instituted, it is likely that the country would have moved back toward the relative prosperity . . . it enjoyed before the 1991 Gulf War and that death and suffering would have been far less."[103]

What were the calculations that led to the implementation of economic sanctions that inflicted widespread suffering on the Iraqi people? In August 1990, sanctions were a cheap and easy alternative to force that could be applied immediately. American leaders seemingly had no qualms about embargoing food, even though President Bush repeatedly argued that the United States had no quarrel with ordinary Iraqis. During the war, although the United States clearly wanted Saddam to fall from power, it was unwilling to risk going to Baghdad and doing the job itself for fear of increased casualties, the probability that the coalition would crumble, and the question of what to do with Iraq once Saddam was overthrown. So the Bush administration turned back to sanctions to achieve its goal of a Saddam-free Iraq. Unwilling to pay the cost of eliminating Saddam with force, the United States chose the indirect approach of going through the Iraqi people. Only after September 11, 2001, when the administration of George W. Bush came to view Saddam's WMD programs and supposed ties to terrorists as an intolerable threat to U.S. national security was it willing to accept the cost in U.S. lives to get rid of him.

This conclusion is broadly consistent with the argument advanced in this book. In war, states turn to civilian victimization when traditional force-on-force strategies fail or are too costly. Economic sanctions potentially provide a way for states to avoid the costs of fighting entirely, or at least to postpone those costs until they can be minimized. Given the perception among U.S. leaders that the public is highly averse to casualties—and given the economic power of the United States—policymakers may view sanctions as an attractive alternative to war.[104]

THE UNITED STATES IN IRAQ SINCE 2003

United States wars since the Persian Gulf have largely been quick and low-cost affairs for the American side. The wars to coerce the Bosnian Serbs to come to the bargaining table in 1995, persuade Slobodan Milošević to stop targeting Kosovo's Albanians, and topple the Taliban regime in Afghanistan in 2001 were all quick and relatively bloodless for two reasons: (1) the United States possessed overwhelming military superiority, and

(2) the U.S. military adopted a "hammer and anvil" approach to warfighting that transferred most of the costs and risks to local allied ground forces while the American contribution was limited to airpower.[105] These factors produced quick U.S. victories with minimal costs, and thus there was little possibility that civilians would be targeted.[106]

Iraq: The Conventional War

The conventional phase of Operation Iraqi Freedom—from the initiation of combat in mid March 2003 until President George W. Bush declared an end to major combat operations on May 1—was another quick and decisive victory for the United States against an overmatched foe. Despite controversy between Secretary of Defense Donald Rumsfeld and some U.S. military officers over the number of troops required for the mission, a relatively small (compared to the Persian Gulf War) American and British force attacking from Kuwait had little trouble defeating Iraq's disintegrating conventional forces.[107] The bulk of Iraqi resistance came instead from an unanticipated direction: the so-called "Saddam Fedayeen," regime loyalists who fought unconventionally. Despite this complication, U.S. forces arrived in the vicinity of Baghdad in less than three weeks, and managed to seize the Iraqi capital via a pair of "Thunder Runs" into the city by U.S. armored forces. By the time U.S. ground commander General David McKiernan arrived in Baghdad on April 12, Saddam Hussein had already fled and his regime had crumbled.

United States forces did not target civilians in the campaign to conquer Iraq; in fact, they went to great lengths to avoid harming noncombatants. Despite these measures, however, at least as many (and perhaps twice as many) civilians died in the war's conventional phase as were killed in the first Gulf War. Partial surveys of Iraqi hospitals in the war zones published in May and June 2003 estimated probable civilian death tolls at between 1,700 and 3,240.[108] A careful report issued several months later by the Project on Defense Alternatives put the figure slightly higher (3,750), while Iraq Body Count tallied 6,882–7,400 civilian fatalities attributable to the United States during the invasion.[109]

Analysts have speculated as to the reason for this upswing in civilian fatalities. Part of the explanation surely lies in a variety of illegal Iraqi practices that put civilians at risk, including the use of noncombatants as shields, operating out of schools, hospitals, and mosques, placing military vehicles and supplies in densely populated neighborhoods, and wearing civilian clothes rather than military uniforms.[110] But other factors also mattered. Carl Conetta, for example, argues that the more ambitious war aim in 2003—the ouster of Saddam Hussein—was responsible because regime change cannot be coerced from outside but must be imposed with brute force. The attainment of this aim required large ground forces to conquer the country and entailed significant fighting in cities where Iraqi forces had holed up, which in turn caused civilian casualties.[111] Human Rights Watch concurs with Conetta's assessment that the increased role of ground forces in 2003 is associated with higher numbers of civilian fatalities but goes further in assigning blame to the coalition's overuse of ground-launched cluster munitions: "While these strikes were directed at Iraqi military targets, the weapons' inaccuracy, broad footprints, and large numbers of submunitions caused hundreds of civilian casualties."[112] Human Rights Watch commends the legal vetting process installed by the army to minimize the effect of artillery fire on civilians but argues that cluster bombs are inherently indiscriminate area weapons because they blanket a large area with bomblets, many of which fail to explode immediately. Human Rights Watch concludes: "The majority of these casualties resulted from the heavy use of cluster munitions in populated areas where soldiers and civilians commingled. The targeting of residential neighborhoods with these area effect weapons represented one of the leading causes of civilian casualties in the war."[113] Cluster bombs, of course, are attractive because they are highly effective at eliminating enemy forces and protecting one's own. As one army officer put it, "If there's a twenty-tank convoy, if you use a precision-guided munition, you get one at a time. If you use a cluster munition, you get twenty in one hit."[114] One study of U.S. combat operations found that the strict rules of engagement regarding the use of artillery and firepower in urban areas fell by the wayside when U.S. troops were heavily engaged.[115]

Iraq: The Insurgency

Although the conventional war to oust Saddam Hussein's regime ended in April 2003, hostilities did not: Saddam loyalists and other Sunni groups opposed to the American occupation intensified the guerrilla warfare they practiced during the invasion and soon a full-scale insurgency was underway. Although U.S. forces have killed several thousand civilians in combating the insurgency, they have not inflicted civilian victimization as defined in this book.

How Many Civilians Have Died in Iraq? This second phase of the conflict has taken the lives of far more Iraqi civilians, although exactly how many is highly disputed. Studies using the two accepted methods for counting civilian casualties—counts and cluster sample surveys—have produced radically different figures. For example, the most thorough estimate using the count method—compiled by Iraq Body Count (IBC)—tallied between 77,500 and 84,500 civilians killed through November 2007.[116] Iraq Body Count researchers use multiple news reports of violent episodes to generate a tally of actual confirmed deaths. This method can be relied on to produce a dependable minimum estimate of civilian casualties. Since violence

[234]

is almost always underreported, however, the actual number of deaths is certainly higher, and there is no sure way to estimate the magnitude of the undercount.

A widely publicized study using the survey method published in the British journal *Lancet,* by contrast, performed by a group of public health scholars based at Johns Hopkins University, estimated total excess deaths in Iraq from the invasion until July 2006 at 655,000. These researchers obtained an estimated death rate for the country during the conflict of 13.3 per 1,000 people per year by interviewing a sample of 1,849 households in forty-seven randomly selected locations across Iraq about deaths in their family since 2002. This death rate represented a major increase over the prewar rate, which the study placed at 5.5 per 1,000 per year. The difference in these two rates applied to the Iraqi population over the forty months of the conflict to July 2006—the number of excess deaths attributable to the war—produced the 655,000 figure.[117]

The *Lancet* study, as it has become known, employs the standard methodology in the field. Although the relatively small sample size opens the study up to the criticism that the random inclusion of one or two high violence clusters could bias the estimated death toll upward, there is no systematic source of bias in the study's methodology.[118] Still, although the IBC figure is almost certainly an undercount, it is highly unlikely that it is off by an order of magnitude. What accounts for the divergence in results? One obvious difference is that IBC strives to count only noncombatant deaths, but the Johns Hopkins survey—owing to the sensitivity of the subject—could not ask whether people who died were insurgents or militia members. Thus, an undetermined (and possibly large) number of the fatalities in the *Lancet* study are combatants.[119]

A second factor that could have caused an inflated estimate of the wartime death rate is the clustered location of the households interviewed. Interviewers randomly chose a house on a residential street to start, and then proceeded down the street until 40 households were interviewed. If a battle, suicide attack, or other violent episode happened to occur on that street, the researchers would be assured of interviewing nearly every family that could possibly have suffered deaths or injuries. If the next street had been chosen, or only a few houses per street, the number of deaths reported could have been zero or a mere handful.[120]

Iraq Body Count and the Johns Hopkins team also disagree on the number of deaths attributable to coalition forces. Based on what the interviewees told their surveyors, the *Lancet* study concluded that the coalition inflicted 31 percent of the postinvasion violent deaths in Iraq, a total of 186,000 fatalities. Iraq Body Count figures, by contrast, indicate that coalition troops (mostly American) killed 12,829 Iraqi noncombatants: 7,400 in the conventional part of the war and 5,429 during the insurgency phase of the conflict stretching from May 2003 to the end of 2006.[121] Given that IBC had counted 54,303 civilian deaths by the end of 2006, these figures translate into 24 percent of total Iraqi civilian deaths, but only 10 percent of the insurgency-phase fatalities.

Given what we know about how the various parties in Iraq fight, the *Lancet* study figure seems like a significant overestimate. Most civilian deaths in Iraq during the insurgency have been inflicted by Iraqis. Sunni insurgents—particularly those affiliated with al-Qaeda in Iraq (AQI)—have adopted deadly car bombings and suicide attacks as their tactics of choice, striking Shi'ite civilians in an attempt to foment chaos and force the United States to withdraw from the country.[122] The war has taken on an increasingly sectarian tone over time, especially since the bombing of the al-Askari Mosque—one of the holiest sites in Shi'a Islam—by AQI in February 2006. Sunni insurgents and Shi'ite militias target each other's civilian populations, which has led to ethnic separation as people flee from vulnerable areas.[123]

American Strategy: Not Clever, But Not Civilian Victimization. United States strategy in Iraq was handicapped initially by the Bush administration's desire for a quick exit from Iraq and its reluctance to recognize the growing resistance as an insurgency and not the lawless acts of a few "dead-enders." Administration officials hoped to rely on the Iraqi Army to provide security in Iraq, but it largely melted away in the conventional war and then was formally disbanded by Coalition Provisional Authority administrator Paul Bremer. The absence of an indigenous force to take over meant that substantial U.S. forces would have to remain. Bush kept troop levels relatively static, however, meaning that the United States has never been able to control the entire country. The insurgency, therefore, has grown and become more deadly, even as a new Iraqi Army has started to take the field.

The United States has not adopted a strategy of civilian victimization in Iraq. It has not, for example, implemented a policy of killing known or suspected civilian supporters of the insurgents, or inflicted indiscriminate reprisal massacres on towns or villages where insurgents are active. Nor has the United States relocated the Sunni population into concentration camps, as it once did in the Philippines and as the British did in South Africa and Italians did in Cyrenaica. Air strikes are generally targeted using precision technology at houses or buildings where guerrillas are thought to be located, such as the attack that killed AQI leader Abu Musab al-Zarqawi in June 2006. Finally, U.S. forces have not attempted to withhold food from Sunni areas of Iraq or used chemicals to destroy food cultivation. None of the classic civilian victimization strategies of counterinsurgency campaigns past, therefore, are being employed by the U.S. forces in Iraq.

The story is not as uncomplicated as it appears, however. Although U.S. troops have not systematically killed civilian supporters of the insurgency, they have detained and imprisoned thousands of people, often with little or no evidence of any wrongdoing. Some fraction of these detainees—as shown by events at Abu Ghraib prison—has been tortured. The Bush administration's attempts to portray torture in Iraq as the misguided actions of a few "bad apples" have been unconvincing, since it was the president's top advisors who argued that the Geneva Conventions should not apply to illegal combatants and who authorized the use of aggressive interrogation techniques.[124] Precision airpower, furthermore, is only as good as the intelligence that guides it, and that intelligence sometimes proves faulty: bombs have fallen on what were later discovered to be civilian gatherings. Applying airpower—no matter how accurate—in urban areas also tends to kill bystanders as well as the specific target.[125]

Moreover, although U.S. troops are guided by specific and restrictive rules of engagement (ROE), when the costs and risks to American soldiers increase, attention to the ROE appears to slacken significantly. Following the murder and mutilation of four military contractors in Fallujah—an insurgent stronghold west of Baghdad—on March 31, 2004, U.S. Marines were ordered to attack the city. In the fierce street-fighting that ensued, media reports claimed that civilian deaths reached six hundred, half of whom were women and children.[126] Marine commanders disputed this toll, but news reports triggered widespread anger among Iraqis as well as armed uprisings in other parts of the country. The United States soon suspended the attack on Fallujah and turned control of the town over to an Iraqi force led by a former Iraqi Army general. After this unit fell apart and control over Fallujah reverted to the insurgents, the United States launched a second operation to seize the city. This time, however, U.S. forces encouraged the civilian population to flee, which allowed U.S. units to use increased firepower but reduce civilian casualties at the same time. It also allowed most of the insurgents to escape. The second battle for Fallujah shows that the U.S. military has learned that large-scale assaults on cities—and the collateral damage they invariably produce—are counterproductive in Iraq. As one U.S. officer commented after the first unsuccessful attempt to take Fallujah, "Destroying a city to save it, is not an option."[127] The battle also shows that U.S. forces are willing to sacrifice combat effectiveness in order to avoid civilian casualties.

Explaining U.S. Conduct in Iraq. Some have argued that this relative restraint on the part of the United States in Iraq indicates a failure of the argument that states target civilians when the costs of fighting increase or the probability of victory declines.[128] The evidence for this view, however, is far from clear cut. Through November 2007, for example, the U.S. military had suffered roughly 3,740 fatalities through 55 months of the insurgency, a loss rate of about 2.2 per day. The fatality rate for Vietnam, by comparison, was more than 8 times higher at 19 per day. The respective rates for World War I, World War II, and Korea were 108, 305, and 48.[129] Deaths of U.S. servicemen, moreover, rarely occur more than one or two at a time; this is increasingly a war of remotely exploded bombs and improvised explosive devices rather than pitched battles. The very low numbers of U.S. battle deaths in Iraq tends to undermine the view that the United States should be targeting civilians.

What about desperation to win the war? As the statistical results in chapter 2 demonstrated, longer wars are more likely to be characterized by civilian victimization and incur larger numbers of civilian casualties. States fighting against guerrilla insurgencies for four years historically have been highly likely to target noncombatants. Yet here, too, the picture is murky. Is the U.S. goal in Iraq to destroy the insurgency by military means? Or is it to hold the insurgents at bay while an Iraqi government can be installed and Iraqi troops are trained and equipped to take over the fight so U.S. troops can be withdrawn? Arguing against the victory objective is the low number of U.S. troops engaged in Iraq. This number has fluctuated between about 120,000 and 160,000 since the fall of Saddam Hussein, and stood at 132,000 in January 2007. President Bush that month announced a "surge" of U.S. troops that increased troop levels to 168,000 by summer but this is a temporary increase designed to stabilize security in Baghdad and encourage political reconciliation rather than a military strategy to defeat the insurgency. Some security gains were evident by September 2007, such as decreased insurgent attacks and fewer Iraqi civilian casualties, yet political progress remained elusive.[130]

Other facets of the political situation in Iraq place restraints on U.S. conduct of the war. Any time U.S. troops inflict civilian casualties on Iraqis, a political furor erupts in Baghdad. After news of a possible massacre by soldiers of the First Marine Regiment's Third Battalion became public in June 2006, for example, the new Iraqi prime minister, Nuri al-Maliki, denounced as "completely unacceptable" the "regular occurrence" of violence by U.S. troops against innocent Iraqis.[131] A similar backlash occurred during the first attack on Fallujah, as discussed above. Avoiding civilian casualties is thus a must for managing relations with the Iraqi regime.

Yet this is clearly not the whole story. Democracies have become markedly more reluctant to target civilians or inflict civilian casualties collaterally in the last thirty to forty years. After about 1970, democracies became significantly less likely to use civilian victimization (although the number of civilians killed by democracies in this time period is not systematically lower than in earlier years). One possible explanation is that the balance between normative and institutional imperatives in democracies has shifted over time, particularly in wars in which strong national interests (or survival) are not at stake. Perhaps now the American public (or the public in any democracy) will truly not stand for policies of civilian victimization inflicted overtly and directly. This is consistent with the rhetoric emanating from Washington and from the U.S. military that the United States never targets civilians and makes every effort to avoid civilian deaths.

Another explanation for U.S. restraint in Iraq is that the organizational culture of the military has embraced and internalized the laws of armed conflict to such a degree that strategies of targeting civilians—or inflicting large numbers of civilian casualties—are simply out of bounds.[132] United States Army units, for example, are now accompanied by judge advocates who render on-the-spot judgments for officers regarding the legality of striking particular targets. Preplanned targets for aerial and artillery bombardment are reviewed using the military's collateral damage estimation methodology and closely vetted by legal advisers. Adjustments are then made to the angle of attack, type of weapon, and timing of the strike to minimize the number of civilian casualties. Targets that exceed a certain threshold of collateral damage require approval by the secretary of defense. The rules of engagement for ground troops in Iraq are restrictive and seek to limit the use of force and the amount of force employed. In short, according to this view, the norm of noncombatant immunity is now an integral part of the culture of the contemporary American military and is responsible for a strong aversion to inflicting civilian casualties.[133]

There is a second, less benevolent, side to American military culture, however. Kahl refers to it as a subculture of annihilation, "which holds that the application of direct and overwhelming force to destroy the enemy is necessary to achieve victory." The coexistence of these two subcultures, what Kahl terms the "annihilation-restraint paradox," explains the high level of technical compliance with the laws of armed conflict by U.S. forces in Iraq but also American overreliance on firepower and aggressive action to kill insurgents, which has produced larger-than-necessary numbers of civilian deaths as a side effect of that approach.[134]

The cultural argument is promising but not fully persuasive. First, as noted above, the rate at which U.S. troops are suffering fatalities in Iraq is unprecedentedly low, and the political goal is to contain but not defeat the insurgency. Second, the argument that the U.S. military—or even the ground forces—is pervaded by a single culture is contradicted by the varied conduct of U.S. units in Iraq. As Thomas Ricks points out, "It was common for observers of U.S. military operations in 2003–04 to note that each division's area of operations felt like a different war." Some units—such as the Fourth Infantry Division in its initial deployment—were highly aggressive, detaining large numbers of people and employing firepower liberally. Other divisions, like the 101st Airborne, employed a far gentler "hearts and minds" approach.[135] This divergence is difficult to explain if the military has a single all-encompassing culture.

Finally, some evidence indicates that U.S. officers and enlisted men alike are not imbued with a culture of restraint in their treatment of Iraqi civilians.

An investigation of the reaction to the Haditha massacre conducted by army major general Eldon A. Bargewell in 2006 concluded the following:

> All levels of command tended to view civilian casualties, even in significant numbers, as routine and as the natural and intended result of insurgent tactics. . . . Statements made by the chain of command during interviews for this investigation, taken as a whole, suggest that Iraqi civilian lives are not as important as U.S. lives, their deaths are just the cost of doing business, and that the Marines need to get "the job done" no matter what it takes.

Rather than investigate the incident, officers at all levels of the Second Marine Division ignored it, attributed it to insurgent propaganda, or simply asserted that "marines are not murderers."[136] Moreover, a survey performed by the army's Mental Health Advisory Team in 2006 of army soldiers and marines in Iraq found some disturbing results. Only 38 percent of marines and 47 percent of soldiers responded affirmatively to the question, "All non-combatants should be treated with dignity and respect." Even more disturbing, only 40 percent of marines and 55 percent of soldiers said they would report a fellow unit member for "injuring or killing an innocent noncombatant."[137] This low level of respect for civilians, reluctance to report buddies who kill civilians, and refusal to investigate reports of civilian casualties seems incompatible with the culture described by Kahl.

It is not possible to adjudicate fully among these competing explanations for U.S. conduct in Iraq. American casualties have not been particularly high, nor is it clear the United States is committed to victory in the traditional sense of defeating the enemy. Even accepting these points, however, U.S. forces have been remarkably protective of civilian life in Iraq. Standard operating procedures within the U.S. military now incorporate stringent methods to avoid civilian casualties, and there is little appetite among political leaders for openly killing noncombatants, even though these same leaders have proved willing to permit aggressive interrogation techniques amounting to torture. In short, with the United States desperate to leave Iraq rather than desperate to win in Iraq, and with the moral inclinations of political leaders and the cultural leanings of the military calling for restraint, the United States has not inflicted civilian victimization in Iraq.

IN THIS chapter I examined several wars in which civilian victimization did not occur. Consistent with my arguments, most of these conflicts were short and low-cost affairs in which states quickly achieved their aims. One exception was the Ethiopian-Eritrean War, in which 100,000 soldiers died. In that case, however, neither belligerent had much capability to target the enemy's civilians; thus it was relatively easy to reach an arrangement to spare noncombatants. The planning and execution of the Persian Gulf War by the United States illustrated how states often go back to the drawing board when their strategy does not promise a quick and decisive victory. When CENTCOM's "high-diddle-diddle-up-the-middle" plan of October 1990 looked as if it would result in high casualties and a war of attrition, the United States opted to double its forces in the region and outflank the Iraqis in the western desert. American airpower pummeled Iraqi forces in Kuwait for weeks before the ground attack, paving the way for the army and marines. The result was a hundred-hour war and one of the most lopsided victories of all time.

The Gulf War, however, also showed how destruction of infrastructure by strategic bombing can contribute to large-scale civilian suffering and also how the desire to avoid the costs of war entirely can lead democracies to target civilians. Bombing infrastructure is supposed to have a bloodless psychological effect on the population, making people uncomfortable and proving the impotence of the regime. Executing this type of campaign is tricky, however, as the large number of civilian fatalities following the Gulf War indicates. In countries (like Iraq) where the public depends on electricity to clean its water supply and treat human waste, pulling the plug can have a disastrous impact on public health and leave the population vulnerable to preventable diseases.

Economic sanctions against Iraq after its conquest of Kuwait—but before any hostilities by the United States or its allies—virtually suffocated Iraqi trade and sought to deny food to civilians. Only when it was deemed that sanctions would fail to oust the Iraqis from Kuwait did the United States decide to proceed to force. Later, rather than pay the costs of ousting Saddam itself, the coalition kept sanctions in place and accepted the suffering of Iraqi civilians this entailed. Sanctions are the modern form of siege and can be just as deadly. Sanctions are attractive, though, because they are casualty-free for the sanctioner, and as this book has demonstrated, if states can achieve results with a policy that avoids casualties on their own side but kills enemy civilians, they will more often than not choose that strategy.

Finally, low casualty rates and desperation to leave rather than to win in Iraq have allowed U.S. political and military leaders to adhere to their values and avoid civilian victimization in the Iraq conflict.

Conclusion

I began this book with a simple question: Why do states target and kill noncombatants in war? I argued that two factors account for the bulk of the variation in civilian victimization. First, desperation to win and to save lives causes civilian victimization in protracted wars of attrition. States seek to win the wars they fight quickly and in an economical fashion. States rarely begin wars with a strategy predicated on targeting civilians: the enemy army is usually viewed as the opponent's center of gravity because coercive strategies that strike at civilians or civilian morale typically do not win wars quickly. Moreover, states are sometimes deterred from targeting noncombatants in a war's opening phases by the opponent's ability to respond in kind or fear of alienating a powerful third party. In relatively short, bloodless wars, therefore, civilian victimization is rare, but when armed conflicts devolve into protracted wars of attrition, the probability mounts that noncombatants will be victimized as a means to reduce costs and avoid defeat.

Second, the appetite to conquer and annex territory from another state leads to the targeting of civilians when the territory contains a population the conqueror views as a threat. Such "enemy" populations tend to be viewed as a fifth column capable of rebelling at any moment in the rear and causing a two-front war. In such cases, attackers often move quickly to eliminate the threat rather than leave it in place where it may cause trouble in the future.

I investigated this question using two complementary methodologies. In the statistical analysis, I compiled data on a number of variables for all interstate war participants between 1816 and 2003. I defined the dependent variable—civilian victimization—as a military policy or strategy in war that targeted noncombatants or refused to discriminate between soldiers and civilians. I also collected data on the number of civilians killed by each state. The results of this analysis strongly supported my hypotheses. Wars of attrition—conflicts characterized by static, positional warfare, sieges, or counterinsurgency—and wars in which a belligerent intended to conquer and annex its neighbor's land each significantly increased the likelihood of civilian victimization and the number of civilian casualties a state inflicted. Deterrence sometimes delays this escalation in particular cases, but is typically unable to head it off altogether. By contrast, the quantitative evidence for the alternative explanations for civilian targeting was more mixed. Larger cultural differences between belligerents, for example—a proxy for the argument that perceptions of the enemy as "barbaric" increase the likelihood of civilian victimization—did not systematically increase the chance that they would harm enemy civilians in a war between them controlling for other factors. Concerning regime type, I found that democracies were more likely than nondemocracies to victimize civilians. This difference was driven by democracies' conduct in wars of attrition, where they were more likely to target noncombatants than nondemocracies. There was also some evidence for the view that democracies have become less likely to target civilians in the post–Vietnam War era, if not inflict fewer civilian casualties.

The case-study portion of this book offered further support for the argument that desperation and territorial annexation lead to civilian victimization. Chapters 3 and 4 each examined a democracy and an autocracy confronting a costly war of attrition, and traced the process whereby the desire to avoid high costs and prevail in the war triggered civilian victimization. In chapter 3, for example, I showed how the rising costs of World War I to Great Britain, and policymakers' realization that they confronted a stalemated war of attrition on the Western Front, caused the British to tighten the naval blockade of Germany to deny food to the civilian population. Similarly, the failure of the Schlieffen Plan in autumn 1914 generated tremendous pressure in Germany to bomb England with zeppelins and wage unrestricted submarine warfare. Fearful that the United States would enter the war on the Entente side, German leaders repeatedly postponed an unlimited U-boat blockade of Britain until the Central Powers' battlefield reverses and fading fortunes in 1916 induced a sense of desperation that everything needed to be tried in order to win the war.

In chapter 4, the prospect of costly invasions of island nations and the failure of bombing against military targets spurred the United States and Germany to unleash civilian victimization. The war of attrition in the Pacific and knowledge of the vulnerability of Japan to fire led to interest in and planning for incendiary bombing of Japanese cities. The trigger that set these plans in motion was the inability of U.S. bombers to do much damage with precision bombing. United States leaders hoped that firebombing would end the Pacific War swiftly and avoid the expense in American lives that would otherwise have been needed to subdue the Japanese. The

German Luftwaffe was generally employed in a counterforce role in support of the German land forces except when the troops confronted an obstacle that delayed a decision or which promised to be costly to assault, such as Warsaw in 1939 or Rotterdam the following year. In the Battle of Britain, Hitler tried to destroy the Royal Air Force to clear the way for a cross-channel invasion, but when this failed he turned his bombers loose against objectives in British cities in the desperate hope that the Blitz would compel the British to come to terms.

Chapter 5 illustrated the desperation argument in a different kind of war of attrition: guerrilla warfare. British forces in South Africa began to institute repressive measures against Boer civilians only when the plucky Boer commandos refused to admit defeat and instead waged a guerrilla campaign that prolonged the war. Tens of thousands of Boers and Africans died from preventable diseases in concentration camps as a result.

In chapter 6, I turned to the argument that the desire to annex territory causes civilian victimization to remove enemy "fifth columns." In the years before 1948, Zionist leaders dreamed of establishing a Jewish state in the whole land of Palestine. Whether or not a master plan for expulsion of the Palestinians existed before the onset of the conflict, the Zionist leadership unanimously embraced the "transfer" of the Palestinian Arabs as the best and only way to establish a viable Jewish state. The reason was that such a state with a large, hostile, internal minority would be forever vulnerable to destruction from within, possibly in coordination with external attacks by neighboring Arab states. During the 1948 war, Israel put transfer into practice. Zionist forces, becoming increasingly desperate and facing probable defeat in the war of the roads in late March 1948, implemented Plan D, which called for the conquest and control of Arab-inhabited areas. Villages that resisted, occupied important lines of communication, or that could not be held were destroyed and their inhabitants expelled. Arab flight was further facilitated by well-publicized massacres by Zionist militias and indiscriminate violence and massacres on the part of the Haganah/IDF. Expulsion became an increasingly explicit policy as the war continued, and the incidence of massacres rose as the Arab inhabitants grew reluctant to flee.

Chapter 7 explored several negative cases—wars in which civilian victimization did not occur—to see if these cases were consistent with my arguments. Most of these cases were indeed quick and decisive victories, or at least limited wars with little loss of life. In the short and low-cost Persian Gulf War, the United States did not target Iraqi civilians, although the Instant Thunder bombing campaign killed about three thousand Iraqi civilians. The Gulf War, however, revealed two disturbing aspects of recent warfare. First, "punishment light"—the U.S. airpower strategy of "turning out the lights" to pressure the civilian population to overthrow Saddam Hussein—had the unforeseen consequence of disabling Iraq's water purification system, which eventually sickened and killed tens of thousands. Although the United States did not intentionally bomb civilians, this episode shows just how fine the line is between imposing psychological pressure versus physical harm. Attempts to remain within the laws of war but still coerce civilians may not actually reduce civilian casualties, but just inflict them in a different way. Second, the Gulf War case suggests that democracies may be increasingly averse to inflicting civilian casualties directly, but that this sensitivity has not affected noncombatant suffering inflicted indirectly. There was no outcry against the 50,000 to 100,000 Iraqi civilians who died from the after-effects of infrastructure bombing, and U.S. leaders turned immediately in August 1990 to economic sanctions—what amounted in effect to a starvation blockade—to compel Saddam Hussein to withdraw from Kuwait. Thus the spread of democracy seems to be something of a mixed blessing for civilian casualties in war: democracies are increasingly disinclined to kill noncombatants directly, but this humanitarian impulse does not always prevent civilian casualties because it does not extend to indirect forms of punishment.

IMPLICATIONS FOR OTHER THEORIES OF CIVILIAN VICTIMIZATION

Regime Type

The argument that democracies are guided by domestic norms that proscribe killing innocent civilians in their conduct of warfare receives little support here. According to the norms strand of democratic peace theory, democracies externalize their domestic norms of peaceful conflict resolution and respect for individual autonomy in their dealings with other democracies. Norms arguments also imply that when democracies fight wars, they should avoid harming innocent people not only because doing so increases the bitterness of the conflict and makes it harder to settle, but because liberal and democratic norms imbue leaders with respect for human rights and prohibit killing those who bear no responsibility for the conflict, namely innocent civilians.

The historical evidence of democracies in interstate wars does not support the argument that democratic states refrain from civilian victimization. This appears to hold true in low-cost wars only. Democracies adhere to their values when it is essentially cost-free for them to do so. When the costs of remaining true to their beliefs rise, however, such states have jettisoned normative restrictions and waged war against noncombatants. All that remains of prewar liberal rhetoric is the way that politicians describe their actions to their domestic audience. Rarely do leaders admit outright that they have adopted a strategy designed or intended to murder enemy noncombatants. This is probably the case because public opinion firmly opposes targeting civilians in peacetime, and leaders assume that this remains the public's preference in wartime as well. Publics in even the most liberal of democracies, however, accept the killing of enemy noncombatants if doing so promises to end the war more quickly and save the lives of their own soldiers. Liberal publics and liberal leaders thus become decidedly illiberal in wartime.

My analysis, therefore, offers further evidence against liberal or democratic norms as an explanation for peace among democracies. This argument has come under increasing fire not only from realists but also from proponents of the main rival explanation, democratic institutions. I find, in agreement with these other analysts, that norms are of secondary importance for explaining the conduct of democracies in wartime.[1] Some studies, however, have argued recently that liberal values are becoming more salient in democratic foreign policy, particularly in small wars when survival is not at stake.[2] Even a hundred years ago in the Boer War, liberal politicians were eventually able to help curtail civilian victimization—if not prevent it initially—in South Africa. The United States, with its massive preponderance of power in the post–Cold War world, may be particularly affected by this trend. I would still argue, however, that sufficiently high costs of fighting or a sense of desperation—even in small wars—or the wish to avoid the costs of war altogether could still trigger civilian victimization by democracies.

The story is more nuanced when it comes to democratic institutions. My theory began with the assumption that all states were equally sensitive to costs. Institutional models of democracy, however, suggest that democracies may be more cost-sensitive in warfare because of the greater ease with which elected leaders may be sanctioned for costly or failed policies. The statistical data tend to support the contention that democracies are more likely than nondemocracies to target civilians, and that this trend is driven by costly wars of attrition. There is some evidence, for example, that democratic leaders worry about the possibility of future punishment by the electorate if they fail to use all the means at their disposal to prevent casualties among their troops and defeat the enemy quickly. Historian Barton Bernstein argues that such fears were evident in the decision to use the atomic bomb in 1945: "Truman, Byrnes, and the other leaders did not have to be reminded of the danger of a political backlash in America if they did not use the bomb and the invasions became necessary. Even if they had wished to avoid its use—and they did not—the fear of later public outrage spurred by the weeping parents and loved ones of dead American boys might well have forced American leaders to drop the A-bomb on Japan."[3] Democratic leaders such as Lord Salisbury and David Lloyd George in the British "khaki" elections of 1900 and 1918—have also been rewarded at the ballot box for advocating and pursuing policies of civilian victimization in war. This book, therefore, supports the time-honored view that while democracies may be slow to anger, once aroused by costly or protracted warfare, they fight with a fury.

Increased sensitivity to costs, however, may not be strictly a function of democracy versus autocracy. Hitler, for example, worried tremendously about British bombs falling on German civilians, and Saddam Hussein exhibited remarkable sensitivity to military costs during the Iran-Iraq War.[4] Process tracing, moreover, turned up relatively few cases of democratic leaders directly citing fears of losing the next election if they did not target enemy civilians. These leaders also resisted public pressure to kill noncombatants when they believed it would trigger enemy retribution or cause uncommitted third parties to enter the war against them. Democratic accountability thus appears to play a supporting role, providing additional incentives for leaders to target civilians in desperate military circumstances. The precise role of democracy in causing (or contributing to) civilian victimization merits further investigation in case studies.

On the other side of the ledger, however, democracies rarely engage in massive, face-to-face killing, preferring to do their killing indirectly via bombing, blockade, or imprisonment in concentration camps. Democracies also do not engage in truly massive killing of civilians, defined as more than 1 million dead, but are at least as likely as nondemocracies to kill more than 500,000, 100,000, or 50,000 noncombatants. Even though democratic publics rarely object to killing enemy noncombatants in wartime, democratic leaders behave as if the public disapproves and tend not to declare openly that they are waging war against civilians. As described above, this is because democratic leaders believe that their constituents oppose such policies when in reality the public often supports them wholeheartedly. Therefore it seems that leaders in democracies pay little if any price for inflicting large-scale harm on civilians in a costly or protracted war. The public is far more likely to turn against a war if they believe it is unwinnable than because it kills significant numbers of noncombatants.[5]

My findings also have implications for the literature on democracy and victory in war. According to the selection-effects argument for democratic victory, the reason democracies are so successful in the wars they initiate is because elected leaders—knowing that going down to defeat in war will likely cost them their job—choose to start only those wars they are sure they will win. If democratic leaders choose correctly, we would expect to find fewer instances of civilian victimization in wars started by democracies because these conflicts should be cheap and easy. On closer examination, however, it turns out that democracies are not significantly less likely to victimize civilians in wars they initiate versus those in which they are attacked. These findings constitute indirect evidence against the selection-effects argument for democratic victory.

Identity

My research also has implications for constructivist arguments in international relations that stress the importance of actors' identity. In the study of violence against civilians, one prominent hypothesis is that civilian victimization is more likely when at least one of the belligerents in a conflict views its opponent as "barbaric," or outside of the community of civilized societies. The rules and customs of civilized nations apply only in conflicts among them, but not to wars involving barbarous nations.

A clear prediction of this argument is that civilian victimization should be more common in colonial/imperial wars—fought mainly between white Europeans and nonwhite Africans, Asians, and Native Americans—than in wars between recognized states. A comparison of the rate of civilian victimization in my dataset of interstate wars with the rate of barbarism in Ivan Arreguín-Toft's dataset of colonial (and some civil) wars, however, contradicts this hypothesis: 30 percent of interstate war participants with the capability to target civilians did so, whereas only 20 percent of states facing nonstate actors used barbarism against them. Moreover, a comparison of the Second Anglo-Boer War and the Zulu War challenges the argument: while the Boers may not have been fully civilized, they were at least white and descended of Europeans, whereas the Zulus were black Africans and widely viewed in Britain as fierce and brutal savages. Yet civilian victimization occurred in the protracted, guerrilla-style Boer War and not in the quick and decisive Zulu War.

A related identity mechanism maintains that to mobilize support for war, elites must demonize the enemy. It is easier to demonize groups that are racially or culturally different from one's own society than people who are culturally similar. Civilian victimization, according to this logic, would be more likely to occur in wars between dissimilar societies because the greater the differences, the easier it is to depict the enemy as racially or culturally inferior.

The evidence discussed above regarding the relative rates of civilian victimization in interstate versus colonial wars also undermines the demonization hypothesis because it should be easier to depict tribal opponents as inferior and savage. Within the category of interstate wars, however, measures of cultural difference, such as belonging to different civilizations or having different religions and skin colors, are not significantly associated with a higher likelihood of civilian victimization. Demonization of the enemy, it seems, is not based on "objective" differences among groups of people; no matter how similar or different the enemy is from oneself, there will always exist some cleavage along which to differentiate self from other and use to denigrate the opponent. This is consistent with the finding from social identity theory that even minimal social groups exert a powerful hold over their members; large differences are not necessary to generate discrimination against an out-group.[6] Moreover, racial or other hatred of the enemy is not strictly necessary for civilian victimization to occur: Americans did not particularly hate Germans in World War II, yet American bombers killed thousands of German civilians. Nor did the British people hold demonic images of the Boers or Germans. Finally, high levels of demonization do not always translate into systematic attacks on noncombatants: deterrence and the threat of great power intervention largely restrained victimization of civilians in the Arab-Israeli wars of 1956, 1967, 1969–70, and 1973.

One conclusion I draw from this evidence is that the attitudes of the mass public are not the determining factor in whether or not a government employs a strategy of civilian victimization. In no case have I observed a vengeful, hate-filled public demand mass slaughter and a government bow to its wishes. Governments do engage in demonization of the enemy, however, either to mobilize public opinion behind the prospect of going to war or to rally the country to contribute to an ongoing war effort. To the extent that such demonization does contribute to public hatred of the enemy, and is more necessary in democracies because public support for war is essential in these societies, the possibility that leaders could be trapped by the "blowback" created by their own overblown rhetoric is thus greater in democracies (although the connection to civilian victimization remains tenuous). Other scholars have argued that myths of imperial aggrandizement are most likely to take hold in cartelized political systems in which groups interested in expansion gain control of the state, logroll their various interests, and engage in self-defeating overextension. These groups propagate "myths of empire" to sell their expansionist program to the public, but often become trapped by their rhetoric, since to abandon it would be to admit that they had been lying all along in pursuit of their narrow interests. Democracies, it is argued, are relatively immune to this problem because the diffusion of political power in democratic systems makes it more difficult for an expansionist coalition to capture the state, and democracies have vibrant marketplaces of ideas that expose such self-serving political programs.[7] But if public support for war is more important in democracies, then elected leaders have greater incentives than unelected leaders to demonize the foe.

Organization Theory

Two hypotheses regarding civilian victimization flow from organization theory. First, if the culture of the military predisposes it toward a punishment strategy, then the state is likely to target civilians. Second, military organizations are likely to inflict civilian victimization if doing so will advance their parochial organizational interests, such as winning independence as a separate service branch.

Organizational culture clearly has an impact on how militaries prepare to fight wars, and its effects continue to be felt during the conflict. In this book I have argued, however, that military culture is not an important factor determining variation in the occurrence of civilian victimization. Most militaries do not have a culture that calls for targeting civilians in war. The few that have such cultures often do not implement them immediately or are not permitted by political leaders to implement them. More frequently, militaries have cultures that prescribe attacking the enemy military and only turn to civilian victimization after counterforce strategies fail to yield results. The effects of culture can still be detected, however, in the way military officers think about or describe their actions. The U.S. Army Air Forces still thought of itself as engaging in precision bombing of Germany, for example, even when half of its tonnage was delivered indiscriminately by radar.

Parochial organizational interests appear to play a role in certain cases—such as the bombing of Japan—but are not necessary for civilian victimization and are of limited general utility. American airmen dearly wanted independence from the army in World War II and strove to win the war with airpower in the Pacific by unleashing firebombing. But was this yearning for organizational independence a necessary condition for civilian victimization? Other, independent, air forces bombed civilians. Moreover, civilians in the U.S. government were at least as enthusiastic about firebombing as was the air force. If the hypothesis is widened to argue that militaries target civilians to gain greater resources and a leg up on their rival services, then it overpredicts civilian victimization, since military organizations are constantly engaged in such competition. In short, parochial organizational interests have contributed to civilian victimization in particular cases, but their broader explanatory power is questionable.

Selective Violence in Counterinsurgency

Existing studies of violence in civil wars argue that violence is intended to punish supporters of one's enemy so as to deter other potential defectors, and that to perform such a function violence must be discriminate. In order to obtain compliance, in other words, compliance must be rewarded with survival. But if compliance does not bring security, and people are killed no matter what their allegiances or loyalties, then one might as well join the other side and at least marginally increase one's chances of survival.

This type of model assumes that the loyalties of the population are fluid and are a function of forceful control: the side that gains a monopoly of force in a particular area, or which establishes enough of a presence to punish (and hence deter) potential defectors, wins the (grudging or willing) support of the people in that territory.[8] This assumes, however, that the belligerents view all members of the population as equally controllable. But in reality, this assumption does not always hold: belligerents often view some groups in society as less susceptible to control than others. When belligerents believe they are unlikely to elicit compliance from a particular ethnic or political group, they do not use force discriminately to deter defection and maintain control as described by the selective violence model. Rather, because a group's very identity labels its members as noncompliant or potentially rebellious, belligerents use violence indiscriminately against all group members to remove them from the territory they hope to control. Such a cleansing strategy gets rid of problematic populations and lowers the costs of the war, and the ensuing occupation of territory.

Several factors probably contribute to perceptions by one group of another that it will be noncompliant and pose a threat. Extreme ethnic, religious, or ideological polarization before the war, for example, can lead to views that the other side is irredeemably hostile and would rebel at the first opportunity. A recent history of conflict between the groups or of oppression by one group at the hands of another may also contribute. In general, however, when indiscriminate "cleansing" violence will be chosen over more discriminate "controlling" violence is poorly understood and begs further research.[9]

IMPLICATIONS FOR THEORIES OF COERCION

A major finding from the coercion literature is that punishment does not work: strategies predicated on hurting civilians in order to convince states to change their behavior or concede an important issue (such as territory) generally fail to produce results.[10] Pape's finding regarding the efficacy of punishment in the context of strategic bombing—while not uncontested—has had a tremendous impact and sparked widespread debate.[11] Pape later extended his argument to include economic sanctions, finding that these, too, produced few concessions on important issues.[12] Pape's research agenda has most recently taken him to the subject of suicide terrorism, where he finds—contrary to his previous work—that light to moderate amounts of punishment do induce concessions by states targeted for suicide attacks.[13] Other scholars have challenged this finding, however, and most follow Pape's earlier argument that punishment is not only ineffective at achieving objectives, it is actually counterproductive because it induces targets to resist more fiercely.[14]

The goal of this book was not to explain the effectiveness of civilian victimization, but rather to explore its causes. The evidence examined herein, however, permits a few general observations on the question of effectiveness. First, Pape is largely correct that coercion by punishment in protracted interstate wars of attrition has a poor track record. Pape contended that this fact was due to the capacity of modern nation-states to absorb high costs; the inability of nonnuclear punishment to inflict sufficient pain to force state leaders to abandon important security goals; states' ability to minimize their vulnerability to punishment; and the fact that suffering inflicted on civilians does not cause them to turn against their own government.[15] Another argument Pape does not mention, however, is that punishment/civilian victimization—because it is caused by desperation—tends to occur in costly

[252]

wars of attrition, that is, the hardest cases, when the adversary is most determined to resist and willing to absorb the most punishment. However, this book revealed at least one case in which large-scale civilian punishment may have convinced a government to end a war: the effects of the British hunger blockade on the German population in World War I contributed to the German government's view that an armistice had to be negotiated rather than a last-ditch defense of the Reich organized. Further qualifying Pape's argument is the efficacy of punishment historically in the form of sieges, where starving the inhabitants of walled towns often paid dividends, as did massacring everyone in towns that resisted, which caused other cities to open their gates to the invaders without a fight. Therefore, one tentative hypothesis about the effectiveness of coercion by punishment in conventional wars of attrition is that the larger the geographic or political unit being coerced, the less likely that punishment will produce concessions.

Second, coercion that inflicts harm on noncombatants is more likely to succeed if it undermines the enemy's ability to fight than if it simply inflicts pain on the general population in the hope that it will overthrow the government and end the war. Pape errs in arguing that strategic bombing that kills civilians is always a punishment strategy. When the United States firebombed Japan, for example, the infliction of mass casualties on the workforce was viewed as a means to destroy Japan's war economy. Furthermore, the true impact of the atomic bomb in August 1945 may not have been on the morale of the Japanese people, but rather on the army's strategy for defending the home islands against an American invasion.[16] Civilian victimization aimed at undermining an adversary's ability to resist rather than its will to resist, therefore, is likely to be more effective.

Third, coercion that targets civilians is liable to be more effective when employed by an invader with immediate access to the civilian population ("eye-to-eye" coercion) than by an attacker projecting force into a state from beyond its borders ("arms'-length" coercion).[17] Such "eye-to-eye" coercion encompasses not only counterinsurgency operations—where killing civilians who aid rebels can deter other civilians from doing likewise, or simply prevent them from doing so (by killing or removing them from the area)— but also wars of territorial expansion in which an aggressor views some of the inhabitants as unreliable and uses violence to expel them. Ethnic cleansing has sometimes paid enormous dividends: witness the founding of the state of Israel in 1948, or the expansion of the Balkan states at the expense of the Ottoman Empire in 1912–13. Taken to an extreme, such as by Nazi Germany, it is counterproductive (not to mention monstrous), but cleansing in measured doses against relatively small groups in specific areas can eliminate people viewed as fifth columns and secure a permanent hold on conquered territory.

Finally, contrary to the claims of some analysts of violence in guerrilla warfare, the effectiveness of civilian victimization does not always depend on its discriminate or indiscriminate character. I have noted above that this generalization does not always hold even in the context of guerrilla/civil war because loyalties are not always viewed as fluid. Outside of the insurgency context, however, it is the very absence of discrimination that induces maximum terror and persuades members of a targeted population that they must flee, such as in a cleansing campaign. The randomness of such violence—being directed at a group, but not at particular members within the group—also may explain the relative success of suicide terrorism. Thus, whether or not discriminate or indiscriminate violence against noncombatants is likely to be effective depends on the context in which the victimization occurs. If the objective is to empty territory of some group, indiscriminate violence is effective because it kills more people and terrifies the rest into flight. If the goal is to keep a population in place but to control them, selective violence against known or suspected defectors is likely to be more effective because of the deterrent effect it has on potential turncoats. Even then, there are circumstances in which indiscriminate violence is effective, such as when the targeted population or the theater of war is small and can be isolated.

IMPLICATIONS FOR POLICY AND THE FUTURE OF WARFARE

Policy

Just as this book has shown that there may be a dark side to democracy in theory—a sensitivity to costs that almost guarantees that democracies will victimize civilians in protracted wars of attrition—so there is a corresponding potential dark side to the spread of democracy. Encouraging the growth of democracy is one of the United States' primary foreign policy goals. Not only is democracy widely touted as the most just and equitable political system for domestic affairs, democracies are also thought not to fight each other. Thus, the more democracies there are in the international system, the greater the zone of peace.

If one's goal is to minimize the likelihood that civilian victimization will occur in interstate wars, however, then spreading democracy—at least in the short run—is not clearly the answer. As we have seen, democracies have been at least as likely to victimize noncombatants in such wars, and probably more likely to do so in costly wars. In a world in which many of the conflict dyads will continue to be mixed (i.e., one democracy, one autocracy), the main restraints on civilian victimization are the costs of the war, how long it goes on, and deterrence. Until such time as the overwhelming majority of states in the world are democracies—which presumably will not fight each other at all—small increases in the number of democracies will only marginally affect the likelihood of civilian victimization.

My research has a second, more direct implication for American policy in the post-9/11 era. The United States has already fought two wars since al-Qaeda terrorists brought down the World Trade Center. The Bush administration has inaugurated a new era in American security affairs by enunciating a policy of prevention, according to which the United States will go to war to prevent the acquisition by terrorists or rogue states of weapons of mass destruction, meaning that the United States will likely find itself at war again in the near future.[18] So far these wars have not imposed a high cost on the United States in terms of fatalities. Should the United States encounter a foe that is capable of exacting a heavy price on American troops, however, enemy civilians could suffer for it.

Should the United States suffer further large-scale terrorist attacks, this would create a permissive environment for potential civilian victimization as part of a counterterrorist campaign. In the wake of 9/11, for example, large majorities of the American public were willing to countenance significant civilian deaths in military strikes against terrorists. Ominously, polls on this question were remarkably insensitive to the number of civilians who would die. The results of a CBS/New York Times poll taken in late September 2001 revealed that 68 percent of the public still favored military action against those responsible for the 9/11 attacks even "if it meant that many thousands of innocent civilians may be killed."[19] A month later, 62 percent supported military action "even if it cost the lives of thousands of civilians in the countries we attack."[20] Given the even greater support expressed in 1945 for the use of atomic weapons against Japan, this ugly public mood should come as no surprise. Should an entire nation or country become identified as having supported a terrorist attack against the United States, however, rather than a nonstate actor being sheltered by a state, American retaliation might not be terribly restrained.

Civilian Victimization in Future Wars

My argument is that the likelihood of civilian victimization in warfare depends mainly on desperation to win and save lives on one's own side, and the appetite for territorial annexation. In that sense, therefore, my view on the possibility that noncombatants will suffer in future wars is pessimistic, or at least agnostic: It all depends on the costs of the war—which are a product of factors that are not easily influenced by human hands—and the territorial ambitions of the belligerents. As far as the United States is concerned, for example, its huge preponderance of power and technological capability over most other states suggest that wars involving the United States will be quick and bloodless. America's opponents, however, knowing this, have incentives to neutralize its advantages by waging guerrilla warfare. Other factors, such as weather and geography, are not possible to manipulate.

Should the United States' technological edge fail it, however, and a war of attrition result, my argument is that civilian victimization is the likely outcome. Alternatively, U.S. leaders, seeking to avoid paying the costs of war altogether, might choose to employ economic embargoes, which can inflict suffering on noncombatants in less direct ways.

One potential danger is that American leaders, possessing overwhelming military power and increasingly accurate weapons, will be drawn into more and more wars. If these conflicts are not won quickly, however, these same leaders will face an unpalatable choice between abandoning the contest—with all of the reputational and electoral consequences inherent in such a choice—or escalating in order to win the war. Escalation, of course, almost always entails less discrimination in the use of force, which can lead to civilian victimization through large-scale collateral damage or the eventual targeting of civilians themselves.

Such an assessment of the future of warfare, one might argue, discounts the power of international norms and media publicity to restrain civilian victimization in warfare. The successful labeling of particular weapons as indiscriminate has greatly facilitated campaigns by political entrepreneurs and nongovernmental organizations to ban these weapons, such as chemical munitions, biological weapons, and antipersonnel land mines.[21] Although not formally banned, a powerful taboo has also developed against using nuclear weapons.[22] The norm that underlies each of these movements is the belief that killing civilians in warfare is wrong, a norm that is increasingly enforced by war crimes tribunals (as in Yugoslavia and Rwanda) and is now formally institutionalized in the International Criminal Court. These developments indicate a growing public distaste for violence against noncombatants in warfare.

Paralleling (and perhaps partially fueling) this preference transformation is an explosion in media coverage of global conflicts, global access to media, and organizations dedicated to publicizing the evil deeds of states with regard to noncombatants. The first two of these factors have combined to create the so-called CNN Effect, whereby the instantaneous relaying of atrocities to millions of people around the world creates imperatives for governments to "do something" that did not exist in the past. In addition, organizations like Human Rights Watch and Amnesty International are devoted to "naming and shaming" both governments that violate human rights but also those that stand by and do nothing to prevent it.

Undoubtedly, states operate in a denser, more constricting normative environment than ever before, but this structure has not been able to prevent massive depredations against noncombatants when governments have felt their power to be threatened by—or have been unable to defeat—domestic foes. Recent examples include the Rwandan genocide, Russia's wars in Chechnya, and the conflict in Darfur. In interstate wars, which often receive greater media attention, some evidence suggests that rather than fully preventing civilian victimization, normative strictures and media effects have combined to drive attacks on noncombatants underground. In the 1991 Persian Gulf War, for example, as we saw earlier, American air strikes attempted to put pressure on Iraqi civilians without killing them by incapacitating Iraq's electrical power grid. These strikes led to widespread civilian suffering, however, by eliminating the country's ability to process sewage and purify water. I did not code this case as civilian victimization because the strategy was not directed at noncombatants themselves and the damage it did was apparently unforeseen, but this attempt to remain within the rules of war (and thus avoid international pressure) while still influencing civilians ended in large numbers of deaths. The economic sanctions on Iraq in the 1990s contributed to the deaths of many more Iraqi civilians but responsibility in this case was even more diffuse, as Western policymakers argued that Saddam was mainly responsible because he continued to defy the international community and hoarded most of the country's oil wealth rather than allow it to be spent on goods for the civilian population. Both of these episodes suggest the emergence of a new, indirect, more deniable means of exercising coercion by punishing noncombatants rather than the extinction of civilian victimization.

My examination of civilian victimization in historical context has revealed that the norm against inflicting widespread and systematic harm on noncombatants in warfare is a frail one. Time and again, when warfare has become costly, or threatened to become so, the interest of states in winning wars at reasonable cost has dictated the sacrifice of enemy innocents. Warfare, particularly in the age of nationalism, follows an inexorable logic of escalation that sets in if victory does not come quickly. Rather than sacrifice their political goals, statesmen employ further means of violence—including mass slaughter of civilians—to achieve them. The coming of democracy and burgeoning international regimes restricting the use of force against noncombatants have not ended this fundamental constant of warfare. Unfortunately, my argument implies that the overwhelming preponderance of power currently wielded by the United States—rather than its liberal beliefs or democratic institutions—has the greatest potential to attenuate civilian victimization in American foreign policy. This predominance, however, is fragile: it can be countered by opponents who wage guerrilla warfare, as in Iraq, or adversaries willing to end their own lives in order to kill and terrorize Americans, as al-Qaeda has done. Liberal democracy and international norms may moderate the escalation toward civilian victimization that inevitably occurs in wars of attrition, but cannot fully prevent it.

Notes

Introduction

1. Quotation is from William T. Sherman, *Memoirs*, vol. 2 (New York: Charles L. Webster, 1892), 126. Figures are from William Eckhardt, "Civilian Deaths in Wartime," *Bulletin of Peace Proposals* 20, no. 1 (March 1989): 90; and Zbigniew Brzezinski, *Out of Control: Global Turmoil on the Eve of the Twenty-First Century* (New York: Scribner's, 1993), 9–10. In a feat of understatement, Eckhardt notes that the massive civilian death toll in modern wars "suggests that the average war over the past three centuries has not been very 'just', as far as the killing of unarmed civilians was concerned." Ibid., 91. Interstate wars are particularly deadly, killing about twice as many noncombatants as civil, colonial, and imperial wars combined. The proportion of civilian to total deaths is highest, however, in civil wars, and has been rising since World War II. Ruth Leger Sivard, *World Military and Social Expenditures* (Washington: World Priorities, 1987 and 1996), 28 and 17, respectively.

2. Civilian victimization in war, of course, is not limited to modern times. A highly abridged history of civilian victimization would no doubt include the slaughter of the men of Melos and the enslavement of the island's women and children after its conquest by Athens in the Peloponnesian War; Rome's destruction of Carthage in the Third Punic War (146 BC); the exploits of Attila and the Huns who, according to Count Marcellinus, notoriously "ground almost the whole of Europe into the dust" in the mid fifth century; the sack of Jerusalem after it fell to the Crusaders in 1099; the massacres of Jenghiz Khan and Tamerlane in the thirteenth and fourteenth centuries; the Thirty Years' War, during which as many as 8 million civilians were killed or driven from their homes; the French devastation of German states on its eastern border in the 1680s and 1690s; the deaths of about 150,000 civilians in the Royalist uprising in the Vendée in France (1793–96); and the hundreds of thousands who perished in colonial wars waged by the Dutch in Java, the Russians in the Caucasus, and the French in Algeria during the first half of the nineteenth century. On these episodes, see Thucydides, *History of the Peloponnesian War*, trans. Rex Warner (London: Penguin, 1972), 408; S. A. Cook, F. E. Adcock, and M. P. Charlesworth, *The Cambridge Ancient History*, vol. 8, *Rome and the Mediterranean, 218 B.C.–133 B.C.* (Cambridge: Cambridge University Press, 1930), 479–84; E. A. Thompson, *The Huns* (Oxford: Blackwell, 1996), 103; Paul K. Davis, *Besieged: 100 Great Sieges from Jericho to Sarajevo* (Oxford: Oxford University Press, 2003), 57–58; on Jenghiz Khan and Tamerlane, René Grousset, *The Empire of the Steppes: A History of Central Asia*, trans. Naomi Walford (New Brunswick: Rutgers University Press, 1970); on the Thirty Years' War and French devastation in the late seventeenth

century, John Childs, *Armies and Warfare in Europe, 1648–1789* (New York: Holmes and Meier, 1982), 9, 152; on the Vendée, Anthony James Joes, "Insurgency and Genocide: La Vendée," *Small Wars and Insurgencies* 9, no. 3 (winter 1998): 37; for the Dutch in Java, Micheal Clodfelter, *Warfare and Armed Conflicts: A Statistical Reference to Casualty and Other Figures, 1500–2000*, 2d ed. (Jefferson, NC: McFarland, 2002), 266; on the Russians in the Caucasus, Ivan Arreguín-Toft, *How the Weak Win Wars: A Theory of Asymmetric Conflict* (Cambridge: Cambridge University Press, 2005), 48–71; and for the French in Algeria, Sivard, *World Military and Social Expenditures 1987–88*, 31.

3. Figures on civilian deaths are drawn from the following sources: the four colonial conflicts, Clodfelter, *Warfare and Armed Conflicts*, 345, 238, 272, and 396; World War I blockades, Avner Offer, *The First World War: An Agrarian Interpretation* (Oxford: Clarendon Press, 1989), 34, and Leo Grebler and Wilhelm Winkler, *The Cost of the World War to Germany and to Austria-Hungary* (New Haven: Yale University Press, 1940), 147; World War II bombing, Robert A. Pape, *Bombing to Win: Air Power and Coercion in War* (Ithaca: Cornell University Press, 1996), 104, 272; Nazi killings, Benjamin A. Valentino, *Final Solutions: Mass Killing and Genocide in the Twentieth Century* (Ithaca: Cornell University Press, 2004), 77, 81; bombing in Korea, Andrew C. Nahm, *Historical Dictionary of the Republic of Korea* (Metuchen, NJ: Scarecrow, 1993), 129; Vietnam and Afghanistan, Guenter Lewy, *America in Vietnam* (New York: Oxford University Press, 1978), 442–53, and Marek Sliwinski, "Afghanistan: The Decimation of a People," *Orbis* 33, no. 1 (winter 1989): 39–56; civil wars, Valentino, *Final Solutions*, 83, 88; and Darfur, Colum Lynch, "Sudan to Allow U.N. Force in Darfur," *Washington Post*, April 17, 2007, A16.

4. Greenberg Research, *The People on War Report: ICRC Worldwide Consultation on the Rules of War* (Geneva: ICRC, 1999), 13, http://www.icrc.org/web/eng/siteeng0.nsf/html/p0758. This belief is not new: the combatant-noncombatant distinction began to develop as early as the late tenth century in the church and in the practice of chivalry, and became well-entrenched in the natural law thinking of Grotius, Locke, and Vattel in the seventeenth and eighteenth centuries. See Richard Shelly Hartigan, *The Forgotten Victim: A History of the Civilian* (Chicago: Precedent, 1982), 65–115.

5. George E. Hopkins, "Bombing and the American Conscience during World War II," *The Historian* 28, no. 3 (May 1966): 453; and "Bush Performance Rating Climbs Back to Low 60s; Americans More Hawkish Over Iraq But Still Considerably Reluctant, Newest Zogby America Poll Reveals," http://www.zogby.com/news/ReadNews.dbm?ID=675, February 9, 2003.

6. Caleb Carr, *The Lessons of Terror: A History of Warfare against Civilians* (New York: Random House, 2002), 12.

7. Pape, *Bombing to Win*; and Robert A. Pape, "Why Economic Sanctions Do Not Work," *International Security* 22, no. 2 (fall 1997): 90–136. See also Michael Horowitz and Dan Reiter, "When Does Aerial Bombing Work? Quantitative Empirical Tests, 1917–1999," *Journal of Conflict Resolution* 45, no. 2 (April 2001): 147–73; and Ivan Arreguín-Toft, "The [F]utility of Barbarism: Assessing the Impact of the Systematic Harm of Non-Combatants in War," paper presented at the annual meeting of the American Political Science Association, Philadelphia, PA, August 2003. On the destructive potential of sanctions, see John Mueller and Karl Mueller, "Sanctions of Mass Destruction," *Foreign Affairs* 78, no. 3 (May/June 1999): 43–53.

8. In this book, I am concerned with states' victimization of foreign civilians in wars, rather than their treatment of noncombatants inside their own borders in war or peace. This category includes civilians residing in enemy states in interstate wars, or the populations of occupied nonstate territories in imperial or colonial wars.

9. Michael J. Engelhardt, "Democracies, Dictatorships and Counterinsurgency: Does Regime Type Really Matter?" *Conflict Quarterly* 12, no. 3 (summer 1992): 52–63; R. J. Rummel, "Democracy, Power, Genocide, and Mass Murder," *Journal of Conflict Resolution* 39, no. 1 (March 1995): 3–26; Arreguín-Toft, "The [F]utility of Barbarism"; Robert A. Pape, "The Strategic Logic of Suicide Terrorism," *American Political Science Review* 97, no. 3 (August 2003): 343–61; Gil Merom, *How Democracies Lose Small Wars: State, Society, and the Failures of France in Algeria, Israel in Lebanon, and the United States in Vietnam* (Cambridge: Cambridge University Press, 2003); and Benjamin Valentino, Paul Huth, and Dylan Balch-Lindsay, "'Draining the Sea': Mass

Killing and Guerrilla Warfare," *International Organization* 58, no. 2 (April 2004): 375–407. President George W. Bush lent support to this view when he declared in 2002 that "targeting innocent civilians for murder is always and everywhere wrong" and asserted that fighting fair is what distinguishes democracies from rogue states, terrorists, and barbarians. George W. Bush, "President Bush Delivers Graduation Speech at West Point." http://www.whitehouse.gov/news/releases/2002/06; and President George W. Bush, *The National Security Strategy of the United States of America* (Washington: White House, 2002).

10. Bruce Bueno de Mesquita et al., "An Institutional Explanation of the Democratic Peace," *American Political Science Review* 93, no. 4 (December 1999): 791–807; and Dan Reiter and Allan C. Stam, *Democracies at War* (Princeton: Princeton University Press, 2002).

11. Mark B. Salter, *Barbarians and Civilization in International Relations* (London: Pluto, 2002), 36–39.

12. Sebastian Balfour, *Deadly Embrace: Morocco and the Road to the Spanish Civil War* (Oxford: Oxford University Press, 2002), 123.

13. Jeffrey W. Legro, "Which Norms Matter? Revisiting the 'Failure' of Internationalism," *International Organization* 51, no. 1 (winter 1997): 35.

14. Jeffrey W. Legro, *Cooperation under Fire: Anglo-German Restraint during World War II* (Ithaca: Cornell University Press, 1995); and Isabel V. Hull, *Absolute Destruction: Military Culture and the Practices of War in Imperial Germany* (Ithaca: Cornell University Press, 2005).

15. This argument is sometimes advanced to explain the escalation of bombing by the U.S. Army Air Forces in the Pacific theater in World War II. See Michael S. Sherry, *The Rise of American Air Power: The Creation of Armageddon* (New Haven: Yale University Press, 1987), 309; and Conrad C. Crane, *Bombs, Cities, and Civilians: American Airpower Strategy in World War II* (Lawrence: University Press of Kansas, 1993), 129.

16. A large academic literature maintains that most episodes of civilian killing constitute genocide or politicide, attempts to "destroy, in whole or part, a communal, political, or politicized ethnic group." See, for example, Barbara Harff, "No Lessons Learned from the Holocaust? Assessing Risks of Genocide and Political Mass Murder since 1955," *American Political Science Review* 97, no. 1 (February 2003): 58.

17. On these categories, see Pape, *Bombing to Win*, 55–79.

18. Ibid., 32–35.

19. The phrase is from Michael Mann, *The Dark Side of Democracy: Explaining Ethnic Cleansing* (Cambridge: Cambridge University Press, 2005). Mann identifies a different dark side of democracy, which occurs when the body politic in a state (the demos) becomes identified with a particular ethnic group (an ethnos). This overlap of demos and ethnos excludes other ethnic groups as foreign, which can eventually lead to violent cleansing depending on other factors.

20. The recent focus on civilian victimization began in the late 1990s in comparative politics, history, and international relations. See, respectively, Stathis N. Kalyvas, "Wanton and Senseless? The Logic of Massacres in Algeria," *Rationality and Society* 11, no. 3 (August 1999): 243–85; Mark Grimsley and Clifford J. Rogers, eds., *Civilians in the Path of War* (Lincoln: University of Nebraska Press, 2002); and Benjamin Valentino, "Final Solutions: The Causes of Mass Killing and Genocide," *Security Studies* 9, no. 3 (spring 2000): 1–59.

21. Kalyvas, "Wanton and Senseless?"; Kalyvas, "The Paradox of Terrorism in Civil War," *Journal of Ethics* 8, no. 1 (March 2004): 97–138; Valentino, Huth, and Balch-Lindsay, "'Draining the Sea'"; Kalyvas, *The Logic of Violence in Civil War* (Cambridge: Cambridge University Press, 2006); Jeremy M. Weinstein, *Inside Rebellion: The Politics of Insurgent Violence* (Cambridge: Cambridge University Press, 2007), 198–259; and Macartan Humphreys and Jeremy M. Weinstein, "Handling and Manhandling Civilians in Civil War," *American Political Science Review* 100, no. 3 (August 2006): 429–47.

22. Valentino, Huth, and Balch-Lindsay, "'Draining the Sea,'" 403.

23. Civilian victimization—although masquerading under other names, such as nuclear deterrence, punishment, and barbarism—is already a key independent variable in security studies. See, for example, Thomas C. Schelling, *Arms and Influence* (New Haven: Yale University Press, 1966); Pape, *Bombing to Win*; and Ivan Arreguín-Toft, "How the Weak Win Wars: A Theory of Asymmetric Conflict," *International Security* 26, no. 1 (summer 2001): 93–128. The targeting

of civilians—under the label terrorism—is also rapidly becoming an important dependent variable. See Mia Bloom, *Dying to Kill: The Allure of Suicide Terrorism* (New York: Columbia University Press, 2005); and Robert A. Pape, *Dying to Win: The Strategic Logic of Suicide Terrorism* (New York: Random House, 2005).

24. William J. Dixon, "Democracy and the Peaceful Settlement of International Conflict," *American Political Science Review* 88, no. 1 (March 1994): 14–32; and Sebastian Rosato, "The Flawed Logic of Democratic Peace Theory," *American Political Science Review* 97, no. 4 (November 2003): 585–602. See also Douglas A. Van Belle, "Dinosaurs and the Democratic Peace: Paleontological Lessons for Avoiding the Extinction of Theory in Political Science," *International Studies Perspectives* 7, no. 3 (August 2006): 287–306.

25. Examples include Richard M. Price, *The Chemical Weapons Taboo* (Ithaca: Cornell University Press, 1997); Nina Tannenwald, "Stigmatizing the Bomb: Origins of the Nuclear Taboo," *International Security* 29, no. 4 (spring 2005): 5–49; Richard Price, "Reversing the Gun Sights: Transnational Civil Society Targets Land Mines," *International Organization* 52, no. 3 (summer 1998): 613–44; and Ward Thomas, *The Ethics of Destruction: Norms and Force in International Relations* (Ithaca: Cornell University Press, 2001). On the question of norm adherence and violation in wartime, see Legro, *Cooperation under Fire.*

26. For an analysis of how developments that make people more civilized and less prone to use violence can be thrown into reverse and result in a "decivilizing" process, see Jonathan Fletcher, *Violence and Civilization: An Introduction to the Work of Norbert Elias* (Cambridge: Polity Press, 1997).

27. Examples include Richard Smoke, *War: Controlling Escalation* (Cambridge: Harvard University Press, 1977); and Eric J. Labs, "Beyond Victory: Offensive Realism and the Expansion of War Aims," *Security Studies* 6, no. 4 (summer 1997): 1–49.

28. Pape, *Dying to Win*, 44.

29. Andrew F. Krepinevich Jr., *The Army in Vietnam* (Baltimore: Johns Hopkins University Press, 1986).

30. George W. Bush, "State of the Union 2007," January 23, 2007, http://www.whitehouse.gov/stateoftheunion/2007.

31. Mark Danner, *Torture and Truth: America, Abu Ghraib, and the War on Terror* (New York: New York Review Books, 2004); and Karen J. Greenberg and Joshua L. Dratel, *The Torture Papers: The Road to Abu Ghraib* (Cambridge: Cambridge University Press, 2005). Some argue that these policies created a permissive environment that led to abuses by American forces of Iraqi detainees such as those committed at Abu Ghraib prison. Danner began making this connection in his articles for *The New York Review of Books* in 2004. See "The Logic of Torture" and "The Secret Road to Abu Ghraib" in *Torture and Truth*, 10–25 and 26–49.

32. Kalyvas, *Logic of Violence in Civil War*, chap. 7, especially 195–207.

33. Quotes are from Valentino, *Final Solutions*, 4, 155.

34. Ibid., 84–88.

35. Ibid., 3.

1. Defining and Explaining Civilian Victimization

1. See *Geneva Convention (IV) relative to the Protection of Civilian Persons in Time of War* (1949) and *Protocol Additional to the Geneva Conventions of August 12, 1949, and relating to the Protection of Victims of International Armed Conflicts* (Protocol I, 1977), http://www.icrc.org/web/eng/siteeng0.nsf/htmlall/genevaconventions. On *jus in bello*—the part of just-war theory that regulates who may be targeted in war—see Michael Walzer, *Just and Unjust Wars: A Moral Argument with Historical Illustrations,* 2d ed. (New York: Basic Books, 1992); and James Turner Johnson, "Maintaining the Protection of Non-Combatants," *Journal of Peace Research* 37, no. 4 (July 2000): 421–48.

2. Benjamin Valentino, *Final Solutions: Mass Killing and Genocide in the Twentieth Century* (Ithaca: Cornell University Press, 2004), 10. Unlike Valentino's definition, however, it is not necessary that a particular number of people die for a case to qualify as civilian victimization.

3. *Protocol Additional (I) to the Geneva Conventions,* Article 43. See also Valentino, *Final Solutions,* 13–14; and Walzer, *Just and Unjust Wars,* 42–43. I exclude prisoners of war from this category mainly for lack of data and to focus sharply on those who are clearly civilians rather than former fighters.

4. Walzer, *Just and Unjust Wars,* 135; see also ibid., 145–46.

5. Theodore J. Koontz, "Noncombatant Immunity in Michael Walzer's *Just and Unjust Wars," Ethics and International Affairs* 11, no. 1 (March 1997): 66–67, 71.

6. Individuals who are functionally assimilated into the military—such as sailors serving on armed merchant ships, or modern-day "civilian" contractors—fall into the combatant category. I acknowledge the difficulty of drawing a clean line between combatants and noncombatants. An alternative would be to create a third category of "quasi-combatants" for those—such as munitions workers or contractors—who build or service weapons but do not actually fight. Such individuals would be accorded greater protections than soldiers but fewer than civilians employed outside the defense industry.

7. Caleb Carr, *The Lessons of Terror: A History of Warfare against Civilians* (New York: Random House, 2002), 47; and Barry Buzan, "Who May We Bomb?" in *Worlds in Collision: Terror and the Future of Global Order,* ed. Ken Booth and Tim Dunne (New York: Palgrave Macmillan, 2002), 85–94.

8. Johnson, "Maintaining the Protection of Noncombatants," 423.

9. John C. Ford, "The Morality of Obliteration Bombing," in *War and Morality,* ed. Richard A. Wasserstrom (Belmont, CA: Wadsworth, 1970), 22–26.

10. Christopher R. Browning, *Ordinary Men: Reserve Police Battalion 101 and the Final Solution in Poland* (New York: Harper Collins, 1992), 160, 161.

11. For a similar definition, see Ivan Arreguín-Toft, "How the Weak Win Wars: A Theory of Asymmetric Conflict," *International Security* 26, no. 1 (summer 2001): 101–02.

12. The bombing directive of February 14, 1942, quoted in Max Hastings, *Bomber Command* (New York: Dial Press, 1979), 133.

13. Richard G. Davis, "German Rail Yards and Cities: U.S. Bombing Policy 1944–1945," *Air Power History* 42, no. 2 (summer 1995): 51; and Thomas R. Searle, "'It Made a Lot of Sense to Kill Skilled Workers': The Firebombing of Tokyo in March 1945," *Journal of Military History* 66, no. 1 (January 2002): 109.

14. On the Al-Firdos episode, see Ward Thomas, *The Ethics of Destruction: Norms and Force in International Relations* (Ithaca: Cornell University Press, 2001), 160–61.

15. Civilian fatalities that result from the simple fact that a war occurred at all rather than from military action by the enemy are excluded. Deaths owing to inevitable outbreaks of disease spread by the marching of armies to and fro—which were terribly common until recent times—are one example. Similarly, the eventual deaths of civilians who flee of their own accord from a war zone are excluded because no one targeted or otherwise used force against them. Diseases spread by a belligerent on purpose, of course, would constitute civilian targeting, and these deaths would count.

16. Avner Offer, *The First World War: An* (Oxford: Clarendon Press, 1989), 227–29; and Barton J. Bernstein, "Understanding the Atomic Bomb and the Japanese Surrender: Missed Opportunities, Little-Known Near Disasters, and Modern Memory," *Diplomatic History* 19, no. 2 (spring 1995): 257–58, 265.

17. Stathis N. Kalyvas, *The Logic of Violence in Civil War* (Cambridge: Cambridge University Press, 2006), 19–20; Valentino, *Final Solutions,* 11

18. Thomas Pakenham, *The Boer War* (New York: Post Road Press, 1979), 524.

19. Instances of domestic violence directed at other groups—such as Turkey's mass killing of Armenians inside Turkey during World War I or Nazi depredations against German Jews—are excluded.

20. This is not to imply that desperation or appetite for conquest do not apply to these types of cases, but merely that for the purposes of this book I test these arguments on international wars.

21. Stathis N. Kalyvas, "Wanton and Senseless? The Logic of Massacres in Algeria," *Rationality and Society* 11, no. 3 (August 1999): 246.

22. Jim Bradbury, *The Medieval Siege* (Woodbridge: Boydell Press, 1992), 317–18.

23. Mark Mazower, *Inside Hitler's Greece: The Experience of Occupation, 1941–44* (New Haven: Yale University Press, 1993), 155–89; and Raul Hilberg, *The Destruction of the European Jews,* Student ed. (New York: Holmes and Meier, 1985), 111, 153.

24. Steven L. Burg and Paul S. Shoup, *The War in Bosnia-Herzegovina: Ethnic Conflict and International Intervention* (Armonk, NY: M. E. Sharpe, 1999), 171–81.

25. Selected examples of naval bombardment include Spain's shelling of the Peruvian port of Callao in 1866 (Chile bombarded the same town during the War of the Pacific, 1879–83), Italian attacks on Libyan coastal towns in the Italo-Turkish War (1911–12), German shelling of English towns in World War I, the French bombing of Haiphong in 1946, and shelling by the U.S.S. *New Jersey* of the Vietnamese and Lebanese coasts.

26. Killing military or political leaders during war—sometimes referred to as decapitation—is not considered civilian victimization, nor does it violate the laws of war. On the legal issue, see Ward Thomas, "Norms and Security: The Case of International Assassination," *International Security* 25, no. 1 (summer 2000): 105–33. On decapitation as a bombing strategy, see Robert A. Pape, *Bombing to Win: Air Power and Coercion in War* (Ithaca: Cornell University Press, 1996), 79–86.

27. Walzer, *Just and Unjust Wars,* 161–65.

28. Harrison E. Salisbury, *The 900 Days: The Siege of Leningrad* (London: Pan Books, 2000), 506, 377.

29. Vice Admiral Charles Ottley, quoted in Offer, *First World War,* 232.

30. Rachel Simon, *Libya between Ottomanism and Nationalism: The Ottoman Involvement in Libya during the War with Italy (1911–1919)* (Berlin: Klaus Schwarz Verlag, 1987), 324.

31. Brigadier Benjamin Adekunle, quoted in John J. Stremlau, *The International Politics of the Nigerian Civil War 1967–1970* (Princeton: Princeton University Press, 1977), 331, n. 53.

32. Vegetius quoted in John France, *Victory in the East: A Military History of the First Crusade* (Cambridge: Cambridge University Press, 1994), 42; ibid., 65–66.

33. John A. Lynn, "A Brutal Necessity? The Devastation of the Palatinate, 1688–1689," in *Civilians in the Path of War,* ed. Mark Grimsley and Clifford J. Rogers (Lincoln: University of Nebraska Press, 2002), 79–110. See also John Childs, *Armies and Warfare in Europe, 1648–1789* (New York: Holmes and Meier, 1982), 152.

34. Quoted in Robert B. Asprey, *War in the Shadows: The Guerrilla in History* (New York: William Morrow, 1994), 99.

35. Lucien-François de Montagnac, quoted in Anthony Thrall Sullivan, *Thomas-Robert Bugeaud, France and Algeria, 1784–1849: Politics, Power, and the Good Society* (Hamden, CT: Archon Books, 1983), 125.

36. Over 100,000 Filipinos probably died in these camps or in the campaigns of devastation designed to compel people to leave their homes. Valentino, *Final Solutions,* 203–4.

37. Quoted in Luzviminda Francisco, "The Philippine-American War," in *The Philippines Reader: A History of Colonialism, Neocolonialism, Dictatorship, and Resistance,* ed. Daniel B. Schirmer and Stephen Rosskamm Shalom (Boston: South End Press, 1987), 16.

38. David E. Stannard, *American Holocaust: Columbus and the Conquest of the New World* (Oxford: Oxford University Press, 1992), 121–25.

39. Quoted in Russell Thornton, *American Indian Holocaust and Survival: A Population History since 1492* (Norman: University of Oklahoma Press, 1987), 116–17.

40. Valentino, *Final Solutions,* 75–77, 157–78.

41. International Commission to Inquire into the Causes and Conduct of the Balkan Wars, *The Other Balkan Wars* (Washington: Carnegie Endowment for International Peace, 1993), 315, 97, 99.

42. R. J. Rummel, "Democracy, Power, Genocide, and Mass Murder," *Journal of Conflict Resolution* 39, no. 1 (March 1995): 5–6; Benjamin Valentino, Paul Huth, and Dylan Balch-Lindsay, "'Draining the Sea': Mass Killing and Guerrilla Warfare," *International Organization* 58, no. 2 (April 2004): 375–407; Michael J. Engelhardt, "Democracies, Dictatorships and Counterinsurgency: Does Regime Type Really Matter?" *Conflict Quarterly* 12, no. 3 (summer 1992): 56; and Gil Merom, *How Democracies Lose Small Wars: State, Society, and the Failures of France in Algeria, Israel in Lebanon, and the United States in Vietnam* (Cambridge: Cambridge University Press,

2003), 24. See also Ivan Arreguín-Toft, "The [F]utility of Barbarism: Assessing the Impact of the Systematic Harm of Non-Combatants in War," paper presented at the annual meeting of the American Political Science Association, Philadelphia, PA, August 2003. On the restraining effect of democracy on domestic human rights violations and genocide, see Christian Davenport and David A. Armstrong II, "Democracy and the Violation of Human Rights: A Statistical Analysis from 1976 to 1996," *American Journal of Political Science* 48, no. 3 (July 2004): 538–54; and Barbara Harff, "No Lessons Learned from the Holocaust? Assessing Risks of Genocide and Political Mass Murder since 1955," *American Political Science Review* 97, no. 1 (February 2003): 57–73.

43. Rummel is the only scholar to emphasize the limits that democratic institutions impose on policymakers, arguing that "the more constrained the power of governments, the more power is diffused, checked, and balanced, the less it will aggress on others and commit democide." R. J. Rummel, *Death by Government* (New Brunswick, NJ: Transaction, 1994), 1–2.

44. Valentino, Huth, and Balch-Lindsay, "'Draining the Sea,'" 382. For a similar hypothesis—but different findings—see Benjamin Valentino, Paul Huth, and Sarah Croco, "Covenants without the Sword: International Law and the Protection of Civilians in Times of War," *World Politics* 58, no. 3 (April 2006): 345–47 and 368–69.

45. Markus Fischer, "The Liberal Peace: Ethical, Historical, and Philosophical Aspects," discussion paper 2000–07 (Cambridge: Belfer Center for Science and International Affairs, John F. Kennedy School of Government, Harvard University, April 2000), 15. See also Michael W. Doyle, *Ways of War and Peace: Realism, Liberalism, and Socialism* (New York: Norton, 1997), 287 n. 81; John Rawls, *The Law of Peoples* (Cambridge: Harvard University Press, 1999), 94–97; and John Locke, *Two Treatises of Government* (Cambridge: Cambridge University Press, 1988), 387–88.

46. Michael W. Doyle, "Kant, Liberal Legacies, and Foreign Affairs, Part 2," *Philosophy and Public Affairs* 12, no. 4 (autumn 1983): 344. He also concedes that liberal norms are not always effective at preventing countercivilian violence: "The terror bombing of civilians—as in the bombings of Dresden, Tokyo, Hiroshima, and Nagasaki—constitute, in this view, violations of these [individual] rights and of Liberal principles and demonstrate weaknesses of Liberal models in these cases." Doyle, *Ways of War and Peace*, 287 n. 81. The role of democratic institutions, according to the norms argument, is to enforce normative restrictions on targeting civilians by threatening leaders who violate the rules with removal from office via regular elections. As Merom puts it, democracies "are restricted by their domestic structure, and in particular by the creed of some of their most articulate citizens and the opportunities their institutional makeup presents such citizens." Merom, *How Democracies Lose Small Wars*, 15.

47. John E. Mueller, *War, Presidents, and Public Opinion* (New York: Wiley, 1973).

48. Bruce Bueno de Mesquita et al., "An Institutional Explanation of the Democratic Peace," *American Political Science Review* 93, no. 4 (December 1999): 798. The authors do not make this claim, but it is consistent with the logic of their argument. Explicitly making the connection are Valentino, Huth, and Croco, "Covenants without the Sword," 347–49.

49. Dan Reiter and Allan C. Stam, *Democracies at War* (Princeton: Princeton University Press, 2002), 19–20. Reiter and Stam also suggest that democratic institutions present no obstacle to "wars of empire or genocide" but do not argue that democracy causes brutal treatment of civilians. Ibid., 163.

50. Sebastian Rosato, "The Flawed Logic of Democratic Peace Theory," *American Political Science Review* 97, no. 4 (November 2003): 585–602; and Samantha Power, *"A Problem From Hell": America and the Age of Genocide* (New York: Basic Books, 2002).

51. On liberal norms and war crimes tribunals, see Gary Jonathan Bass, *Stay the Hand of Vengeance: The Politics of War Crimes Tribunals* (Princeton: Princeton University Press, 2000).

52. Rosato, "Flawed Logic of Democratic Peace Theory," 588–92; and Reiter and Stam, *Democracies at War*, 159–62.

53. John Mueller, "Public Opinion as a Constraint on U.S. Foreign Policy: Assessing the Perceived Value of American and Foreign Lives," paper presented at the annual meeting of the International Studies Association, Los Angeles, CA, March 2000. Public opinion surveys have found that in hypothetical scenarios, Americans routinely consider protecting foreign civilian lives to be at least as important as preserving American combatant lives. When asked about this trade-off during an ongoing war, however, this restraint disappears. A minority usually

responds that the United States is doing too much to protect civilians, or that it should escalate the use of force against noncombatants.

54. Reiter and Stam, *Democracies at War*, 151–58, 163.

55. H. E. Goemans, *War and Punishment: The Causes of War Termination and the First World War* (Princeton: Princeton University Press, 2000).

56. Rosato, "Flawed Logic of Democratic Peace Theory," 593–94; and Kenneth A. Schultz, *Democracy and Coercive Diplomacy* (Cambridge: Cambridge University Press, 2001), 14–15. See also Giacomo Chiozza and H. E. Goemans, "International Conflict and the Tenure of Leaders: Is War Still *Ex Post* Inefficient?" *American Journal of Political Science* 48, no. 3 (July 2004): 604–19.

57. For an argument that this autonomy depends on democracies' differing institutional structures, see Norrin M. Ripsman, *Peacemaking by Democracies: The Effect of State Autonomy on the Post–World War Settlements* (University Park, PA: Pennsylvania State Press, 2002).

58. Matthew A. Baum, "The Constituent Foundations of the Rally-Round-the-Flag Phenomenon," *International Studies Quarterly* 46, no. 2 (June 2002): 263–98.

59. Mueller, *War, Presidents, and Public Opinion*, 45, 54.

60. One study found that opposition parties go along at a rate of 84 percent when a democratic government issues a deterrent threat. Schultz, *Democracy and Coercive Diplomacy*, 167–68.

61. John W. Dower, *War without Mercy: Race and Power in the Pacific War* (New York: Pantheon, 1986).

62. Quotations are from Childs, *Armies and Warfare in Europe*, 102; Jürgen Osterhammel, quoted in Mark B. Salter, *Barbarians and Civilization in International Relations* (London: Pluto, 2002), 38; and International Commission, *Other Balkan Wars*, 95.

63. Bradbury, *Medieval Siege*, 189, 297. The Thirty Years' War, as well as the First and Second World Wars were all intra-European affairs.

64. On the similar treatment meted out to both Western POWs and Asian POWs and laborers by the Japanese, including episodes like the Bataan Death March and the building of the Burma Railway, see Dower, *War without Mercy*, 43–52. The most notorious single incident of Japan's war in Asia was the Nanking Massacre in December 1937, where Japanese forces killed about 300,000 people after occupying the city. See Iris Chang, *The Rape of Nanking: The Forgotten Holocaust of World War II* (New York: Basic Books, 1997). The Japanese also killed large numbers of civilians fighting Mao's communists in North China and experimented with germ warfare. See Lincoln Li, *The Japanese Army in North China 1937–1941: Problems of Political and Economic Control* (Tokyo: Oxford University Press, 1975), 13–14, 209; and Sheldon H. Harris, *Factories of Death: Japanese Biological Warfare, 1932–1945, and the American Cover-up*, Rev. ed. (New York: Routledge, 2002).

65. The term *extrasystemic* refers to wars fought between a state and a nonstate actor outside of the state's own territory. Imperial and colonial wars fall into this category.

66. I thank Ivan Arreguín-Toft for kindly providing this data. For details on his analysis, see Arreguín-Toft, "How the Weak Win Wars," and his book of the same title (Cambridge University Press, 2005).

67. Demonization in this view is instrumental and often has little or nothing to do with leaders' views regarding the enemy's actual identity.

68. Ido Oren, "The Subjectivity of the 'Democratic' Peace: Changing U.S. Perceptions of Imperial Germany," *International Security* 20, no. 1 (fall 1995): 147–84. Another example is the change in American leaders' depiction of Joseph Stalin from evil Marxist dictator in the 1930s to the benign "Uncle Joe" after the United States and USSR allied in opposition to Nazi Germany during World War II.

69. According to the commission that investigated the war, "Day after day the Bulgarians were represented as a race of monsters, and public feeling was roused to a pitch of chauvinism which made it inevitable that war, when it came, should be ruthless." International Commission, *Other Balkan Wars*, 95. For examples of anti-Bulgarian propaganda, see ibid., 95–98.

70. It may therefore be the case that dehumanization is necessary psychologically for individuals to be able to murder civilians, but it does not appear to be necessary for state policy. On the importance of dehumanization in overriding individuals' moral inhibitions against

committing violence, see Herbert C. Kelman, "Violence without Moral Restraint: Reflections on the Dehumanization of Victims and Victimizers," *Journal of Social Issues* 29, no. 4 (winter 1973): 48–52.

71. Jeffrey W. Legro, *Cooperation under Fire: Anglo-German Restraint during World War II* (Ithaca: Cornell University Press, 1995), 28.

72. Ibid., 27–28.

73. Ibid., 115, 142. Powerful militaries with a strong sense of honor—whose culture has been permeated by respect for noncombatant immunity—would similarly eschew strategies of civilian victimization because such strategies violate the organizational culture. See, for example, Colin H. Kahl, "How We Fight," *Foreign Affairs* 85, no. 6 (November/December 2006): 83–101. Kahl develops this argument in greater detail in Colin H. Kahl, "In the Crossfire or the Crosshairs? Norms, Civilian Casualties, and U.S. Conduct in Iraq," *International Security* 32, no. 1 (summer 2007): 7–46.

74. Isabel V. Hull, *Absolute Destruction: Military Culture and the Practices of War in Imperial Germany* (Ithaca: Cornell University Press, 2005); and Isabel V. Hull, "Military Culture and the Production of 'Final Solutions' in the Colonies: The Example of Wilhelminian Germany," in *The Specter of Genocide: Mass Murder in Historical Perspective,* ed. Robert Gellately and Ben Kiernan (Cambridge: Cambridge University Press, 2003), 141–62.

75. Jack Snyder, "Civil-Military Relations and the Cult of the Offensive, 1914 and 1984," *International Security* 9, no. 1 (summer 1984): 108–46.

76. On the RAF's adoption of area bombing, see Tami Davis Biddle, *Rhetoric and Reality in Air Warfare: The Evolution of British and American Ideas about Strategic Bombing, 1914–1945* (Princeton: Princeton University Press, 2002), 69–128. On the New Look and massive retaliation, see Peter J. Roman, *Eisenhower and the Missile Gap* (Ithaca: Cornell University Press, 1995), 63–111. I thank an anonymous reviewer for bringing this case to my attention. Other exceptions, such as the Kommissar and Barbarossa Orders issued before Germany's invasion of the Soviet Union in 1941, were the product of civilian minds, not military culture.

77. A further important issue concerns the origins of military cultures. It could be argued, for example, that the British preference for strategic bombing and the German preference for close air support in the 1930s stemmed from the countries' respective strategic situations. Britain, an offshore power, traditionally maintained a small army and relied on a strong navy to defend itself and exert power abroad. For Germany, by contrast, a land power in the center of Europe, depending on coercive instruments like naval and air power was a luxury it could not afford: without a large army, the country might be overrun before coercion could have any effect. For continental powers, therefore, security has usually meant ground forces. To the extent that strategic factors like these account for variation in military culture, the independent effect of such cultures is weakened.

78. These two mechanisms are obviously related: protracted wars are often costly; rising costs can contribute to desperation to win; and civilian victimization implemented to conserve costs is also intended to help win the war. They do not always go together, however, and thus I present them separately.

79. Hastings, *Bomber Command,* 128.

80. Searle, "'It Made a Lot of Sense to Kill Skilled Workers,'" 117–18.

81. Conrad C. Crane, *American Airpower Strategy in Korea, 1950–1953* (Lawrence: University Press of Kansas, 2000), 47.

82. V. E. Tarrant, *The U Boat Offensive, 1914–1945* (Annapolis: Naval Institute Press, 1989), 15. See also Germany's note to the U.S. government, delivered the day before the campaign began, quoted in R. H. Gibson and Maurice Prendergast, *The German Submarine War, 1914–1918* (New York: Richard R. Smith, 1931), 137.

83. For a similar logic, which maintains that governments target civilians when the guerrilla force is large and has widespread support among the population, both of which make the rebellion more threatening, see Valentino, Huth, and Balch-Lindsay, "'Draining the Sea.'" Incumbents also have incentives to hold down their costs so as to be able to prosecute a long war. Directing force at civilians helps to achieve this goal.

84. Kalyvas, *Logic of Violence in Civil War,* 195–207.

85. George Kennan, "Morality and Foreign Policy," *Foreign Affairs* 64, no. 2 (winter 1985–86): 206.

86. Thomas, *Ethics of Destruction*, 185.

87. Merom, *How Democracies Lose Small Wars*, 42–46.

88. Gary Shandroff, "The Evolution of Area Bombing in American Doctrine and Practice," Ph.D. diss., New York University, 1972, 97–98.

89. John J. Mearsheimer, *Conventional Deterrence* (Ithaca: Cornell University Press, 1983).

90. I am indebted to Tanya Schreiber for suggesting this phrase.

91. Exceptions—such as the German bombing of Belgrade in April 1941—may occur when a state finds itself under tremendous pressure to win quickly and cannot spare the forces to execute an alternative conventional strategy (such as a blitzkrieg). In spring 1941, for example, the Wehrmacht—feverishly preparing for Operation Barbarossa—was tasked by Hitler to assist Italy against Greece and conquer Yugoslavia at the same time. German bombers struck Belgrade on the first day of the invasion to frighten the Yugoslav government into an early capitulation. For an explanation along these lines, see Matthew Cooper, *The German Air Force 1933–1945: An Anatomy of Failure* (London: Jane's, 1981), 197–98.

92. Pape, *Bombing to Win*, 21–27, 32–35.

93. George H. Quester, *Deterrence before Hiroshima: The Airpower Background of Modern Strategy* (New York: John Wiley and Sons, 1966), 82–122.

94. On the difference between constitutive versus instrumental effects of norms, see Nina Tannenwald, "The Nuclear Taboo: The United States and the Normative Basis of Nuclear Non-Use," *International Organization* 53, no. 3 (summer 1999): 440.

95. For United States and British examples with regard to Italian, German, and Japanese bombing in the 1930s, see Dower, *War without Mercy*, 38–39.

96. The United States did immediately declare unrestricted submarine warfare since American leaders knew the war would undoubtedly be a long one. See Clay Blair Jr., *Silent Victory: The U.S. Submarine War against Japan* (Philadelphia: J. B. Lippincott, 1975), 106. The United States also launched the Doolittle Raid in 1942, but this was an act of psychological warfare rather than the beginning of sustained bombing of Japan.

97. Geoffrey Wawro, *The Franco-Prussian War: The German Conquest of France in 1870–1871* (Cambridge: Cambridge University Press, 2003), 304.

98. Although this "fifth column" logic is distinct from the desperation logic, in practice the two sometimes occur in the same war when the target state's resistance turns the conflict into a war of attrition. Several examples are noted in table 2.13 and discussed in appendix 2.2.

99. Avraham Ussishkin, quoted in Benny Morris, *The Birth of the Palestinian Refugee Problem Revisited*, 2d ed. (Cambridge: Cambridge University Press, 2004), 50.

100. Ibid., 227.

101. International Commission, *Other Balkan Wars*; and Justin McCarthy, *Death and Exile: The Ethnic Cleansing of Ottoman Muslims, 1821–1922* (Princeton: Darwin, 1995), 135–77.

102. On Stalin's deportations, see Robert Conquest, *The Nation Killers: The Soviet Deportation of Nationalities* (London: Macmillan, 1970); and Terry Martin, "The Origins of Soviet Ethnic Cleansing," *Journal of Modern History* 70, no. 4 (December 1998): 820.

103. Massacres by North and South Korea in the early stages of the Korean War are examples.

104. Pape, *Bombing to Win*; Michael Horowitz and Dan Reiter, "When Does Aerial Bombing Work? Quantitative Empirical Tests, 1917–1999," *Journal of Conflict Resolution* 45, no. 2 (April 2001): 147–73; Robert A. Pape, "Why Economic Sanctions Do Not Work," *International Security* 22, no. 2 (fall 1997): 90–136; Arreguín-Toft, "[F]utility of Barbarism"; and Ivan Arreguín-Toft, "Self-Inflicted Wounds: Evaluating the Costs of Barbarism as a Coercive Strategy in War," paper presented at the annual meeting of the International Studies Association, Honolulu, HI, March 2005. On the self-defeating effect of indiscriminate violence in guerrilla warfare and counterinsurgency, see Kalyvas, "Wanton and Senseless?" 251; and Stathis N. Kalyvas, "The Paradox of Terrorism in Civil War," *Journal of Ethics* 8, no. 1 (2004): 112–23.

105. Michael Ignatieff, "Barbarians at the Gates: Warfare against Civilians, Caleb Carr Argues, Should Always be Viewed as Terrorism," *New York Times Book Review*, February 17, 2002, 8.

106. Robert Baldick, *The Siege of Paris* (London: The History Book Club, 1965), 222. Fear of insurrection by communards inside Paris also contributed to the decision to seek an armistice. Alistair Horne, *The Fall of Paris: The Siege and the Commune 1870–71* (New York: St. Martin's Press, 1965), 239.

107. Offer, *First World War*, 72.

108. Kenneth P. Werrell, *Blankets of Fire: U.S. Bombers over Japan during World War II* (Washington: Smithsonian Institution Press, 1996), 233–34.

109. Mancur Olson Jr., *The Economics of the Wartime Shortage: A History of British Food Supplies in the Napoleonic War and in World Wars I and II* (Durham: Duke University Press, 1963).

110. Kalyvas, "Paradox of Terrorism in Civil War," 100, 137. On the effectiveness of the Phoenix Program, see also Mark Moyar, *Phoenix and the Birds of Prey: The CIA's Secret Campaign to Destroy the Viet Cong* (Annapolis: Naval Institute Press, 1997), 258–59, 262–64.

111. On the Boer War, see Byron Farwell, *The Great Boer War* (Hertfordshire: Wordsworth Editions, 1999), 371; and S. B. Spies, *Methods of Barbarism? Roberts and Kitchener and Civilians in the Boer Republics, January 1900–May 1902* (Cape Town: Human and Rousseau, 1977), 284. On the U.S.–Filipino War, see Timothy K. Deady, "Lessons from a Successful Counterinsurgency: The Philippines, 1899–1902," *Parameters* 35, no. 1 (spring 2005): 53–68. On the Italo-Sanusi War, see E. E. Evans-Pritchard, *The Sanusi of Cyrenaica* (Oxford: Clarendon Press, 1949), 188

112. On the counterproductive effects of Nazi indiscriminate violence, see Matthew Cooper, *The Nazi War against Soviet Partisans, 1941–1944* (New York: Stein and Day, 1979), 19–29; Kalyvas, "Paradox of Terrorism in Civil War," 113–14; and Paul N. Hehn, *The German Struggle Against Yugoslav Guerrillas in World War II: German Counter-Insurgency in Yugoslavia, 1941–1943* (Boulder: East European Quarterly, 1979), 143.

113. This difference is statistically significant ($p = 0.04$). The difference between barbarism and conventional strategies in general is not.

114. Neither of these differences is statistically significant.

115. The former relationship is significant ($p < 0.01$) whereas the latter is not ($p = 0.16$). Civilian victimization remains an important correlate of victory in multivariate regression even controlling for other factors known to be associated with winning, such as relative power, allied contributions, military strategy, terrain, quality of forces, regime type, and war initiation. Using a dataset of interstate wars assembled by Reiter and Stam in chapter 2 of their book *Democracies at War*, I added a variable indicating whether each state targeted enemy civilians. Civilian victimization was consistently positive and significant ($p < 0.01$), meaning that it significantly increases the likelihood of victory for states that use it.

116. Several of the case studies also show how adopting strategies of civilian victimization reduced belligerents' costs of fighting.

117. I was not able to obtain variation in military culture—none of the militaries examined here had a culture that prescribed civilian victimization, but many of them targeted noncombatants anyway, offering evidence against the cultural argument.

118. Alexander L. George and Andrew Bennett, *Case Studies and Theory Development in the Social Sciences* (Cambridge: MIT Press, 2005), 166–67, 221.

2. *Statistical Tests*

1. Correlates of War Interstate War Data, 1816–1997, version 3, http://cow2.la.psu.edu. See also Meredith Reed Sarkees, "The Correlates of War Data on War: An Update to 1997," *Conflict Management and Peace Science* 18, no. 1 (2000): 123–44.

2. Dan Reiter and Allan C. Stam, *Democracies at War* (Princeton: Princeton University Press, 2002), 39.

3. This list is identical to the one that appears in an article I published in 2006 in the journal *International Security* with one exception, involving Turkish participation in World War I. COW codes Turkey's belligerency as ending with the collapse of Russia in 1917, but this is incorrect: as the Russian Army crumbled, Turkey invaded Transcaucasia in 1918 and continued its massacre

of Armenians—begun inside Turkey in 1915—outside its prewar borders. See Christopher J. Walker, *Armenia: Survival of a Nation*, 2d ed. (New York: St. Martin's Press, 1980), 247–63. Under my coding rules—the killing of enemy civilians in an interstate war—the domestic genocide of the Armenians is not included, but the killing of 75,000 Armenians in the Caucasus later on does qualify for inclusion and is also a case of mass killing. For my earlier analysis, see Alexander B. Downes, "Desperate Times, Desperate Measures: The Causes of Civilian Victimization in War," *International Security* 30, no. 4 (spring 2006): 152–95.

4. Benjamin A. Valentino, *Final Solutions: Mass Killing and Genocide in the Twentieth Century* (Ithaca: Cornell University Press, 2004).

5. Benjamin Valentino, Paul Huth, and Sarah Croco, "Covenants without the Sword: International Law and the Protection of Civilians in Times of War," *World Politics* 58, no. 3 (April 2006): 360.

6. It should be noted that using a different coding of democracy, this difference disappears and the two regime types are about equally likely to target civilians. I explore the reasons for this disparity in appendix 2.1.

7. Only Israel—ironically in the War of Attrition (1969–70)—did not target civilians in a war of attrition.

8. Both of these findings are from Benjamin Valentino, Paul Huth, and Dylan Balch-Lindsay, "'Draining the Sea': Mass Killing and Guerrilla Warfare," *International Organization* 58, no. 2 (April 2004): 375–407.

9. See, for example, Christian Davenport and David A. Armstrong II, "Democracy and the Violation of Human Rights: A Statistical Analysis from 1976 to 1996," *American Journal of Political Science* 48, no. 3 (July 2004): 538–54; and Barbara Harff, "No Lessons Learned from the Holocaust? Assessing Risks of Genocide and Political Mass Murder since 1955," *American Political Science Review* 97, no. 1 (February 2003): 57–73.

10. British conduct in the Mau Mau Rebellion in Kenya may also be a case of civilian victimization. See Caroline Elkins, *Imperial Reckoning: The Untold Story of Britain's Gulag in Kenya* (New York: Henry Holt, 2005).

11. This is consistent with the finding that democracies engaged in mass killing in two out of the three cases when insurgents posed a serious threat to the government and had high levels of civilian support. Valentino, Huth, and Balch-Lindsay, "'Draining the Sea,'" 399, n. 49. I do not know how many civil wars in democracies were wars of attrition in this period, and how often they induced civilian victimization. Some scholars, of course, treat colonial wars as civil wars, which would make some of the wars mentioned above cases of civilian victimization by democracies in civil wars. See James D. Fearon and David D. Laitin, "Ethnicity, Insurgency, and Civil War," *American Political Science Review* 97, no. 1 (February 2003): 75–90.

12. Obviously it is not possible to have a negative number of civilian casualties. However, the slope of the regression line with all variables at their average values—which is what the "mfx compute" command in Stata is calculating—could be steep enough that a one-unit change in a variable—in this case cultural differences—results in a decrease in casualties larger than the initial predicted value, thus producing this seemingly strange negative outcome.

13. Valentino, Huth, and Croco, "Covenants without the Sword," 366.

14. James Mahoney and Gary Goertz, "The Possibility Principle: Choosing Negative Cases in Comparative Research," *American Political Science Review* 98, no. 4 (November 2004): 653–69.

15. Clearly there are also cases where no choice is involved, such as those where geography or the current state of technology make targeting enemy civilians impossible. Dropping such cases would not introduce bias into the analysis.

16. Additional tables containing full results with the reduced dataset are available on the author's website, http://www.duke.edu/~downes.

17. The only conflict in the dataset in which states employed counterinsurgency is Vietnam (United States, South Vietnam). Excluding these cases from the analysis does not change the substantive results.

18. See, for example, Jeffrey W. Legro, *Cooperation under Fire: Anglo-German Restraint during World War II* (Ithaca: Cornell University Press, 1995), 94–103; Isabel V. Hull, *Absolute Destruction: Military Culture and the Practices of War in Imperial Germany* (Ithaca: Cornell University

Press, 2005); Colin H. Kahl, "How We Fight," *Foreign Affairs* 85, no. 6 (November/December 2006): 83–101; Colin H. Kahl, "In the Crossfire or the Crosshairs? Norms, Civilian Casualties, and U.S. Conduct in Iraq," *International Security* 32, no. 1 (summer 2007): 7–46; and Alexander B. Downes, "Military Culture and Civilian Victimization: The Case of American Strategic Bombing in World War II," paper presented at the annual meeting of the American Political Science Association, Philadelphia, PA, September 2006.

19. Monty G. Marshall and Keith Jaggers, *Polity IV Project: Political Regime Characteristics and Transitions, 1800–2000* (College Park, MD: Center for International Development and Conflict Management, 2001).

20. See Michael W. Doyle, *Ways of War and Peace: Realism, Liberalism, and Socialism* (New York: Norton, 1997), 261–64. As a practical matter, the lists of states these two different coding procedures yield are very similar (correlation coefficient = 0.83). Some have argued that insular states—countries that do not share land borders with neighbors that could potentially invade them, such as Britain, the United States, Japan, and Australia—are more secure and hence likely to develop liberal democratic regimes that are more cost-sensitive. Insular states would also seem to be more likely to develop military forces capable of projecting force across water, such as navies and air forces, which also happen to be good tools for targeting civilians via blockade and bombing. Such states would thus have both greater motivation and opportunity to victimize civilians in war. A dummy variable for insular states generally performs similarly to the variable for democracy in the analyses below, but the two are highly correlated, which makes including them both in the same model problematic. I thus set aside the question of whether democracies are prone to civilian victimization because they are also insular states and flag it for future research. I would simply note that democracies that are not insular (France, Israel) have targeted civilians, and some insular states are not democratic (Imperial Japan) and have victimized noncombatants. I thank Barry Posen for bringing this argument to my attention. See Otto Hintze, *The Historical Essays of Otto Hintze*, ed. Felix Gilbert (New York: Oxford University Press, 1975), 174, 199.

21. Samuel Huntington, *The Clash of Civilizations and the Remaking of World Order* (New York: Simon and Schuster, 1996). I also coded religious difference without separating the Eastern and Western versions of Christianity, as well as racial differences. Finally, I used COW's country codes to identify states from different areas of the world: Latin America, Europe (including the U.S., Canada, Australia, and New Zealand), Africa, the Middle East, and Asia. Results for these variables are consistently insignificant.

22. Attrition normally involves ground forces, but one could imagine attrition warfare on the seas or in the air. A conflict that was primarily naval and entailed repeated large-scale destructive battles between fleets would qualify as attrition. The costs of such battles could persuade leaders to turn to blockade instead. Similarly, attrition sometimes occurs in aerial warfare. The best example is the Battle of Britain, during which the German Luftwaffe tried to destroy Britain's fighter force in large-scale aerial battles to open the way for a cross-Channel invasion (not as an alternative to an invasion). Fierce English resistance and untenable German aircraft losses led the Luftwaffe to abandon the "dour campaign of attrition" and turn to night bombing of English cities. Richard Overy, *The Battle of Britain: The Myth and the Reality* (New York: Norton, 2000), 86. On the battle as a war of attrition, see also Williamson Murray, *Luftwaffe* (Baltimore: Nautical and Aviation Publishing Company of America, 1985), 52–53.

23. Valentino, Huth, and Croco, "Covenants without the Sword," 362. These authors also combine attrition and counterinsurgency in their analysis.

24. Readers may wonder why I did not make use of existing measures of attrition, such as the one used in Reiter and Stam, *Democracies at War*, chapter 2. This variable, however, does not necessarily measure what I want to measure: the nature of the fighting over the course of the war rather than the initial strategy chosen. Furthermore, attrition strategies are very common in their data: over 70 percent of the war participants are coded as using attrition strategies, whereas only 24 percent of belligerents in my data are coded as fighting in wars of attrition.

25. Valentino, Huth, and Croco, "Covenants without the Sword," 355.

26. For the analysis of numbers of civilian fatalities, I substitute a dummy variable signifying whether belligerents suffered casualties among their own civilian population instead of whether they were targeted for civilian victimization.

27. Ward Thomas, *The Ethics of Destruction: Norms and Force in International Relations* (Ithaca: Cornell University Press, 2001), 185.

28. J. Scott Long, *Regression Models for Categorical and Limited Dependent Variables* (Thousand Oaks, CA: Sage Publications, 1997), 217–50.

29. On these points, see Gary King, *Unifying Political Methodology: The Likelihood Theory of Statistical Inference* (Cambridge: Cambridge University Press, 1989), 53–54; and Rainer Winkelmann, *Econometric Analysis of Count Data*, 4th ed. (Berlin: Springer-Verlag, 2003), 63.

30. Valentino, Huth, and Croco, "Covenants without the Sword," 364. It is not clear this interpretation is correct, however. Although multiple civilians are often killed per attack—and sometimes hundreds or thousands—each one of them is either killed or not killed. The process generating the data, in other words, is still binary even though we only observe the total numbers of casualties rather than particular deaths. Distributions like the Poisson or negative binomial specifically deal with variables like these, where we observe only the total number of events rather than each individual underlying event.

31. Negative binomial is preferred to Poisson because the variance exceeds the mean, indicating that casualties are positively correlated with each other: the occurrence of one civilian casualty is likely to lead to more.

32. Substituting the continuous version of the Polity variable (–10 to +10) for the dummy variable produces consistently positive yet insignificant results: B = 0.05, Pr = 0.26 in model 1, for example. I explain the reason for this weaker result below in the section on specification checks.

33. My reading of the secondary literature tends to confirm the Polity coding. The Greek military, fed up with governmental corruption and incompetence (and several other professional matters), forced the prime minister to resign by staging a peaceful revolution in 1909 that one historian describes as having "the overtones of a comic opera." At the military's urging, King George then appointed Cretan politician Eleftherios Venizelos to the premiership. Venizelos's Liberal Party obtained a large majority in the December 1910 elections and proceeded to revise the constitution to guarantee more liberal rights and protections. Venizelos's government was reelected in March 1912 and remained in power until tensions between the prime minister and the new king Constantine over Greece's stance in World War I induced the National Schism in 1915. One could argue that the "coup" of 1909 is what led Doyle to code Greece as nonliberal, but Doyle does not remove Greece from the ranks of liberal democracies until 1912. See D. George Kousoulas, *Modern Greece: Profile of a Nation* (New York: Scribner's, 1974), 94 (quote), and 94–111; and Richard Clogg, *A Concise History of Greece*, 2d ed. (Cambridge: Cambridge University Press, 2002), 73–90.

34. The British cases are the Crimean (1854–56) and Anglo-Persian (1856–57) wars; the Italian cases are the Crimean, Italian Unification (1859), Italo-Roman (1860), Italo-Sicilian (1860–61), Seven Weeks (1866), and Italo-Turkish (1911–12) wars.

35. The smaller coefficient for deterrence when only capable states are included in the analysis (models 3–4) supports this interpretation.

36. This difference is significant: Pearson Chi^2(1) = 12.7685, Pr < 0.001. The gap between democracies and autocracies is not quite as striking using Doyle's coding of liberal states, 65 versus 44 percent (Pr = 0.11).

37. This same sensitivity, however, does not seem to have made democracies more attractive targets for civilian victimization. Democracies are actually somewhat less likely (12 percent) than autocracies (14 percent) to have civilian victimization used against them (p = 0.59).

38. These cases include Britain, France, and the United States in the Boxer Rebellion; Romania in the Hungarian War; France and Turkey in the Franco-Turkish War; the Soviet Union in the Sino-Soviet War and the Russo-Finnish War; and Iraq in the Persian Gulf War.

39. Data on war initiation is taken from COW except for those conflicts that are in my dataset but not in COW (recent conflicts plus the various components of the two World Wars), for which I relied on secondary historical accounts to code initiation. COW codes as the initiator the first state to use force in a dispute. I followed this definition even though it produces some odd results, such as coding the great powers that intervened in China during the Boxer Rebellion as initiators, whereas most historical accounts agree that the Boxers started the conflict by

besieging the foreign legations in Beijing. For this criticism of the COW coding, see Sebastian Rosato, "The Flawed Logic of Democratic Peace Theory," *American Political Science Review* 97, no. 4 (November 2003): 585–602. The reason to code the case this way, however, is that the great powers were the first state actors to use force, whereas the Boxers were a nonstate actor. I thank Christopher Gelpi for reminding me of this definition.

40. H. E. Goemans, *War and Punishment: The Causes of War Termination and the First World War* (Princeton: Princeton University Press, 2000).

41. Using a version of the Polity variable that ranges from 0 to 20 in model 1, the coefficient is negative (B = −0.41, p < 0.01) while the square of this variable is positive (B = 0.02, p < 0.01), indicating a U-shaped relationship.

42. Some readers may find this nonresult puzzling given the brutal behavior of the Nazi regime. The answer has to do with the way the dependent variable is coded. Civilian victimization is intended to detect intentional and indiscriminate violence against enemy noncombatants during ongoing interstate wars. Many Nazi atrocities were perpetrated against populations in countries against which Germany was not at war, such as Hungary, or against the populations of defeated adversaries after the interstate phase of the conflict was over, including France, Yugoslavia, and Greece. The guerrilla campaigns in those states were initiated after the government had been deposed and the country occupied. They technically belong in the "extrasystemic" category of imperial or colonial wars pitting a state against a nonstate actor. Nazi Germany victimized noncombatants in the interstate phases of wars against Poland (1939), Britain (1940–45), Yugoslavia (1941), and the Soviet Union (1941–45), but did not against Norway/Denmark (1940), in the Battle of France (1940), or in the defeat of Greece (1941).

43. Valentino, Huth, and Balch-Lindsay, "'Draining the Sea.'" My result is not sensitive to changes in coding. Doyle's version of liberal democracy, for example, yields the same result. France and the United States in World War I are coded as committing mass killing via their participation in the British-led blockade of the Central Powers. Reversing this coding decision only slightly reduces the coefficient (B = 2.00) and the significance level (p < 0.02).

44. The actual figures are 44 percent vs. 29 percent (p = 0.25). The relationship using Doyle's coding of liberal democracy is slightly stronger: 53 percent vs. 26 percent (p = 0.06).

45. As was the case with civilian victimization, mixed regimes are significantly less likely than democracies or dictatorships to engage in mass killing (B = −2.55, p < 0.01). Further tests indicate that the relationship between regime type and mass killing is curvilinear. Democracies committed mass killing in 12 percent of their wars, compared to 6 percent for dictatorships and 2 percent for mixed regimes. Regression results support this: the sign on democracy is negative (B = −0.47) whereas the sign on the squared value of democracy is positive (B − 0.03). Both are significant. Finally, democratic war initiators are not significantly less likely to commit mass killing than autocratic initiators (B = −2.40, p = 0.26).

46. An examination of the data indicates that World Wars I and II on the Western Front account for most of the cases of mass killing among belligerents from the same civilization. Dropping these cases reverses the sign on cultural differences, but it does not become significant.

47. Country-specific effects do not appear to affect the results: dummy variables for Germany, Nazi Germany, and the United States, for example, are each insignificant.

48. Again, as with the analysis of mass killing, the western fronts of the two World Wars account for several large counts of civilian deaths in conflicts between states from the same civilizations. Dropping several of these counts halves the size of the cultural differences coefficient, but it remains negative. Eliminating the attrition and annexation variables reverses the sign of cultural differences, but the coefficient is essentially zero. It is thus difficult to avoid the conclusion that cultural differences are not an important determinant of civilian deaths in interstate wars.

49. B = −1.77 (p = 0.14) for democracy after 1945, and B = −0.60 (p = 0.54) for democracy after 1970. Unlike with civilian victimization and mass killing, oligarchies do not kill fewer civilians than other regime types (B = 0.31, p = 0.60). There is no significant evidence to support a curvilinear relationship between regime type and civilian casualties, although the coefficients are correctly signed.

50. In terms of country-specific effects, dummy variables for Nazi Germany (p = 0.10) and the United States (p < 0.01) are positive and significant. Including the U.S. dummy causes the sign on democracy to become negative, but not nearly significant. Other variables are unaffected.

51. An alternative categorization—1–1,000; 1,001–10,000; 10,001–50,000; 50,001–100,000; 100,001–1 million; and greater than 1 million—yielded similar results.

52. The variable for mixed regimes regains a negative sign using ordinal logit (–0.66, p = 0.12).

53. Dummy variables for Germany (p < 0.10) and the United States (p < 0.01) are also positive and significant. Including the U.S. dummy makes democracy slip below the significance line (p = 0.17).

54. Oligarchies kill somewhat fewer civilians than other regime types (B = –0.28, p = 0.26).

55. Valentino, Huth, and Croco, "Covenants without the Sword," 358. For their exact coding rules on coalitions, see ibid., 358, n. 58.

56. One other possible reason for the disparity between our results is that Valentino, Huth, and Croco count munitions workers as civilians whereas I do not. Given the quality of the data, however, I doubt this difference has much of an effect.

57. Justin McCarthy, *Death and Exile: The Ethnic Cleansing of Ottoman Muslims* (Princeton, NJ: Darwin Press, 1995), 68.

3. *The Starvation Blockades of World War I*

1. Conservative Party leader Andrew Bonar Law speaking in the House of Commons on March 1, 1915. See *The Parliamentary Debates*, 5th ser., vol. 70, *House of Commons, Third Volume of Session 1914–15* (London: His Majesty's Stationery Office), 607.

2. Major-General Thabit Sultan, commander of the Iraqi Fourth Corps, quoted in Dilip Hiro, *The Longest War: The Iran-Iraq Military Conflict* (London: Grafton, 1989), 135.

3. Thomas R. Searle, "'It Made a Lot of Sense to Kill Skilled Workers': The Firebombing of Tokyo in March 1945," *Journal of Military History* 66, no. 1 (January 2002): 103–33.

4. Michael Walzer, *Just and Unjust Wars: A Moral Argument with Historical Illustrations*, 2d ed. (New York: Basic Books, 1992), 161.

5. Ibid., 167, 166. The Soviets eventually evacuated about a million people, mostly across Lake Ladoga. Artillery bombardment of besieged towns can act as a further prod to induce surrender, as the Prussian bombardment of Paris did in the Franco-Prussian War.

6. John de St. Jorre, *The Brothers' War: Biafra and Nigeria* (Boston: Houghton Mifflin, 1972), 237.

7. Joseph E. Thompson, *American Policy and African Famine: The Nigeria-Biafra War, 1966–1970* (Westport, CT: Greenwood Press, 1990), 147–48.

8. One reason for this is that states can adapt to shortages by cultivating more land or substituting other goods for those lost. See Mancur Olson Jr., *The Economics of the Wartime Shortage: A History of British Food Supplies in the Napoleonic War and in World Wars I and II* (Durham: Duke University Press, 1963).

9. Estimates on the Nigerian case range widely, but center on 1 million. See R. J. Rummel, *Statistics of Democide: Genocide and Mass Murder Since 1900* (Münster: Lit Verlag, 1998), 245–46. On the Iraq sanctions, see Mohamed M. Ali and Iqbal H. Shah, "Sanctions and Childhood Mortality in Iraq," *The Lancet* 355, no. 9218 (May 2000): 1851–57; and Richard Garfield, "Morbidity and Mortality among Iraqi Children from 1990 through 1998: Assessing the Impact of the Gulf War and Economic Sanctions," Unpublished MS, Columbia University, March 1999.

10. The mechanics of the blockade and rationing agreements are thoroughly recounted in the British official history: A. C. Bell, *A History of the Blockade of Germany and of the Countries Associated with Her in the Great War, Austria-Hungary, Bulgaria, and Turkey, 1914–1918* (London: Her Majesty's Stationery Office, 1961).

11. Rye and barley production also fell by about one-third. Louis Guichard, *The Naval Blockade, 1914–1918*, trans. and ed. Christopher R. Turner (New York: D. Appleton, 1930), 285.

12. *Kriegsbrot* initially contained 10 to 20 percent potato flour, but this was replaced by turnip flour after the failure of the potato crop in 1916. The rye and wheat flour used the entire grain, which made the bread "difficult to digest and assimilate." In 1917 the ration of even this meager fare was reduced from 225 to 160 grams per day. C. Paul Vincent, *The Politics of Hunger: The Allied Blockade of Germany, 1915–1919* (Athens: Ohio University Press, 1985), 127.

13. Ibid., 128.

14. Figures are from Avner Offer, *The First World War: An Agrarian Interpretation* (Oxford: Clarendon Press, 1989), 33; Bell, *Blockade of Germany*, 672; and Vincent, *Politics of Hunger*, 140. Rickets affects the skeletal system, causing bones to become brittle, teeth to fall out, jawbones to break, and joints to ache.

15. Figures are from Vincent, *Politics of Hunger*, 141; and Offer, *First World War*, 34.

16. Leo Grebler and Wilhelm Winkler, *The Cost of the World War to Germany and to Austria-Hungary* (New Haven: Yale University Press, 1940), 147.

17. The German female death rate per thousand in 1918 was 21.6 compared to 14.3 in 1913, and 14.6 in England in 1918. Offer, *First World War*, 35. Interestingly, infant mortality (one year or younger) actually declined for most of the war. As children grew older, however, their chances of dying prematurely increased. Babies born during the war, moreover, were underweight, averaging between four and five pounds. Nigel Hawkins, *The Starvation Blockades* (Barnsley: Leo Cooper, 2002), 237.

18. Scheidemann, quoted in Offer, *First World War*, 76.

19. Ibid., 72.

20. Samuel R. Williamson Jr., *The Politics of Grand Strategy: Britain and France Prepare for War, 1904–1914* (Cambridge: Harvard University Press, 1969), 318.

21. John W. Coogan, *The End of Neutrality: The United States, Britain, and Maritime Rights, 1899–1915* (Ithaca: Cornell University Press, 1981), 153.

22. David French, *British Strategy and War Aims, 1914–1916* (London: Allen and Unwin, 1986), 22.

23. The belief that a Prussian "military party" was responsible for the war is aptly stated in Viscount Grey of Fallodon, *Twenty-Five Years, 1892–1916*, vol. 2 (New York: Frederick A. Stokes, 1925), 28. See also Lorna S. Jaffe, *The Decision to Disarm Germany: British Policy towards Postwar German Disarmament, 1914–1919* (Boston: Allen and Unwin, 1985), 7–20.

24. Quotes are from Eric J. Labs, "Beyond Victory: Offensive Realism and the Expansion of War Aims," *Security Studies* 6, no. 4 (summer 1997): 42; and French, *British Strategy and War Aims*, 23. The British began the process of raising a large army (Kitchener's New Armies) immediately after the declaration of war, but the plan was to withhold these forces until the land powers had worn themselves out. Britain's armies could then deploy to the continent "to deliver the final blow against the Germans and allow the British to dictate their peace terms to allies and enemies alike." Ibid., 25.

25. Quotations are from Geoffrey Blainey, *The Causes of War*, 3d ed. (New York: Free Press, 1988), 37; Oliver, Viscount Esher, ed., *Journals and Letters of Reginald, Viscount Esher*, vol. 3, 1910–1915 (London: Ivor, Nicholson and Watson, 1938), 177; and Grey, *Twenty-Five Years*, 71. See also Coogan, *End of Neutrality*, 152. Reinforcing the "short war illusion" was the widespread view that belligerents' economies would collapse under the strain of war, and thus a Europeanwide conflagration would of necessity end quickly. Grey, *Twenty-Five Years*, 20 and 71; and Esher, *Journals and Letters*, 177.

26. Paul M. Kennedy, *The Rise and Fall of British Naval Mastery* (London: Ashfield Press, 1976), 230–31; and Offer, *First World War*, 301.

27. Restrictions on the cotton and copper trades proved particularly contentious since both were dominated by American producers. Bell, *History of the Blockade*, 46–58, 119–42.

28. Ibid., 50–51 and 228–29.

29. Telegram of September 29, 1914, quoted in ibid., 115.

30. Grey, quoted in Robert K. Massie, *Castles of Steel: Britain, Germany, and the Winning of the Great War at Sea* (New York: Random House, 2003), 509.

31. Coogan, *End of Neutrality*, 170. Coogan argues, however, that U.S. leaders were in fact highly accommodating of Britain's blockade policies even though these measures interrupted American trade with much of Europe because Wilson and his closest advisers favored the

Allied cause. According to this interpretation, Wilson sought cosmetic concessions by the British not to protect U.S. rights under international law, but rather to placate American public opinion. Ibid., 178–85.

32. Offer, *First World War*, 276; and Vincent, *Politics of Hunger*, 31. Although Britain was not a signatory to the declaration in 1914, its rules had been incorporated into the Admiralty's regulations on how it would wage war.

33. On the categories of contraband, see Vincent, *Politics of Hunger*, 30–31.

34. Coogan, *End of Neutrality*, 164.

35. Figures in this paragraph are from Martin Gilbert, *The First World War: A Complete History* (New York: Henry Holt, 1994), 68 (early casualties); John Keegan, *The First World War* (London: Hutchinson, 1998), 143 (Ypres); and Spencer C. Tucker, *The Great War, 1914–18* (Bloomington: Indiana University Press, 1998), 38 (total 1914 casualties).

36. Quotations are from David French, "Allies, Rivals and Enemies: British Strategy and War Aims during the First World War," in *Britain and the First World War*, ed. John Turner (London: Unwin Hyman, 1988), 25; French, *British Strategy and War Aims*, 57; Esher, *Journals and Letters*, 192; and Earl of Oxford and Asquith, *Memories and Reflections, 1852–1927* (Boston: Little, Brown, 1928), 52.

37. David Lloyd George, *War Memoirs of David Lloyd George*, vol. 1 (Boston: Little, Brown, 1933), 369–80; and Martin Gilbert, *Winston S. Churchill*, vol. 3, *1914–1916: The Challenge of War* (Boston: Houghton Mifflin, 1971), 225–26.

38. For these quotations, see David Lloyd George, "Suggestions as to the Military Position," CAB 42/1/8, 2; *H. H. Asquith Letters to Venetia Stanley*, ed. Michael and Eleanor Brock (Oxford: Oxford University Press, 1982), 345; and Lord Esher, "The War: After Six Months," January 29, 1915, CAB 42/1/29.

39. The French figure is from Tucker, *Great War*, 38; the Russian from French, *British Strategy and War Aims*, 57.

40. French, "Allies, Rivals, and Enemies," 25.

41. Ibid., 26.

42. Marion C. Siney, *The Allied Blockade of Germany, 1914–1916* (Ann Arbor: University of Michigan, 1957), 22.

43. Bell, *History of the Blockade*, 53.

44. Coogan, *End of Neutrality*, 161, 162.

45. This threat helped to induce Germany's neutral neighbors to enter into negotiations to restrict voluntarily their export trade with Germany. This practice, known as rationing, became a key part of the blockade.

46. Coogan, *End of Neutrality*, 165; see also ibid., 195.

47. Vincent, *Politics of Hunger*, 38 and 54, n. 38; and Bell, *History of the Blockade*, 44. Of merchant ships sailing from the United States to neutral European countries, only eight were impounded from August 1914 to January 1915. Massie, *Castles of Steel*, 509. On the difference between "arrest" and "detention" of neutral ships, see Coogan, *End of Neutrality*, 167, n. 73. Coogan asserts that focusing on arrest understates Britain's interference with neutral trade. Early in the war, it appears that the navy simply detained many ships for extended periods. As evidence, Coogan cites a diary entry by Lord Esher on August 31, 1914, stating that 52 ships loaded with grain destined for Germany or Holland had been interned by the end of August. Coogan, *End of Neutrality*, 163.

48. Bell, *History of the Blockade*, 51; see also Siney, *Allied Blockade of Germany*, 25.

49. Churchill in *Parliamentary Debates*, 5th ser., vol. 69, *House of Commons, Second Volume of Session 1914–15*, 937–38.

50. Coogan, *End of Neutrality*, 199.

51. Lloyd George memo of January 1, 1915, quoted in Lloyd George, *War Memoirs*, 1:373.

52. Siney, *Allied Blockade of Germany*, 67.

53. Quoted in Bell, *History of the Blockade*, 233.

54. Vincent, *Politics of Hunger*, 38.

55. Churchill quoted in *Parliamentary Debates*, 5th ser., vol. 69, *House of Commons, Second Volume of Session 1914–15*, 937; Viscount Haldane quoted in Coogan, *End of Neutrality*, 222. Indeed,

the German submarine campaign of 1915 was hardly unrestricted. See the section below on the German blockade; and Philip K. Lundeberg, "The German Naval Critique of the U-Boat Campaign, 1915–1918," *Military Affairs* 27, no. 3 (autumn 1963): 110, n. 35.

56. David Stevenson, *Cataclysm: The First World War as Political Tragedy* (New York: Basic Books, 2004), 202.

57. Bonar Law and Asquith, respectively, are quoted in *Parliamentary Debates*, 5th ser., vol. 70, *House of Commons, Third Volume of Session 1914–15*, 609, and 600–601. For Hankey's words, see his memo "The Apparent Deadlock on the Western Front," December 28, 1914, CAB 37/122/194, 3–4.

58. On official British silence regarding the blockade, see Offer, *First World War*, 227–29.

59. "Memorandum by Lord Crewe," June 18, 1915, CAB 37/130/15, 1.

60. "Notes on Lord Crewe's Memorandum," June 23, 1915, CAB 37/130/25, 1; 2.

61. "The New Blockade," *Times* (London), October 5, 1917.

62. Bell, *History of the Blockade*, 117.

63. M.P.A. Hankey, G. Herbert Fowler, and Mervyn O'Gorman, "Proposed Devastation of the Enemy's Crops," April 1, 1915, CAB 42/2/16, 8.

64. The report also recommended using incendiaries carried by balloons, but the cabinet ruled this out as being too indiscriminate. See M.P.A. Hankey, "Proposed Devastation of the Enemy's Crops: Report of a Conference," September 28, 1915, CAB 42/3/32, 3–4. The British made much of the humanity of burning German crops and blockade compared to the brutality of the enemy's practice of sinking merchant ships and tried to shift the blame for any harm done to civilians by these policies to the German government's refusal to surrender. Hankey, Fowler, and O'Gorman, "Proposed Devastation of the Enemy's Crops"; and A. J. Balfour, *The British Blockade* (London: Darling and Son, 1915), 4.

65. See "Proposed Devastation of the Enemy's Crops: Report of a Conference," 4. References to this plan disappear after 1915.

66. Lloyd George, "Suggestions as to the Military Position," 6.

67. See "Food Supplies of Germany," June 2, 1915, CAB 37/129/7, 4; and "Report on the Working of Food Legislation in Germany during the War, August to December 1914," July 1915, CAB 42/3/13, 2.

68. "House of Commons: The Blockade," *Times* (London), March 16, 1917.

69. Coogan, *End of Neutrality*, 164.

70. Bell, *History of the Blockade*, 408, 449–52; and Siney, *Allied Blockade of Germany*, 101–2, 129–32.

71. "Full Use of Sea Power," *Times* (London), December 2, 1916.

72. "Two Blockade Debates," *Times* (London), March 28, 1917.

73. Wile quoted in Werner Schaeffer, *War Against Women and Children* (Scotch Plains, NJ: Flanders Hall, 1941), 1.

74. Quoted in Harold Nicolson, *Peacemaking, 1919* (London: Constable, 1933), 61.

75. Vincent, *Politics of Hunger*, 79.

76. Offer, *First World War*, 77.

77. Coogan, *End of Neutrality*, 165; 195.

78. Matthew Stibbe, *German Anglophobia and the Great War, 1914–1918* (Cambridge: Cambridge University Press, 2001), 55.

79. John Horne and Alan Kramer, *German Atrocities, 1914: A History of Denial* (New Haven: Yale University Press, 2001), 179, 217.

80. The *Report of the Committee on Alleged German Outrages* (1915), headed by Lord Bryce, was one of the most influential pieces of British propaganda of the entire war, owing partially to Bryce's stature as a scholar and former ambassador to the United States.

81. Stuart Wallace, *War and the Image of Germany: British Academics 1914–1918* (Edinburgh: John Donald, 1988), 183, quoting J. H. Morgan, *German Atrocities: An Official Investigation* (1916).

82. M. L. Sanders and Philip M. Taylor, *British Propaganda during the First World War, 1914–18* (London: Macmillan, 1982), 162. The French also produced a wide variety of drawings depicting Germany as barbaric, but it was the Americans who generated some of the most famous

images after their entry into the war in 1917. One American propaganda poster, for example, depicted Germany as a gorilla wielding a club labeled "Kultur" underneath the caption "Destroy this mad brute," while another portrayed a German soldier as demonic and bloodstained while urging people to "Beat back the Hun" by buying Liberty Bonds. H. R. Hopps, "Destroy this Mad Brute," circa 1917; and Frederick Strothmann, "Beat Back the Hun with Liberty Bonds," 1918.

83. Offer, *First World War,* 234–35.

84. Wilson quoted in Williamson, *Politics of Grand Strategy,* 106. That these strategic ideas are not mutually exclusive is demonstrated by Fisher's view—despite his firm advocacy of the economic strategy—that the army should be put at the disposal of the navy to threaten or implement amphibious landings, "a projectile to be fired by the navy." Fisher memo to Selborne quoted in P. Haggie, "The Royal Navy and War Planning in the Fisher Era," in *The War Plans of the Great Powers, 1880–1914,* ed. Paul M. Kennedy (London: George Allen and Unwin, 1979), 126.

85. CID quoted in Offer, *First World War,* 243.

86. Vincent, *Politics of Hunger,* 34.

87. Coogan, *End of Neutrality,* 244.

88. Fisher quoted in Williamson, *Politics of Grand Strategy,* 109.

89. At the culmination of the Anglo-German naval race in 1912, for example, Churchill announced in Parliament that "the Admiralty would maintain a sixty percent margin over the dreadnoughts authorized by the 1908 German Naval Law, and any increases above that law would be met on a two-to-one basis." Ibid., 257.

90. Coogan, *End of Neutrality,* 156–57.

91. George H. Quester, *Deterrence before Hiroshima: The Airpower Background of Modern Strategy* (New York: Wiley, 1966), 28, 42; Gilbert, *First World War,* 279. Civilian deaths resulted mainly from the sinking of passenger liners, such as *Lusitania* (1,198), *Arabic* (44), *Hesperian* (32), and *Sussex* (50). Ibid., 157, 188, 191, 236. Thirty-seven unarmed liners were sunk in the course of the 1915 and 1916 campaigns, but few of these were passenger liners. V. E. Tarrant, *The U-Boat Offensive 1914–1945* (Annapolis: Naval Institute Press, 1989), 30.

92. Stibbe, *German Anglophobia and the Great War,* 136.

93. Before the outbreak of war in 1914, German leaders were confident that, as Kaiser Wilhelm II famously told German troops, the Schlieffen Plan would defeat France in a few weeks and that they "would be home before the leaves have fallen from the trees." Quoted in Stephen Van Evera, "The Cult of the Offensive and the Origins of the First World War," *International Security* 9, no. 1 (summer 1984): 67.

94. On Falkenhayn's pessimism, see Gordon A. Craig, *Germany, 1866–1945* (New York: Oxford University Press, 1978), 347–48; on Bethmann's view, see H. E. Goemans, *War and Punishment: The Causes of War Termination and the First World War* (Princeton: Princeton University Press, 2000), 84.

95. The Germans actually experienced their first episode of desperation in the opening days and weeks of the war. The success of the Schlieffen Plan depended on speed, which meant that Belgium had to be subdued immediately and traversed quickly. Stubborn Belgian resistance and exaggerated German fears of a repeat of the *franc-tireur* resistance of the Franco-Prussian War, however, resulted in widespread massacres of Belgian (and French) civilians in August and September of 1914. While many incidents were triggered by German battlefield reverses, and some spontaneous resistance by civilians no doubt occurred, the scale and uniformity of the German response reveals a powerful belief in the ubiquity of *franc-tireur* resistance that in reality did not exist. The foremost historians of German atrocities in 1914 argue that the violence stemmed from "German *belief* in a People's War, which constituted a massive case of collective self-suggestion, probably unparalleled in a modern army." German officers and soldiers perceived themselves to be confronting a people in arms, and responded—in an atmosphere where time was of the essence—by attempting to suppress the resistance with violence. Horne and Kramer, *German Atrocities,* 77.

96. Quoted in Douglas H. Robinson, *The Zeppelin in Combat: A History of the German Naval Airship Division, 1912–1918,* 3d ed. (Henley-on-Thames: Foulis, 1971), 52.

97. Quester, *Deterrence before Hiroshima,* 26.

98. The remaining 22 merchantmen were sent to the bottom by submerged torpedo shots; of these, 12 were identified as belonging to the enemy while 10 were neutrals. Lundeberg, "German Naval Critique of the U-Boat Campaign," 110, n. 35.

99. *Lusitania* was torpedoed on May 7, *Arabic* on August 19. One hundred twenty-eight of those killed on board *Lusitania* were Americans, as were three of *Arabic*'s passengers. Tarrant, *U-Boat Offensive*, 21.

100. General von Falkenhayn, *The German General Staff and Its Decisions* (New York: Dodd, Mead, 1920), 178. Nor was inflicting serious losses on British shipping within German capabilities: the 750,000–850,000 tons sunk represented at most 4 percent of what Britain had available, and the 1.3 million tons of new construction in 1915 more than compensated for these losses. See John Terraine, *Business in Great Waters: The U-Boat Wars 1916–1945* (London: Leo Cooper, 1989), 10; and Holger H. Herwig, *"Luxury" Fleet: The Imperial German Navy, 1888–1918* (London: Allen and Unwin, 1980), 165.

101. On land, Falkenhayn planned to assault the French fortress city of Verdun, hoping to draw the French into a battle of attrition that would bleed them white. At sea, the chief of the General Staff proposed to launch a second battle of attrition by unleashing the U-boats in an unrestricted campaign to cut off British imports.

102. Falkenhayn, *German General Staff*, 241.

103. Goemans, *War and Punishment*, 88.

104. Quoted in Konrad H. Jarausch, *The Enigmatic Chancellor: Bethmann Hollweg and the Hubris of Imperial Germany* (New Haven: Yale University Press, 1973), 281.

105. Quoted in Admiral Scheer, *Germany's High Sea Fleet in the World War* (London: Cassell, 1920), 241; and R. H. Gibson and Maurice Prendergast, *The German Submarine War, 1914–1918* (New York: Richard R. Smith, 1931), 83.

106. Herwig, *Luxury Fleet*, 166.

107. French losses were similar. Roger Chickering, *Imperial Germany and the Great War, 1914–1918* (Cambridge: Cambridge University Press, 1998), 68.

108. Also contributing to pessimism regarding German chances in the war was the increasingly desperate food situation on the German home front in 1916. For good descriptions, see Laurence Moyer, *Victory Must Be Ours: Germany in the Great War, 1914–1918* (New York: Hippocrene Books, 1995), 156–72; Robert B. Asprey, *The German High Command at War: Hindenburg and Ludendorff Conduct World War I* (New York: Morrow, 1991), 258–61; and Chickering, *Imperial Germany and the Great War*, 140–46.

109. Quoted in Tarrant, *U-Boat Offensive*, 35.

110. General Ludendorff, *My War Memories, 1914–1918*, vol. 1 (London: Hutchinson, 1919), 243. See also Asprey, *German High Command at War*, 266 67; and Martin Kitchen, *The Silent Dictatorship: The Politics of the German High Command under Hindenburg and Ludendorff* (New York: Holmes and Meier, 1976), 112.

111. Bell, *Blockade of Germany*, 599.

112. Terraine, *Business in Great Waters*, 14.

113. Gibson and Prendergast, *German Submarine War*, 119.

114. Scheer, *Germany's High Sea Fleet*, 194.

115. Quoted in Bell, *Blockade of Germany*, 600.

116. Tarrant, *U-Boat Offensive*, 45.

117. Chickering, *Imperial Germany and the Great War*, 71.

118. Asprey, *German High Command at War*, 284. This realization was also behind the "all-out assault by the Naval Airship Division on the British capital" described by Robinson in late 1916. He mentions each of the four hammer blows just discussed. Robinson, *Zeppelin in Combat*, 165.

119. Center Party leader Matthias Erzberger, quoted in Jarausch, *Enigmatic Chancellor*, 297.

120. Craig, *Germany*, 380.

121. Jarausch, *Enigmatic Chancellor*, 297–98.

122. Bethmann was largely free-lancing in this maneuver, as he had consulted neither the Reichstag nor the military command in its preparation, and the Duo at Pless opposed the peace move when they learned of it.

123. Asprey, *German High Command at War*, 289.

124. Ironically, Levy got most of his ideas from the British Royal Commission on Food Supply, an inquiry into Britain's vulnerability to an embargo on its food imports that took place from 1903 to 1905. See Offer, *First World War,* 220–25.

125. Ibid., 356.

126. Ibid., 356.

127. Ibid., 356–57.

128. For the full text of this document, see Carnegie Endowment for International Peace, *Official German Documents Relating to the World War,* vol. 2 (New York: Oxford University Press, 1923), 1214–19.

129. North America provided 90 percent of Great Britain's wheat imports in 1915. Offer, *First World War,* 359.

130. Holtzendorff realized that Britain actually had about 20 million tons of cargo space. He argued, however, that 8.6 million tons had been taken into military service, another 500,000 tons was plying the coastal trade, about 1 million was under repairs, and 2 million tons were being used to help other Entente powers. This left 8 million tons, but statistics on British commerce showed that only 6.75 million tons per month actually docked in English ports. Adding the 900,000 tons of seized vessels and 3 million tons of neutral hulls yields almost 10.75 million.

131. Tarrant, *U-Boat Offensive,* 148–49.

132. Carnegie Endowment, *Official German Documents Relating to the World War,* 2:1216.

133. Offer, *First World War,* 360.

134. Massie, *Castles of Steel,* 519, 703.

135. The Germans actually assumed that 100,000 tons of shipping sent to the bottom destroyed 240,000 tons of wheat. Offer, *First World War,* 359.

136. Ibid., 366.

137. Quoted in Asprey, *German High Command at War,* 293.

138. Besides the works cited below, see Goemans, *War and Punishment,* 94–98; and Kitchen, *Silent Dictatorship,* 123.

139. Ludendorff, *My War Memories,* 1:307, 312.

140. Scheer, *Germany's High Sea Fleet,* 255.

141. Quoted in Gibson and Prendergast, *German Submarine War,* 137.

142. Tarrant, *U-Boat Offensive,* 45.

143. Michael W. Doyle, "Kant, Liberal Legacies, and Foreign Affairs, Part I," *Philosophy and Public Affairs* 12, no. 3 (summer 1983): 216, n. 8.

144. Christopher Layne, "Kant or Cant: The Myth of the Democratic Peace," *International Security* 19, no. 2 (fall 1994): 42–44; and Ido Oren, "The Subjectivity of the 'Democratic' Peace: Changing U.S. Perceptions of Imperial Germany," *International Security* 20, no. 2 (fall 1995): 153.

145. Tirpitz quoted in Bell, *Blockade of Germany,* 211.

146. Craig, *Germany,* 369. See also Jarausch, *Enigmatic Chancellor,* 273; and Massie, *Castles of Steel,* 540, 552.

147. Quoted in Stibbe, *German Anglophobia,* 144.

148. Moyer, *Victory Must Be Ours,* 185.

149. Craig, *Germany,* 381.

150. Jarausch, *Enigmatic Chancellor,* 307.

151. David Welch, *Germany, Propaganda and Total War, 1914–1918: The Sins of Omission* (New Brunswick: Rutgers University Press, 2000), 58, 61.

152. Quoted in Stibbe, *German Anglophobia,* 21, 17.

153. Ibid., 55.

154. Welch, *Germany, Propaganda and Total War,* 62.

155. Ivo Nikolai Lambi, *The Navy and German Power Politics, 1862–1914* (Boston: Allen and Unwin, 1984), 401.

156. Lundeberg, "German Naval Critique of the U-Boat Campaign," 106–7.

157. Tarrant, *U-Boat Offensive,* 15.

158. In February and March 1917 the volume of ships arriving in and departing from British ports fell to about 25 percent of the traffic from the year before. Tarrant, *U-Boat Offensive,* 47. At

the height of the campaign, a merchant vessel departing from England had only a one in four chance of returning safely!

159. For the despondent views of Winston Churchill and First Sea Lord John Jellicoe, see Terraine, *Business in Great Waters*, 47–48.

160. Tami Davis Biddle, *Rhetoric and Reality in Air Warfare: The Evolution of British and American Ideas about Strategic Bombing, 1914–1945* (Princeton: Princeton University Press, 2002), 46–47.

4. Strategic Bombing in World War II

1. LeMay and his predecessor at Twenty-first Bomber Command, General Haywood Hansell, had already launched several "experimental" fire raids on Japanese cities with incendiary weapons. The attack on March 9, however, signaled a shift in U.S. bombing practice. The objective remained the same: shut down Japanese war production. The method used to achieve that goal, however, changed dramatically: rather than trying to destroy specific factories with high explosive bombs, U.S. aircraft began to burn out large sections of urban areas with incendiary devices. Far more debate has been devoted to the decision to drop atomic bombs on Hiroshima and Nagasaki in August 1945 than to the initiation of incendiary bombing in March. As Kenneth Werrell points out, however, "The critical step was not the decision authorizing the use of the atomic bombs, but the earlier decisions that allowed cities and civilians to be the targets of area bombing, first by Japan and German [sic], then against Germany and Japan." For this reason, I focus on the initial choice to aim at civilians in Japan, not the later culmination of this decision in the atomic bombings. Kenneth P. Werrell, *Blankets of Fire: U.S. Bombers over Japan during World War II* (Washington: Smithsonian Institution Press, 1996), 219. See also Tami Davis Biddle, *Rhetoric and Reality in Air Warfare: The Evolution of British and American Ideas About Strategic Bombing, 1914–1945* (Princeton: Princeton University Press, 2002), 270.

2. Richard B. Frank, *Downfall: The End of the Imperial Japanese Empire* (New York: Random House, 1999), 3–19; Wesley Frank Craven and James Lea Cate, eds., *The Army Air Forces in World War II*, vol. 5, *The Pacific: Matterhorn to Nagasaki, June 1944 to August 1945* (Washington: Office of Air Force History, 1983), 614–18; and Werrell, *Blankets of Fire*, 159–63. By March 1945, 1.7 million people had left Tokyo; it is unclear how much this flight reduced the population density in the targeted area. Six million people remained in the city. Gordon Daniels, "The Great Tokyo Air Raid, 9–10 March 1945," in *Modern Japan: Aspects of History, Literature and Society*, ed. W. G. Beasley (Berkeley: University of California Press, 1975), 122.

3. Quotes are from Michael S. Sherry, *The Rise of American Air Power: The Creation of Armageddon* (New Haven: Yale University Press, 1987), 276; Ronald Schaffer, *Wings of Judgment: American Bombing in World War II* (New York: Oxford University Press, 1985), 135; and Conrad C. Crane, *Bombs, Cities, and Civilians: American Airpower Strategy in World War II* (Lawrence: University Press of Kansas, 1993), 132. Figures on fatalities and homeless are estimates by the U.S. Strategic Bombing Survey (USSBS), in Schaffer, *Wings of Judgment*, 132. On the amount of physical destruction inflicted, see Frank, *Downfall*, 16–17. For eyewitness accounts and descriptions of the raid, see Edwin P. Hoyt, *Inferno: The Firebombing of Japan, March 9–August 15, 1945* (Lanham, MD: Madison Books, 2000), 7–35.

4. Werrell, *Blankets of Fire*, 168. LeMay expressed pride over the 0.9 percent loss rate achieved by his forces in the March fire raids. Curtis E. LeMay with MacKinlay Kantor, *Mission with LeMay: My Story* (Garden City, NY: Doubleday, 1965), 367. Indeed, in attacks on cities of less than 100,000 people, B-29s destroyed 3.5 square miles per bomber lost to any cause. See *The War Reports of General of the Army George C. Marshall, Chief of Staff, General of the Army H. H. Arnold, Commanding General, Army Air Forces [and] Fleet Admiral Ernest J. King, Commander-in-Chief, United States Fleet and Chief of Naval Operations* (Philadelphia: Lippincott, 1947), 441–42.

5. Arnold, "Report on Army Air Operations in the War against Japan," JCS 1421, July 16, 1945, quoted in Barton J. Bernstein, "Understanding the Atomic Bomb and the Japanese Surrender: Missed Opportunities, Little-Known Near Disasters, and Modern Memory," *Diplomatic History* 19, no. 2 (spring 1995): 249.

6. Werrell, *Blankets of Fire*, 328, n. 1; and Craven and Cate, *Army Air Forces in World War II*, 5:655, 749–50. According to Craven and Cate, 104,000 tons of bombs out of 147,000 tons total delivered by B-29s were dropped on urban areas. By contrast, only 22 percent of total bomb weight fell on "precision industrial targets." Werrell, *Blankets of Fire*, 226.

7. Ibid., 226–27. Japanese estimates range from 268,157 to 330,000 killed, but estimates done by the USSBS using polling techniques put the death toll at 900,000 (with an additional 1.3 million wounded). For discussion of these estimates, see Sherry, *Rise of American Airpower*, 413.

8. United States Strategic Bombing Survey, *Summary Report (Pacific War)* (Washington: GPO, 1946), 26, 29.

9. American pilots flying B-25 bombers launched from the aircraft carrier U.S.S. *Hornet* did strike Tokyo in April 1942 in the Doolittle Raid, but this was a one-time event that was staged as much for its impact on domestic morale as for any material damage it did to Japan.

10. Frank, *Downfall*, 28–29.

11. General Alexander Archer Vandegrift, quoted in ibid., 28.

12. John W. Dower, *War without Mercy: Race and Power in the Pacific War* (New York: Pantheon, 1986), 45.

13. Frank, *Downfall*, 28.

14. The struggle for Iwo Jima was ongoing when LeMay decided to shift to incendiary bombing.

15. Quoted in Frank, *Downfall*, 143. Truman made this comment during a meeting with his military advisors at the White House on June 18, 1945.

16. Ibid., 30.

17. JCS 924/2, "Operations Against Japan Subsequent to Formosa," August 30, 1944, 120, quoted in Frank, *Downfall*, 30. For further discussion of this document and its importance, see D. M. Giangreco, "Casualty Projections for the U.S. Invasions of Japan, 1945–1946: Planning and Policy Implications," *Journal of Military History* 61, no. 3 (July 1997): 521–81. As many readers are undoubtedly aware, estimates of U.S. casualties likely to result from an invasion of Japan are hotly contested. President Truman and Secretary of War Henry L. Stimson, for example, each asserted that the number of American lives saved by the bomb was on the order of 250,000 to 500,000. Harry S. Truman, *Memoirs*, vol. 1, *1945, Year of Decisions* (Garden City, NY: Doubleday, 1955), 417; J. Samuel Walker, *Prompt and Utter Destruction: Truman and the Use of Atomic Bombs Against Japan* (Chapel Hill: University of North Carolina Press, 1997), 103–4; and Henry L. Stimson, "The Decision to Use the Atomic Bomb," *Harper's Magazine* 194, no. 1161 (February 1947): 102.

18. Two studies compiled by the military in spring 1945 estimated U.S. casualties from an invasion at 193,500 (43,000 dead) and 456,611 (119,516 dead). Frank, *Downfall*, 139, 136. Historians arguing for lower figures include Barton J. Bernstein, "The Atomic Bombings Reconsidered," *Foreign Affairs* 74, no. 1 (January/February 1995): 149. See also Barton J. Bernstein, "A Postwar Myth: 500,000 U.S. Lives Saved," *Bulletin of the Atomic Scientists* 42, no. 6 (June/July 1986): 38–40; and Rufus E. Miles Jr., "Hiroshima: The Strange Myth of Half a Million American Lives Saved," *International Security* 10, no. 2 (fall 1985): 121–40. Frank argues that U.S. military officials, particularly army general George C. Marshall, conspired to keep the numbers down and avoided presenting firm estimates to the president. Frank, *Downfall*, 138–39, 145–48.

19. Bernstein, "Atomic Bombings Reconsidered," 149. On the Japanese buildup, see John Ray Skates, *The Invasion of Japan: Alternative to the Bomb* (Columbia: University of South Carolina Press, 1994), 136–44; and Frank, *Downfall*, 197–213. Indeed, Bernstein, a proponent of lower numbers, noted in a 1999 article that "the distressing evidence by early August 1945 of the large Japanese buildup would have unsettled, and substantially increased, those mid-June casualty estimates. The important point, put bluntly, is that American officials' expectations and fears in August 1945 were very different from their mid-June attitudes." Barton J. Bernstein, "The Alarming Japanese Buildup on Southern Kyushu, Growing U.S. Fears, and Counterfactual Analysis: Would the Planned November 1945 Invasion of Southern Kyushu Have Occurred?" *Pacific Historical Review* 68, no. 4 (November 1999): 564.

20. Quoted in Sherry, *Rise of American Air Power*, 58. Mitchell's sentiments were shared by some inside the military as well. Ibid., 39–40.

21. Werrell, *Blankets of Fire*, 41.

22. Quoted in Thomas R. Searle, "'It Made a Lot of Sense to Kill Skilled Workers': The Fire-bombing of Tokyo in March 1945," *Journal of Military History* 66, no. 1 (January 2002): 115–16.

23. Charles L. McNichols and Clayton D. Carus, "One Way to Cripple Japan: The Inflammable Cities of Osaka Bay," *Harper's Magazine* 185, no. 1105 (June 1942): 35, 36.

24. Biddle, *Rhetoric and Reality*, 160. See also Robert A. Pape, *Bombing to Win: Air Power and Coercion in War* (Ithaca: Cornell University Press, 1996), 62–64.

25. Biddle, *Rhetoric and Reality*, 162.

26. Crane, *Bombs, Cities, and Civilians*, 14–15. This argument is made at length in Schaffer, *Wings of Judgment*.

27. Pape, *Bombing to Win*, 262. AWPD is short for Air War Plans Division. Among the authors of the document were several mid-ranking officers who went on to become prominent wartime commanders, among them Haywood Hansell. American air strategy also assumed civilians would die and sought to capitalize on the fear this would cause. See the document entitled "Air Force: National Economic Structure" written by Major Muir S. Fairchild, an instructor at the Air Corps Tactical School (ACTS), in Schaffer, *Wings of Judgment*, 31.

28. Pape, *Bombing to Win*, 62; Arnold and Eaker quoted in ibid., 66.

29. Quoted in Werrell, *Blankets of Fire*, 43.

30. Arnold's staff, however, had compiled target folders by February 1942 that "included areas of Tokyo ranked in order of 'vulnerability to incendiary attack.'" See "Priorities: Japanese Objective Folder Material," February 19, 1942, quoted in Crane, *Bombs, Cities, and Civilians*, 126. The Intelligence Division of the AAF had begun compiling information on Japanese economic targets even before the war began. Biddle, *Rhetoric and Reality*, 262.

31. Searle, "'It Made a Lot of Sense to Kill Skilled Workers,'" 117. See also E. Bartlett Kerr, *Flames over Tokyo: The U.S. Army Air Forces' Incendiary Campaign against Japan* (New York: Donald I. Fine, 1991), 40–45. On a separate memo in mid October 1943 to Laurence Kuter making essentially the same points, see Werrell, *Blankets of Fire*, 51–52.

32. Werrell, *Blankets of Fire*, 48–49; and Mike Davis, *Dead Cities, and Other Tales* (New York: New Press, 2002), 65–83. Further tests in the humid environment at Elgin Field in Florida confirmed the effectiveness of the M-69.

33. Schaffer, *Wings of Judgment*, 111, 112.

34. Quoted in Sherry, *Rise of American Air Power*, 171.

35. JCS 742/6, "Optimum Use, Timing, and Deployment of Very Long Range Bombers in the War Against Japan," April 6, 1944, quoted in Searle, "'It Made a Lot of Sense to Kill Skilled Workers,'" 118; ibid., 119. A later COA report designated urban areas—to be attacked with incendiary bombs—as second only to aircraft production in priority as a target for B-29s.

36. Committee of Operations Analysts, "Economic Effect of Successful Area Attacks on Six Japanese Cities," September 4, 1944, quoted in Sherry, *Rise of American Air Power*, 229. See also Schaffer, *Wings of Judgment*, 116.

37. Sherry, *Rise of American Air Power*, 229, 228, referring to the "Revised Report of the Committee of Operations Analysts on Economic Targets in the Far East," October 10, 1944.

38. Ibid., 230. The COA had already recommended the March 1945 time frame for a "general attack on Japanese urban industrial areas." Memorandum, Colonel Guido R. Perera to Brigadier General Hansell, May 9, 1944, quoted in Searle, "'It Made a Lot of Sense to Kill Skilled Workers,'" 119. Some contest the conclusion that a fire campaign was by this time inevitable: "Nothing had as yet been settled. The groundwork for urban incendiary attacks had been established, but the AAF's instinct for selective targeting continued to coexist with it." Biddle, *Rhetoric and Reality*, 265.

39. Ewell memo to Vannevar Bush, head of the Office of Scientific Research and Development at the NRDC, October 12, 1944, quoted in Schaffer, *Wings of Judgment*, 120.

40. COA memo of May 9, 1944, quoted in Searle, "'It Made a Lot of Sense to Kill Skilled Workers,'" 119; 120. The COA report of October 10, 1944, made a similar recommendation and proposed precision attacks against war production in the meantime. Craven and Cate, *Army Air Forces in World War II*, 5:133; and Schaffer, *Wings of Judgment*, 120.

41. Quoted in Sherry, *Rise of American Air Power*, 248.

42. Searle, "'It Made a Lot of Sense to Kill Skilled Workers,'" 121.

43. The B-29 represented a significant improvement over the B-17 and B-24 in speed, range, and payload. Werrell, *Blankets of Fire*, 55–83. The B-29 was also expensive: the design, testing, and production of the nearly 4,000 B-29s delivered during World War II cost over $3 billion, easily surpassing the $2 billion spent on the atomic bomb. Kerr, *Flames over Tokyo*, 26. By May 8, 130 B-29s were at their new bases west of Calcutta. Attack missions were flown out of bases near Chengtu, the capital of Szechuan province.

44. Werrell, *Blankets of Fire*, 101–02.

45. Frank, *Downfall*, 50. Fuel was the major problem: B-29s that were converted into tankers owing to a shortage of C-46 transport aircraft could deliver 8 tons of fuel and other supplies, but burned 28 tons getting it there. Werrell, *Blankets of Fire*, 98.

46. Ibid., 119, and Craven and Cate, *Army Air Forces in World War II*, 5:170–71.

47. Craven and Cate, *Army Air Forces in World War II*, 5:558–59.

48. Ibid., 561, 564–65.

49. Sherry, *Rise of American Air Power*, 257.

50. Frank, *Downfall*, 58. See also Searle, "'It Made a Lot of Sense to Kill Skilled Workers,'" 123–33.

51. Werrell, *Blankets of Fire*, 135.

52. Ibid., 135–36.

53. Ibid., 140, and Searle, "'It Made a Lot of Sense to Kill Skilled Workers,'" 127.

54. Werrell, *Blankets of Fire*, 151. Given this unspectacular performance, Arnold fully expected Twentieth Air Force to be transferred to one of the Pacific theater commands under Admiral Nimitz or General MacArthur and devoted to tactical missions. Frank, *Downfall*, 60.

55. On the imprecision of radar bombing in World War II, see W. Hays Parks, "'Precision' and 'Area' Bombing: Who Did Which, and When?" in *Airpower: Theory and Practice*, ed. John Gooch (London: Frank Cass, 1995), 145–74.

56. Werrell, *Blankets of Fire*, 147.

57. Over Germany in 1943 there were on average between six and ten days per month when cloud cover over the target area was less than three-tenths of the sky, the minimum thought necessary to bomb visually; for perfectly clear conditions, the airmen could hope for about three days per month. Gary Shandroff, "The Evolution of Area Bombing in American Doctrine and Practice," Ph.D diss., New York University, 1972, 90–91.

58. Haywood S. Hansell Jr., *The Strategic Air War against Germany and Japan: A Memoir* (Washington: Office of Air Force History, 1986), 203; and LeMay, *Mission with LeMay*, 343–44.

59. As Thomas Searle observes, "The Norden bombsight could not compensate for crosswinds of such magnitude. Bombing runs conducted downwind had ground speeds of over five hundred miles per hour, making it impossible for bombardiers to line up their sights in time. Flying into the wind devoured fuel and left the aircraft over the target, exposed to antiaircraft fire, for too long." Searle, "'It Made a Lot of Sense to Kill Skilled Workers,'" 112.

60. Werrell, *Blankets of Fire*, 51. More than half of all Japanese industry was contained in the country's six largest cities.

61. LeMay, *Mission with LeMay*, 384.

62. Werrell, *Blankets of Fire*, 141.

63. For LeMay's thinking on these changes, see LeMay, *Mission with LeMay*, 344–52.

64. Werrell, *Blankets of Fire*, 157.

65. Sherry, *Rise of American Air Power*, 271; see also ibid., 282–83. On the reduction in U.S. losses, see ibid., 288.

66. Arnold, Norstad, and Barney Giles (another of Arnold's deputies) each wrote to congratulate LeMay. Crane, *Bombs, Cities, and Civilians*, 134. Norstad termed the raid "nothing short of wonderful," while Arnold wrote: "Congratulations. This mission shows your crews have got the guts for anything." Schaffer, *Wings of Judgment*, 138, 132.

67. Sherry, *Rise of American Air Power*, 220.

68. Ibid., 159, 160.

69. Quoted in Werrell, *Blankets of Fire*, 238–39.

70. Sherry, *Rise of American Air Power*, 309.

71. Ibid., 183.

72. Schaffer, *Wings of Judgment*, 152. Norstad and Colonel Harry F. Cunningham quoted in ibid., 138, 142.

73. LeMay, *Mission with LeMay*, 347.

74. Quoted in Sherry, *Rise of American Air Power*, 270.

75. Quoted in Richard H. Kohn and Joseph P. Harahan, ed., *Strategic Air Warfare: An Interview with Generals Curtis E. LeMay, Leon W. Johnson, David A. Burchinal, and Jack J. Catton* (Washington: Office of Air Force History, 1988), 59.

76. Quoted in Searle, "'It Made a Lot of Sense to Kill Skilled Workers,'" 121.

77. Ibid., 122. That American air officers conceived of killing Japanese noncombatants in this way is ironic given that the American blockade had already strangled the Japanese economy by the time the firebombing began. The Japanese merchant fleet, which began the war with about 6 million tons of shipping, had been reduced to 2 million by the beginning of 1944. Overall, American submarines and mines sank 8.1 million tons of Japanese shipping. "Even without the air attack," Kenneth Werrell observes, "Japanese production in August 1945 would have been 40 to 50 percent below its 1944 peak solely because of the blockade." Werrell, *Blankets of Fire*, 233. In many cases, therefore, the B-29s simply wiped out idle production capacity and workers who were already out of a job.

78. LeMay, *Mission with LeMay*, 384.

79. Quoted in Thomas M. Coffey, *Iron Eagle: The Turbulent Life of General Curtis LeMay* (New York: Crown, 1986), 163.

80. Quoted in Kerr, *Flames over Tokyo*, 212–13.

81. LeMay, *Mission with LeMay*, 352. LeMay expressed similar sentiments regarding the atomic bombs: "If those bombs shortened the war only by days, they rendered an inestimable service, and so did the men who were responsible for their construction and delivery." Ibid., 388.

82. Hansell, *Strategic Air War against Germany and Japan*, 228.

83. George E. Hopkins, "Bombing and the American Conscience During World War II," *The Historian* 28, no. 3 (May 1966): 459.

84. Ibid., 462.

85. Crane, *Bombs, Cities, and Civilians*, 31.

86. Dower, *War without Mercy*, 41. An example of the condemnation of those opposed to bombing was the public outcry provoked by Vera Brittain's pamphlet *Massacre by Bombing*. See Crane, *Bombs, Cities, and Civilians*, 29.

87. Hadley Cantril and Mildred Strunk, *Public Opinion, 1935–1946* (Princeton: Princeton University Press, 1951), 1067. See also Conrad C. Crane "Evolution of U.S. Strategic Bombing of Urban Areas," *The Historian* 50, no. 1 (November 1987): 20.

88. Quoted in Hopkins, "Bombing and the American Conscience," 463.

89. Dower, *War without Mercy*, 55. For further evidence of exterminationist sentiments toward the Japanese, see ibid., 53–54, and Cantril and Strunk, *Public Opinion*, 1118, 392. Eighty-five percent of Americans favored the use of the A-bomb, while 23 percent regretted that Japan surrendered before more bombs could be dropped. A mere 4.5 percent of those polled felt that the United States should not have used any atomic weapons. Ibid., 20, 23.

90. Sherry, *Rise of American Air Power*, 143; see also ibid., 245–46.

91. Quoted in Crane, *Bombs, Cities, and Civilians*, 31–32.

92. Hopkins, "Bombing and the American Conscience," 453.

93. Quoted in Schaffer, *Wings of Judgment*, 88.

94. Sherry, *Rise of American Air Power*, 102, 156.

95. Crane, *Bombs, Cities, and Civilians*, 120. See also Jack Couffer, *Bat Bomb: World War II's Other Secret Weapon* (Austin: University of Texas Press, 1992).

96. Quoted in Hopkins, "Bombing and the American Conscience," 451.

97. On these episodes, see Sherry, *Rise of American Air Power*, 262, 294–95.

98. Bernstein, "Atomic Bombings Reconsidered," 147.

99. In the European theater, for example, most American military objections to British practices were practical, but a few officers—such as Colonel Richard Hughes and General Charles

P. Cabell—argued that bombing civilians was immoral. Indeed, Cabell condemned Operation Clarion—a plan to bomb small German towns—as "the same old baby killing plan of the get-rich quick psychological boys, dressed up in a new Kimono." Quoted in Schaffer, *Wings of Judgment*, 92.

100. Quoted in ibid., 92.

101. Sherry, *Rise of American Airpower*, 258.

102. Searle, " 'It Made a Lot of Sense to Kill Skilled Workers,' " 126.

103. Several attempts to bomb specific industrial targets also turned into area bombing because poor weather over the target forced many bombers to divert to the secondary target, usually an urban area.

104. Quoted in Bernstein, "Understanding the Atomic Bomb," 268.

105. Dower, *War without Mercy*.

106. Shandroff, "Evolution of Area Bombing," 102; Parks, " 'Precision' and 'Area' Bombing," 162; and Richard G. Davis, "German Rail Yards and Cities: U.S. Bombing Policy 1944–1945," *Air Power History* 42, no. 2 (summer 1995): 60.

107. Werrell, *Blankets of Fire*, 25. On the losses incurred in these raids, see, respectively, Thomas M. Coffey, *Decision over Schweinfurt: The U.S. 8th Air Force Battle for Daylight Bombing* (New York: David McKay, 1977), 76, 78; and Wesley Frank Craven and James Lea Cate, eds., *The Army Air Forces in World War II*, vol. 2, *Europe: Torch to Pointblank, August 1942 to December 1943* (Washington: Office of Air Force History, 1983), 695–706, 850.

108. The false dichotomy of U.S. precision versus British area bombing still persists, however, even in very recent works. See, for example, A.C. Grayling, *Among the Dead Cities: The History and Moral Legacy of the WWII Bombing of Civilians in Germany and Japan* (New York: Walker, 2006), 21, 76.

109. Sherry, *Rise of American Air Power*, 168.

110. Frank, *Downfall*, 336; and Werrell, *Blankets of Fire*, 209. Searle points out that American documents do not support the assertion that "U.S. firebombing was the result of U.S. racism." Searle, " 'It Made a Lot of Sense to Kill Skilled Workers,' " 122–23, n. 62.

111. Dower, *War without Mercy*, 11 (emphasis added). These views probably played a much larger role in explaining the prevalence of battlefield atrocities, murdering of prisoners, and the collection of grisly "trophies" from dead foes in the Pacific. Ibid., 62–71.

112. Searle, " 'It Made a Lot of Sense to Kill Skilled Workers,' " 105.

113. Skates, *Invasion of Japan*, 50.

114. Crane, *Bombs, Cities, and Civilians*, 124–26.

115. Searle, " 'It Made a Lot of Sense to Kill Skilled Workers,' " 115, 126–27.

116. Hansell, *Strategic Air War against Germany and Japan*, 218. This report raised urban objectives to second on the priority list of targets behind aircraft production.

117. Richard M. Titmuss, *Problems of Social Policy* (London: His Majesty's Stationery Office, 1976), 559–60.

118. Campaign statistics for the Blitz (including Coventry), unless otherwise noted, are from Matthew Cooper, *The German Air Force, 1933–1945: An Anatomy of Failure* (London: Jane's, 1981), 164–74.

119. *X-Gerät* was the second navigational system invented by the Luftwaffe. In the first, known as *Knickebein*, aircraft flew along a radio beam and released their bombs when this beam was intersected over the target by a second beam sent from a different location. When the British discovered this tactic and began jamming the transmissions, the Germans countered with System X, which released bombs automatically after an aircraft passed through the third of three beams intersecting the initial beam. *Knickebein* could deliver bombs to within about 380 meters of the aim point, while the circular error probable of System X was 260–300 meters. On these systems, see Alfred Price, *Blitz on Britain 1939–45* (Phoenix Mill: Sutton, 2000), 37–42, 95–99.

120. Horst Boog, "The Luftwaffe and Indiscriminate Bombing up to 1942," in *The Conduct of the Air War in the Second World War: An International Comparison*, ed. Horst Boog (New York: Berg Publishers, 1992), 391.

121. Each German incendiary weapon held 36 bombs each weighing one kilogram. See Derek Wood and Derek Dempster, *The Narrow Margin: The Battle of Britain and the Rise of Air*

Power, 1930–40 (London: Hutchinson, 1961), 481, n. 1. Therefore, a total of 31,716 kilograms of incendiaries was dropped in this attack. As one kilogram equals 2.2 pounds, this yields a total of 69,775 pounds, or slightly less than 35 tons of the 538 tons that fell on Coventry.

122. Cooper, *German Air Force*, 165. See also Basil Collier, *The Defence of the United Kingdom* (London: Her Majesty's Stationery Office, 1957), 261.

123. Richard Overy, *The Battle of Britain: The Myth and the Reality* (New York: Norton, 2000), 109.

124. Boog, "Luftwaffe and Indiscriminate Bombing," 392.

125. Figures are from Cooper, *German Air Force*, 165, 174.

126. Boog, "Luftwaffe and Indiscriminate Bombing," 384. The American air force, also dedicated to precision bombing of military targets, had no such technology when it entered the war, and in fact never developed the means to deliver ordnance accurately at night or through overcast.

127. Important German doctrinal documents on airpower may be found in translation in James S. Corum and Richard R. Muller, *The Luftwaffe's Way of War: German Air Force Doctrine, 1911–1945* (Baltimore: Nautical and Aviation, 1998). See also James S. Corum, *The Luftwaffe: Creating the Operational Air War, 1918–1940* (Lawrence: University Press of Kansas, 1997).

128. R. J. Overy, "From 'Uralbomber' to 'Amerikabomber': The Luftwaffe and Strategic Bombing," *Journal of Strategic Studies* 1, no. 2 (September 1978): 158.

129. Corum, *Luftwaffe*, 7.

130. Michael Alfred Peszke, *Battle for Warsaw, 1939–1944* (Boulder, CO: East European Monographs, 1995), 25. For the military balance in the west, see Nicholas Bethell, *The War Hitler Won: The Fall of Poland, September 1939* (New York: Holt, Rinehart and Winston, 1972), 169–70. On Hitler's fears of delay, see ibid., 114, 139; Erich von Manstein, *Lost Victories*, ed. and trans. Anthony G. Powell (Chicago: Henry Regnery Company, 1958), 58–59; and Andrew Borowiec, *Destroy Warsaw! Hitler's Punishment, Stalin's Revenge* (Westport, CT: Praeger, 2001), 14.

131. Quoted in Ernest R. May, *Strange Victory: Hitler's Conquest of France* (New York: Hill and Wang, 2000), 17.

132. Over 400 Luftwaffe aircraft dropped 572 tons of bombs (but only 72 tons of incendiaries) on military targets in the city's western area. On the amateur nature of the attack and the unsuitable aircraft used, see Cooper, *German Air Force*, 101; and Boog, "Luftwaffe and Indiscriminate Bombing," 386.

133. Bethell, *The War Hitler Won*, 140. The German air raid on Warsaw, however, was perfectly legal at the time: the city was held by Polish troops, was actively resisting, and contained valuable military targets.

134. The only bombing the Luftwaffe did in Norway was aimed at British and French bridgeheads established on the coast at Namsos and Aandalsnes. See Adam R. A. Claasen, *Hitler's Northern War: The Luftwaffe's Ill-Fated Campaign, 1940–1945* (Lawrence: University Press of Kansas, 2001), 105–19.

135. On the shift in German strategy from a potentially costly frontal attack to a blitzkrieg that promised a quick and decisive victory, see Manstein, *Lost Victories*, 94–126; and John J. Mearsheimer, *Conventional Deterrence* (Ithaca: Cornell University Press, 1982), 99–133.

136. Walter B. Maass, *The Netherlands at War: 1940–1945* (London: Abelard-Schuman, 1970), 21; and Cooper, *German Air Force*, 114.

137. On this episode and the confusion surrounding it, see Cooper, *German Air Force*, 114–15; Boog, "Luftwaffe and Indiscriminate Bombing," 386–87; and Maass, *Netherlands at War*, 40. The attack killed about 900 civilians, injured several thousand, and rendered 78,000 homeless. Maass, *Netherlands at War*, 40. Although viewed at the time as a treacherous terror attack, Rotterdam was not an open city and thus was not protected by international law against bombardment from the air. Moreover, German aircraft flew low, exposing themselves to ground fire in order to bomb more accurately, and dropped only high explosive bombs, not incendiaries. Indeed, 18th Army commander, General Georg von Kuechler, cautioned the attacking forces to use "all means to prevent unnecessary bloodshed among the Dutch population." Quoted in Cooper, *German Air Force*, 114.

138. John Ray, *The Battle of Britain: New Perspectives: Behind the Scenes of the Great Air War* (London: Arms and Armour, 1994), 40.

139. Despite the Führer's prohibition, 12 German bombers, having lost their way on a night mission, accidentally struck the British capital on the night of August 24. This mishap prompted British prime minister Winston Churchill to unleash his own bombers on Berlin.

140. George H. Quester, *Deterrence before Hiroshima: The Airpower Background of Modern Strategy* (New York: Wiley, 1966), 111.

141. Hitler repeated this instruction in all of his directives in the war's first month. See H. R. Trevor-Roper, ed., *Hitler's War Directives* (London: Sidgwick and Jackson, 1964), 5; and H. W. Koch, "The Strategic Air Offensive against Germany: The Early Phase, May-September 1940," *Historical Journal* 34, no. 1 (March 1991): 124.

142. Trevor-Roper, *Hitler's War Directives*, 19.

143. Cooper, *German Air Force*, 126.

144. Trevor-Roper, *Hitler's War Directives*, 29; Cooper, *German Air Force*, 126.

145. Cooper, *German Air Force*, 126.

146. Ray, *Battle of Britain*, 35.

147. Cooper, *German Air Force*, 121.

148. Ibid., 126.

149. Cajus Bekker, *The Luftwaffe War Diaries: The German Air Force in World War II*, trans. and ed. Frank Ziegler (Garden City, NY: Doubleday, 1968), 148.

150. In general, when referring to German aircraft, Do stands for Dornier, Ju for Junkers, He for Heinkel, and Bf for Messerschmitt (Bayerische Flugzeugwerke AG, the Bavarian Aircraft Works).

151. Quoted in Wood and Dempster, *Narrow Margin*, 220.

152. Peter Townsend, *Duel of Eagles* (New York: Simon and Schuster, 1970), 273.

153. Cooper, *German Air Force*, 129; and Townsend, *Duel of Eagles*, 308.

154. See Directive No. 17, issued August 1, in Bekker, *Luftwaffe War Diaries*, 150. Luftwaffe leaders argued that the best way to lure British fighters into the air was to attack London. Hitler's prohibition torpedoed the idea. Townsend, *Duel of Eagles*, 297–98.

155. Trevor-Roper, *Hitler's War Directives*, 34.

156. Germany's airmen thus found themselves attempting to do what they had already concluded they could not do: bring Britain to its knees with airpower alone. Ray, *Battle of Britain*, 42.

157. Townsend, *Duel of Eagles*, 301. Altogether the British had 576 single-engine fighters ready for action.

158. On this raid, see Townsend, *Duel of Eagles*, 329–31; Bekker, *Luftwaffe War Diaries*, 155–63; and Wood and Dempster, *Narrow Margin*, 279–85.

159. Williamson Murray, *Luftwaffe* (Baltimore: Nautical and Aviation Publishing Company of America, 1985), 52. Overall losses on August 15 were 75 for the Luftwaffe and 34 for the RAF. Townsend, *Duel of Eagles*, 337.

160. Townsend, *Duel of Eagles*, 345–50; Bekker, *Luftwaffe War Diaries*, 165; Wood and Dempster, *Narrow Margin*, 288–90, 299. For a detailed account of the actions on this day, see Alfred Price, *Battle of Britain: The Hardest Day, 18 August 1940* (New York: Scribner's, 1979).

161. Cooper, *German Air Force*, 140. German aircraft lost and damaged from all causes, August 13–18, numbered 350. Ibid., 141. The Luftwaffe lost a total of 167 bombers August 10–23. Wood and Dempster, *Narrow Margin*, 299.

162. Murray, *Luftwaffe*, 53.

163. Cooper, *German Air Force*, 140, 145, 146; Townsend, *Duel of Eagles*, 388. Figures in this paragraph are from Cooper, *German Air Force*, 146, except for German bombers lost, which is from Wood and Dempster, *Narrow Margin*, 330.

164. Murray, *Luftwaffe*, 54.

165. Figures for civilian dead are from Townsend, *Duel of Eagles*, 406, 409, 410.

166. Ibid., 391.

167. Quoted in Boog, "Luftwaffe and Indiscriminate Bombing," 390.

168. On the Luftwaffe, Cooper, *German Air Force*, 148; and Collier, *Defence of the United Kingdom*, 463–67; for the RAF, Wood and Dempster, *Narrow Margin*, 463.

169. For full details, see Alfred Price, *Battle of Britain Day: 15 September 1940* (London: Sidgwick and Jackson, 1990).

170. Cooper, *German Air Force*, 158.

171. Telford Taylor, *The Breaking Wave: The Second World War in the Summer of 1940* (New York: Simon and Schuster, 1967), 170.

172. Ibid., 175.

173. Cooper, *German Air Force*, 165.

174. Wood and Dempster, *Narrow Margin*, 285; and Taylor, *Breaking Wave*, 145.

175. Cooper, *German Air Force*, 167. From early November 1940 to late February 1941 the Germans lost only 75 bombers out of 12,000 sorties. Ibid., 170.

176. Ibid., 167. See also Taylor, *Breaking Wave*, 175–76.

177. Frederick Taylor, *Dresden: Tuesday, February 13, 1945* (New York: HarperCollins, 2004), 99.

178. Harvey B. Tress, "Churchill, the First Berlin Raids, and the Blitz," *Militärgeschichtliche Mitteilungen* 32, no. 2 (1982): 65–78; and Quester, *Deterrence before Hiroshima*, 117–18.

179. Taylor, *Breaking Wave*, 158.

180. Overy, "From 'Uralbomber' to 'Amerikabomber,'" 160. The internal quote is from the war diary of General Halder.

181. The decision to send German bombers against London (September 1940), attack sites of cultural significance (the so-called Baedeker Raids of 1942), and launch the V-weapons (1944) all fall in this category.

182. Development of a heavy four-engine bomber was hindered by the requirement—bizarre to outsiders but sensible to those immersed in Luftwaffe culture—that it be capable of dive bombing. See Edward L. Homze, "The Luftwaffe's Failure to Develop a Heavy Bomber Before World War II," *Aerospace Historian* 24, no. 1 (March 1977): 20–26.

183. Jeffrey W. Legro, *Cooperation under Fire: Anglo-German Restraint during World War II* (Ithaca: Cornell University Press, 1995), 115.

184. Townsend, *Duel of Eagles*, 297–98; and Boog, "Luftwaffe and Indiscriminate Bombing," 390.

185. Max Hastings, *Bomber Command* (New York: Dial Press, 1979), 98.

186. Taylor, *Dresden*, 101. For more on the events summarized in this paragraph, see Robin Neillands, *The Bomber War: The Allied Air Offensive Against Nazi Germany* (New York: Barnes and Noble, 2001), 34–59.

187. Davis, "German Rail Yards and Cities," 52.

188. Shandroff, "Evolution of Area Bombing," 99.

189. Ibid., 100.

190. Bernstein, "Atomic Bombings Reconsidered," 151–52.

5. Guerrilla Warfare, Counterinsurgency, and Civilian Victimization

1. In addition to the works cited below, see Stathis N. Kalyvas, *The Logic of Violence in Civil War* (Cambridge: Cambridge University Press, 2006); and Benjamin A. Valentino, *Final Solutions: Mass Killing and Genocide in the Twentieth Century* (Ithaca: Cornell University Press, 2004), 196–233.

2. Benjamin Valentino, Paul Huth, and Dylan Balch-Lindsay, "'Draining the Sea': Mass Killing and Guerrilla Warfare," *International Organization* 58, no. 2 (spring 2004): 375–407.

3. Analysis performed by author in "Democracy and Destruction: Regime Type and Civilian Victimization in Small Wars," paper presented at the annual meeting of the International Studies Association, Montreal, Québec, March 2004. My thanks to Ivan Arreguín-Toft for providing this data, which forms the basis of his article "How the Weak Win Wars: A Theory of Asymmetric Conflict," *International Security* 26, no. 1 (summer 2001): 93–128.

4. Michael J. Engelhardt, "Democracies, Dictatorships and Counterinsurgency: Does Regime Type Really Matter?" *Conflict Quarterly* 12, no. 3 (summer 1992): 56.

5. Downes, "Democracy and Destruction," 18–19. These results hold for both the Polity and Doyle coding of regime type. In a later paper, Arreguín-Toft finds that democracies

(15 percent) are slightly less likely than nondemocracies (21 percent) to use barbarism in inter-state and colonial/imperial wars. See Ivan Arreguín-Toft, "The [F]utility of Barbarism: Assessing the Impact of the Systematic Harm of Non-Combatants in War," paper presented at the annual meeting of the American Political Science Association, Philadelphia, PA, August 2003, 14.

6. Engelhardt, "Democracies, Dictatorships and Counterinsurgency," 55.

7. Support in this context should not be confused with loyalty. Civilians who provide mate-riel or intelligence to rebels may do so because they are "true believers" in the cause, or because the insurgents have guns and helping them is a good way to ensure survival.

8. Guenter Lewy, *America in Vietnam* (New York: Oxford University Press, 1978), 82–83.

9. Hence the title of Valentino, Huth, and Balch-Lindsay's article on the subject, " 'Draining the Sea.' "

10. Discriminate massacres have the added bonus that they eliminate real guerrilla support-ers, thus damaging the insurgents' infrastructure.

11. Report of General Breuillac, quoted in Gil Merom, *How Democracies Lose Small Wars: State, Society, and the Failures of France in Algeria, Israel in Lebanon, and the United States in Vietnam* (Cambridge: Cambridge University Press, 2003), 94. On the Setif massacre, see Anthony Clayton, "The Setif Uprising of May 1945," *Small Wars and Insurgencies* 3, no. 1 (spring 1992): 1–21.

12. Tom Marks, "Making Revolution: *Sendero Luminoso* in Peru," *Small Wars and Insurgencies* 3, no. 1 (spring 1992): 43; and Stathis N. Kalyvas, "Wanton and Senseless? The Logic of Mas-sacres in Algeria," *Rationality and·Society* 11, no. 3 (August 1999): 257. See also Kalyvas, "The Paradox of Terrorism in Civil War," *Journal of Ethics* 8, no. 1 (March 2004): 97–138. Some argue that indiscriminate killing is less effective in gaining compliance because by definition it takes the lives of guilty and innocent alike. If there is a good chance the incumbents will kill you whether you support the rebels or not, you might as well support the insurgents and hence improve your chances of survival, if only marginally. Kalyvas, "Paradox of Terrorism in Civil War," 104–5. The indiscriminate nature of German "reprisal" massacres in the Soviet Union during World War II, for example, drove large numbers to join the partisans: "Ruthless meth-ods, instead of subduing, fuelled resistance and created it where none existed; without German barbarity to aid its cause, the Soviet partisan movement might well have been still-born." Matthew Cooper, *The Nazi War Against Soviet Partisans, 1941–1944* (New York: Stein and Day, 1979), 1. Such massacres, however, can be effective in reducing resistance under certain conditions, a point I elaborate on in the conclusion.

13. Ali Abdullatif Ahmida, *The Making of Modern Libya: State Formation, Colonization, and Re-sistance, 1830–1932* (Albany: State University of New York Press, 1994), 107; and E. E. Evans-Pritchard, *The Sanusi of Cyrenaica* (Oxford: Clarendon Press, 1949), 188. Hunger, disease, and privation exacted a fearsome toll from the population languishing in the camps: only 35,000 people emerged from the camps after the war. In addition to the sources cited in this note, see Giorgio Rochat, *Guerre Italiane in Libia e in Etiopia: Studi Militari 1921–1939* (Treviso: Pagus Edizione, 1991), 84–85.

14. Lewy, *America in Vietnam*, 229.

15. Kelly M. Greenhill, "The Use of Refugees as Political and Military Weapons in the Kosovo Conflict," in *Yugoslavia Unraveled: Sovereignty, Self-Determination, Intervention*, ed. Raju G. C. Thomas (Lanham, MD: Lexington, 2003), 205–42.

16. Mark Danner, *The Massacre at El Mozote: A Parable of the Cold War* (New York: Vintage, 1994), 42–43.

17. Evans-Pritchard, *Sanusi of Cyrenaica*, 163. Cyrenaica was the region of northern Libya in which the war was fought.

18. For a firsthand description of the camps in the first few months of 1900, see Emily Hobhouse, *The Brunt of the War and Where It Fell* (London: Methuen, 1902), 114–25.

19. Fransjohan Pretorius, "The Fate of the Boer Women and Children," in *Scorched Earth*, ed. Fransjohan Pretorius (Cape Town: Human and Rousseau, 2001), 46.

20. Thomas Pakenham, *The Boer War* (New York: Post Road Press, 1979), 523. See also S. B. Spies, *Methods of Barbarism? Roberts and Kitchener and Civilians in the Boer Republics, January 1900–May 1902* (Cape Town: Human and Rousseau, 1977), 199.

21. Owen Coetzer, *Fire in the Sky: The Destruction of the Orange Free State, 1899–1902* (Weltevreden Park: Covos-Day, 2000), 116.

22. One problem was that the number of camps did not increase with the number of people confined in them: 27 camps held 35,000 people in March 1901; just six months later 34 camps held 110,000 people. Pretorius, "Fate of the Boer Women and Children," 49.

23. Ibid., 44; and Pakenham, *Boer War*, 548.

24. Pakenham, *Boer War*, 524. At one point Kitchener even considered deporting the entire Boer population to some remote location, such as the Dutch East Indies, Fiji, or Madagascar. Ibid., 530.

25. Ibid., 515–16. His restrained views on how the war should be conducted did not extend to the terms Milner thought Britain should exact from the Boers, as he insisted on unconditional surrender. Kitchener blamed the High Commissioner for repeatedly torpedoing his efforts to negotiate a moderate peace. Paradoxically, therefore, the architect of the concentration camp system in South Africa sought a reasonable peace of conciliation, whereas the champion of humane conduct in war pursued a punitive peace.

26. Stowell V. Kessler, "The Black and Coloured Concentration Camps," in *Scorched Earth*, 135, 137.

27. Ibid., 149–52.

28. Ibid., 147–48.

29. Ibid., 151–52.

30. British annexation of the Transvaal in 1877 sparked the first war. On February 27, 1881, Colley led a detachment of his force up Majuba Hill—which commanded the Boer positions below—during the night, but failed to make any preparations for battle. Rather than flee, the Boers ascended the hill and destroyed the British force, killing Colley in the process. See Oliver Ransford, *The Battle of Majuba Hill: The First Boer War* (London: John Murray, 1967). This victory earned nominal independence for the Transvaal, although it remained subject to British supervision in its relations with foreign powers.

31. The Boer rural economy at the time relied heavily on slave labor, not to mention the fact that the Boers' strict Calvinist beliefs sanctioned a racial hierarchy with whites at the apex. On the Boers' early history and their Great Trek out of British-governed Cape Colony in the 1830s, see Barbara Villet, *Blood River: The Passionate Saga of South Africa's Afrikaners and of Life in their Embattled Land* (New York: Everest House, 1982), 37–89.

32. Kruger extended the residency requirement for earning citizenship—and hence the right to vote—from 5 to 14 years in 1888, meaning that as late as 1898 few *Uitlanders* had been given the franchise.

33. Cecil Rhodes, the prime minister of Cape Colony, with the assent of his boss, British colonial secretary Joseph Chamberlain, hatched a plot to stage an *Uitlander* uprising in Johannesburg, which would in turn be used to justify intervention to protect "endangered" British citizens. The raid—led by Dr. Leander Starr Jameson and launched on January 1, 1896—was a total failure and served only to strengthen Kruger's hand domestically and bind the two Boer republics closer together. On the raid and its consequences see Pakenham, *Boer War*, xxv–xxix, 21–24, 33–34.

34. The British Army in 1899 counted about 320,000 men, but only 20,000 of these were in South Africa, with 13,000 of these troops stationed close to the borders of the Boer republics. For these figures, see, respectively, Bill Nasson, *The South African War, 1899–1902* (London: Arnold, 1999), 75, 61; and Pakenham, *Boer War*, 106

35. Nasson, *South African War*, 68.

36. Pakenham, *Boer War*, 35. Altogether, the Transvaal spent one-third of its budget between 1896 and 1899 on defense. Nasson, *South African War*, 57.

37. The Boers defeated the British Field Force at Dundee, forcing the stunned Britons to retreat to Ladysmith, where they were trapped and besieged for four months. On the western front, meanwhile, Boer forces laid siege to the Cape Colony border towns of Mafeking and Kimberley. There was civilian suffering during the sieges, to be sure: at Kimberley indiscriminate Boer shelling killed a small but steady stream of noncombatants. Altogether, about 1,500

civilians died in the siege of Kimberley, all but a handful of them blacks. Nasson, *South African War,* 104–5.

38. Ibid., 114.

39. In the west, smaller Boer forces defeated British detachments at Magersfontein and Stormberg, and Boer troops under Louis Botha similarly checked General Redvers Buller's attempt to relieve Ladysmith at Colenso on the Tugela River.

40. British troops in South Africa totaled 180,000 by early 1900. Nasson, *South African War,* 149.

41. Ibid., 183. The British captured a further 4,500 commandos under Marthinus Prinsloo in mid July. These men became known to commandos who continued to fight as *Hensoppers,* or "hands-uppers."

42. Ibid., 166–67.

43. A British public notice issued in Krugersdorp on July 9, 1900, reproduced in Fransjohan Pretorius, "The Anglo-Boer War: An Overview," in *Scorched Earth,* 22.

44. Nasson, *South African War,* 193. De Wet and his fellow commanders also hoped to relieve some of the pressure at home and rally support in British territory by invading Natal and the Cape Colony, but these sorties—which drew massive numbers of British troops in pursuit—failed to have much of an impact on the course of the war. Most of the military clashes in the last two years of the war consisted of Boer ambushes and British pursuit of the elusive commandos.

45. Pakenham, *Boer War,* 351.

46. Ibid., 466. Much of the destruction inflicted was contrary to Roberts's standing orders, but "it would appear that he did not find the actions particularly objectionable." Pretorius, "Fate of the Boer Women and Children," 37.

47. Roberts's first proclamation, quoted in Hobhouse, *Brunt of the War,* 2.

48. The March proclamation was more carefully worded, and specified more conditions that would have to be met before a former commando received amnesty. Spies, *Methods of Barbarism,* 34. The May announcement further omitted the guarantee that Boers who surrendered would be able to keep their property.

49. Quoted in ibid., 50.

50. Quoted in Coetzer, *Fire in the Sky,* 88.

51. For the text of this proclamation, see Spies, *Methods of Barbarism,* 102. Roberts further decreed in September that following an attack on rail or telegraph communications, all foodstuffs within a 16km (10 mile) radius would be destroyed, and further in October that all farmhouses in the same area should be burned. Pretorius, "The Fate of the Boer Women and Children," 39; and Spies, *Methods of Barbarism,* 110.

52. Coetzer, *Fire in the Sky,* 88.

53. Quoted in ibid., 91.

54. Pakenham, *Boer War,* 467.

55. Quoted in Spies, *Methods of Barbarism,* 112.

56. Ibid., 121.

57. Quoted in ibid., 122.

58. General Hunter to General Bruce Hamilton, September 29, 1900, quoted in ibid., 122.

59. Quoted in ibid., 175.

60. Coetzer, *Fire in the Sky,* 87.

61. Pakenham, *Boer War,* 500–01.

62. Quoted in Spies, *Methods of Barbarism,* 120.

63. Ibid., 120.

64. Quoted in Coetzer, *Fire in the Sky,* 94.

65. Captain March Phillipps, quoted in Hobhouse, *Brunt of the War,* 20.

66. British troops under General Hunter, for example, burned 45 houses in Bothaville, a town in northwestern Orange River Colony (formerly the Orange Free State) on October 23, 1900. Spies, *Methods of Barbarism,* 119. The supply difficulties resulting from this systematic devastation partially caused the Boer invasions of Cape Colony and Natal: the commandos calculated that the British would not be so promiscuous in burning property in their own territory. Pakenham, *Boer War,* 501.

67. Coetzer, *Fire in the Sky*, 105; Pakenham, *Boer War*, 608; and André Wessels, "Afrikaners at War," in *The Boer War: Direction, Experience, and Image*, ed. John Gooch (London: Frank Cass, 2000), 101. Following the war, Boers filed 63,000 claims for damage compensation with their new government. Pakenham, *Boer War*, 608.

68. Quoted in Nasson, *South African War*, 192.

69. Quoted in ibid., 192.

70. Ibid., 192. Nor did the farm-burning policy reduce the number of attacks on British lines of communication, which increased from June to November 1900. "It cannot therefore be said that the burning of farms was an effective deterrent against attacks on communications." Spies, *Methods of Barbarism*, 114.

71. Byron Farwell, *The Great Boer War* (Hertfordshire: Wordsworth Editions, 1999), 372, 371.

72. Spies, *Methods of Barbarism*, 287. Provisions were in particularly short supply in eastern Transvaal, whereas many guerrillas in the Orange River Colony and western Transvaal felt they could still somehow make do.

73. On Roberts's expulsion of Boer civilians, see Pretorius, "Fate of the Boer Women and Children," 39. After burning the town of Ventersburg, British general Bruce Hamilton declared: "The Boer women and children who are left behind should apply to the Boer commandants for food, who will supply them unless they wish to see them starve. No supplies will be sent from the railway to the town." Quoted in Coetzer, *Fire in the Sky*, 93.

74. Hobhouse, *Brunt of the War*, 37.

75. Coetzer, *Fire in the Sky*, 107.

76. Spies, *Methods of Barbarism*, 188.

77. Pakenham, *Boer War*, 522.

78. Ibid., 523; and Pretorius, "Fate of the Boer Women and Children," 41.

79. Pretorius, "Fate of the Boer Women and Children," 44.

80. Spies, *Methods of Barbarism*, 190.

81. Kitchener also copied Weyler's system of covering the country with closely connected blockhouses to deny the rebels free movement.

82. Indeed, the extent of the outcry over "Butcher" Weyler's methods contributed to American intervention and the resulting Spanish-American War.

83. Pretorius, "Fate of the Boer Women and Children," 43. Less often noted is the disastrous toll that disease exacted from the Spanish expeditionary forces: over 53,000 soldiers died of yellow fever and other illnesses, compared to only about 9,000 killed in combat. See Micheal Clodfelter, *Warfare and Armed Conflicts: A Statistical Reference to Casualty and Other Figures, 1500–2000*, 2d ed. (Jefferson, NC: McFarland, 2002), 345.

84. Stanley G. Payne, *Politics and the Military in Modern Spain* (Stanford: Stanford University Press, 1967), 74.

85. Spies, *Methods of Barbarism*, 148; and Coetzer, *Fire in the Sky*, 115.

86. Nasson, *South African War*, 212. Contributing to this constriction of space was the denial to the Boers of a territorial sanctuary outside of their republics that historically has been so essential for the waging of successful guerrilla campaigns.

87. Ibid., 223.

88. Sebastian Rosato, "The Flawed Logic of Democratic Peace Theory," *American Political Science Review* 97, no. 4 (November 2003): 585–602.

89. Nasson, *South African War*, 37.

90. Ibid., 236.

91. Ibid., 236.

92. The *Cape Times*, July 22, 1901, quoted in Coetzer, *Fire in the Sky*, 131.

93. Pakenham, *Boer War*, 493.

94. Campbell-Bannerman caused a sensation when he first uttered this phrase at a Liberal dinner party on June 14, 1901.

95. Pakenham, *Boer War*, 533; and Coetzer, *Fire in the Sky*, 118.

96. Pakenham, *Boer War*, 540.

97. Ibid., 540.

98. Hobhouse, *Brunt of the War*, 127–28.

99. The intrepid humanitarian nevertheless attempted another visit to South Africa in late October 1901, when Kitchener and Milner denied her entry and had her forcibly placed on an outbound ship and deported back to England. These events provoked a storm of controversy, with Hobhouse bringing suit against Kitchener and Milner, but the matter was eventually dropped.

100. Pakenham, *Boer War*, 548–49.

101. Ibid., 549.

102. Of course, it is not possible to discern the extent to which Liberal politicians were motivated by their desire to embarrass the government and to gain power for themselves versus sympathy with and outrage over the treatment of innocent Boer civilians. Campbell-Bannerman, Lloyd George, and others may have simply used the humanitarian crisis to score political gains at the government's expense.

103. Likewise, there is no evidence that the government took a harsher line toward Boer civilians at the public's behest.

104. Quoted in Spies, *Methods of Barbarism*, 255.

105. Hobhouse, *Brunt of the War*, 286.

106. For a development of the idea of hypocrisy costs, see Kelly M. Greenhill, "People Pressure: Strategic Engineered Migration as an Instrument of Statecraft and the Rise of the Human Rights Regime," Ph.D diss., Massachusetts Institute of Technology, 2003.

107. Alternatively, one could argue that the imperatives of democratic institutions in small wars reinforce liberal norms rather than contradicting them as they do in more costly wars. I thank Kelly Greenhill for this insight.

108. Clearly there are exceptions to this rule, such as the German response to the Herero uprising in Southeast Africa in 1904, but even here racism probably did not cause the violence. On this case, see Isabel V. Hull, *Absolute Destruction: Military Culture and the Practices of War in Imperial Germany* (Ithaca: Cornell University Press, 2005), 5–90.

109. Quoted in Robert B. Edgerton, *Like Lions They Fought: The Zulu War and the Last Black Empire in South Africa* (New York: Free Press, 1988), 24.

110. Kalyvas, "Paradox of Terrorism in Civil War," 104–5.

6. *Territorial Annexation and Civilian Victimization*

1. "When war begins in the Balkans," writes one author, "the local civilian population of the defeated nation immediately assumes a strategic threat to the victorious fighters." Misha Glenny, *The Fall of Yugoslavia: The Third Balkan War*, 3d rev. ed. (New York: Penguin, 1996), 186.

2. For descriptions, see Steven L. Burg and Paul S. Shoup, *The War in Bosnia-Herzegovina: Ethnic Conflict and International Intervention* (Armonk, NY: M.E. Sharpe, 1999), 171–81, and Ed Vulliamy, *Seasons in Hell: Understanding Bosnia's War* (New York: St. Martin's Press, 1994), 85–97. Regarding the territorial nature of the wars in the former Yugoslavia, Glenny comments: "At the heart of the wars lies the struggle for territorial acquisition and not blood-lust." Glenny, *Fall of Yugoslavia*, 183. See also David Rieff, *Slaughterhouse: Bosnia and the Failure of the West* (New York: Touchstone, 1996), 100.

3. Hugh Thomas, *The Spanish Civil War* (New York: Harper and Brothers, 1961), 165, 176.

4. Julio de la Cueva, "Religious Persecution, Anticlerical Tradition, and Revolution: On Atrocities against the Clergy during the Spanish Civil War," *Journal of Contemporary History* 33, no. 3 (July 1998): 355–69.

5. British military attaché Harold Armstrong, quoted in Ben Lieberman, "Ethnic Cleansing in the Greek-Turkish Conflicts from the Balkan Wars through the Treaty of Lausanne: Identifying and Defining Ethnic Cleansing," in *Ethnic Cleansing in Twentieth-Century Europe*, ed. Steven Béla Várdy and T. Hunt Tooley (Boulder: Social Science Monographs, 2003), 190.

6. "Reports in the District of Yalova and Geremlek and in the Ismid Peninsula," quoted in Norman M. Naimark, *Fires of Hatred: Ethnic Cleansing in Twentieth-Century Europe* (Cambridge: Harvard University Press, 2001), 45.

7. Lieberman, "Ethnic Cleansing in the Greek-Turkish Conflicts," 187.

8. See Justin McCarthy, *Death and Exile: The Ethnic Cleansing of Ottoman Muslims, 1821–1922* (Princeton: Darwin Press, 1995), 255–332; and Naimark, *Fires of Hatred*, 46–56.

9. Treitschke's essay "What Do We Demand from France?" quoted in Geoffrey Wawro, *The Franco-Prussian War: The German Conquest of France in 1870–1871* (Cambridge: Cambridge University Press, 2003), 304.

10. Prussia's demand for the two provinces, however, did contribute to civilian victimization in another way: it steeled French determination to fight on even after disastrous early defeats deprived France of the bulk of its regular army. Continued French resistance necessitated the prolonged siege and starvation of Paris, and the rise of irregular *franc-tireurs* led to harsh reprisals meant to deter attacks on Prussian troops.

11. McCarthy, *Death and Exile*, 153–54; Justin McCarthy, *The Ottoman Peoples and the End of Empire* (London: Arnold, 2001), 40, 94; and International Commission to Inquire into the Causes and Conduct of the Balkan Wars, *The Other Balkan Wars* (Washington: Carnegie Endowment for International Peace, 1993), 155–58.

12. Autocracies sought to annex territory in 11.4 percent of wars, compared to 10.1 percent for democracies, a difference that is not significant ($p = 0.77$).

13. This picture changes slightly when Doyle's indicator for liberal democracy is used, owing to his coding of Greece in 1912–13 as a nonliberal state. The relevant percentages then become 86 for autocracies and 50 for democracies (significant at $p < 0.08$).

14. One reason that democracies have fought relatively few wars of territorial annexation against other states is that several were active imperial powers, expanding into areas unclaimed by other states. Britain and France, for example, established colonies in Asia and Africa, whereas the United States expanded into territorially contiguous areas of North America where there were no recognized states. On the general relationship between democracy and colonial/imperial wars, see Hilde Ravlo, Nils Petter Gleditsch, and Han Dorussen, "Colonial War and the Democratic Peace," *Journal of Conflict Resolution* 47, no. 4 (August 2003): 520–48.

15. International Commission, *Other Balkan Wars*, 126, 309, and 99.

16. Samih K. Farsoun with Christina E. Zacharia, *Palestine and the Palestinians* (Boulder: Westview Press, 1997), 78.

17. On these outbursts see, respectively, Tom Segev, *One Palestine, Complete: Jews and Arabs Under the British Mandate*, trans. Haim Watzman (New York: Metropolitan Books, 1999), 138; Benny Morris, *Righteous Victims: A History of the Zionist-Arab Conflict, 1881–1999* (New York: Alfred A. Knopf, 1999), 101–2; and Richard Allen, *Imperialism and Nationalism in the Fertile Crescent: Sources and Prospects of the Arab-Israeli Conflict* (New York: Oxford University Press, 1974), 299–300.

18. Quoted in Nur Masalha, *Expulsion of the Palestinians: The Concept of "Transfer" in Zionist Political Thought, 1882–1948* (Washington: Institute for Palestine Studies, 1992), 31.

19. On the Arab Revolt, see Morris, *Righteous Victims*, 121–60. On how the failure of the revolt contributed to the Palestinian collapse in 1948, see Rashid Khalidi, "The Palestinians and 1948: The Underlying Causes of Failure," in *The War for Palestine: Rewriting the History of 1948*, ed. Eugene L. Rogan and Avi Shlaim (Cambridge: Cambridge University Press, 2001), 25–32. On the impact of Jewish immigration on Arab fears of being relegated to minority status, see Segev, *One Palestine, Complete*, 361. On British excesses in suppressing the revolt, see ibid., 416–26.

20. Morris, *Righteous Victims*, 184. Conversely, the Arab state of 800,000 people contained almost no Jews.

21. Avi Shlaim, *The Iron Wall: Israel and the Arab World* (New York: Norton, 2000), 25.

22. Sami Hadawi, *Bitter Harvest: A Modern History of Palestine*, Rev. ed. (New York: Olive Branch Press, 1990), 67. The new Arab state would comprise 43 percent of the land (4,476 square miles), while the Jerusalem International Zone took up about 1 percent (68 square miles).

23. On Haganah strength, see Chaim Herzog, *The Arab-Israeli Wars: War and Peace in the Middle East* (New York: Random House, 1982), 20. On the Arabs, see Yoav Gelber, *Palestine 1948: War, Escape and the Emergence of the Palestinian Refugee Problem* (Brighton: Sussex Academic Press, 2001), 12.

24. Morris, *Righteous Victims*, 215–18.

25. In fact, King Abdullah of Transjordan had engaged in intermittent negotiations with Zionist leaders before the war regarding how to divide Palestine between them. See Avi Shlaim, *Collusion Across the Jordan: King Abdullah, the Zionist Movement, and the Partition of Palestine* (New York: Columbia University Press, 1988). Abdullah intended to annex the parts of Palestine that abutted his kingdom, and instructed his forces to seize as much of the West Bank as possible. The Egyptians, confronted with this plan, altered their strategy in the hope of gaining some of the West Bank for themselves. See David Tal, *War in Palestine 1948: Strategy and Diplomacy* (London: Routledge, 2004), 16–18, and Morris, *Righteous Victims*, 220–22.

26. On territory annexed, see Nadav Safran, *Israel: The Embattled Ally* (Cambridge: Belknap Press, 1978), 60; on villages destroyed, see Walid Khalidi, ed., *All That Remains: The Palestinian Villages Occupied and Depopulated by Israel in 1948* (Washington: Institute for Palestine Studies, 1992), xxxi. For various estimates of the number of Palestinian refugees, see Martin Gilbert, *Israel: A History* (New York: William Morrow, 1998), 255.

27. On Arab fatalities, see Ilan Pappe, *The Ethnic Cleansing of Palestine* (Oxford: Oneworld Publications, 2006), 150; for Israeli deaths, see Martin van Creveld, *The Sword and the Olive: A Critical History of the Israeli Defense Force* (New York: Public Affairs, 1998), 99.

28. Gelber, *Palestine 1948*, 74–83.

29. Quoted in Shabtai Teveth, *Ben-Gurion and the Palestinian Arabs: From Peace to War* (Oxford: Oxford University Press, 1985), 188.

30. Ibid., 189–90, 188.

31. Quoted in Simha Flapan, *The Birth of Israel: Myths and Realities* (New York: Pantheon, 1987), 22.

32. Quoted in ibid., 52–53.

33. Quoted in Shabtai Teveth, *Ben-Gurion: The Burning Ground, 1886–1948* (Boston: Houghton Mifflin, 1987), 613.

34. Quoted in Masalha, *Expulsion of the Palestinians*, 62. The Peel plan allocated less than 20 percent of Palestine to a Jewish state.

35. Quoted in Flapan, *Birth of Israel*, 23, 24.

36. Quoted in ibid., 32.

37. Quoted in Uri Milstein, *History of Israel's War of Independence*, vol. 4, *Out of Crisis Came Decision*, trans. and ed. Alan Sacks (Lanham, MD: University Press of America, 1988), 187–88.

38. In particular, see Masalha, *Expulsion of the Palestinians*.

39. Herzl's diary entry for June 12, 1895, quoted in Benny Morris, "Revisiting the Palestinian Exodus of 1948," in *War for Palestine*, 41.

40. Benny Morris, *The Birth of the Palestinian Refugee Problem Revisited*, 2d ed. (Cambridge: Cambridge University Press, 2004), 43.

41. Quoted in Masalha, *Expulsion of the Palestinians*, 37.

42. Ibid., 67–80.

43. Quoted in Teveth, *Ben-Gurion and the Palestinian Arabs*, 189.

44. Morris, *Birth Revisited*, 50. On the protransfer consensus of the JAE, see also Masalha, *Expulsion of the Palestinians*, 106–19.

45. Quoted in Masalha, *Expulsion of the Palestinians*, 117.

46. Quoted in Morris, *Birth Revisited*, 54.

47. Quoted in ibid., 55.

48. Segev, *One Palestine, Complete*, 407.

49. Quoted in Morris, *Righteous Victims*, 168–69.

50. Quote is from Segev, *One Palestine, Complete*, 407. Segev notes that some have tried to disassociate Ben-Gurion from the transfer idea, but that such "interpretations are unprincipled: Ben-Gurion's stand on deportations, like that of other Zionist leaders, is unambiguous and well-documented" (ibid.).

51. Indeed, leading Zionists were very much aware of the Sudeten precedent and invoked it as a reason to eliminate the Arab component from the Jewish state. See Masalha, *Expulsion of the Palestinians*, 108.

52. Quoted in Morris, *Birth Revisited*, 50.

53. Quoted in Masalha, *Expulsion of the Palestinians*, 115.

54. Benny Morris, *The Birth of the Palestinian Refugee Problem, 1947–1949* (Cambridge: Cambridge University Press, 1987), 28. See also Masalha, *Expulsion of the Palestinians,* 175–76.

55. Quoted in Flapan, *Birth of Israel,* 31–32.

56. Morris, in an article that appeared in the Israeli newspaper *Ha'aretz* on May 9, 1989, quoted in Nur Masalha, "A Critique of Benny Morris," *Journal of Palestine Studies* 21, no. 1 (autumn 1991): 92.

57. Morris, *Birth Revisited,* 43–44.

58. Morris, "Revisiting the Palestinian Exodus of 1948," 48–49. See also Morris, *Birth Revisited,* 60.

59. Masalha, "Critique of Benny Morris," 93.

60. Morris, *Birth Revisited,* 588. For a recent work that argues there was what amounted to a master plan, see Pappe, *Ethnic Cleansing of Palestine.*

61. On events at Tantura on May 22–23, during which 200 Arabs were allegedly killed, see Ilan Pappé, "The Tantura Case in Israel: The Katz Research and Trial," *Journal of Palestine Studies* 30, no. 3 (spring 2001): 19–39; and Morris, *Birth Revisited,* 247. On the killings in Abu Shusha (May 13–14), see *Birth Revisited,* 257. Haganah massacres also occurred at Nasr al-Din, 'Ein al Zeitun, and Tirat Haifa. Pappe, *Ethnic Cleansing of Palestine,* 110–11.

62. *Birth Revisited,* 70.

63. Ibid., 71; Tal, *War in Palestine,* 57; Morris, *Birth Revisited,* 71, 76.

64. Tal, *War in Palestine,* 61. The massacre of 60–80 Arabs at Sa'sa on February 14–15 demonstrates the Haganah's increased aggressiveness. Overall, by the end of January, 1,500 Palestinians had been killed. Pappe, *Ethnic Cleansing of Palestine,* 77–78, 72.

65. See the map on population distribution that originally appeared in the Anglo-American Committee of Inquiry's *A Survey of Palestine* (1946), reprinted in Khalidi, *All That Remains,* xxviii.

66. Morris, *Birth Revisited,* 163. For a contrary view that the Yishuv was not in danger of annihilation and Ben-Gurion was confident in victory, see Pappe, *Ethnic Cleansing of Palestine,* 80–85, 46–47.

67. Safran, *Israel,* 46; and Chaim D. Kaufmann, "When All Else Fails: Ethnic Population Transfers and Partitions in the Twentieth Century," *International Security* 23, no. 2 (fall 1998): 144–46.

68. "Text of Plan Dalet (Plan D), 10 March 1948: General Section," in *Journal of Palestine Studies* 18, no. 1 (autumn 1988): 24.

69. Ibid., 29.

70. Morris, *Birth Revisited,* 163–64.

71. While Morris contends that "Plan D was not a political blueprint for the expulsion of Palestine's Arabs," this conclusion is contradicted by other statements he makes, such as "given the nature of the war and the admixture of populations, securing the interior of the Jewish State and its borders in practice meant the depopulation and destruction of the villages that hosted the hostile militias and irregulars." Ibid., 164. Other scholars go further and interpret Plan D as a master plan to clear the territories awarded to the Jews by the UN partition plan—and the Arab-populated areas between them—of unwanted inhabitants. See Norman G. Finkelstein, *Image and Reality of the Israel-Palestine Conflict* (London: Verso, 2001), 64, and Shlaim, *Iron Wall,* 31. Still others argue that Plan D "was not the principal reason for intensification of the mass flight of Palestinians," emphasizing instead the fear induced by unauthorized massacres like Deir Yassin and the general weakness of Palestinian Arab society. See Gelber, *Palestine 1948,* 98, 99–116.

72. Morris, *Birth Revisited,* 166–67, 171; and Pappe, *Ethnic Cleansing of Palestine,* 82.

73. Morris, *Birth Revisited,* 190 and 200; 213; and 183, 222–24, 227, 249–51, 256, and 259.

74. Ibid., 235, 256, 257, 227, and 228.

75. Ibid., 236.

76. Ibid., 236.

77. Ibid., 257, 222, 289, and 220.

78. Matthew Hogan, "The 1948 Massacre at Deir Yassin Revisited," *The Historian* 63, no. 2 (winter 2001): 330–31.

79. Cited in Morris, *Birth Revisited*, 240.

80. Shlaim, *Collusion Across the Jordan*, 164.

81. Morris, *Birth Revisited*, 189. Although the Arab defenders had the upper hand in terms of numbers, they were poorly trained, equipped, and organized. Their morale—and that of the Arab population more generally—was sapped by the departure on the first day of the battle of several high-ranking Arab officials, such as Ahmad Bey Khalil, the town's chief magistrate, and Amin Bey Azzadin, the commander of Haifa's fighting men.

82. Quoted in Pappe, *Ethnic Cleansing of Palestine*, 95. About 15,000–20,000 of Haifa's 70,000 Arab citizens had already fled by April 1948.

83. Quoted in Morris, *Birth Revisited*, 207.

84. Quoted in Finkelstein, *Image and Reality*, 66. On Ben-Gurion's bewilderment regarding the Haifa exodus, see ibid., 191, n. 31.

85. Morris, *Birth Revisited*, 191–92.

86. Quoted in ibid., 200.

87. Ibid., 200.

88. Uri Milstein, an Israeli military historian, quoted in Finkelstein, *Image and Reality*, 67. This interpretation is supported by the Carmeli Brigade's history of its operations. See Pappe, *Ethnic Cleansing of Palestine*, 96.

89. Quoted in Morris, *Birth Revisited*, 191.

90. Ibid., 202, 207.

91. Ibid., 202–03.

92. Four IDF brigades participated in Operation DANI, whereas the legion had one company stationed in Lydda/Ramle, and a second company positioned to the north at Beit Nabala.

93. Benny Morris, "Operation Dani and the Palestinian Exodus from Lydda and Ramle in 1948," *Middle East Journal* 40, no. 1 (winter 1986): 84; and Pappe, *Ethnic Cleansing of Palestine*, 158. IDF commanders may have assumed that the population would flee, as had the inhabitants of other Arab or mixed towns previously attacked by Jewish forces. Morris, "Operation Dani," 85.

94. Morris, "Operation Dani," 86; and Morris, *Birth Revisited*, 425.

95. Quoted in Morris, *Birth Revisited*, 425.

96. Ibid., 424–25.

97. Quoted in ibid., 425.

98. Ibid., 426.

99. Ibid., 426.

100. Ibid., 427, 428.

101. Finkelstein, *Image and Reality*, 55.

102. Morris, "Operation Dani," 90.

103. Ibid., 90.

104. Morris, *Birth Revisited*, 429. Gelber disputes this account, instead stressing the punitive attitudes of IDF soldiers toward Palestinian civilians. Gelber, *Palestine 1948*, 162–63.

105. Morris, *Birth Revisited*, 429. Similar orders were also sent to the Kiryati Brigade with respect to Ramle's population.

106. Morris, "Operation Dani," 96.

107. A major massacre occurred on this front on October 28 or 29 at Dawayima. See Morris, *Birth Revisited*, 469–71, and "Another Deir Yassin?" *Journal of Palestine Studies* 14, no. 2 (winter 1985): 207–12. See also Pappe, *Ethnic Cleansing of Palestine*, 195–97.

108. Morris, "Revisiting the Palestinian Exodus of 1948," 51.

109. Quoted in Morris, *Birth Revisited*, 464; see also Morris, "Revisiting the Palestinian Exodus of 1948," 52.

110. Morris, "Revisiting the Palestinian Exodus of 1948," 52.

111. Tal, *War in Palestine*, 423–24.

112. One exception to this trend was the Maronite village of 'Eilabun, where Golani troops killed 12–15 civilians after the village surrendered. Morris, *Birth Revisited*, 479–80.

113. Ibid., 482. On these massacres, see ibid., 477–81, 500–501; and Ari Shavit, "Survival of the Fittest (An Interview with Historian Benny Morris)," *Haaretz*, Magazine Section, January 9, 2004.

114. Tal, *War in Palestine*, 424–25; and Gelber, *Palestine 1948*, 227.

115. Quoted in Morris, "Revisiting the Palestinian Exodus of 1948," 52.

116. Ibid., 54.

117. Howard M. Sachar, *A History of Israel: From the Rise of Zionism to Our Time*, 2d ed. (New York: Alfred A. Knopf, 1996), 191; Ilan Pappe, *A History of Modern Palestine: One Land, Two Peoples* (Cambridge: Cambridge University Press, 2004), 90; and General Sir Henry Maitland Wilson, quoted in Sachar, *History of Israel*, 246. The World Zionist Organization initially served as the body called for under the terms of the Mandate to work with the British in developing the Jewish National Home. Not until 1929 was this function taken over by the Jewish Agency.

118. Morris, *Righteous Victims*, 193.

119. Anglo-American Committee of Inquiry, *A Survey of Palestine*, vol. 2 (1946), 910. Over time, however, Palestine-based Zionist groups came to dominate the council and the executive.

120. Ilan Pappé, *The Making of the Arab-Israeli Conflict, 1947–51* (London: I. B. Tauris, 1992), 48.

121. Sachar, *History of Israel*, 354, 355.

122. Morris, *Birth Revisited*, 169–70, 320, 347–56, 486–90.

123. Ibid., 356, 487, 488, 320.

124. Ben Gurion quoted in Teveth, *Ben-Gurion and the Palestinian Arabs*, 174, 174–75; and Morris, *Birth Revisited*, 486.

125. It could be argued that the right-wing militias—IZL and LHI—were competing elements, but this would be incorrect. These militias were not controlled by the Jewish Agency or the Provisional Government until Ben-Gurion forced them to submit and be incorporated into the IDF during the Second Truce. Since they worked for different masters before that, there was no point in competing since doing so could not have made a difference in the organization's influence or budget.

126. Morris, *Birth Revisited*, 81.

127. Ibid., 71; see also Tal, *War in Palestine*, 57.

128. Masalha, "Critique of Benny Morris," 96. See also Finkelstein, *Image and Reality*, 85.

129. Indeed, Morris recently faulted Ben-Gurion for failing to expel the entire Arab population in 1948. Shavit, "Survival of the Fittest."

130. Quoted in Morris, *Birth Revisited*, 317. See also Flapan, *Birth of Israel*, 105.

131. Laila Parsons, "The Druze and the Birth of Israel," in *War for Palestine*, 60–78.

7. Negative Cases

1. Alexander B. Rossino, *Hitler Strikes Poland: Blitzkrieg, Ideology, and Atrocity* (Lawrence: University Press of Kansas, 2003). Most of the victims of this strategy were not Jews. Ibid., 234.

2. Micheal Clodfelter, *Warfare and Armed Conflicts: A Statistical Reference to Casualty and Other Figures, 1500–2000*, 2d ed. (Jefferson, NC: McFarland, 2002), 228.

3. Elaine Unterhalter, "Confronting Imperialism: The People of Nquthu and the Invasion of Zululand," in *The Anglo-Zulu War: New Perspectives*, ed. Andrew Duminy and Charles Ballard (Pietermaritzburg: University of Natal Press, 1981), 105.

4. John Coates, *Suppressing Insurgency: An Analysis of the Malayan Emergency, 1948–1954* (Boulder: Westview Press, 1992), 202. On the Malayan case, see also Benjamin A. Valentino, *Final Solutions: Mass Killing and Genocide in the Twentieth Century* (Ithaca: Cornell University Press, 2004), 229–30.

5. Neville Maxwell, *India's China War* (London: Jonathan Cape, 1970).

6. King C. Chen, *China's War with Vietnam, 1979: Issues, Decisions, and Implications* (Stanford, CA: Hoover Institution Press, 1987); and Hemen Ray, *China's Vietnam War* (New Delhi: Radiant, 1983).

7. D. George Boyce, *The Falklands War* (Houndmills: Palgrave Macmillan, 2005), 10.

8. Michael Parsons, *The Falklands War* (Phoenix Mill: Sutton, 2000), 80.

9. Ashok Krishna, "The Kargil War," in *Kargil: The Tables Turned,* ed. Ashok Krishna and P. R. Chari (New Delhi: Manohar, 2001), 104.

10. For this and other fatality estimates, see Tekeste Negash and Kjetil Tronvoll, *Brothers at War: Making Sense of the Eritrean-Ethiopian War* (Oxford: James Currey, 2000), 90, 99.

11. Patrick Gilkes and Martin Plaut, *War in the Horn: The Conflict between Eritrea and Ethiopia* (London: Royal Institute of International Affairs, 1999), 52.

12. Negash and Tronvoll, *Brothers at War,* 47.

13. Quoted in Gilkes and Plaut, *War in the Horn,* 56.

14. Ibid., 28.

15. Ibid., 28–29, and Karl Vick, "Civilian Attack Stuns Ethiopians," *Washington Post Foreign Service,* June 7, 1998, in *Dispatches from the Electronic Front: Internet Responses to the Ethio-Eritrean Conflict* (Addis Ababa: Walta Information Center, 1999), 156.

16. Gilkes and Plaut, *War in the Horn,* 33, 34–35.

17. Saddam Hussein's regime, by contrast, fired Scud missiles indiscriminately at Saudi and Israeli cities, hoping to shatter the fragile U.S.–led coalition. This qualifies as a marginal case of civilian victimization (only 14 total civilians died). See Robert A. Pape, *Bombing to Win: Air Power and Coercion in War* (Ithaca: Cornell University Press, 1996), 357–58.

18. Stephen T. Hosmer, *Psychological Effects of U.S. Air Operations in Four Wars 1941–1991: Lessons for U.S. Commanders* (Santa Monica: RAND, 1996), 155.

19. American forces deployed to the gulf numbered 235,215 as of November 15, 1990, supported by 1,000 aircraft and 857 tanks. On troops and tanks, see Gulf War Air Power Survey (henceforth GWAPS), *A Statistical Compendium and Chronology of the Gulf War* (Washington: GPO, 1993), vol. 5, part 2, 105–6. On aircraft, see Department of Defense, *Conduct of the Persian Gulf War: Final Report to Congress* (Washington: GPO, 1992), 77–78.

20. H. Norman Schwarzkopf, with Peter Petre, *It Doesn't Take a Hero* (New York: Linda Grey/ Bantam, 1992), 315.

21. Michael R. Gordon and Bernard E. Trainor, *The Generals' War: The Inside Story of the Conflict in the Gulf* (Boston: Little, Brown, 1995), 132–33.

22. Ibid., 141, and Colin L. Powell with Joseph E. Persico, *My American Journey* (New York: Random House, 1995), 485.

23. Gordon and Trainor, *Generals' War,* 142–45.

24. GWAPS, *Statistical Compendium and Chronology,* vol. 5, part 1, 51.

25. Anthony H. Cordesman and Abraham R. Wagner, *The Lessons of Modern War,* vol. 4, *The Gulf War* (Boulder: Westview Press, 1996), 94.

26. Ibid., 140–41, 94. The number of Air Force planes committed to the air campaign when it began was over 1,300. DoD, *Conduct of the Persian Gulf War,* 164. The total number of U.S. fixed-wing aircraft in theater when the air war began was 1,847. GWAPS, *Statistical Compendium and Chronology,* vol. 5, part 2, 154.

27. Gordon and Trainor, *Generals' War,* 78.

28. On the five rings, see John A. Warden III, "Employing Air Power in the Twenty-first Century," in *The Future of Air Power in the Aftermath of the Gulf War,* ed. Richard H. Shultz Jr., and Robert L. Pfaltzgraff Jr. (Maxwell Air Force Base, AL: Air University Press, 1992), 57–82; Mark Clodfelter, "Of Demons, Storms, and Thunder: A Preliminary Look at Vietnam's Impact on the Persian Gulf Air Campaign," *Airpower Journal* 5, no. 4 (winter 1991): 23; and GWAPS, *Planning and Command and Control,* vol. 1, part 1 (Washington: GPO, 1993), 115–22.

29. GWAPS, *Operations and Effects and Effectiveness,* vol. 2, part 2 (Washington: GPO, 1993), 87.

30. Colonel Michael F. Reavy, an aide to CENTCOM's air commander, quipped: "Not to imply that we were trying to assassinate Saddam, but we were trying to kill him." Quoted in Gordon and Trainor, *Generals' War,* 314. Because of the political sensitivity of assassination, Air Force chief of staff General Michael Dugan was dismissed by Cheney in September 1990 for basically admitting that the Air Force hoped to kill Saddam Hussein. Yet it was common knowledge that air planners were targeting all the places Saddam might be, and President Bush raised no objections to this strategy. As the president wrote in his diary on January 31, 1991, "This is a war and if he [Saddam] gets hit with a bomb in his headquarters, too bad." George Bush and Brent Scowcroft, *A World Transformed* (New York: Alfred A. Knopf, 1998), 464. See also

Lawrence Freedman and Efraim Karsh, *The Gulf Conflict, 1990–1991: Diplomacy and War in the New World Order* (Princeton: Princeton University Press, 1993), 323.

31. Dugan quoted in Clodfelter, "Of Demons, Storms, and Thunder," 26.

32. Gordon and Trainor, *Generals' War*, 80.

33. Pape, *Bombing to Win*, 221.

34. Quoted in Gordon and Trainor, *Generals' War*, 84.

35. Quoted in Pape, *Bombing to Win*, 224.

36. John A. Warden III, "Instant Thunder: A Strategic Air Campaign Proposal for CINCENT," August 17, 1990, quoted in Pape, *Bombing to Win*, 222.

37. Warden quoted in ibid., 223.

38. Daniel T. Kuehl, "Airpower vs. Electricity: Electric Power as a Target for Strategic Air Operations," in *Airpower: Theory and Practice*, ed. John Gooch (London: Frank Cass, 1995), 252.

39. Quotations from Barton Gellman, "Allied Air War Struck Broadly in Iraq; Officials Acknowledge Strategy Went Beyond Purely Military Targets," *Washington Post*, June 23 1991, A1.

40. For a summary of these estimates, some of which ranged as high as 50,000 American deaths, see Jacob Weisberg, "Gulfballs: How the Experts Blew It, Big-Time," *New Republic*, March 25, 1991, 17, 19; Freedman and Karsh, *Gulf Conflict*, 286, and 468, n. 8; and Bush and Scowcroft, *A World Transformed*, 389, 425. On CIA chief William Webster's views, based on disagreements over the Pentagon's bomb damage assessment, see Gordon and Trainor, *Generals' War*, 335.

41. Powell, *My American Journey*, 498–99.

42. Tom Mathews, "The Secret History of the War," *Newsweek*, March 18, 1991; and Freedman and Karsh, *Gulf Conflict*, 391.

43. Freedman and Karsh, *Gulf Conflict*, 391.

44. Bob Woodward, *The Commanders* (New York: Simon and Schuster, 1991), 376. One political scientist also predicted a short war with fewer than 1,000 American deaths. See John J. Mearsheimer, "Will Iraq Fight or Fold Its Tent? Liberation in Less Than a Week," *New York Times*, February 8, 1991, A31.

45. Bush and Scowcroft, *A World Transformed*, 412.

46. Ibid., 462. See also ibid., 469.

47. Ibid., 462; and Gordon and Trainor, *Generals' War*, 337.

48. DoD, *Conduct of the Persian Gulf War*, 85–86.

49. Out of a total of 41,309 strikes, 22,790 were sent against the Iraqi ground order of battle. GWAPS, *Statistical Compendium and Chronology*, vol. 5, part 1, 418.

50. Pape, *Bombing to Win*, 242, 250.

51. GWAPS estimates that the desertion rate for Iraqi forces in the KTO was about 25–30 percent, totaling perhaps 100,000 men. GWAPS, *Operations and Effects and Effectiveness*, vol. 2, part 2, 220. In addition, the bombing killed or injured 30,000–60,000 troops, leaving only about 200,000–222,000 Iraqi soldiers when the coalition ground attack began. Pape, *Bombing to Win*, 247; and GWAPS, *Operations and Effects and Effectiveness*, vol. 2, part 2, 220. A U.S. Army intelligence report written shortly after the war shows that many regular Iraqi divisions along the front lines, and even some Republican Guard divisions, suffered massive desertions, in certain cases reducing their manpower by over 50 percent. Gordon and Trainor, *Generals' War*, 351–52. Many of those who did not desert during the air campaign surrendered once the ground war began: coalition forces captured nearly 87,000 Iraqi prisoners. DoD, *Conduct of the Persian Gulf War*, 577. Air strikes also destroyed or disabled about one-fifth of Iraq's armored vehicles and artillery. Pape, *Bombing to Win*, 249 (based on postwar studies). CENTCOM assessed on the day before the ground assault kicked off that its air component had destroyed 39 percent of the Iraqi army's tanks in the KTO, 32 percent of its armored personnel carriers, and 47 percent of its artillery. GWAPS, *Operations and Effects and Effectiveness*, vol. 2, part 2, 211.

52. See sources in notes 24–26 above.

53. Stephen Biddle, *Military Power: Explaining Victory and Defeat in Modern Battle* (Princeton: Princeton University Press, 2004), 136.

54. For details, see Daryl G. Press, "The Myth of Air Power in the Persian Gulf War and the Future of Warfare," *International Security* 26, no. 2 (fall 2001): 13, n. 24. The American tanks also

had thermal sites allowing them to fight at night, and a special stabilizer system that enabled them to shoot on the move.

55. This lack of skill was revealed when fighting commenced. Even the best Iraqi forces committed major blunders, such as piling up sand around their armored vehicles (which revealed their positions but provided no protection) rather than digging them in below ground, and allowing themselves to be taken by surprise because their screening forces failed to provide warning of approaching U.S. units. Biddle, *Military Power*, 137–39.

56. Press, "Myth of Air Power," 14. By one estimate, Shi'ites composed 70 percent and Kurds 20 percent of Iraq's frontline divisions. Ibid., 14, n. 25.

57. Ward Thomas, *The Ethics of Destruction: Norms and Force in International Relations* (Ithaca: Cornell University Press, 2001), 159; and GWAPS, *Statistical Compendium*, vol. 5, part 1, 418.

58. GWAPS, *Operations and Effects and Effectiveness*, vol. 2. part 2, 270.

59. William M. Arkin, "Baghdad: The Urban Sanctuary in Desert Storm?" *Airpower Journal* 11, no. 1 (spring 1997): 5–7. This accounted for 3 percent of all PGMs delivered in the war.

60. Middle East Watch, *Needless Deaths in the Gulf War: Civilian Casualties during the Air Campaign and Violations of the Laws of War* (New York: Human Rights Watch, 1991), 96–110.

61. Ibid., 201–24.

62. Gordon and Trainor, *Generals' War*, 326–27.

63. Thomas, *Ethics of Destruction*, 159. The official Iraqi government figure is 2,278 deaths.

64. GWAPS, *Operations and Effects and Effectiveness*, vol. 2, part 2, 268–69.

65. John Mueller, *Policy and Opinion in the Gulf War* (Chicago: University of Chicago Press, 1994), 317.

66. Ibid., 318.

67. Ibid., 123.

68. Quoted in Powell, *My American Journey*, 499.

69. Bush and Scowcroft, *A World Transformed*, 375.

70. Gordon and Trainor, *Generals' War*, 77.

71. Thomas, *Ethics of Destruction*, 148. Thomas acknowledges that most of the wars fought in the post-1945 period have not challenged the central interests of the major powers, those with the greatest ability to employ airpower, but still maintains that "attitudes concerning the appropriate conduct of war have changed." Ibid., 170.

72. Eliot A. Cohen, "The Meaning and Future of Air Power," *Orbis* 39, no. 2 (spring 1995): 200.

73. Thomas, *Ethics of Destruction*, 172.

74. GWAPS, *Operations and Effects and Effectiveness*, vol. 2, part 2, 291–92. Targeting electricity has been central to American strategic bombing thought and practice since the 1930s. Kuehl, "Airpower vs. Electricity," 237–50.

75. GWAPS, *Operations and Effects and Effectiveness*, vol. 2, part 2, 300–302; and Kuehl, "Airpower vs. Electricity," 253–55.

76. International Study Team (IST), *Health and Welfare in Iraq after the Gulf Crisis* (International Study Team: 1991), chap. 3, "Electrical Facilities Survey." See also GWAPS, *Operations and Effects and Effectiveness*, vol. 2, part 2, 306, for a summary of this damage.

77. The International Study Team (IST), for example, conducted a survey in late August and early September 1991 in which they sampled 9,034 households in all 18 governates of Iraq. The study found that mortality among children under the age of five had increased 3.8 times over the rate in 1990. IST, *Health and Welfare in Iraq*, 1. In a later article based on the same study, the authors estimated excess deaths in the under-five age group at approximately 47,000 for the period January–August 1991. See Alberto Ascherio et al., "Effect of the Gulf War on Infant and Child Mortality in Iraq," *New England Journal of Medicine* 327, no. 13 (September 1992): 933. A separate survey, which estimated total excess deaths for the entire population in 1991, found that 111,000 people had died from health effects caused by the war, 70,000 of whom were 15 or younger or over 65. Beth Osborne Daponte, "A Case Study in Estimating Casualties from War and Its Aftermath: The 1991 Persian Gulf War," *Physicians for Social Responsibility Quarterly* 3 (1993): 57–66.

78. About 75–80 percent of these facilities had backup diesel generators but many were unreliable owing to a lack of fuel and spare parts.

79. Rick Atkinson, *Crusade: The Untold Story of the Persian Gulf War* (Boston: Houghton Mifflin, 1993), 282. See also Richard G. Davis, "Strategic Bombardment in the Gulf War," in *Case Studies in Strategic Bombardment*, ed. R. Cargill Hall (Air Force History and Museums Program, 1998), 565; IST, *Health and Welfare in Iraq*, "Water and Wastewater Systems Survey," 6; and Middle East Watch, *Needless Deaths in the Gulf War*, 182.

80. Ascherio et al., "Effect of the Gulf War on Infant and Child Mortality in Iraq," 935. See also Harvard Study Team, *Harvard Study Team Report: Public Health in Iraq after the Gulf War* (May 1991), 12–13.

81. This document also cites a UNICEF report, which estimated that potable water in Baghdad was "less than 5 percent of the original supply." DIA, "Medical Problems in Iraq," March 15, 1991, http://www.gulflink.osd.mil/declassdocs/dia/19951016/951016_0me018_91. html. For similar conclusions, see Armed Forces Medical Intelligence Center, Epidemiology Branch, "Health Conditions in Iraq and Prospects for the Future," http://www.gulflink.osd. mil/declassdocs/dia/19950825/950825_0131pgv_91d.html

82. Kuehl, "Airpower vs. Electricity," 254, 265, n. 57, and GWAPS, *Operations and Effects and Effectiveness*, vol. 2, part 2, 307. For a contrary view that the U.S. military should have foreseen the effects of eliminating electric power on the civilian population, see Middle East Watch, *Needless Deaths in the Gulf War*, 179–80.

83. Ward Thomas, "Victory by Duress: Civilian Infrastructure as a Target in Air Campaigns," *Security Studies* 15, no. 1 (January–March 2006): 7.

84. Arkin quoted in GWAPS, *Operations and Effects and Effectiveness*, vol. 2, part 2, 307, n. 87.

85. UN Security Council Resolution 661, August 6, 1990, Article 3 (c).

86. Geoff Simons, *The Scourging of Iraq: Sanctions, Law and Natural Justice*, 2d ed. (Houndmills: Macmillan, 1998), 38–39.

87. Freedman and Karsh, *Gulf Conflict*, 196.

88. Defense Intelligence Agency, "Iraq Water Treatment Vulnerabilities," January 18, 1991, http://www.gulflink.osd.mil/declassdocs/dia/19950901/950901_511rept_91.html.

89. Joy Gordon, "Accountability and Global Governance: The Case of Iraq," *Ethics and International Affairs* 20, no. 1 (April 2006): 83.

90. It should be noted, however, that a slight increase in infant and under-five mortality rates occurred during the last five months of 1990 compared to the 12 months before sanctions were levied. Richard Garfield, "Morbidity and Mortality among Iraqi Children from 1990 through 1998: Assessing the Impact of the Gulf War and Economic Sanctions," Unpublished MS, Columbia University, March 1999, 9.

91. Quoted in Freedman and Karsh, *Gulf Conflict*, 191.

92. John Mueller and Karl Mueller, "The Methodology of Mass Destruction: Assessing Threats in the New World Order," *Journal of Strategic Studies* 23, no. 1 (March 2000): 172.

93. Quoted in Freedman and Karsh, *Gulf Conflict*, 426.

94. UN Security Council Resolution 687, April 3, 1991, Article 20.

95. Sarah Graham-Brown, *Sanctioning Saddam: The Politics of Intervention in Iraq* (London: Tauris, 1999), 70–78.

96. Ibid., 75; Simons, *Scourging of Iraq*, 100; and Graham-Brown, *Sanctioning Saddam*, 90.

97. Gordon, "Accountability and Global Governance," 85.

98. The original claim—of 567,000 dead Iraqi children, to be exact—was based on a survey published in *The Lancet* in 1995. Follow-up surveys performed by one of the authors of the original study, however, failed to replicate its results, instead finding much lower mortality rates. See Sarah Zaidi and Mary C. Smith-Fawzi, "Health of Baghdad's Children," *The Lancet* 346, no. 8988 (December 1995): 1485; and Sarah Zaidi, "Child Mortality in Iraq," *The Lancet* 350, no. 9084 (October 1997): 1105. For higher estimates, see Simons, *Scourging of Iraq*, xiii; and Anthony Arnove, ed., *Iraq Under Siege: The Deadly Impact of Sanctions and War* (Cambridge: South End Press, 2000), 181, 185.

99. "Iraq Surveys Show 'Humanitarian Emergency,'" UNICEF News Release, August 12, 1999, http://fas.org/news/iraq/1999/08/99pr29.htm. Excess deaths in the under-five age range would have numbered approximately 420,000 if the mortality rates from the 1980s had stayed level instead of continuing to decline. Matt Welch, "The Politics of Dead Children:

Have Sanctions against Iraq Murdered Millions?" *reasononline,* March 2002, http://www.reason.com/0203/fe.mw.the.shtml. For the UNICEF survey, see UNICEF and Ministry of Health (Iraq), *Child and Maternal Mortality Survey 1999: Preliminary Report* (Iraq: July 1999), http://www.fas.org/news/iraq/1999/08/990812-unicef.htm.

100. Garfield, "Morbidity and Mortality among Iraqi Children," 1. Garfield later updated his figure to 350,000 through 2000. David Cortright, "A Hard Look at Iraq Sanctions," *The Nation,* December 3, 2001, 21.

101. Amatzia Baram, "The Effect of Iraqi Sanctions: Statistical Pitfalls and Responsibility," *Middle East Journal* 54, no. 2 (spring 2000): 204.

102. For these and other criticisms, see ibid., 205–19.

103. Mueller and Mueller, "Methodology of Mass Destruction," 173.

104. Whether sanctions achieve much success is another matter. Pape, for example, argues that the 34 percent success rate found by the leading study of economic sanctions is wrong; sanctions succeeded in only 5 percent of the cases. See Gary Clyde Hufbauer, Jeffrey J. Schott, and Kimberly Ann Elliott, *Economic Sanctions Reconsidered,* 2d ed. (Washington: Institute for International Economics, 1990); and Robert A. Pape, "Why Economic Sanctions Do Not Work," *International Security* 22, no. 2 (fall 1997): 90–137. Others have since argued that sanctions are much more successful than Pape allows because many potential targets of sanctions concede at the threat stage before sanctions are ever imposed. Daniel Drezner, "The Hidden Hand of Economic Coercion," *International Organization* 57, no. 3 (summer 2003): 643–59.

105. On the hammer and anvil approach, see Robert A. Pape, "The True Worth of Air Power," *Foreign Affairs* 83, no. 2 (March/April 2004): 116–30. On the late phases of the Bosnian War, see Richard Holbrooke, *To End a War* (New York: Random House, 1998), 79–227. On Kosovo, see Wesley K. Clark, *Waging Modern War: Bosnia, Kosovo, and the Future of Combat* (New York: Public Affairs, 2001); and Andrew J. Bacevich and Eliot A. Cohen, ed., *War over Kosovo: Politics and Strategy in a Global Age* (New York: Columbia University Press, 2001). On the Afghan War, see Michael E. O'Hanlon, "A Flawed Masterpiece," *Foreign Affairs* 81, no. 3 (May/June 2002): 47–63; Stephen Biddle, "Afghanistan and the Future of Warfare," *Foreign Affairs* 82, no. 2 (March/April 2003): 31–45; Richard B. Andres, Craig Wills, and Thomas Griffith Jr., "Winning with Allies: The Strategic Value of the Afghan Model," *International Security* 30, no. 3 (winter 2005/6): 124–60; and Stephen D. Biddle, "Allies, Airpower, and Modern Warfare: The Afghan Model in Afghanistan and Iraq," *International Security* 30, no. 3 (winter 2005/06): 161–76.

106. Pressures for escalation were present in Yugoslavia: Milošević's failure to capitulate as expected in the first few days led to a gradual expansion of the target set and the acceptance of increased risk to civilian life. Clark, *Waging Modern War,* 430. Indeed, top Serbian leaders, including Milošević and General Nebojsa Pavković, stated after the war that they feared NATO would escalate the bombing and obliterate Serbia's cities. See Stephen Biddle, "The New Way of War? Debating the Kosovo Model," *Foreign Affairs* 81, no. 3 (May/June 2002): 141.

107. A total of 307,747 U.S. ground forces deployed in Operation Iraqi Freedom, but the attack began with a strike force of about 140,000. See, respectively, U.S. Central Air Forces Assessment and Analysis Division, *Operation IRAQI FREEDOM—By the Numbers,* April 30, 2003, http://www.globalsecurity.org/military/library/report/2003/uscentaf_oif_report_30apr2003.pdf; and Michael R. Gordon and General Bernard E. Trainor, *Cobra II: The Inside Story of the Invasion and Occupation of Iraq* (New York: Pantheon Books, 2006), 168.

108. One survey of 27 Baghdad-area hospitals found 1,700 killed and 8,000 wounded, plus as many as 1,000 undocumented civilian deaths between March 19 and April 24. Laura King, "Baghdad's Death Toll Assessed," *Los Angeles Times,* May 18, 2003, 1. A second survey found 1,101 civilians killed, an additional 1,255 probable civilians killed, and 6,800 wounded in Baghdad, March 19–April 9. Matthew Schofield, Nancy A. Youssef, and Juan O. Tamayo, "Civilian Deaths in Baghdad Total at Least 1,101," *Knight-Ridder News Service,* May 4, 2003. The most thorough of the press surveys, conducted by the Associated Press, estimated a minimum civilian figure of over 3,000: Niko Price, "AP Tallies 3,240 Civilian Deaths in Iraq," *Associated Press,* June 11, 2003. This tally canvassed 60 hospitals across Iraq, and probably still represents an undercount, as it excluded figures that did not differentiate between military

and civilian deaths, as well as totals from hospitals that did not have daily counts but only gross figures.

109. Carl Conetta, *The Wages of War: Iraqi Combatant and Noncombatant Fatalities in the 2003 Conflict*, Research Monograph #8 (Cambridge, MA: Project on Defense Alternatives, October 20, 2003), 3, http://www.comw.org/pda/0310rm8.html; Iraq Body Count, *A Dossier of Civilian Casualties 2003–2005*, http://reports.iraqbodycount.org/a_dossier_of_civilian_casualties_2003–2005.pdf; and Iraq Body Count, "Year Four: Simply the Worst," Press Release 15, March 18, 2007, http://www.iraqbodycount.org/press/pr15.php.

110. Human Rights Watch (HRW), *Off Target: The Conduct of the War and Civilian Casualties in Iraq* (New York: Human Rights Watch, 2003), 66–79.

111. Conetta, *Wages of War*, 40–42.

112. HRW, *Off Target*, 80. According to CENTCOM, U.S. ground forces fired 10,782 cluster munitions carrying between 1.7 and 2 million submunitions. British forces fired an additional 2,100 such weapons containing 102,900 submunitions. Ibid., 81–82.

113. Ibid., 85.

114. Quoted in ibid., 83.

115. Gordon and Trainor, *Cobra II*, 246, 257. Although not a leading cause of civilian injury, the Air Force's 50 fruitless attacks on leadership targets did result in several instances of noncombatant fatalities. HRW, *Off Target*, 24.

116. See the figures compiled at http://www.iraqbodycount.net.

117. Gilbert Burnham et al., "Mortality after the 2003 Invasion of Iraq: A Cross-Sectional Cluster Survey Sample," *Lancet* 368, no. 9545 (October 2006): 1421–28. For another estimate using the same methods applied to Iraq from the time of the invasion through September 2004, which found that as many as 100,000 excess deaths may have occurred, see Les Roberts et al., "Mortality before and after the 2003 Invasion of Iraq: Cluster Sample Survey," *Lancet* 364, no. 9448 (November 2004): 1857–64.

118. One might argue that the prewar death rate used in the study—5.5 per 1,000 per year—is too low. One critic argues that the correct figure is more than twice that used in the study. See Jim Lacey, "A Damned Statistic," *National Review*, November 6, 2006, 26. The rate provided by the U.S. Census for 2002, however, is only slightly higher: 6.02 per 1,000 per year. Even if one calculates excess deaths using the upper bound of the 95 percent confidence interval given in the study for the prewar war death rate (7.1) and the lower bound of this interval for the wartime death rate (10.9), the number of fatalities remains alarmingly high: 330,756. Although this figure is half what the *Lancet* authors report, it is still five times the IBC estimate for the same time period.

119. Indeed, males between the ages of 15 and 44 comprise 59 percent of all postinvasion violent deaths in the study; men between the ages of 15 and 59 account for 78 percent of such deaths. Burnham et al., "Mortality after the 2003 Invasion of Iraq," 1425, 1423.

120. This selection method, however, is not open to "main street bias," the argument that violence is more common on main thoroughfares because of higher traffic, which increases the possibility of car bombs or attacks on convoys. See Sarah Boseley, "UK Scientists Attack Lancet Study over Death Toll," *The Guardian*, October 24, 2006, 17. The researchers specifically did not choose main streets, but rather residential streets off the main roads. Burnham et al., "Mortality after the 2003 Invasion of Iraq," 1422.

121. The latter figure is adjusted upward from 4,399 by Colin Kahl to account for deaths inflicted by U.S. forces at checkpoints and during convoys, which he claims are underreported by IBC. Colin H. Kahl, "In the Crossfire or the Crosshairs? Norms, Civilian Casualties, and U.S. Conduct in Iraq," *International Security* 32, no. 1 (summer 2007): 11–12.

122. One study counted 514 suicide attacks in Iraq from March 2003 to August 2006. Mohammed M. Hafez, *Suicide Bombers in Iraq: The Strategy and Ideology of Martyrdom* (Washington: United States Institute of Peace Press, 2007), 89.

123. Department of Defense, "Measuring Stability and Security in Iraq," Report to Congress, November 2006, 17–24, http://www.defenselink.mil/home/features/Iraq_Reports/Index.html; Chaim Kaufmann, "Separating Iraqis, Saving Lives," *Foreign Affairs* 85, no. 4 (July/August 2006): 156–60; and Chaim Kaufmann, "America's Final Mission in Iraq," *Boston*

Globe, February 11, 2007, E9. For a sampling of the many news articles on the subject, see Sudarsan Raghavan and Nancy Trejos, "Sunni Arabs Flee Homes in Baghdad," *Washington Post,* December 10, 2006, A24; Solomon Moore, "The Conflict in Iraq: 'Sectarian Cleansing' in Baghdad," *Los Angeles Times,* January 12, 2007, 1; and Larry Kaplow, "Uprooted by Iraq War, They Wander," *Atlanta Journal-Constitution,* February 4, 2007, 1A.

124. For documents concerning this issue, see Mark Danner, *Torture and Truth: America, Abu Ghraib, and the War on Terror* (New York: New York Review Books, 2004); and Karen J. Greenberg and Joshua L. Dratel, *The Torture Papers: The Road to Abu Ghraib* (Cambridge: Cambridge University Press, 2005).

125. For examples, see Ellen Knickmeyer and Salih Saif Aldin, "U.S. Raid Kills Family North of Baghdad," *Washington Post,* January 4, 2006, A12; Ellen Knickmeyer, "U.S. Airstrikes Take Toll on Civilians," *Washington Post,* December 24, 2005, A1; and Dan Murphy, "Fallujah Strike Under Scrutiny," *Christian Science Monitor,* June 21, 2004. There are also many instances of U.S. air strikes killing civilians in IBC's database, http://www.iraqbodycount.org/database.

126. Christina Asquith, "Refugees Tell of Rising Anger in Fallujah," *Christian Science Monitor,* April 14, 2004. See also Iraq Body Count, "No Longer Unknowable: Falluja's April Civilian Toll is 600," Press Release 9, October 26, 2004, http://www.iraqbodycount.org/analysis/reference/press-releases/9.

127. Scott Peterson, "US Tests Way out of Fallujah," *Christian Science Monitor,* April 30, 2004.

128. Kahl, "In the Crossfire or the Crosshairs?" 36. For a more detailed argument, see Colin H. Kahl, "Annihilation, Restraint, and U.S. Military Conduct in Iraq," paper presented at the annual meeting of the International Studies Association, Chicago, IL, March 2007.

129. Jeffrey Record and W. Andrew Terrill, *Iraq and Vietnam: Differences, Similarities, and Insights* (Carlisle, PA: U.S. Army War College, 2004), 11–12. Calculations for the United States in Iraq performed by the author using figures from http://icasualties.org/oif. The figure of roughly two U.S. deaths per day is similar to that cited by Record and Terrill as of spring 2004.

130. "President's Address to the Nation," January 10, 2007, http://www.whitehouse.gov/news/releases/2007/01/20070110-7.html. For various views on the progress of the surge in Iraq, see General David H. Petraeus, "Report to Congress on the Situation in Iraq," September 10–11, 2007, http://www.foreignaffairs.house.gov/110/peto91007.pdf; Michael E. O'Hanlon and Jason H. Campbell, "Iraq Index: Tracking Variables of Reconstruction and Security in Post-Saddam Iraq," Brookings Institution, September 10, 2007, http://www.brookings.edu/iraqindex; United States Government Accountability Office, "Securing, Stabilizing, and Rebuilding Iraq: Iraqi Government Has Not Met Most Legislative, Security, and Economic Benchmarks," September 2007, http://www.gao.gov/new.items/do71195.pdf; and Michael R. Gordon, "Hints of Progress, and Questions, in Iraq Data," *New York Times,* September 8, 2007. On the lack of political progress, see James Glanz, "Compromise on Oil Law in Iraq Seems to Be Collapsing," *New York Times,* September 13, 2007; and Thomas E. Ricks, "Iraqis Wasting an Opportunity, U.S. Officers Say," *Washington Post,* November 15, 2007, Al.

131. Richard A. Oppel Jr., "Iraqi Assails U.S. for Strikes on Civilians," *New York Times,* June 2, 2006.

132. Kahl, "In the Crossfire or the Crosshairs?"; and Colin H. Kahl, "How We Fight," *Foreign Affairs* 85, no. 6 (November/December 2006): 83–101. Kahl stresses the role of the My Lai massacre and the Vietnam War more generally in stimulating the military's emphasis on the laws of war. Specifically the Department of Defense's Law of War Program greatly increased the role of judge advocates, improved training in the laws of war, and reoriented weapons procurement toward precision munitions.

133. The army even has a video game it uses for recruiting that enjoins players to observe the laws of armed conflict and penalizes them if they harm noncombatants. Colin H. Kahl, "Compliance with the Norm of Noncombatant Immunity: The Case of Iraq," paper presented at the annual meeting of the American Political Science Association, Washington, D.C., September 2005, 1–2.

134. Kahl, "In the Crossfire or the Crosshairs?" 38, 42–45.

135. Quote is from Thomas E. Ricks, *Fiasco: The American Military Adventure in Iraq* (New York: Penguin, 2006), 227; description of operations is from ibid., 228–34.

136. Quotes are from Josh White, "Report on Haditha Condemns Marines," *Washington Post*, April 21, 2007, A1. On November 19, 2005, U.S. Marines allegedly killed two dozen Iraqi civilians in Haditha after their convoy was struck by a roadside bomb, killing one soldier. Tim McGirk, "One Morning in Haditha," *Time*, March 27, 2006, 34–36.

137. Mental Health Advisory Team (MHAT) IV Operation Iraqi Freedom 05–07, *Final Report*, November 17, 2006, 35, 37, http://www.armymedicine.army.mil.

Conclusion

1. See, for example, Dan Reiter and Allan C. Stam, *Democracies at War* (Princeton: Princeton University Press, 2002).

2. Gil Merom, *How Democracies Lose Small Wars: State, Society, and the Failures of France in Algeria, Israel in Lebanon, and the United States in Vietnam* (Cambridge: Cambridge University Press, 2003).

3. Barton J. Bernstein, "The Atomic Bombings Reconsidered," *Foreign Affairs* 74, no. 1 (January/February 1995): 149.

4. On Saddam's cost-sensitivity, see Stephen C. Pelletiere and Douglas V. Johnson II, *Lessons Learned: The Iran-Iraq War* (Carlisle, PA: U.S. Army War College, 1991), 9; Anthony H. Cordesman and Abraham R. Wagner, *The Lessons of Modern War*, vol. 2, *The Iran-Iraq War* (Boulder: Westview Press, 1990), 109; and Efraim Karsh, *The Iran-Iraq War: A Military Analysis* (London: International Institute for Strategic Studies, 1987), 35–36.

5. On this point, see Christopher Gelpi, Peter D. Feaver, and Jason Reifler, "Success Matters: Casualty Sensitivity and the War in Iraq," *International Security* 30, no. 3 (winter 2005/06): 7–46.

6. See, for example, Henri Tajfel, ed., *Differentiation between Social Groups: Studies in the Social Psychology of Intergroup Relations* (London: Academic Press, 1978). For an application in international relations, see Jonathan Mercer, "Anarchy and Identity," *International Organization* 49, no. 2 (spring 1995): 229–52.

7. Jack Snyder, *Myths of Empire: Domestic Politics and International Ambition* (Ithaca: Cornell University Press, 1991), 31–52.

8. Stathis N. Kalyvas, *The Logic of Violence in Civil War* (Cambridge: Cambridge University Press, 2006).

9. For one attempt to explain this variation, see James Ron, *Frontiers and Ghettos: State Violence in Serbia and Israel* (Berkeley: University of California Press, 2003).

10. Robert A. Pape, *Bombing to Win: Air Power and Coercion in War* (Ithaca: Cornell University Press, 1996).

11. For a good summary of the debate and a critique of Pape's argument, see Karl Mueller, "Strategies of Coercion: Denial, Punishment, and the Future of Air Power," *Security Studies* 7, no. 3 (spring 1998): 182–228.

12. Robert A. Pape, "Why Economic Sanctions Do Not Work," *International Security* 22, no. 2 (fall 1997): 90–136.

13. Robert A. Pape, "The Strategic Logic of Suicide Terrorism," *American Political Science Review* 97, no. 3 (August 2003): 343–61; and Pape, *Dying to Win: The Strategic Logic of Suicide Terrorism* (New York: Random House, 2005). Pape argues that suicide terrorism succeeds more often than other forms of punishment because its perpetrators seek to extract relatively minor concessions from their targets, and because they target democracies, which are more sensitive to casualties.

14. For criticisms of Pape's argument that suicide terrorism is effective, see Assaf Moghadam, "Suicide Terrorism, Occupation, and the Globalization of Martyrdom: A Critique of *Dying to Win*," *Studies in Conflict and Terrorism* 29, no. 8 (December 2006): 707–29; and Max Abrahms, "Why Terrorism Does Not Work," *International Security* 31, no. 2 (fall 2006): 42–78. On the general ineffectiveness of punishment, see Caleb Carr, *The Lessons of Terror: A History of Warfare Against Civilians* (New York: Random House, 2002); and Ivan Arreguín-Toft, "The [F]utility of Barbarism: Assessing the Impact of the Systematic Harm of Non-Combatants in War," paper

presented at the annual meeting of the American Political Science Association, Philadelphia, PA, August 2003.

15. Pape, *Bombing to Win*, 21–27.

16. For this argument, see Sadao Asada, "The Shock of the Atomic Bomb and Japan's Decision to Surrender—A Reconsideration," *Pacific Historical Review* 67, no. 4 (November 1998): 477–512; and Richard B. Frank, *Downfall: The End of the Japanese Empire* (New York: Random House, 1999), 347–48.

17. I am grateful to Robert Pape for suggesting these terms.

18. George W. Bush, *The National Security Strategy of the United States of America* (Washington: The White House, 2002).

19. CBS/New York Times poll, September 20–23, 2001, http://www.americans-world.org/digest/global_issues/terrorism/data_milAct.cfm.

20. Fox News poll, October 17–18, 2001, available at same source as in previous note.

21. Richard Price, *The Chemical Weapons Taboo* (Ithaca: Cornell University Press, 1997); and Price, "Reversing the Gun Sights: Transnational Civil Society Targets Land Mines," *International Organization* 52, no. 3 (summer 1998): 613–44. The most recent target of norms activists is cluster bomb units.

22. Nina Tannenwald, "The Nuclear Taboo: The United States and the Normative Basis of Nuclear Non-Use," *International Organization* 53, no. 3 (summer 1999): 433–68; and Tannenwald, "Stigmatizing the Bomb: Origins of the Nuclear Taboo," *International Security* 29, no. 4 (spring 2005): 5–49.

Index